Judicial Politics in Polarized Times

Judicial Politics in Polarized Times

THOMAS M. KECK

THE UNIVERSITY OF CHICAGO PRESS   CHICAGO AND LONDON

THOMAS M. KECK is the Michael O. Sawyer Chair of Constitutional Law and Politics at Syracuse University's Maxwell School of Citizenship and Public Affairs. He is the author of *The Most Activist Supreme Court in History*, also published by the University of Chicago Press.

The University of Chicago Press, Chicago 60637
The University of Chicago Press, Ltd., London
© 2014 by The University of Chicago
All rights reserved. Published 2014.
Printed in the United States of America

23 22 21 20 19 18 17 16 15 14   1 2 3 4 5

ISBN-13: 978-0-226-18238-4 (cloth)
ISBN-13: 978-0-226-18241-4 (paper)
ISBN-13: 978-0-226-18255-1 (e-book)
DOI: 10.7208/chicago/9780226182551.001.0001

Library of Congress Cataloging-in-Publication Data

Keck, Thomas Moylan, author.
   Judicial politics in polarized times / Thomas M. Keck.
       pages ; cm
   Includes bibliographical references and index.
   ISBN 978-0-226-18238-4 (cloth : alk. paper) — ISBN 978-0-226-18241-4 (pbk. : alk. paper) — ISBN 978-0-226-18255-1 (e-book)   1. Political questions and judicial power — United States. 2. Judicial process — United States.   I. Title.
   KF8775.K43 2014
   342.73'04—dc23   2014029539

FOR SASHA AND RUBY

Contents

Preface   ix

INTRODUCTION   Three Stories about Courts   1

PART I   **Rights on the Left, and Rights on the Right**

ONE   Rights on the Left   19

TWO   Rights on the Right   69

PART II.   **Courts, Democracy, and Policy Change**

THREE   Are Judges Umpires?   129

FOUR   Are Judges Tyrants?   164

FIVE   Are Judges Sideshows?   198

CONCLUSION   Judicial Politics in Polarized Times   240

Appendix A   Coding Procedures for Polarization Analysis   259

Notes   263

References   317

Index   337

Online at http://press.uchicago.edu/sites/keck/

Appendix B   Judicial Decisions Coded for Polarization Analysis

Appendix C   Congressional Votes Coded for Polarization Analysis

Preface

This book has been a decade in the making, and I have incurred a great many debts during that time. My intellectual home throughout this decade has been the Maxwell School of Citizenship and Public Affairs at Syracuse University, where my thoughts about the political significance of contemporary courts (and about politics more broadly) have been shaped by countless interactions with colleagues and students.

Many of these students have aided the production of the book more directly, by providing invaluable research assistance. In this regard, I would like to thank Amanda DiPaolo, Cyril Ghosh, Keneshia Grant, Sam Knehans, Yale Leber, Brandon Metroka, Jason Plume, John Ryan, Nilesh Sinha, and especially Richard Price, who has graduated from research assistant to colleague and collaborator. Richard read and provided comments on the full manuscript and taught me much of what I know about state constitutional litigation.

In addition to Richard, a number of friends and colleagues have read and commented on various portions of the manuscript or, in some cases, earlier projects that eventually evolved into this one. I would like to thank Jeb Barnes, Elizabeth Cohen, Kevin den Dulk, David Garrow, Bill Haltom, Ron Kahn, Ken Kersch, Art Leonard, Dan Lipson, Suzanne Mettler, Lisa Miller, Julie Novkov, Sarah Pralle, Grant Reeher, Hans Peter Schmitz, Carroll Seron, Ken Sherrill, Stephen Siegel, Miriam Smith, Jeff Stonecash, Brian Taylor, Steve Wasby, Erika Wilkens, Amanda Winkler, and especially Keith Bybee and Mark Graber. Keith provided detailed comments on multiple chapters, and Mark read the full manuscript not once but twice. The book is immeasurably better as a result of their efforts. It might be better still if I had accepted more of their suggestions. I did not impose the manuscript on my friend Kevin McMahon, but our ongoing collaborative work has shaped my views regarding the law and politics of abortion rights, the influence of the presidency on constitutional development, and much more.

Along the way, I presented early versions of many of the arguments in this book at the Annual Meetings of the American Political Science Association, the American Studies Association, the Association of American Law Schools, the Law and Society Association, the Southern Political Science Association, and the Western Political Science Association, as well as talks at Carleton, Hobart & William Smith, Moravian, and Oberlin Colleges; at DePaul, Grand Valley State, Harvard, Princeton, and Rutgers Universities; and at SUNY Albany. I have not kept track of the panelists and attendees at all of these venues, but I hope some of them will recognize the fruits of their questions and comments in this book.

Once upon a time, this was going to be a book about affirmative action litigation. (It still is a book about affirmative action litigation, but it has grown to encompass abortion, gay rights, and gun rights litigation as well.) At that time, I imposed on a number of participants in the legal and political conflict over affirmative action to talk to me about their experiences. The book project evolved in ways that prevented me from giving those experiences significant attention, but I would nonetheless like to thank Nancy Cantor, Glynn Custred, Michael Greve, Kirk Kolbo, Rick Lempert, and Diane Schachterle for being so generous with their time.

In addition to providing the intellectual environment in which the book was written, the Maxwell School has supported my efforts in more concrete ways. I have been particularly fortunate to have at my disposal the resources of the Michael O. Sawyer Chair for Constitutional Law and Politics, which was endowed by former students of the legendary Michael O. Sawyer. I have lost count of how many times I have been introduced as holder of the Sawyer Chair, prompting a member of the audience to track me down before the event concluded, shake my hand, and introduce herself or himself as one of Michael's students and eternal fans. For those who knew him, I would like to assure you that his legacy lives on at Maxwell, and that we are always happy to hear from you. I have also received invaluable support for my work from Syracuse University's Department of Political Science (with a special thanks to my predecessors as department chair, Jeff Stonecash and Mark Rupert), from the Dean's Office in the Maxwell School (with a special thanks to Mike Wasylenko, Mitch Wallerstein, and Jim Steinberg), and from the Institute for the Study of the Judiciary, Politics, and the Media (with a special thanks to its director,

Keith Bybee). Last but certainly not least, the book would still be unfinished if I had not received support for a year of full-time writing from the American Philosophical Society.

At the University of Chicago Press, John Tryneski has supported this project through many iterations, gently steering me back from several missteps along the way. It has been a pleasure to work with him throughout the process. I would also like to thank Melinda Kennedy, Rodney Powell, Joel Score, Meg Wallace, Lisa Wehrle, and an anonymous reviewer for guiding the project from manuscript to book.

On a more personal note, the pleasures of writing a book for ten years don't always feel like pleasures, and the process would in fact be unbearable were it not for a great community of friends here in Central New York. I hesitate to list folks by name, for fear of repeating Justice Blackmun's mistake with Mel Ott, but here goes: Tanya Bowen and Althea Henry (and Jonah, Kingston, and Jaden!), Tim Brower and Holly Greenberg (and Gulliver and Eisen!), Keith Bybee and Jen Champa (and Evan and Ava!), Joe Cota and Jennifer Waters (and Juliette!), Pete Couvares and Gladys McCormick (and Amelia and Lucia!), Mike Goode and Jolynn Parker (and Dash!), Mary Hageman and Paul Otteson (and Max and Alaira!), Brenden and Lisa Kuerbis (and Henry and Lucy!), Norman Kutcher and Richard Wallach, Katherine Lieber and Katherine Biers, Jen Margulies and Jackie Cuevas (and Avital!), Laurie Marhoefer and Stephanie Clare, Jesse Nissim and Gretchen Purser, Jasmine Pryor and Earl Hardy (and Elodie and Nyla, and go Ravens!), Chris and Heather Scanlon (and Jude, Luke, and Sophie!), and Brian Taylor and Renee de Nevers (and Anatol and Lucian!).

More far flung, and thus less helpful in providing regular distractions from my writing, my many extended families nonetheless deserve recognition for their constant support. To the Kecks, the Poggis, the Drosnins, the Gozans, the Imels, the Dobkins, and the Schwartz-Howerdds, my thanks and my love.

In thanking those who helped with my previous book, I noted that just one person had had to live with me day in and day out while I wrote it. That one is now three, and Sasha, Ruby, and Julie deserve more thanks than anyone. It's one thing to put up with me being holed up in my office, typing away, but even more unjust is having to suffer through all the times I've been walking through the house, making breakfast, eating dinner, playing Sleeping Queens, while my mind races away, composing sentences about law and courts. Sasha, thank you for keeping me company while

I'm at my computer, and for keeping me on my toes with your persistent skepticism of why anyone would want to write a book about the Supreme Court. I love reading books with you (Bilbo, Frodo, Harry, and Septimus!) and talking about books that you've read and I haven't (Laura and Mary, and all those warrior cats and owls!). I can't wait to see what the books will be about when you start writing them. Ruby, thank you for introducing me to Mr. Magutwin, Boggy and Seekie, tickle class, and (most especially) Pablo and Zebra. I love reading and talking about books with you too (Batty and Hound, Caveman and Zero, Paddington Bear, and the Rooster Prince!), and I can't wait 'til you start reading them to me. Now that I think about it, if you're reading this, you might have started already. Goz, thank you for your many close readings of the manuscript, but even more so for your companionship, every day. Remember when we used to read books together? You're the best company.

Three Stories about Courts

In this era of intensely polarized politics, three stories about courts and judges have emerged. When the US Supreme Court (SCOTUS) upheld most provisions of the Affordable Care Act (ACA, also known as Obamacare) in June 2012, some observers emphasized that a chief justice appointed by Republican president George W. Bush had joined the Court's four Democratic appointees to uphold the statute, characterizing the decision as a textbook example of neutral judging according to law. Others emphasized that the Court's four other justices, all Republican appointees, had voted to strike down in its entirety a 900-page statute that represented the signature domestic policy achievement of a sitting Democratic president; these observers fretted about the latest example of partisan justice. And still others emphasized that the ACA's ultimate fate appeared to hinge less on the justices' views than on the outcome of the 2012 election, suggesting that the Court's role was relatively inconsequential. Each of these stories captures part of what is significant about *National Federation of Independent Businesses v. Sebelius* (2012)—and about contemporary courts more broadly—but none of them paints the full picture.

Consider the first story, told most often by judges themselves. When we ask judges to describe their work, they invariably say that they are doing their utmost to apply the law as written. As John Roberts put it in 2005, "judges are like umpires." Testifying before the Senate Judiciary Committee on his nomination as chief justice of the United States, Roberts insisted that as a judge, his job was simply to call balls and strikes, not to root for either team. Like an umpire, he would not write the rules, but merely apply them.[1] With or without the sports analogy, this story has long been a central rhetorical feature of the written opinions issued

by appellate courts, and judges regularly revert to it when speaking to
the public in other settings. It is, after all, the textbook account of the
role of federal judges in our constitutional system. The framers of our
Constitution wisely provided that these judges would be appointed, not
elected, and that they would serve life terms. These provisions ensure that
federal judges have the independence necessary to apply the law as written, without regard to the popularity of the result.

It is not surprising that judges describe their work this way. Some of
them actually believe it, and all of them recognize that saying anything different might get them into trouble. Four years after Roberts sat before the
Judiciary Committee, Sonia Sotomayor found herself in the same seat,
where she faced repeated criticism for two recorded speeches in which
she had acknowledged that appellate judges make policy and that the
race and gender of those judges might sometimes make a difference in
their decisions. Most famously, she had indicated that the decisions of "a
wise Latina" judge might sometimes be different from those issued by
white male judges. A number of Republican senators denounced these
comments, and given the stakes involved, it is no surprise that Judge
Sotomayor indicated that her words had been misunderstood, that she
did "not believe that any ethnic, racial or gender group has an advantage in sound judging," and that throughout her seventeen-year tenure
on the federal bench, she had simply applied the law to the facts of the
cases before her. When Senator Herb Kohl referenced Roberts's umpire
analogy, Sotomayor agreed that the role of judges, "like umpires, is to be
impartial and bring an open mind to every case before them."[2]

On both sides of the aisle, partisan senators have echoed this story
of judges as umpires, but only when talking about judicial nominees
put forward by a president from their own party. When President Bush
nominated Samuel Alito to the Court, his Republican allies in the Senate
repeatedly emphasized that Alito had "more judicial experience than any
Supreme Court nominee in more than 70 years" and that his record on the
federal bench demonstrated a politically neutral commitment to the rule
of law. In support, Republican senators offered several examples of cases
in which Judge Alito had reached liberal results because those were what
the law commanded.[3] Three years later, Democratic senators emphasized
that Judge Sotomayor had even more judicial experience than Alito,
indeed more "than any Justice in the past 100 years." They touted the
nominee's neutral commitment to the rule of law and highlighted cases
in which she had reached conservative results. Indeed, Democratic sen-

ator Charles Schumer indicated that "any objective review of Judge Sotomayor's record on the Second Circuit leaves no doubt that she has simply
called balls and strikes for 17 years, far more closely than Chief Justice
Roberts has during his four years on the Supreme Court."[4]

When describing judicial nominees from the opposite party, the senators at these hearings told a different story, repeatedly characterizing the
judges before them as unaccountable judicial activists. In Alito's case,
Democratic senators emphasized that in legal disputes between individuals and the government or powerful corporations, Alito hardly ever sided
with the individual; when he did do so, it was invariably to support an individual rights claim that conservatives widely endorsed.[5] In Sotomayor's
case, Republican senators worried aloud that she would impose the platform of the Puerto Rican Legal Defense Fund on the nation at large.[6]
According to partisan critics of the courts, many judges are essentially
tyrants in robes. They are *supposed* to just apply the law as written, but
what they *really* do is impose their own preferences on the nation—
making up new constitutional rights as they go along, thwarting the
democratic will, and (because of their lifetime appointments) leaving the
people with no recourse when they do so. Partisan conservatives have told
this story for almost half a century, and they have shown no signs of abandoning it even when a majority of federal judges have been appointed
by Republican presidents.[7] If anything, the story of unaccountable activist judges has become *more* prominent in recent years because partisan
liberals now tell it as well. They are not criticizing the same decisions, of
course. Conservatives shout "judicial activism" when the courts issue an
abortion rights decision, and liberals shout it when the courts issue a gun
rights decision. But they are all shouting the same thing: that judges are
abusing their power by imposing their own political preferences on the
nation. Indeed, judges increasingly tell the same story themselves—not
when describing their own decisions but when characterizing the objectionable rights-protecting decisions of their colleagues.[8]

The third story is less prominent in public discourse, but those who
pay close attention to courts and judges have probably heard it. This story
is told by a number of scholars who have rejected both the umpire and
tyrant narratives as hopelessly out of touch with reality. Insisting that
courts are relatively weak and inconsequential, and hence neither to be
feared nor praised, these scholars emphasize that judicial decisions rarely
challenge popular sentiment and are almost always ineffective when they
do so. In a widely influential 1957 article, Robert Dahl emphasizes that

"the policy views dominant on the Court are never for long out of line with the policy views dominant among the lawmaking majorities of the United States" (1957, 285). In an equally influential 1991 book, Gerald Rosenberg emphasizes that the Court lacks the capacity to enforce decisions on an unwilling public. In the long run, federal judges are unlikely to impose limits on the popular will—either for good or for ill—because they are appointed by elected presidents and confirmed by elected senators. State judges are even less likely to do so because many of them are elected, and even those who are appointed generally serve for shorter terms than their federal counterparts. Given these electoral connections, judges can be expected to share the public's views on most significant questions. And on the rare occasions when judges do not share those views, their attempts to challenge the public will are likely to fail, as unpopular judicial decisions tend to provoke such a strong political backlash that they are effectively ignored, resisted, or overturned. On this account, we should not spend much time worrying about judicial power, as courts are the "least dangerous branch," but neither should we waste much effort defending it, as it achieves nothing of value that we could not achieve just as well in its absence.

In this book, I build on a variety of recent scholarly accounts of judicial politics—and draw on my own analysis of two decades of litigation regarding abortion, affirmative action, gay rights, and gun rights—to tell a more nuanced story about the role of courts in times of political polarization. In polarized America, advocates on both the left and the right engage in litigation more or less constantly to achieve their ends. This fact is not likely to change because none of these advocates have any incentive to engage in unilateral disarmament. Judges have responded to this unending litigation not simply as umpires, tyrants, or servants of whoever won the last election, but partly in light of distinctive judicial values and practices. The result is that the policies and politics of the contemporary culture wars are significantly different than they would have been in the absence of constitutional litigation.

Courts and the Culture Wars during the Clinton, Bush, and Obama Eras

In August 1992, Pat Buchanan declared to the delegates at the Republican National Convention that "[t]here is a religious war going on in our country for the soul of America. It is a cultural war, as critical to the kind of nation we will one day be as was the Cold War itself." Calling an end to his primary campaign against incumbent president George H. W. Bush, Buchanan urged conservatives of all stripes to come together for the November election. He warned that if Bill Clinton and Al Gore were elected—with Hillary Clinton coming to power as part of the package—the nation would continue down a disastrous road toward abortion on demand, same-sex marriage, radical feminism, environmental extremism, pornography, and lawless violence (Buchanan 1992). Buchanan's speech was widely criticized, his candidate lost in November, and some national Republican leaders since then have sought to soften the edges of his war against liberalism. Still, the polarizing social and cultural issues that Buchanan highlighted remain a central focus of national political conflict.

And this despite one Democratic president's concerted effort to call the culture war to an end. Speaking to the delegates at the Democratic National Convention in August 2008, Barack Obama urged voters to lay aside the polarized conflicts of the Clinton and Bush eras, and to come together on common ground:

> We may not agree on abortion, but surely we can agree on reducing the number of unwanted pregnancies in this country. The reality of gun ownership may be different for hunters in rural Ohio than for those plagued by gang-violence in Cleveland, but don't tell me we can't uphold the Second Amendment while keeping AK-47s out of the hands of criminals. I know there are differences on same-sex marriage, but surely we can agree that our gay and lesbian brothers and sisters deserve to visit the person they love in the hospital and to live lives free of discrimination. . . . This too is part of America's promise—the promise of a democracy where we can find the strength and grace to bridge divides and unite in common effort. (Obama 2008)

This call to move past the culture wars was a consistent theme of Obama's 2008 campaign. Earlier in the year, he had praised the Supreme Court's decision in *District of Columbia v. Heller* (2008) by emphasizing that the Court was both protecting the individual right to bear arms and leaving room for continued legislative efforts to regulate gun possession. If elected, Obama promised that he would "uphold the constitutional rights of law-abiding gun-owners, hunters, and sportsmen" but would also work "to enact common-sense laws, like closing the gun show loophole and improving our background check system, so that guns do not fall into the hands of terrorists or criminals" (Littau 2008). Likewise, whenever he was asked about same-sex marriage during the 2008 campaign, he emphasized his continued opposition but pledged to seek full federal recognition of civil unions for same-sex couples (Nagourney 2008).

President Obama may have hoped to use his position of national leadership to forge broadly acceptable compromises on issues that had long polarized the country, and his first term did witness some successes on this front. He signed two significant gay rights policies into law, and in the midst of his reelection campaign, with public support for same-sex marriage having surpassed 50 percent, he came out in favor of full legal equality for gay and lesbian couples.[9] Still, at the end of his first term, a number of his promises to the LGBT (lesbian, gay, bisexual, and transgender) community remained unfulfilled. On gun rights, Obama's first-term record was even thinner; indeed, he did not act on any of the policy promises he made when praising the *Heller* decision. Shortly after his reelection in November 2012, a horrific school shooting in Newtown, Connecticut, led him to move the issue of gun control to the top of his legislative agenda, but even then, he was unable to push any significant policy changes through a divided Congress.

President Obama's limited progress in resolving the culture wars resulted in part from his attention often being elsewhere. He inherited two wars and a devastating economic crisis, and his top domestic policy priority (the ACA) unexpectedly consumed nearly the entirety of his first term. His relative lack of success on the culture war front is also traceable to the intense polarization of contemporary partisan politics. At every turn, his efforts to forge compromise—in dropping the so-called public option from the ACA, in tightening border security before pursuing comprehensive immigration reform, in selecting widely respected moderates for the federal bench—brought grief from the left with no corresponding credit from the right. But perhaps most significant, certain institutional features of the contemporary American political system provide the president with at best limited control of the national agenda, especially on culture war issues like gay rights and gun rights. Indeed, one of the key defining features of these issues, as they play out in American politics, is that they are the focus of extensive litigation. Hence their trajectories are shaped more by lawyers and judges than by elected presidents and legislators. As a result, not even a popular president with large partisan majorities in both houses of Congress can control the timing or scope of conflicts surrounding these issues.

Most of the culture war issues that Buchanan and Obama highlighted in their speeches have witnessed significant policy change since 1992, and courts have played a central role in these processes. When Buchanan raised the "amoral" specter that "gay and lesbian couples should have the same standing in law as married men and women," he seemed to be tilting at windmills. No judge in the country had endorsed this idea, and no legislative institution was even considering it. But just eighteen years later, a federal judge appointed by President George H. W. Bush himself held that same-sex couples have a constitutional right to marry.[10] On the abortion issue, Buchanan's speech came in the wake of a notorious Supreme Court decision in which five Republican-appointed justices had flatly rejected the Bush administration's call to overturn *Roe v. Wade* (1973).[11] *Roe* has remained on the books ever since, but conservative judges have persistently chipped away at the scope of its protections, and state and federal legislators have taken this opportunity to impose an ever-proliferating variety of restrictions on abortion providers. Abortion rights advocates have tirelessly challenged these laws in court, and though these efforts have been less successful with each passing year, they continue to win some victories.

Meanwhile, policy advocates on the right have made similar use of litigation. During the Clinton era, a small group of conservative litigators launched a concerted effort to persuade the courts to ban race-conscious affirmative action policies once and for all. They have not reached this broad goal, but their lawsuits (along with a parallel set of ballot initiative campaigns) have succeeded in curtailing the scope of such policies to a significant degree, and the effort has not yet run its course. The Clinton era also witnessed the emergence of nationally significant gun rights litigation, sparked in particular by President Clinton's signing of the Brady Bill in 1993 and a federal ban on assault weapons the following year. Gun rights advocates escalated these litigation efforts during the George W. Bush era, challenging not just newly enacted federal gun restrictions, but state and local policies that had been in place for many years.

In this book, I hope to shed fresh light on the significance and legitimacy of these lawsuits. On both the left and the right, policy advocates regularly appeal to courts to advance their aims. How effective are these efforts? Do they prove consequential in either intended or unintended ways? Are the lawyers who bring these suits to be celebrated or bemoaned? How about the judges who sometimes endorse them? And perhaps most important, should we be concerned that calling on courts to settle so many polarizing political conflicts might have some negative impact on judicial institutions themselves?

In the chapters that follow, I describe and evaluate the patterns of nationally significant litigation on four key culture war issues—abortion, affirmative action, gay rights, and gun rights—from the beginning of the Clinton presidency in 1993 through the first seven months of President Obama's second term. Two of these issues involve widespread and well-known litigation on the left, while the other two involve similar litigation on the right. One thing I hope to make clear, however, is that all four issues have witnessed both judicial politics and democratic politics on both sides of the aisle. On the abortion issue, for example, the most familiar story line involves conservative efforts to regulate abortion via state legislation, which then spark left-liberal efforts to defend reproductive rights via litigation. At various points in the conflict, however, abortion rights advocates have themselves made headway in the legislative arena, and when they have done so, abortion opponents have often responded with litigation of their own. To note just one instance, when President Clinton signed the Freedom of Access to Clinic Entrances Act in May 1994, pro-life advocates responded with multiple constitutional challenges to the statute on free speech grounds. The gay rights picture is similar in many ways. The most well-known lawsuits have originated on the left, and conservative opponents of gay rights have regularly denounced these suits as efforts to use the courts to thwart the democratic will. But when LGBT rights advocates have instead won policy victories in state or federal legislatures, their conservative opponents have invariably challenged these policies in court.

On affirmative action and gun rights, the roles are reversed, but the story is the same. With affirmative action, the most well-known lawsuits have involved conservative rights advocates calling for courts to dismantle policies enacted by Congress, by local city councils and school boards, and by state university systems. Affirmative action supporters have denounced these suits, but whenever it seemed like it might help, they have turned to the courts themselves. Most notably, when color-blind advocates have tried to ban affirmative action via ballot initiative, affirmative action supporters have regularly challenged these initiatives in court. Finally, gun rights advocates have long defended the right to bear arms primarily via electoral and lobbying efforts, but in recent years they have won some landmark victories in court as well. Meanwhile, their opponents on the left have sought the enactment of gun control policies primarily via legislative politics, but they too have been willing to try their hand at litigation.

In addition to being initiated by advocates across the political spectrum, constitutional litigation is also directed at policymakers across the political spectrum. The textbook account of such litigation suggests that it is a tactic engaged in by political losers and directed against political winners. Depending on your vantage, this tactic is likely to seem praiseworthy on some occasions and to merit denunciation on others. Are the litigators asking judges to heroically defend minority rights against an electoral majority that is trampling on those rights? Or are they asking judges to substitute their own preferred policies for the contrary policies that are favored by a majority of our fellow citizens? Either way, we have been led to expect electoral and legislative losers to turn to court in an effort to block or reverse the policies enacted by electoral and legislative winners. On the issues that I examine here, we might expect to see conservative litigation on affirmative action and gun rights during the Clinton era, supplanted by liberal litigation on abortion and gay rights during the Bush era, and then reverting to the prior pattern during the Obama era. In actual fact, however, the patterns are independent of partisan control of the elected branches. Indeed, there is both liberal and conservative litigation on all four issues across the full time frame. This is partly because a great deal of constitutional litigation is directed at state lawmaking institutions that are controlled by the party currently out of power at the national level (Klarman 1996). But it is also because rights advocates litigate against their ostensible friends as well as their enemies. In the famously fragmented and decentralized system of American lawmaking, litigation is an ever-present tool, no different in kind from electioneering or lobbying. In any given context, policy advocates will choose the combination of tools that seems most likely to advance their aims. On both the left and the right, that combination will often include litigation (Cummings 2013, 179–80).

What Do Rights Advocates Want from Courts?

In part 1 of the book, I survey the key litigation developments regarding abortion, affirmative action, gay rights, and gun rights during the Clinton, Bush, and Obama eras. One goal of this survey is descriptive. After all, we cannot evaluate a set of judicial decisions without first knowing what the judges actually did, and in the sort of polarized legal conflicts I examine here, popular descriptions of the key cases have sometimes borne only a passing resemblance to what actually happened. But readers who are already well versed in the subject—those who know immediately what I mean when I refer to "*Carhart I* and *II*" or to "*Heller* and *McDonald*"—will find something of value in this section as well, as I have situated the landmark cases within a much larger sea of less well-known judicial holdings. Some readers are already well aware that courts in California, Connecticut, Iowa, and Massachusetts legalized same-sex marriage but may not know that courts in Alaska, Montana, New Hampshire, and Oregon ordered the extension of health benefits to the same-sex domestic partners of state employees during this same period. Or that courts in Georgia, Massachusetts, Michigan, Minnesota, and Virginia ordered public officials to *cease* providing such benefits to same-sex partners. Because rights advocates are engaged in a constant struggle to advance their policy aims, I treat their most well-known courtroom victories and defeats as part of a larger story in which courts are a more or less constant presence.

Assessing this larger story requires an expanded vantage along three dimensions. First, I emphasize the policy goals of change-seeking litigation campaigns rather than their doctrinal underpinnings. On the issues that I examine in this book, the leading rights advocates (on both the left and the right) care first and foremost about policy results. From the beginning, gun rights advocates would have loved to persuade the courts to adopt a more robust understanding of the Second Amendment—because that would aid their policy aims across multiple fronts and would likely have some additional symbolic value as well—but in the meantime, if they could persuade courts to invalidate gun control laws on commerce clause, Tenth Amendment, or even commercial speech grounds, they would happily count those as victories. Thus, when I survey the landscape of "gun rights litigation," I look not just to Second Amendment lawsuits but to any and all efforts by gun rights advocates to use courts to push existing policy in their preferred direction.

Second, I examine a range of litigation initiated by organized rights advocates (again, on both the left and the right), but also a variety of overlapping and intersecting lawsuits filed by private litigants and attorneys. For example, legal challenges to affirmative action are sometimes filed by political organizations dedicated to dismantling race-conscious government policies, but they are sometimes filed by rejected university applicants whose families have retained private counsel. These latter suits, which I refer to as "wildcat litigation" throughout the book, have regularly complicated the efforts of movement attorneys to lead the courts down a preferred path.[12]

Third, I survey a number of well-known decisions issued by SCOTUS, but I pay equal or even greater attention to decisions issued by state and federal judges below this level. These decisions are important because they regularly settle conflicts (or at least attempt to settle conflicts) that do not make it to SCOTUS. And even for issues that do make it to the high court, their earlier treatment by state and federal judges often constructs and constrains the options with which the Supreme Court justices are presented. These lower court decisions are also important because the lawsuits that produce landmark SCOTUS decisions are just the tip of an iceberg that, once revealed, provides a fuller picture of the range of goals that motivate change-seeking litigation.

Perhaps the most original contribution of part 1 is its demonstration that this range of goals is shared by advocates across the political spectrum. Indeed, the central goal of the first half of the book is to make clear that advocates on the left and the right are more or less equally likely to frame their demands in the language of rights, that they are more or less equally likely to appeal to courts to vindicate these demands, and that they call on courts to do so in parallel circumstances. The existing scholarly literature includes scores of valuable treatments of litigation by left-liberal social movements and an increasing number of such treatments of litigation by conservative movements, but it includes very few studies that treat these two categories as examples of the same phenomenon.[13] By treating them together, I hope to emphasize that whatever judgments we adopt regarding the legitimacy and significance of rights-protecting judicial decisions, those judgments are likely to apply to some such decisions that each of us agrees with and to others that we reject.

As such, I use part 1 to detail three distinct strategic circumstances in which advocates regularly conclude that litigation is worth pursuing. On both sides of the political spectrum, advocates routinely call on judges to block new and unwanted policy changes, to dismantle existing policies to which they object, and to facilitate efforts to change policy legislatively. In the first scenario, advocates turn to litigation when faced with newly enacted, rights-restricting policies that they have been unable to block in the electoral and legislative arenas. For example, when the Clinton-era Democratic Congress enacted a federal ban on gun possession by persons subject to a domestic violence restraining order, gun rights advocates immediately challenged the provision in federal court. Likewise, when the Bush-era Republican Congress enacted a federal ban on so-called partial-birth abortion, abortion rights advocates immediately challenged that provision in federal court. In these and similar cases, rights advocates call on judges to enjoin newly enacted statutes, thus preserving the policy status quo. In short, they seek to use courts as veto points.

In the second scenario, advocates litigate because they think the courts might be willing to dismantle rights-restricting policies that are already on the books. When gay rights advocates challenged Texas's criminal prohibition of consensual sodomy, the policy had been in place for decades, but they nonetheless persuaded the Supreme Court that it was time for it to go. Likewise for the gun rights suits targeting local bans on handgun possession in Washington, DC, and Chicago, which also persuaded the high Court to invalidate policies that had been in force for many years. Most anti–affirmative action suits fit this mold as well, with advocates of color blindness calling on judges to enjoin existing policies in the areas of higher education, government contracting, and public employment. Here, advocates call on courts to disrupt the policy status quo rather than preserve it.

In the third scenario, advocates litigate not to reverse a democratically enacted policy directly but to buttress their own efforts to change policy via democratic channels. Put another way, even when relying on more conventional forms of democratic politics, rights advocates often find themselves drawn into court in an effort to facilitate the success of these democratic campaigns. These suits take a variety of forms, including litigation designed to remove impediments to the electoral success of ballot initiative campaigns, litigation designed to enforce policy victories previously won via electoral and legislative channels, and litigation initiated by democratically elected policymakers themselves when other policy avenues are closed off. In these circumstances and others, advocates seek to change policy the "normal" way—via electoral and legislative politics—but nonetheless find it necessary to call on judges for assistance. Here, advocates are using courts to clear the channels of political change.

Throughout the book, I refer to these distinct forms of judicial politics as category 1, 2, and 3 litigation, respectively, but I should note at the outset that the lines dividing these three categories are not sharp. Indeed, the careful reader will notice some lawsuits that fit within more than one category. In *Doe v. Reed* (2010), for example, the Supreme Court rejected a First Amendment challenge to a provision of Washington's 1972 Public

Records Act that required state election officials to publish the names of all signatories to ballot petitions. (The ballot measure at issue would have repealed a recently enacted domestic partnership law.) As a constitutional challenge to a statutory provision that had long been on the books, this case would fit comfortably in category 2. But as an effort to dismantle a state-imposed obstacle to the success of a pending ballot measure on the rights of same-sex partners, it likewise fits in category 3. Despite these porous boundaries, the three modes of change-seeking litigation represent distinct types that should each be evaluated on its own terms.

After all, each mode bears a distinct relationship to norms of constitutional interpretation and democratic legitimacy. Some judges and constitutional scholars have long argued that the active assertion of judicial power is justified when, and only when, judges are seeking to clear the channels of political change (Ely 1980), so it may be that rights-protecting decisions in category 3 are less in tension with democratic theory than those in category 1 or 2. Likewise, it could be the case that the American public is suspicious of judicial efforts to thwart policy changes that are supported by popular majorities in the here and now, but willing to have judges dismantle age-old rights-restricting policies that have survived past their time. In similar fashion, judges might be more effective at dismantling outdated policies than they are at thwarting newly popular ones or, conversely, more effective at blocking policies than at removing them once they have taken root.

Umpires, Tyrants, or Sideshows?

In part 2 of the book, I turn directly to these evaluative questions, framing the inquiry in terms of the three stories about courts that I noted at the outset. In chapter 3, I take up the question of whether judges are usefully understood as neutral umpires, concluding that this judicial narrative is misleading in many ways, but that it does carry a seed of truth. Focusing primarily on the culture war decisions issued by federal appellate courts, I find that the votes of Democratic and Republican appointees diverge in these cases, but not as sharply as the votes of Democratic and Republican legislators on similar issues. In other words, federal judges are indeed polarized on partisan lines, but not as badly as members of Congress. As such, it is misleading to characterize judges as neutral umpires, but judicial institutions nonetheless remain a site of potential cross-partisan agreement within our polarized political system. I support this account with aggregate data on judicial vote patterns, but I also reexamine a number of the legal disputes introduced in part 1, detailing a variety of cases in which courts managed to mark out broadly acceptable compromises on issues that have badly polarized the nation's other political institutions. I close by emphasizing that this judicial centrism was far from inevitable, and that it remains vulnerable in the face of persistent partisan pressure on the courts.

In chapter 4, I turn to the story of judges as activist tyrants. If the judicial defense of rights is inherently undemocratic, then there is indeed a substantial degree of illegitimate judicial activism in the contemporary United States, as state and federal courts regularly invalidate policies that had been democratically enacted. I describe a number of such decisions that can fairly be characterized as thwarting the popular will, with the judges invalidating policies that are supported by the median voter but that run afoul of constitutional principle (in the textbook version) or the judges' own values (in the more cynical account). But I also document repeated instances in which judges invalidated policies that had been democratically enacted but that nonetheless lacked support from popular majorities before, during, and after their invalidation. In these cases, the exercise of judicial review appears to have pushed the policy status quo closer to the public will. And I document several additional cases in which judges invalidated policies that were supported by popular majorities at the time, but whose support was on a downward trajectory and subsequently dipped below 50 percent. In these cases, the courts may have been out in front of public opinion, but they were moving in the same direction.

Many scholars agree that even controversial rights-protecting judicial decisions often have broad public support, and they usually conclude that such decisions are therefore relatively insignificant. After all, we should not need courts to enact policies that are broadly popular because those policies can presumably be enacted via normal democratic channels. In fact, however, the patterns of litigation I describe in part 1 have repeatedly altered policy outcomes in significant ways. This is not because judicial decisions are always and immediately complied with; in fact, they are often successfully resisted, at least for a time. But the widespread scholarly attention to rights-protecting decisions that provoke a public backlash has tended to obscure other rights-protecting decisions that have provoked different reactions. As such, I use chapter 5 to detail the full range of responses by other policymakers to rights-protecting decisions issued by judges. Four such responses recur regularly enough to merit significant attention: resistance, compliance, compromise, and innovation. Judicial decisions of the sort I examine in this book are rarely final in any meaningful sense, and we certainly should not treat them as Olympian pronouncements from on high. But neither should we treat them as "hollow hopes" that fall on deaf ears.[14] Rather, our assessment of their legitimacy and significance should turn on their actual role in ongoing processes of policy change. Again and again, the rights-protecting decisions that I survey in chapters 1 and 2 have altered policy trajectories in measureable ways. Indeed, when I compare the broad policy landscapes on the issues of abortion, affirmative action, gay rights, and gun rights at the outset of the Clinton era and the beginning of Obama's second term, the patterns of change are literally incomprehensible without sustained attention to the influence of lawyers and judges.

*   *   *

If all of this is true, then three important conclusions about contemporary American courts follow. First, no matter how much political denunciation or scholarly skepticism they face, political advocates are unlikely to withdraw from judicial politics. In a world of constant litigation by friend and foe, any decision not to litigate would amount to an act of unilateral disarmament, leaving the field entirely to their ideological opponents. Second, these frequent appeals to courts are no cause for handwringing about democratic legitimacy because judges usually respond to them in ways that are broadly acceptable to the American public. No evidence suggests that rights-based litigation is producing regular acts of judicial "tyranny" in which judges impose their unpopular views on the nation at large. Third and finally, an important normative concern *is* raised by the operation of contemporary courts, but it is not the one that is usually expressed. Constitutional scholars have long fretted that judicial review is a countermajoritarian and hence deviant institution in a democratic system (Bickel 1986). My principal concern with contemporary courts is not that they might protect rights in the face of public opposition, but that they might protect some categories of broadly supported rights while failing to protect other such categories. This concern is rooted in the possibility not of countermajoritarianism but of partisan capture.

PART I

Rights on the Left, and Rights on the Right

CHAPTER ONE

Rights on the Left

The mid-twentieth-century effort by the NAACP Legal Defense and Education Fund to use the courts to advance the cause of civil rights has long been the chief template for litigation in pursuit of policy change. The NAACP's lawyers found litigation to be a potentially fruitful avenue in three distinct circumstances. When southern legislatures and school boards adopted new and innovative policies to curtail African American rights, the NAACP regularly called on the federal courts to enjoin such policies.[1] Of course, many discriminatory policies in the South were of long standing (rather than newly enacted), and the NAACP regularly called on the federal courts to invalidate these policies as well.[2] Third and finally, even where the organization was engaged primarily in democratic politics, its litigators regularly called on the federal courts to enable these efforts by preventing state governments from enforcing laws that hindered the key mobilization and protest tactics engaged in by the organization and its allies.[3]

More recently, LGBT rights advocates have turned to courts in similar circumstances. When red-state legislatures have enacted new statutory or constitutional restrictions on partnership or parenting rights, movement lawyers have called on courts to preserve the policy status quo by enjoining these new laws.[4] When the timing seemed right, the advocates likewise called on courts to dismantle existing rights-restrictive policies—particularly criminal bans on consensual sodomy and discriminatory marriage laws—some of which had been on the books for decades.[5] The timing of their category 1 suits was dictated by the enactment of new legislation, but with these category 2 suits, the advocates did their best to wait until the combination of public support and legal precedent marked out a clear path to victory. Finally, even where they were pursuing their policy aims primarily via legislative channels, they sometimes faced legal barriers that were best hurdled with some assistance from courts.[6]

On both the left and the right, and across a broad range of issues, policy advocates have continued to appeal to courts in each of these three scenarios: to preserve the policy status quo by enjoining new and unwanted policies, to disrupt the policy status quo by dismantling existing policies, and to enable democratic politics by clearing the channels of political change. In this chapter and the next, I survey a range of such examples drawn from the universe of culture war litigation during the Bill Clinton, George W. Bush, and Barack Obama presidencies. I focus here on the policy goals sought by left-liberal advocates in court, the legal arguments they crafted in pursuit of those goals, and the judicial holdings that came in response to these arguments. In chapter 2, I canvas similar ground for suits initiated by conservative advocates. In the second half of the book, I turn my attention from the advocates to the judges, examining the partisan dynamics that have influenced the judicial responses to the lawsuits described in part 1, the degree to which those responses have been consistent with the democratic will, and the impact of those responses on subsequent patterns of policy development and political conflict.

Using Courts as Veto Points

On both the left and the right, legislative losers turn to the courts as a matter of course. Day in and day out, they call on judges to preserve the policy status quo by enjoining new policies that the rights advocates had been unable to block in the legislative arena. Judges usually reject these calls, but on the occasions when they heed them, they provide advocates with a veto point that can have consequential policy effects. Indeed, as Gordon Silverstein has noted, this sort of "blocking function" has long been "the courts' primary power" (2009, 30–33).

Consider the case of abortion regulation. During the Clinton era, no antiabortion legislation could pass at the federal level (because it would be vetoed by President Clinton), but there was fairly widespread legislative activity in the states. Most of this new legislation represented state efforts to copy (and incrementally expand on) the Pennsylvania abortion restrictions that the Supreme Court had upheld in its June 1992 decision in *Planned Parenthood v. Casey*. In the mid-1990s, however, abortion opponents opened a new legislative front whose constitutional status was uncertain, with more than half the state legislatures voting to ban so-called partial-birth abortion. During George W. Bush's first term, Congress enacted a federal ban on the procedure as well. During Bush's second term and Obama's first, state legislatures enacted an expanded range of abortion regulations that went beyond those upheld in *Casey*, with a few of them once again experimenting with outright abortion bans. Virtually all of these new statutes sparked what I have characterized as category I litigation.

Blocking criminal bans on abortion procedures

State legislatures have only rarely tried to enact the sort of sweeping abortion bans that the Supreme Court struck down in *Roe v. Wade* (1973), but when they have done so, the federal courts have prevented these laws from taking effect. The year before the Court reaffirmed *Roe* in *Casey*, both Louisiana and Utah had banned abortion except in cases of rape, incest, severe fetal deformity, or severe threats to the pregnant woman's health. Lawyers with the Center for Reproductive Law and Policy (CRLP) filed immediate constitutional challenges to each of these laws, and the federal courts eventually enjoined them both.[7] In *Casey*'s wake, state legislatures refrained from enacting such clearly unconstitutional abortion bans for fourteen years, until South Dakota sought to push the constitutional envelope in 2006. The statute's proponents were hoping to provoke a lawsuit that would provide a vehicle for SCOTUS to reconsider *Roe*, but abortion rights advocates foiled this strategy by launching an initiative campaign that successfully repealed the law in November 2006. If the initiative had failed, the abortion rights advocates would then have litigated the issue, and the federal courts would surely have invalidated this law as well.

Meanwhile, abortion opponents had begun persuading state legislatures to enact a new set of criminal bans on a particularly controversial late-term abortion procedure that they dubbed "partial-birth abortion." The procedure, medically known as "dilation and extraction" (D&X), involved the partial delivery of a living fetus prior to the completion of the abortion. The first ban on this procedure was enacted by Ohio in 1995, and federal judges quickly divided over whether these laws were consistent with *Casey*. A divided Sixth Circuit panel struck down the Ohio law in 1997, but the year after that, a divided Fourth Circuit panel went the other way, lifting an injunction against Virginia's law.[8] In September 1999, an Eighth Circuit panel managed unanimity in three companion cases striking down the Nebraska, Arkansas, and Iowa bans, but the following month, an en banc Seventh Circuit panel split 5–4 in upholding the Illinois and Wisconsin bans.[9] Collectively, these decisions focused on two potential constitutional defects with the state bans on partial-birth abortions. First, the statutes were sometimes drafted in such a way as to apparently restrict not just the controversial D&X procedure, but also an alternative procedure known as "dilation and evacuation" (D&E). The D&E procedure is the most common method for performing second-trimester abortions, and providers argued that whether intended or not, the statutory bans on this procedure imposed an undue burden on many women seeking to terminate a pregnancy prior to viability. In addition, many of the statutes lacked an adequate exception for situations in which a late-term abortion was necessary to protect maternal health, which abortion providers identified as a second and independent ground for striking them down.

The Seventh Circuit decision is particularly noteworthy because Circuit Judge Frank Easterbrook spelled out a line of argument that would be adopted by SCOTUS some eight years later, and because his colleague Richard Posner responded to this argument with a scathing dissent. Judge Easterbrook rejected facial challenges to the Illinois and Wisconsin laws, but enjoined both states from applying those statutes too broadly and outlined several possible narrowing constructions that the state courts might legitimately adopt. (Easterbrook also held that there was no per se constitutional requirement for all abortion regulations to include health exceptions.) In dissent, Posner observed that "[c]ompromise holds seductive allure for a court faced with a hot issue," but objected that "[t]he court's decision is not a real compromise. It leaves intact the core of the statutory prohibitions, which unlawfully burden the right of abortion." Remarking on "the peculiar and questionable character of these statutes," Posner argued that "[i]f any fetal lives are saved . . . , it will only be by scaring physicians away from performing any late-term abortions, an effect particularly likely in Wisconsin, whose statute imposes a punishment of life imprisonment for its violation." The recent wave of partial-birth abortion bans, Posner continued, "does not exhibit the legislative process at its best, whatever one thinks of abortion rights. Whipped up by activists who wanted to dramatize the ugliness of abortions and deter physicians from performing them, the public support for the laws was also based . . . on sheer ignorance of the medical realities of late-term abortion." These statutes, Posner concluded, "can fairly be described as irrational." They "are not concerned with saving fetuses, with protecting fetuses from a particularly cruel death, with protecting the health of women, with protecting viable fetuses, or with increasing the Wisconsin population (as intimated, surely not seriously, by Wisconsin's counsel). They are concerned with making a statement in an ongoing war for public opinion. . . . The statement is that fetal life is more valuable than women's health."[10]

Faced with this conflict among (and within) the circuits, the Supreme Court granted certiorari in the Nebraska case in January 2000. The plaintiff in this case was Dr. Leroy Carhart, one of a small number of doctors nationwide who regularly performed late-term abortions. Representing Dr. Carhart, CRLP Litigation Director Simon Heller argued that for certain abortions conducted after fifteen weeks of pregnancy, the D&X procedure was the safest method available. By banning this procedure with no exception for maternal health, the state was forcing women to undergo a greater degree of medical risk, with no attendant benefit for either themselves or their fetuses. The district court, the Eighth Circuit, and the Clinton administration all endorsed this line of argument, with the administration also objecting that Nebraska's statutory definition of partial-birth abortion was so broad as to cover the conventional D&E procedure and perhaps the even more common suction curettage procedure in some instances.[11]

In June 2000, a bare five-justice majority sided with Dr. Carhart and the Clinton administration, with Justice Stephen Breyer holding that the Nebraska statute was unconstitutional both because the operative definition of the banned procedure appeared to include the widespread D&E method and because the ban lacked an exception for maternal health, thus compelling some doctors to use an alternative procedure that (in their judgment, under certain circumstances) posed a greater risk of injury to the pregnant woman.[12] Justice Sandra Day O'Connor wrote separately to emphasize that if a state carefully limited its ban to the D&X method and provided an adequate health exception, such a statute would be constitutional under *Casey*.

The most widely noted aspect of the decision, however, was Justice Anthony Kennedy's dissenting opinion. The case represented the Court's first direct engagement with the abortion issue since *Casey*, and during that time, Clinton's replacement of Justice Byron White with Ruth Bader Ginsburg had appeared to increase the Court's pro-*Roe* bloc from five justices to six. (President Clinton had also replaced *Roe*'s author, Harry

Blackmun, with Stephen Breyer, but that appointment had no effect on the Court's balance of power in abortion cases.) But by abandoning his colleagues from the *Casey* decision, Kennedy rendered the Court once again divided by a single vote. Moreover, his opinion opened with a lengthy and graphic description of the abortion procedure at issue and ended by noting that "many decent and civilized people find [it] so abhorrent as to be among the most serious of crimes against human life."[13] Unlike his fellow dissenters, Kennedy did not call *Casey* into question, and there was no reason to suppose that he had changed his mind on the merits of that decision.[14] Still, the tone of his opinion left abortion rights advocates uneasy (Greenhouse 2000b, A1).

Despite these fears for the future, the most immediate impact of *Stenberg v. Carhart* (*Carhart I*) (2000) was a series of decisions enjoining the state partial-birth bans that had so far taken effect.[15] A secondary impact of the decision was to prompt several state legislatures to modify their existing bans in an effort to satisfy judicial scrutiny. These legislative efforts sparked yet further litigation. Ohio was the first state to revise its law, doing so shortly before *Carhart I* came down (but three years after Ohio's first partial-birth ban had been invalidated). Federal District Judge Walter Herbert Rice issued a preliminary injunction in September 2000, holding that the revised statute still lacked a constitutionally adequate health exception—as *Carhart I* by that point required—but in December 2003, a divided Sixth Circuit panel reversed.[16] In doing so, the appellate panel endorsed the Bush administration's judgment that the statute's health exception was constitutionally adequate after all.[17] The administration's lawyers were particularly concerned with this issue in 2002 because they were then in the midst of seeking to enact a federal partial-birth abortion ban that also lacked a robust exception for maternal health. In 2003 and 2004, three other states tried modifying their partial-birth bans to satisfy the Court's constitutional scrutiny. Utah added a health exception to its existing ban. Virginia enacted a law closely modeled on the 2003 federal ban, providing a more careful definition of the banned procedure than Virginia's prior law, but still lacking a health exception. And Michigan declared any partially delivered fetus to be "a legally born person for all purposes under the law." The Michigan statute subjected doctors to civil and criminal liability for aborting any such partially delivered fetus, except in cases where they acted to "save the life of the mother" or to "avert an imminent threat to [her] physical health," and even there required doctors to make "every reasonable effort . . . to preserve the life of" the fetus. Federal courts enjoined all three of these statutes, though two of these decisions were reversed after SCOTUS revised its assessment of partial-birth bans in *Gonzales v. Carhart* (*Carhart II*) (2007).[18]

During President Obama's first term, with the battle over partial-birth bans having run its course, abortion opponents opened yet another legislative front, with legislatures in nine states enacting statutory bans on all abortions performed after twenty weeks' gestation, on the (disputed) grounds that this was the point at which fetuses developed the capacity to feel pain. Texas followed suit in 2013, following a widely noted state legislative filibuster that delayed enactment of the law for several weeks. Two additional states pushed the envelope even further that year, with Arkansas banning abortion after twelve weeks' gestation and North Dakota doing so after a fetal heartbeat is detected, typically around six weeks' gestation. In response, the American Civil Liberties Union (ACLU) and the Center for Reproductive Rights (as CRLP was by this point known) filed federal constitutional challenges in Arizona, Arkansas, Georgia, and North Dakota. In 2012 and 2013, state or federal judges enjoined all four of these laws.[19]

In addition to working through state legislatures, abortion opponents have on occasion turned to the ballot initiative process, calling on the voters themselves to enact state constitutional provisions designed to severely curtail the availability of abortion. Faced with these measures, abortion rights advocates have sometimes turned to the courts even before election day, filing preemptive suits to keep these initiatives off the ballot. Judges have generally been reluctant to review substantive constitutional objections to ballot measures that have not yet been enacted, but in 2012, the ACLU and the Center for Reproductive Rights persuaded the Oklahoma high court that a pending ballot measure that would have amended the state constitution to grant legal personhood to fetuses was inconsistent with *Planned Parenthood v. Casey.*[20] In other cases, abortion rights advocates have relied on state law procedural requirements in persuading judges to exclude nonconforming initiatives from the ballot.[21]

Blocking state-imposed burdens on abortion access

With the exception of the partial-birth cases, most abortion rights litigation during the Clinton era challenged not outright bans on abortion procedures, but instead a wide range of state legislative restrictions on when, by whom, and on whom abortions may be performed. The 1992

Casey decision held that such restrictions were permissible so long as they did not impose an "undue burden" on the constitutionally protected right to terminate a pregnancy, but this standard left room for substantial legal wrangling regarding the precise practical effects of any particular restriction. In *Casey* itself, for example, SCOTUS rejected a facial challenge to Pennsylvania's requirement that women seeking an abortion be provided with certain state-mandated information at least twenty-four hours before the abortion is conducted. On remand, the abortion providers argued that the requirement should not take effect until they had had a chance to prove that it imposed an undue burden on some women in actual practice. Federal District Judge Daniel H. Huyett III agreed, but a Third Circuit panel reversed this holding in January 1994, and after Justice David Souter denied the clinics' request for an emergency stay, these provisions of the 1989 statute finally took effect. In issuing this decision, Souter noted that the clinics still had the option of pursuing as-applied challenges demonstrating that in practice, the law did indeed impose an undue burden.[22]

One issue that quickly divided the federal courts was whether and how they should take account of practical issues of abortion access that might make the effect of an informed consent/waiting period requirement differ from state to state. After all, many states had fewer abortion providers than Pennsylvania, and the providers claimed that mandatory waiting periods would impose a greater practical burden in these states because women seeking abortions would often have to travel significant distances not once but twice. Just two months after *Casey* came down, a unanimous Fifth Circuit panel upheld Mississippi's informed consent/waiting period requirements, noting that these 1991 provisions were "substantially identical" to the Pennsylvania requirements upheld in *Casey*.[23] A similar challenge to North Dakota's 1991 statute was likewise unsuccessful, but not before some justices had noted their continued concern that such requirements might impose an undue burden in practice. After Federal District Judge Rodney S. Webb dismissed the constitutional challenge in February 1993, the North Dakota clinic appealed to the Eighth Circuit, which scheduled arguments for April but refused to issue a stay in the meantime. The Supreme Court likewise refused to issue a stay, but four justices wrote or joined separate opinions addressing the merits of the case. Most notable was O'Connor's concurring opinion, joined by Souter, which objected that the lower courts had failed to undertake the analysis called for by *Casey*. In O'Connor's view, the practical question to be addressed was whether, "in a large fraction of the cases in which [the law] is relevant, it will operate as a substantial obstacle to a woman's choice to undergo an abortion."[24] Later that spring, the Eighth Circuit heeded O'Connor's observations and temporarily enjoined the law, but in early 1994, a unanimous panel allowed the law to take effect, holding that even with only one part-time abortion provider in the state, the law did not unduly burden the right to terminate a pregnancy.[25]

A different Eighth Circuit panel upheld South Dakota's informed consent/waiting period requirement the following year—noting that it was "substantially similar to provisions upheld by the Supreme Court in *Casey*"—but abortion rights advocates briefly had greater success in a case from Indiana.[26] There, they persuaded Federal District Judge David F. Hamilton to permanently enjoin Indiana's 1995 informed consent/eighteen-hour law. Relying primarily on a study of the impact of the Mississippi provisions, which were the first such requirements to have taken effect, Judge Hamilton held that by effectively requiring two separate visits to a clinic, the Indiana law would unduly burden the ability of some women to obtain an abortion.[27] This suit dragged on for a number of years, but a divided Seventh Circuit panel eventually reversed Judge Hamilton's holding, with Circuit Judge Easterbrook noting that the text of the Indiana law was "materially identical" to the Pennsylvania law upheld in *Casey* and holding that the plaintiffs had failed to establish that the law would impose more of a burden in the former state than the latter.[28] Circuit Judge Diane Wood dissented from Easterbrook's holding, reflecting a doctrinal disagreement that had divided the Seventh Circuit for several years. In a similar suit regarding Wisconsin's informed consent/ waiting period law, which had been enacted in 1996, Federal District Judge Barbara B. Crabb heard virtually the same expert testimony regarding the impact of Mississippi's law. She agreed with Judge Hamilton that such requirements appeared to reduce the incidence of abortion, but she held that the plaintiffs had failed to prove that this reduction resulted from an impermissible burden imposed by the mandatory twenty-four-hour waiting period. On Judge Crabb's reading, the declining abortion rate may well have resulted from the persuasive effect of the law's informed consent provisions, which were intentionally (and permissibly) designed to persuade some women to choose childbirth over abortion.[29] A divided Seventh Circuit panel affirmed this holding in August 1999, and the full circuit then split down the middle—a 5–5 vote—on whether to rehear the case en banc.[30]

Though the decisions were not unanimous, the Clinton-era informed consent/waiting period laws virtually all survived federal judicial review.[31] Since most of them were modeled on the Pennsylvania statute upheld in

Casey, this result is not surprising. Given this pattern of federal judicial decisions, abortion rights advocates sometimes turned to state constitutional litigation instead (Kolbert and Miller 1998; Wharton 2009). They won with this strategy in Montana and Tennessee, but as with their federal litigation, most of their state suits ultimately failed.[32] For example, after their unsuccessful federal constitutional challenges in Mississippi and Indiana, abortion providers filed state constitutional challenges seeking the same end. These challenges were rejected by the state high courts in 1998 and 2005, respectively, and state constitutional challenges were unsuccessful in Ohio, Michigan, Florida, and Missouri, as well.[33]

When a number of red-state legislatures enacted a new wave of informed consent requirements during the Bush and Obama eras, abortion rights advocates returned to court, but the judicial response was again largely unsympathetic. South Dakota modified its informed consent requirement in 2005, markedly expanding the range of state-mandated information that abortion providers were required to present to their patients. Planned Parenthood immediately filed a federal constitutional challenge, and Federal District Judge Karen Schreier enjoined the law before it took effect.[34] A divided Eighth Circuit panel affirmed this preliminary injunction, but the state petitioned for rehearing, and an en banc panel lifted the injunction in June 2008, remanding the case for trial.[35] On remand, an Eighth Circuit panel unanimously upheld the statutory requirement that abortion providers inform each of their patients "that the abortion will terminate the life of a whole, separate, unique, living human being," that the patient "has an existing relationship with that unborn human being and that the relationship enjoys protection under the United States Constitution and under the laws of South Dakota," and that "by having an abortion, her existing relationship and her existing constitutional rights with regards to that relationship will be terminated." The panel invalidated the statute's additional requirement that patients be told that abortion is associated with "[i]ncreased risk of suicide ideation and suicide," but in July 2012, an en banc panel reversed this latter holding by a 7–4 vote, allowing the full statute to take effect.[36]

By this time, South Dakota legislators had tightened their informed consent requirements still further, expanding the waiting period to seventy-two hours and requiring all women seeking abortions to first undergo counseling at an antiabortion "pregnancy help center." This statute was enacted in 2011, and Judge Schreier again enjoined the law before it took effect, holding that "forcing a woman to divulge to a stranger at a pregnancy help center the fact that she has chosen to undergo an abortion humiliates and degrades her as a human being."[37] The state appealed this holding, and if the Eighth Circuit responds the same way it responded with respect to the 2005 legislation, the 2011 law has a good chance of eventually taking effect.

In addition to requiring abortion clinics to provide patients with specified information orally and in writing, South Dakota and a number of other states began requiring them to provide patients with an ultrasound image of their fetus before conducting an abortion as well. Most such statutes required providers simply to offer patients the option of viewing such an image, but in 2008, Oklahoma enacted a law requiring providers to situate the monitor such that the patient could view the image, whether she wanted to or not, and to describe various specified elements of the fetal anatomy while doing so. After abortion rights advocates successfully challenged this law on the grounds that it violated the state constitutional requirement that statutes be limited to a single subject, the legislature reenacted the requirement in 2010.[38] The Center for Reproductive Rights immediately filed a new challenge in state court, and a unanimous state high court invalidated the law in December 2012.[39] By this point, federal constitutional challenges to similar laws had reached mixed results in cases from North Carolina and Texas.[40]

The SCOTUS holdings on parental involvement laws, like the holdings on informed consent requirements, left significant room for continued litigation. In a series of decisions culminating in *Casey*, abortion rights advocates had repeatedly failed to persuade SCOTUS that parental notification or consent laws were unconstitutional per se, but they had won a number of holdings that imposed some limits on such laws. In particular, the Court had repeatedly held that states could not constitutionally require parental notification or consent unless they provided a so-called judicial bypass option by which a minor could avoid parental involvement if she persuaded a judge that she was mature enough to make the decision on her own or that the abortion was in her best interest.[41]

As Clinton-era state legislatures modified their parental involvement requirements in *Casey*'s wake, they generally included such a bypass option. Where they did not do so, the federal courts had little difficulty striking such laws down.[42] Likewise, so long as an adequate bypass provision was present, Clinton-era courts had little difficulty upholding such laws.[43] Of course, the mere presence of a judicial bypass provision in a parental involvement statute does not guarantee that, in practice, the state is adequately protecting the constitutional rights of pregnant minors. Indeed, as Helena Silverstein (2007) has demonstrated at some length, many local trial judges are either unaware of or irredeemably opposed to the judicial bypass provisions of their states' parental involvement laws. As such, some judges repeatedly fail to entertain bypass requests that appear to have substantial merit.

Abortion rights advocates sometimes litigated on this point, contending that the statutory wording of a particular bypass provision was constitutionally inadequate. These suits achieved mixed success. In 1997, CRLP's attorneys persuaded a Fifth Circuit panel to enjoin Louisiana's 1995 parental consent statute on the grounds that it left "juvenile court judges [with] the discretion to deny an abortion to a minor even though the minor demonstrates that she is mature, well-informed, or that the abortion would be in her best interest."[44] A Ninth Circuit panel reached a similar result with respect to Arizona's parental involvement requirements in 1999.[45] But similar suits challenging Clinton-era statutes from Illinois, Montana, and Tennessee ultimately proved unsuccessful, as did a subsequent suit challenging a Bush-era parental notification law in Oklahoma. The Illinois suit, litigated by the ACLU, prevented the statute's enforcement for more than a decade, but a unanimous Seventh Circuit panel eventually upheld the provision, as construed by the state's courts.[46] The Tennessee suit, also brought by the ACLU, produced a passionate thirty-page opinion from Sixth Circuit Judge Damon Keith emphasizing that the onerous requirements of the state's bypass option "make it a practical impossibility for a minor to obtain an abortion without first consulting or notifying a parent to seek the parent's permission."[47] But this opinion came in dissent, and the full Sixth Circuit subsequently denied rehearing by an equally divided vote.[48] The Montana suit, litigated by CRLP, persuaded a Ninth Circuit panel that the state's judicial bypass option was inadequate, but SCOTUS reversed that holding.[49] And the Oklahoma suit, also litigated by CRLP (known by this point as the Center for Reproductive Rights) was rejected by a unanimous Tenth Circuit panel, though the holding did note that pregnant minors remained free to challenge the statute as applied.[50]

As they did with informed consent/waiting period requirements, abortion rights advocates sometimes turned to state constitutional litigation when they were unable to persuade federal courts to impose adequate limits on state parental involvement mandates. Indeed, the 1998 Mississippi high court decision noted above rejected challenges to both the informed consent and the parental involvement provisions of the state's abortion laws.[51] Elsewhere, such state constitutional litigation was sometimes successful, with the Massachusetts high court holding in 1997 that the state could not constitutionally require the consent of *both* parents (even with a bypass option), and four other state high courts invalidating recently enacted parental involvement laws over the next ten years.[52]

Despite these holdings, most states that wanted to require parental involvement for minors seeking abortions proved able to do so in ways that satisfied judicial scrutiny. Abortion providers regularly complained that these requirements worked in practice to prevent some pregnant minors from exercising their constitutional rights, but that complaint rarely made it onto the public radar, at least during the Clinton years. In June 2000, the Texas Supreme Court drew significant local attention to the issue when it broke into open and sharp division regarding its role in reviewing a trial court decision denying a bypass. The state high court voted 6–3 to reverse such a denial, on the grounds that the pregnant minor had conclusively established the statutory requirement that she was "'mature and sufficiently well informed' to consent to an abortion without parental notification." In response, the three dissenting justices denounced their colleagues in unusually harsh terms for thwarting the legislative will, and concluded on the basis of their own lengthy review of the record that the pregnant teenager at issue lacked the requisite maturity to make such a decision on her own. This conclusion rested, at least in part, on their judgment that she had not sought "advice or counseling from anyone who was inclined to thoroughly explore with her the adverse emotional and psychological impact that an abortion may have," and their view that "a minor cannot be well informed if the only information she has is from people who favor abortion." Responding in turn, two members of the majority published concurring opinions objecting to the intemperate language in their colleagues' dissents and asserting that by "constru[ing] the Parental Notification Act so narrowly as to eliminate bypasses, or to create hurdles that simply are not to be found in the words of the statute," these colleagues were engaged in "an unconscionable act of judicial activism."[53]

This decision drew little national attention when it came down, though the *New York Times* eventually addressed it in the context of Texas Governor George W. Bush's ongoing campaign for the presidency (Yardley 2000). One year later, however, the national media discovered the case. By this time, Bush was in the White House, one member of the Texas high court that had issued the decision was serving as his White House counsel, and another member was awaiting confirmation to a seat on the Fifth Circuit. The Fifth Circuit nominee was Texas Supreme Court Justice Priscilla Owen, and Democratic senators used her dissenting opinion in the parental notification case as exhibit A in their campaign to block her confirmation. In this effort, they regularly reiterated the charge, which had been advanced by future White House counsel Alberto Gonzales, that Owen and her fellow dissenters were unconscionable judicial activists. Despite the notoriety of this case, abortion providers continued to have no more than occasional success in persuading appellate courts that existing judicial bypass provisions failed to adequately safeguard the constitutional rights of pregnant minors. The campaign against Owen was likewise unsuccessful, though Democratic senators did delay her confirmation for four years.

When SCOTUS invalidated Nebraska's partial-birth abortion ban in 2000, the holding opened up a new legal question with regard to parental involvement laws. Recall that Breyer's opinion for the Court in *Carhart I* rested in part on the fact that the statute lacked an exception for situations in which the abortion was medically necessary to protect the pregnant woman's health. Some parental involvement statutes lacked such health exceptions as well, and by 2004, abortion rights advocates had persuaded federal appellate courts to invalidate such laws that had recently been enacted in Colorado, Idaho, and New Hampshire.[54] In May 2005, SCOTUS granted certiorari in the New Hampshire case, and the following January, the Court endorsed the near-unanimous opinion of federal judges that its recent precedents required all abortion regulations to include an exception for maternal health. In a striking example of judicial minimalism, however, Justice O'Connor's opinion also held that statutes lacking such exceptions need not be invalidated on their face, thereby remanding the case for further proceedings on whether some narrower remedy was workable.[55] More important, this opinion was O'Connor's last on the Court. John Roberts had replaced William Rehnquist four months earlier, and just two weeks after the New Hampshire decision came down, Samuel Alito replaced O'Connor.

Blocking federal abortion restrictions

This judicial turnover quickly altered the Supreme Court's approach to abortion rights, and the first battleground was on the field of partial-birth abortion bans. While those bans had been proliferating in state legislatures in the 1990s, President Clinton had twice vetoed such statutes at the federal level. But in January 2001, pro-life advocates had taken simultaneous control of the White House and both houses of Congress for the first time since *Roe v. Wade*. The GOP had temporarily lost control of the Senate when Vermont Republican James Jeffords switched parties later that year, but had regained full control in the midterm elections of 2002. When the Republican Congress enacted a partial-birth ban for the third time in November 2003, President Bush signed it into law.

By failing to include a maternal health exception in this ban, Congress and the president issued a direct challenge to the Court's holding in the Nebraska case. As a result, lower court judges were virtually unanimous in invalidating the federal law.[56] When the issue reached SCOTUS, however, the justices upheld the law, with Alito reversing O'Connor's decisive vote from *Carhart I*. Justices Clarence Thomas and Antonin Scalia wrote separately to observe "that the Court's abortion jurisprudence, including *Casey* and *Roe v. Wade*, has no basis in the Constitution," but Justice Kennedy and the two recent Bush appointees followed Solicitor General Paul Clement's lead in upholding the federal ban without upsetting any of the Court's abortion precedents.[57] Indeed, while Kennedy's opinion is most notorious for adopting much of the rhetoric of the contemporary pro-life movement, it was narrowly drawn in several respects. Kennedy voiced the increasingly prominent pro-life argument that abortion harms the women who choose it, often leading to "regret," "severe depression," and "loss of esteem,"[58] but he declined the opportunity to reverse *Carhart I* or *Casey*, and he took pains to emphasize that the banned D&X procedure was quite rare; that the statute did not ban the separate and more widely used D&E procedure; and that even the ban on D&X remained vulnerable to further legal challenges. He also relied on the Court's recent (and unanimous) opinion in *Ayotte v. Planned Parenthood* (2006) in assuming that "the Act would be unconstitutional . . . if it subjected women to significant health risks."[59] As such, the decision's immediate policy implications were quite limited (Garrow 2007). Still, though the step was a small one, Kennedy's opinion marked an unmistakable change in direction. Federal judges had been nearly unanimous in finding the federal ban inconsistent with existing precedent, and SCOTUS reached a contrary conclusion only by abandoning its long-standing holdings that regulations promoting the government's interest in fetal life could be imposed only after viability and that both pre- and postviability regulations must provide an exception for maternal health.

Gonzales v. Carhart was the only challenge to a federal antiabortion policy that drew significant national attention, but abortion rights advocates challenged at least two other Bush administration policies in federal court, one issued in the opening weeks of President Bush's tenure and the other at its tail end. On his third day in office, President Bush reinstated the so-called Mexico City policy—the Reagan-era prohibition, rescinded by Clinton in 1993, on federal support for international family planning groups that promote abortion. (This day was January 22, 2001, the twenty-eighth anniversary of *Roe v. Wade*.) Nearly eight years later, following the 2008 elections, the lame-duck Bush administration promulgated a federal regulation expanding the rights of health-care workers to refuse to participate in abortions or contraceptive services to which they objected on moral or religious grounds. Abortion rights advocates filed immediate federal legal challenges to each of these policies. In September 2002, Second Circuit Judge Sonia Sotomayor wrote for a unanimous panel in rejecting the challenge to the Mexico City policy, and in early 2009, the challenge to the so-called provider conscience regulation was stayed when the Obama administration announced plans to repeal the rule.[60]

Blocking antigay initiatives

LGBT rights advocates, like their abortion rights counterparts, have made heavy use of litigation across a range of strategic circumstances. Most antigay policies are of long standing, but when the people or their elected representatives have enacted new ones, LGBT rights advocates have regularly filed suit to block enforcement of these laws. In the early 1990s, for example, a wave of antigay ballot initiatives sought to prevent the extension of state and local civil rights laws to cover sexual orientation. Beginning in the late 1990s, a second wave of antigay ballot initiatives sought to block the expansion of partnership rights for same-sex couples. On both occasions, LGBT rights advocates sometimes challenged these measures in court, both before and after election day. As with antiabortion initiatives, these measures sometimes ran afoul of state law procedural requirements in ways that led state judges to exclude them from the ballot. In 1994, for example, the Lambda Legal Defense and Education Fund (Lambda Legal) persuaded the Florida Supreme Court that a proposed antigay initiative violated the state's single-subject requirement.[61] Fourteen years later, the same organization persuaded the Maryland high court to block a proposed referendum seeking to repeal a local antidiscrimination law, with the court accepting Lambda Legal's contention that the referendum's supporters had submitted insufficient valid signatures.[62]

Such preballot challenges were not always successful. In 2002, Gay and Lesbian Advocates and Defenders (GLAD) failed to persuade the Massachusetts high court to block a pending ballot initiative that would have prohibited the recognition of same-sex marriage (SSM) or any similar relationship status.[63] GLAD and its allies subsequently succeeded in blocking the initiative in the state legislature, and the following year, the state high court legalized SSM in *Goodridge v. Department of Public Health* (Mass. 2003). When SSM opponents launched an initiative campaign to reverse *Goodridge*, GLAD again filed suit to prevent the measure from reaching the ballot. The state high court again declined to enjoin the proposed ballot measure, but SSM advocates again managed to block it in the state legislature.[64] SSM supporters in California likewise called on the state high court to block a ballot measure designed to reverse the court's own decision legalizing SSM, but the court declined to do so, and Proposition 8 appeared on the ballot in November 2008.[65]

When preballot challenges were unavailing, LGBT rights advocates tried to defeat these initiatives at the polls, and they were sometimes successful.[66] When that failed, they often challenged the new laws in court. The most significant such case was *Romer v. Evans* (1996), in which LGBT rights litigators successfully blocked enforcement of Colorado's Amendment 2, a state constitutional provision that would have prevented the enactment or enforcement of any governmental policies protecting gays and lesbians from discrimination anywhere in the state. The state's voters adopted the amendment in November 1992, but gay rights advocates immediately filed suit in state court, and the amendment never took effect. The Colorado Supreme Court struck it down in 1994, and SCOTUS affirmed (on different grounds) two years later.[67] Writing for a six-justice majority in *Romer*, Justice Kennedy held that Amendment 2 bears no "rational relation to [any] legitimate end" and "seems inexplicable by anything but animus toward the class it affects." Noting that "a bare . . . desire to harm a politically unpopular group cannot constitute a legitimate governmental interest," Kennedy concluded that "[a] State cannot . . . deem a class of persons a stranger to its laws."[68] This holding, issued by a high Court with seven Republican-appointed justices, authored by a Reagan appointee, and coming in the midst of a nationwide legislative assault on SSM, gave renewed hope to LGBT rights advocates that the courts might be on their side. Still, Kennedy's opinion was cautious in many respects, and the federal courts continued to uphold some antigay initiatives even after *Romer*.[69]

Meanwhile, gay rights opponents turned their attention to the marriage issue, where they had even broader success. Beginning with Alaska and Hawaii in 1998, thirty-two state electorates voted to ban SSM, some of them more than once.[70] In a number of states, these voter-enacted constitutional bans on SSM were supplemented by additional statutory or administrative restrictions on gays and lesbians' spousal or parenting rights. For strategic reasons, LGBT rights advocates refrained from challenging most of these rights-restrictive policies in court, but they did choose some battles that seemed winnable and/or strategically important. In November 2000, for example, Nebraska voters enacted a state constitutional amendment that was particularly troubling to LGBT rights advocates in two respects. It made Nebraska the first state not threatened by litigation to enact a constitutional (rather than statutory) ban on SSM, and it included prohibitory language that reached beyond marriage itself: "Only marriage between a man and a woman shall be valid or recognized in Nebraska. The uniting of two persons of the same sex in a civil union, domestic partnership, or other similar same-sex relationship shall not be valid or recognized in Nebraska."[71] Adopted in the wake of Vermont's enactment of the nation's first civil union law, at a time when SSM itself did not yet exist anywhere in the country, the Nebraska amendment represented a substantial barrier to even incremental advancements in partnership rights for same-sex couples. As such, the ACLU and Lambda Legal made an exception to their general rule against supporting federal constitutional litigation on the marriage issue, jointly filing a lawsuit that was eventually rejected by a unanimous Eighth Circuit panel in 2006.[72]

The vast majority of SSM litigation, however, has taken place in state courts, with LGBT rights advocates almost universally regarding those institutions (in certain states) as more hospitable than the federal judiciary. Most of these lawsuits have challenged policies that had been in place for as long as civil marriage has existed. On several occasions, however, SSM litigators tried their luck against recently enacted bans as well. In Oregon, Wisconsin, and California, when voters enacted anti-SSM constitutional amendments in 2004, 2006, and 2008, respectively, LGBT rights advocates unsuccessfully challenged each measure in state court.[73] Because these suits called on judges to invalidate recently enacted provisions of their state constitutions on state constitutional grounds, the movement litigators recognized from the beginning that they faced long odds. They supported these suits principally because they had no better strategic options available. The Wisconsin suit was an example of wildcat litigation—social reform litigation that is initiated by private litigants and attorneys rather than movement litigators—and Lambda Legal and the ACLU joined it as amici only after it had been filed by private counsel. The LGBT rights groups launched the California suit on their own, but they did so in part because they hoped that the state constitutional challenge to Proposition 8 would help preempt calls for a federal constitutional challenge, which the litigators continued to think premature and strategically unwise (Cummings and NeJaime 2010).

Once the California Supreme Court rejected their state constitutional challenge in *Strauss v. Horton* (Cal. 2009), the movement litigators' cautious approach was thwarted when two nonmovement lawyers immediately filed the most high-profile wildcat suit in all the culture war conflicts that I have examined. In a press conference the day after *Strauss* came down, Ted Olson and David Boies—two of the leading litigators in the country, who had squared off against each other in the presidential election controversy of November 2000—announced that they were challenging Proposition 8 in federal court. (The suit was litigated by Olson and Boies, but it was the brainchild of Chad Griffin, a California-based LGBT rights advocate who objected to the LGBT rights bar's reluctance to file such a challenge (Cummings and NeJaime 2010, 1299–1301).) Given the stature of Olson and Boies, the suit immediately drew widespread media attention, and the national LGBT rights organizations, unable to make the suit go away, joined in with amicus briefs and a public media campaign designed to help Olson and Boies win their case. After a closely watched bench trial, Federal District Judge Vaughn R. Walker invalidated Proposition 8 on due process and equal protection grounds in August 2010.[74] The governor and attorney general of California declined to appeal Walker's holding, but supporters of Proposition 8, who had successfully intervened in the case, appealed to the Ninth Circuit and, when they lost there as well, to the Supreme Court.[75] In June 2013, SCOTUS held that these nonstate supporters of Proposition 8 lacked standing to appeal Walker's holding.[76] Two days later, the Ninth Circuit lifted its stay of Judge Walker's injunction, and SSMs resumed in California (Melvin, Kurhi, and Peele 2013).

Blocking antigay policies enacted by state legislatures and executives

In addition to those enacted by voters, antigay policies enacted by state legislative and executive institutions sometimes provoked legal challenges by gay rights advocates. In 2007, for example, Lambda Legal persuaded a Tenth Circuit panel to invalidate Oklahoma's 2004 Adoption Invalidation Law, which purported to deny state recognition to any adoptions by same-sex couples that were issued by sister states or foreign jurisdictions.[77] And when Arizona governor Jan Brewer signed a law repealing domestic partnership benefits for state employees in 2009, Lambda Legal persuaded a unanimous Ninth Circuit panel to enjoin the repeal.[78]

This sort of federal constitutional challenge remains infrequent, as LGBT rights advocates generally tried to keep the issues of marriage, partnership, and parenting rights out of federal court, at least until 2009. When faced with newly enacted policies that merited legal challenge, they preferred to file such challenges in state court. In 1999, for example, when the Arkansas Child Welfare Agency Review Board adopted a regulation providing that "[n]o person may serve as a foster parent if any adult member of that person's household is a homosexual," the ACLU responded with a state constitutional challenge, and the state high court invalidated the regulation in 2006.[79] When the state's voters responded by enacting a statutory ban on adoption by unmarried cohabitants, straight or gay, the ACLU filed another state constitutional challenge, and in April 2011, a unanimous state high court invalidated the provision on state constitutional privacy grounds.[80]

On the marriage issue, the most well-known antigay policies have been enacted directly by the voters, but a number of state legislatures have enacted statutory bans on SSM as well, and LGBT rights advocates have occasionally responded with state constitutional challenges. For example, when the Washington state legislature enacted such a ban in 1998, SSM advocates persuaded a state trial court to enjoin the law, but a closely divided state high court reversed in July 2006.[81]

Blocking enforcement of "Don't Ask, Don't Tell"

At the outset of the Clinton era, the US military had explicitly banned gays and lesbians from service since the Cold War. This ban had faced repeated legal challenges throughout that time, but Congress sparked a new wave of litigation when it codified (and modified) the policy in 1993. This first gay rights skirmish involving the Clinton White House began with the newly elected president announcing that he would issue an executive order rescinding the military ban but ended with him signing a federal statute declaring that "the presence in the armed forces of persons who demonstrate a propensity or intent to engage in homosexual acts would create an unacceptable risk to the high standards of morale, good order and discipline, and unit cohesion that are the essence of military capability."[82] President Clinton sought to frame this new law as a compromise, as it ended the practice of asking all military inductees whether they were homosexual and purported to allow gays and lesbians to continue serving as long as they successfully kept their sexual orientation hidden. But gay rights advocates uniformly regarded this Don't Ask, Don't Tell (DADT) policy as a significant defeat, and Lambda Legal, the ACLU, and the newly formed Service Members Legal Defense Network (SLDN) repeatedly challenged the policy on federal constitutional grounds (Rimmerman 1996, 119–20). Despite a blatantly discriminatory policy, an army of sympathetic plaintiffs, and a carefully planned litigation strategy, these Clinton-era legal challenges were almost entirely unsuccessful.

As I note above, LGBT rights litigators were never particularly eager to pursue their claims in federal court. After all, at the time DADT was enacted, roughly 60 percent of sitting federal judges had been appointed by Republican presidents, and the leading federal constitutional decision on gay rights was *Bowers v. Hardwick* (1986).[83] Still, early signs indicated that the military cases might be winnable. Public opinion was on the side of gay rights on this issue, and the first two years of the Clinton era witnessed several courtroom victories. In late January 1993, Federal District Judge Terry J. Hatter Jr. ruled in favor of Keith Meinhold, who had been discharged from the navy under the pre-Clinton policy for declaring his homosexuality—"Yes, I am in fact gay"—in a nationally televised interview.[84] President Clinton praised the decision when it came down, but by early March, his Justice Department was urging the Ninth Circuit to reverse it, with administration officials concerned that the litigation would preempt the compromise they were then negotiating with supporters of the ban (Schmitt 1993). In September, Judge Hatter expanded his ruling from earlier in the year by permanently enjoining the Defense Department from "taking any action[] whatsoever . . . against gay or lesbian service members, or prospective service members, that in any way affects, impedes, interferes with, or influences their military status, advancement, evaluation, duty assignment, duty location, promotion, enlistment or reenlistment based upon their sexual orientation in the absence of . . . sexual conduct [that is] . . . proven to interfere with the military mission of the armed forces."[85] As a result, the Pentagon was forced to temporarily suspend enforcement of the new policy, which had been scheduled to take effect on October 1. Answering the Clinton administration's urgent plea, the Supreme Court lifted the injunction in late October, insofar as it applied to persons other than Meinhold himself, pending the disposition of the government's appeal.[86]

In November, in another case involving the discharge of an otherwise highly qualified naval officer, a DC Circuit panel struck down the pre-Clinton policy because it was "not rationally related to any legitimate goal." Writing for a unanimous panel in *Steffan v. Aspin* (D.C. Cir. 1993), Chief Judge Abner Mikva held that "[i]t is fundamentally unjust to abort a most promising military career solely because of a truthful confession of a sexual preference different from that of the majority, a preference untarnished by even a scintilla of misconduct."[87] The following June, yet another court found the pre-Clinton policy unconstitutional, with Federal District Judge Thomas S. Zilly holding that "there is no rational basis for the Government's underlying contention that homosexual orientation equals 'desire or propensity to engage' in homosexual conduct."[88] After the Ninth Circuit rejected the Clinton administration's request for a stay pending appeal, the Washington National Guard reinstated Colonel Margarethe Cammermeyer in July. The following month, a unanimous Ninth Circuit panel agreed with Judge Hatter that Keith Meinhold's discharge had been unlawful, holding that the pre-Clinton policy's ban on homosexual conduct was constitutional but that the military had provided no evidence of such conduct on Meinhold's part.[89]

Opponents of the ban were not winning every case, but the litigation campaign looked promising at this point.[90] In November 1994, however, just weeks after the GOP recaptured Congress in the midterm elections, the DC Circuit reversed the panel decision in *Steffan* by a 7–3 vote.[91] In the *Meinhold* case, the Ninth Circuit panel had been willing to defer to the military's judgment that homosexual conduct was incompatible with service, but it held that the navy could not discharge Meinhold simply for saying publicly that he was gay. In contrast, the DC Circuit held in *Steffan* that the military was indeed free to presume homosexual conduct on the part of service members who had made such statements. This conflict in circuits made the issue ripe for SCOTUS review, but the Clinton administration decided not to appeal the Ninth Circuit's *Meinhold* decision, and the LGBT rights groups decided not to appeal in *Steffan*. On each side, the lawyers were now determined to focus on the new policy, which had taken effect in February 1994.

The lead test case against DADT was *Able v. United States*, filed jointly by several national LGBT rights organizations in federal district court in Brooklyn, New York. In April 1994, Federal District Judge Eugene Nickerson enjoined the new policy, and later in the year, he rejected the Clinton administration's motion to dismiss the case, thus clearing the way for trial.[92] After trial, Nickerson held the policy unconstitutional, emphasizing that its ban on public declarations of homosexuality was inconsistent with the First Amendment.[93] The administration appealed to the Second Circuit, but the first appellate holding on DADT came in a different case in April 1996, when Chief Judge J. Harvie Wilkinson wrote for a divided Fourth Circuit in rejecting Navy Lieutenant Paul Thomasson's constitutional challenge.[94] About six weeks later, the Supreme Court's decision in *Romer* gave new hope to opponents of DADT, but those hopes did not pan out. The Second Circuit reversed Judge Nickerson's free speech holding in July, and when Nickerson invalidated the policy once again on remand, relying this time on *Romer*'s equal protection analysis, the Second Circuit reversed him again.[95] By this point, the Eighth and Ninth Circuits had rejected constitutional challenges to DADT as well.[96]

Given their lack of success so far and their pessimistic assessments of the Supreme Court at the time—despite *Romer*, the Court seemed unlikely to challenge the military on DADT—the national LGBT rights groups were sometimes willing to let these defeats stand. When they (or private counsel) did petition for certiorari, the Supreme Court repeatedly refused to enter the fray.[97] Having failed in court, opponents of DADT returned to the political process, waging a long campaign to educate Congress and the public about the harms that the policy was imposing on gay and lesbian service members and, by extension, on national security (Neff and Edgell 2013). This effort had positive effects on public opinion, where opposition to the policy continued to increase throughout the Clinton and Bush eras, but it made no headway in the Republican Congress. As such, the advocates returned to court once again, with SLDN attorneys filing a new test case in 2004. The prospects for success seemed better this time, in part because SCOTUS had overturned *Bowers* in 2003 and in part because additional evidence had emerged "to show that the factual premise of DADT is simply false. For example, . . . service members known to be gay, lesbian, or bisexual had served with distinction in Kosovo, Afghanistan, Iraq, and elsewhere, with no basis for claiming that their presence harmed morale, good order and discipline, or unit cohesion."[98]

Despite this new evidence, a First Circuit panel rejected the SLDN suit in June 2008, holding that even after the Court's reversal of *Bowers v. Hardwick*, the military context counseled substantial deference to Congress.[99] At this point, the rights advocates decided not to appeal because a better vehicle had emerged in the Ninth Circuit. When one of the First Circuit plaintiffs disagreed and filed a certiorari petition pro se, the national LGBT rights groups opposed the petition, urging the Court to wait for the Ninth Circuit case—*Witt v. Department of the Air Force*—which promised to have a better-developed factual record.[100] The Obama administration opposed the pro se petition as well, arguing that the existing policy was constitutional, but also emphasizing that *Witt* would be a better vehicle for reviewing that policy.

In the *Witt* case, a Ninth Circuit panel had held in May 2008 that the military ban was subject to heightened scrutiny under *Lawrence v. Texas* (2003), the case in which SCOTUS had overturned *Bowers*.[101] The Bush administration requested en banc review, which was denied in December 2008.[102] The Obama administration then decided against petitioning for certiorari, which allowed the case to proceed to trial under heightened scrutiny. This is what the LGBT rights advocates wanted, and it had the added advantage for the administration of delaying any final resolution of the case. Obama had publicly committed to repealing DADT on the presidential campaign trail in 2008, and every time his administration defended the policy in court, LGBT rights advocates responded with outrage. In this way, the pressure imposed by the lawsuits reportedly led the administration to move forward with a repeal bill in 2010 (Bumiller 2010a, A1). When that bill stalled in the Senate that fall, attention returned to the federal courts once again. In yet another federal constitutional challenge, this one filed by the Log Cabin Republicans in October 2004, Federal District Judge Virginia A. Phillips issued a permanent injunction against enforcement of DADT in October 2010.[103] Two months later, the lame-duck Democratic Congress repealed the law, leading the Ninth Circuit to vacate Judge Phillips's holding as moot.[104]

Blocking anti–affirmative action initiatives

The most prominent litigation on the affirmative action issue has been initiated by the right (and hence is reviewed in chapter 2), but left-liberal supporters of affirmative action have sometimes launched lawsuits of their own. In particular, when faced with state ballot initiatives seeking to outlaw race-conscious government policies, they have responded just as LGBT rights advocates did in such circumstances: first by trying to persuade the courts to keep the initiatives off the ballot, or at least to modify their language to make them less appealing to the voters; then by trying to win at the polls; and then by returning to court in an effort to invalidate the newly enacted policies.

The first such conflict involved the California Civil Rights Initiative (CCRI), an effort that was launched by two conservative professors, Glynn Custred and Thomas Wood, and subsequently led by a prominent member of the University of California (UC) Board of Regents, Ward Connerly. Under Connerly's leadership, the campaign collected sufficient signatures to be placed on the ballot in November 1996, where it would be known as Proposition 209. Fearful of losing at the polls, affirmative action supporters sought to block the vote with a preelection legal challenge. The initiative asked voters whether to amend the state constitution to provide that "[t]he state shall not discriminate against, or grant preferential treatment to, any individual or group on the basis of race, sex, color, ethnicity, or national origin in the operation of public employment, public education, or public contracting." Professors Custred and Wood had drawn most of this language from the 1964 Civil Rights Act, but their adversaries objected that it was misleading and should be revised to indicate explicitly that the initiative would ban "affirmative action." A state trial judge agreed in August 1996, but that judgment was quickly reversed on appeal.[105] Proposition 209 appeared on the ballot as scheduled and was adopted with 54.6 percent of the vote.

At this point, the ACLU, the NAACP, and a number of other civil rights organizations filed a federal constitutional challenge, and Federal District Judge Thelton Henderson issued a temporary restraining order that prevented Proposition 209 from taking effect.[106] In late December, the Clinton administration announced that it was joining the constitutional challenge, and a few days later, Judge Henderson issued a preliminary injunction preventing the state from enforcing the ballot measure until the challenge was resolved.[107] On the other side, the initiative's supporters had been content to let the state attorney general's office handle the defense in the preelection challenge, but this time, Custred and Wood's organization, Californians Against Discrimination and Preferences, Inc. (CADP), intervened in the case. CADP was represented by the Center for Individual Rights (CIR), the conservative public interest law firm that was then litigating against affirmative action in other states. In January 1997, the Proposition 209 defense team was joined by Connerly's newly established organization, the American Civil Rights Institute (ACRI), which was dedicated to carrying the ballot initiative strategy nationwide. Later in the year, they were joined also by a group of conservative faculty and students at Boalt Hall (University of California (UC), Berkeley's law school), who submitted an amicus brief drafted largely by Professor John Yoo (Guerrero 2002, 123). Heeding the calls of the initiative's supporters to respect the popular will, a unanimous Ninth Circuit panel vacated Judge Henderson's preliminary injunction in April, holding that Proposition 209 passed constitutional muster.[108] When the full circuit denied rehearing in August, Proposition 209 finally took effect. When SCOTUS denied certiorari in November, the federal constitutional battle was over.

Despite this defeat, affirmative action supporters never fully gave up on the hope that the courts might provide some relief from the limits imposed by Proposition 209. After the abandonment of race-conscious admissions policies resulted in a significant decline in African American and Latino enrollments at UC's flagship campuses, the civil rights organizations returned to court in February 1999, contending that the new race-neutral policies had a discriminatory impact on minority applicants (Equal Justice Society 2004, 64; Miksch 2008).

When Connerly sought to reprise Proposition 209's success in Michigan, affirmative action supporters again filed legal challenges to his initiative both before and after it was enacted by the state's voters.[109] Connerly launched the campaign for a Michigan Civil Rights Initiative (MCRI) immediately after SCOTUS upheld the race-conscious admissions policy at the University of Michigan College of Law in *Grutter v. Bollinger* (2003), but supporters of affirmative action sought to derail the campaign with multiple legal challenges before it reached the ballot. In one case, a local trial judge dismissed a substantive constitutional objection to the measure, holding that that claim could be considered only after enactment (Klein 2004). But in a separate case, a different judge invalidated the initiative on procedural grounds, holding in March 2004 that its language provided inadequate warning that the proposal would "alter or abrogate" the state constitution. The Michigan Court of Appeals reversed this holding a few months later, but by that point, the signature deadline was so close that the organizers announced that they would delay the ballot measure until 2006.[110] After they submitted the necessary signatures in January 2005, the measure was scheduled for the November 2006 ballot, where it would be known as Proposal 2. Affirmative action supporters, led by the Coalition to Defend Affirmative Action by Any Means Necessary (BAMN), again filed suit to block the election, alleging that MCRI supporters had engaged in fraudulent signature-gathering practices. In August 2006, Federal District Judge Arthur Tarnow agreed that the MCRI campaign had engaged in widespread fraud but declined to enjoin the election.[111] In September, a Sixth Circuit panel likewise declined to block the vote, and in November, 57.9 percent of the state's voters supported Proposal 2.[112]

The day after the election, BAMN filed a new challenge, alleging that Proposal 2 was inconsistent with federal constitutional and statutory civil rights guarantees.[113] The following month, the state's public universities filed a motion in the suit, requesting permission to delay implementation of the ballot measure until the conclusion of their current annual admissions cycle. In December, Federal District Judge David M. Lawson issued a preliminary injunction, preventing the amendment from taking effect until July 1, 2007.[114] This decision ratified an agreement between the universities and state attorney general Mike Cox, under which the universities agreed to forgo any further challenges. But CIR was not a party to the deal, and its lawyers were representing Eric Russell, a white applicant to Michigan's law school who had intervened in the case. Russell appealed to the Sixth Circuit, which then stayed the district court's mandate, allowing Article I, Section 26, of the Michigan Constitution to take immediate effect.[115] On remand, Judge Lawson rejected the constitutional and statutory challenges to Proposal 2 in March 2008.[116]

Three years later, a divided Sixth Circuit panel reversed, with Circuit Judges R. Guy Cole, Jr. and Martha Craig Daughtrey holding that Proposal 2 violated federal equal protection principles, at least in the context of public university admissions.[117] Attorney General Cox's successor, Bill Schuette, petitioned for en banc reconsideration, but in November 2012, the full circuit reaffirmed the panel holding by a vote of 8–7.[118] On both the three-judge panel and the full circuit, these holdings sparked incredulity from the dissenting judges, and it is unlikely that they will survive Supreme Court review. As with the postelection challenge to Proposition 209 in California, this lawsuit was a long shot from the beginning, as it appeared to call on the courts to hold that the federal Constitution *required* states to maintain race-conscious affirmative action policies. The Ninth Circuit had been unwilling to do so in 1997, but a bare majority of the Sixth Circuit held that when banning affirmative action, the state's voters were not free to "reorder[] the political process in a way that places special burdens on racial minorities." Relying on the Supreme Court's holdings in *Hunter v. Erickson* (1969) and *Washington v. Seattle School District No. 1* (1982), the Circuit's eight-judge majority held that "the Equal Protection Clause prohibits requiring racial minorities to surmount more formidable obstacles than those faced by other groups to achieve their political objectives. . . . Because less onerous avenues to effect political change remain open to those advocating consideration of non-racial factors in admissions decisions, Michigan cannot force those advocating for consideration of racial factors to traverse a more arduous road without violating the Fourteenth Amendment."[119] SCOTUS granted certiorari in March 2013, and the justices will almost certainly reverse the Sixth Circuit holding.[120]

Meanwhile, when Connerly followed up his ballot victory in Michigan by pledging to wage similar initiative campaigns across the country in November 2008—in what he billed as a "Super Tuesday" for racial equality—affirmative action supporters again responded with preelection challenges, with BAMN's Shanta Driver observing, "We have had a fair amount of discussion with both civil-rights and lesbian and gay groups, and it is our view that what we have to do is stop these ballot initiatives before they get on the ballot" (Schmidt 2007d).[121] When Connerly sought to extend his campaign still further in 2010, BAMN sought to preempt these efforts with a federal constitutional challenge to California's Proposition 209 (Schmidt 2010). A unanimous Ninth Circuit panel rejected this challenge in April 2012.[122]

In sum, left-liberal policy advocates regularly seek to reverse their legislative defeats by persuading judges to block the enforcement of recently enacted policies or even (in the case of ballot initiatives) to block the enactment of new policies in the first place. Most such efforts are unsuccessful—the failed lawsuits surveyed in this section outnumber the successful ones—but these lawsuits are nonetheless likely to continue for the foreseeable future, for at least two reasons. First, so long as judges prove willing to heed such calls from advocates at least occasionally, the advocates will have sufficient strategic incentive to litigate; after all, once they have already lost in the elected branches, the courts will often seem a last, best hope that is worth pursuing. Second, from the advocates' perspective, even courtroom defeats have the potential to benefit the cause by drawing publicity, shaping the political agenda, and the like; in other words, advocates may sometimes win even when they lose (McCann 1994; NeJaime 2011).

Using Courts to Dismantle Existing Policies

In addition to using courts as veto points, advocates sometimes appeal to judges to disrupt an entrenched policy status quo that is proving otherwise resistant to change. Put another way, advocates use courts not only to block new legislative restrictions on rights, but also to dismantle such restrictions that are already in place. As Gordon Silverstein has noted, courts can sometimes operate as battering rams, "break[ing] through profound political and institutional barriers that can be broken in no other way short of violent or massive systemic, institutional, or constitutional change" (2009, 245). Much of the well-known liberal judicial activism from the Warren and early Burger Courts fits this description. When the Supreme Court held that local school districts could no longer segregate students by race, that state criminal courts must exclude all illegally seized evidence, and that state legislatures could no longer ban contraceptives or abortion, the justices were effectively reversing policies that had been in place for decades.

Such efforts are a recurrent feature of American politics. When advocates are unable to repeal undesirable policies via legislative and electoral means—or, in some cases, when such avenues appear so closed as to not be worth an attempt—they regularly turn to courts as an alternative. In the LGBT rights context, for example, most significant legal disabilities faced by gays and lesbians have reflected policies of long standing, and movement litigators have targeted many of these policies for judicial invalidation. As compared to category 1 litigation, one of the key distinguishing features of these category 2 lawsuits is that their optimal timing is uncertain. In category 1 cases, movement lawyers are able to challenge objectionable statutes immediately on enactment, thus claiming the field and preempting any competing suits. But with category 2 cases, the timing of a constitutional challenge is wide open. Movement lawyers will typically wait for (or try to orchestrate) a favorable conjunction of judicial doctrine and public support, but in the meantime, they run the risk that private litigants will file suit before the time is right. As such, wildcat litigation plays a potentially greater role in this context.

Decriminalizing consensual sodomy

From its inception, one of the chief legal goals of the gay rights movement was the dismantling of long-standing criminal prohibitions on consensual sexual activity (Andersen 2005, 58–97). After a widely noted federal constitutional challenge failed in *Bowers v. Hardwick*, movement leaders regrouped and eventually launched a series of state constitutional challenges. This shift in strategy began to bear fruit in September 1992, when the Kentucky Supreme Court invalidated the state's criminal sodomy law on state constitutional grounds.[123] After this initial victory, similar challenges reached unsuccessful conclusions in Texas and Louisiana in 1994, and then Oklahoma and Rhode Island in 1995.[124] Beginning in 1996, however, LGBT rights lawyers won a rapid series of victories, with state courts following Kentucky's lead in Tennessee in 1996, Montana in 1997, Georgia and Maryland in 1998, Missouri in 1999, Minnesota in 2001, and Arkansas and Massachusetts in 2002.[125] Virtually all of these suits were filed by the organized LGBT rights bar, and these advocates achieved several policy victories outside of court as well (Andersen 2005, 98–142).

With the ground thus laid, the litigators returned to federal court with the case of *Lawrence v. Texas*, which had a set of facts that closely paralleled *Bowers*. (In both cases, the litigants had been arrested for engaging in private, consensual sexual activity in one of their own homes.) In June 2003, delivering an opinion that evoked tears of joy from the LGBT rights advocates present in the courtroom, Justice Kennedy noted that most states had already repealed their sodomy statutes, either legislatively or judicially, and he held that the remaining laws were inconsistent with the evolving conception of liberty guaranteed by the Fourteenth Amendment's due process clause.[126]

Pursuing marriage equality

Beginning in May 1993, all LGBT rights conflicts proceeded in the shadow of SSM, as the Hawaii Supreme Court unexpectedly held that the state's refusal to grant marriage licenses to same-sex couples was subject to strict judicial scrutiny and hence probably unconstitutional.[127] As with the effort to repeal the military ban, the campaign for SSM was not launched by the national LGBT rights organizations. President Clinton had put the military issue on the table in an effort to attract gay votes in 1992, and the marriage issue emerged from wildcat litigation by ordinary gay and lesbian couples seeking legal rights and benefits for their own families. The suit that led to the Hawaii decision in *Baehr v. Lewin* (Haw. 1993) had been filed in 1991 by three same-sex couples and their private counsel, and both Lambda Legal and the ACLU had declined a request from the local counsel to join the case, although Lambda Legal did submit an amicus curiae brief in support (Andersen 2005, 178).[128]

Once the Hawaii court placed the issue on the national agenda in 1993, however, the advocates recognized that it was there to stay, in part because wildcat litigation was likely to proliferate. In 1995, having been inspired by the recent Hawaii victory, a same-sex couple in Alaska filed a similar suit, again represented by private counsel. Earlier that same year, an Alaska trial court had issued a statutory holding (in a different case) requiring the extension of domestic partnership benefits to all state employees, and the judge in the subsequent case likewise proved willing to follow Hawaii's lead, issuing a state constitutional holding that seemed likely to legalize SSM in the near future.[129] In this context, the leaders of the LGBT public interest bar signed onto the SSM campaign, laying the groundwork for legal challenges of their own. In particular, they established the Marriage Project in 1994, with the explicit goal of integrating their litigation efforts with a broader public campaign of education, lobbying, and the like (Andersen 2005, 178–85). Under the auspices of this joint initiative, the leading national LGBT rights groups—principally Lambda Legal, the ACLU, GLAD, and the National Center for Lesbian Rights (NCLR)—agreed to litigate only where the odds seemed most in their favor and, in the meantime, to devote significant resources to nonlegal strategies as well. As their first test case, they selected Vermont, with GLAD's Mary Bonauto joining local lawyers Susan Murray and Beth Robinson to file suit in 1997 on behalf of three same-sex couples seeking to marry.

In developing and implementing this strategy, the litigators learned several lessons from the Alaska and Hawaii events. In November 1998, the voters in both states adopted constitutional amendments preempting the judicial legalization of SSM. As such, the litigators responded by intentionally selecting state targets whose constitutions were more difficult to amend, and even then, they did not file suit until significant political groundwork had been laid. When the first of these test cases resulted in a landmark victory in *Baker v. Vermont* (Vt. 1999), it became clear that judges as well as litigators had drawn lessons from the Alaska and Hawaii experience. Writing for a unanimous state high court, Vermont's Chief Justice Jeffrey L. Amestoy held that the state's exclusion of same-sex couples from the benefits of civil marriage was inconsistent with the state constitution's promise of equal treatment to all persons. One member of the court thought this constitutional analysis required the immediate legalization of SSM, but Chief Justice Amestoy instead held that it was up to the state legislature to decide whether to include same-sex couples "within the marriage laws themselves or [in] a parallel 'domestic partnership' system or some equivalent statutory alternative."[130] In reaching this holding,

Amestoy expressly referenced the Alaska and Hawaii backlashes, cautioned against "confus[ing] . . . judicial authority with finality," and quoted constitutional scholar Cass Sunstein for the proposition that "[c]ourts do best by proceeding in a way that is catalytic rather than preclusive, and that is closely attuned to the fact that courts are participants in the system of democratic deliberation."[131]

The Vermont decision altered the dynamics of the marriage conflict in several key respects. It confirmed the viability of the test case strategy, reversing the momentum of the national conflict and leading the attorneys affiliated with the Marriage Project to immediately identify their next targets. It called attention to the idea of a compromise granting the benefits of marriage but not the name, a policy that would in the short run prove significantly more politically viable than SSM itself. It forced the state legislature to enact such a compromise—unless the legislators were willing to directly challenge the state court's authority—thus shifting some of the political blame for the decision back onto the legislators' shoulders. And of course, it provoked a political reaction from SSM opponents. Like the earlier rulings in Hawaii and Alaska, *Baker v. Vermont* sparked a political backlash, but it seems to have sparked a "forelash" as well, with SSM supporters building on the Vermont decision to achieve unprecedented victories. As Ellen Ann Andersen (2005, 186–88) puts it, the decision served as a "mobilizing agent" for both supporters and opponents.

In 2001, GLAD filed a SSM suit in Massachusetts, with Bonauto again serving as lead attorney, and in 2002, Lambda Legal filed one in New Jersey. As with Vermont, these states were selected because their constitutions were difficult to amend, because their high courts had proven willing to support gay rights claims in the past, and because their political cultures seemed supportive enough that any potential backlash to a judicial victory could be contained.[132] In Massachusetts, the suit also represented an effort to preempt an ongoing campaign to amend the state constitution to ban SSM (Bonauto 2005, 19–21; Klarman 2013, 89). In *Goodridge v. Department of Public Health*, the Massachusetts Supreme Judicial Court became the first in the nation to order full marriage equality for same-sex couples, though it stayed its order for six months to allow time for a legislative response.[133]

As with the Alaska, Hawaii, and Vermont decisions, *Goodridge* provoked significant countermobilization by SSM opponents. Most notably, these opponents succeeded in enacting anti-SSM constitutional amendments in eleven states in November 2004, and some evidence suggests that judges retreated in the face of this electoral backlash (Klarman 2013, 116–18). In the first half of 2005, appellate courts in Oregon, Indiana, and New Jersey rejected state constitutional challenges to their states' discriminatory marriage laws.[134] New York's highest court joined them in July 2006, and over the next several months, SSM advocates suffered courtroom defeats in Nebraska, Washington, and California as well.[135]

As of early October 2006, the SSM movement appeared to be in trouble. Even in blue states like New York, most judges now seemed unwilling to accept legal arguments in support of SSM that appeared quite strong to their advocates. To some extent, judges continued to rely on long-standing and familiar—and, in the view of LGBT rights advocates, flatly false and discriminatory—arguments against SSM. In *Hernandez v. Robles* (NY 2006), for example, the New York Court of Appeals held that "[t]he Legislature could rationally believe that it is better, other things being equal, for children to grow up with both a mother and a father." Perhaps even more notable, however, appellate judges seemed to go out of their way to come up with novel justifications for their states' discriminatory marriage laws. In New York, the *Hernandez* court identified a second legitimate interest as well: "[T]he Legislature could rationally decide that, for the welfare of children, it is more important to promote stability, and to avoid instability, in opposite-sex than in same-sex relationships" because members of the former, but not the latter, can get pregnant by accident. This second argument, with its odd suggestion that heterosexual couples are in greater need of state support for their relationships than are same-sex couples, had been advanced by the Indiana Court of Appeals in 2005, and it was subsequently endorsed by a unanimous Eighth Circuit panel and by five of the nine justices on the Washington Supreme Court.[136] As Kenji Yoshino (2006) notes, the judicial enthusiasm for this argument seemed like an increasingly "desperate" attempt to articulate a nondiscriminatory purpose for the states' discriminatory marriage laws. As New York's Chief Justice Judith Kaye pointed out in dissent, the desire to promote the stability of heterosexual relationships does not explain in any obvious way the denial of marriage licenses to gay and lesbian couples; after all, "[t]here are enough marriage licenses to go around for everyone."[137] Given the judges' resort to such arguments, these appellate rulings reinforced the impression that the judiciary was now simply unwilling to enter this political minefield. Regardless of the legal arguments, most judges were determined to abstain.

Even in the wake of the 2004 ballot initiatives, however, some courts

remained willing to move forward, particularly on expansions of partnership rights that fell short of full marriage equality. In December 2004, the
Montana Supreme Court held on state constitutional grounds that public
universities must provide health benefits to same-sex partners of employees.[138] The Alaska Supreme Court issued a similar holding in October
2005, as did a New Hampshire trial court in May 2006, in a decision that
the state ultimately chose not to appeal.[139] In June 2006, the Arkansas
Supreme Court unanimously held that the state could not ban homosexuals from serving as foster parents, and in October 2006, the New Jersey
Supreme Court gave the movement its biggest victory since *Goodridge*. In
Lewis v. Harris (NJ 2006), the New Jersey court unanimously held that the
state must provide same-sex couples with all the rights and responsibilities
of marriage, with three of the seven justices insisting that it must provide
same-sex couples with access to marriage itself.[140] Movement litigators
suffered another significant defeat the following year, with the Maryland
high court narrowly rejecting the ACLU's SSM suit in *Conaway v. Deane*
(Md. 2007), but in May 2008, the California Supreme Court became the
second state high court to order full marriage equality and the first to hold
that discrimination on the basis of sexual orientation, like discrimination
on the basis of race, was constitutionally "suspect."[141] In October 2008,
the Connecticut Supreme Court became the third to legalize SSM, and in
April 2009, the Iowa Supreme Court became the fourth.[142]

In addition to the judicial victory in Iowa, SSM advocates won a number of significant legislative victories in 2009 as well. The Connecticut
legislature codified the recent state high court decision by enacting a marriage equality bill, and the legislatures of Maine, New Hampshire, and
Vermont enacted such bills without judicial compulsion. The city council
of Washington, DC, did likewise. In addition, Nevada and Washington
State enacted statutes granting all state law rights of marriage without
the name; Colorado enacted a Designated Beneficiary Agreement Act,
which provided a legal status and a small number of specified rights to
unmarried couples, both straight and gay; and California enacted a bill
extending all state law rights of marriage to same-sex couples who were
lawfully married in other jurisdictions.

These legislative successes were remarkable, but where such a path
proved unavailing, SSM advocates remained ready and willing to return
to court. When Hawaii's Republican governor, Linda Lingle, vetoed a
civil union bill in July 2010, Lambda Legal filed a lawsuit seeking all state
law rights of marriage. Likewise in New Jersey, where a Civil Union Act

had been in place since shortly after the state high court's 2006 holding in *Lewis v. Harris,* the legislature considered and rejected a marriage equality bill in 2009. In response, Lambda Legal moved to reopen the case, alleging that the existing law failed to provide the fully equal treatment required by the state constitution. When the state high court declined to reopen the case, indicating that "[t]his matter cannot be decided without the development of an appropriate trial-like record," Lambda's attorneys followed up with a new state constitutional challenge, filed in June 2011.[143] In the spring of 2012, Lambda Legal filed new SSM suits in Nevada and Illinois, alleging in each case that the state's provision of the rights of marriage without the name fell short of full constitutional equality, and in March 2013, the ACLU and NCLR jointly filed a SSM suit in New Mexico.[144]

Similarly, at the federal level, LGBT rights advocates used litigation to maintain pressure on the Obama administration to live up to the president's campaign promises from 2008, which included the repeal of the 1996 Defense of Marriage Act (DOMA) and federal recognition of civil unions. Most notably, GLAD filed a carefully planned test case against DOMA in March 2009. Seeking to force the administration's hand, GLAD's attorneys argued that the federal government's failure to recognize Massachusetts SSMs for purposes of Social Security, federal taxes, federal employment benefits, and the issuance of passports was inconsistent with the Fourteenth Amendment's promise of equal treatment. Massachusetts attorney general Martha Coakley followed up with a similar suit filed on the state's behalf, and in May 2012, a unanimous First Circuit panel ruled in the plaintiffs' favor in both cases.[145] Even before this victory, GLAD extended the effort to a neighboring circuit by filing a similar suit on behalf of same-sex couples lawfully married in Connecticut, New Hampshire, and Vermont, and the ACLU filed a separate suit on behalf of the surviving member of a New York same-sex couple lawfully married in Canada. As in the Massachusetts case, the litigators in these cases argued that the federal government's refusal to recognize these marriages violated the Fourteenth Amendment. They targeted the Second Circuit in part because it included additional states that had legalized SSM, thus enabling their complaint about the federal government's nonrecognition of those marriages, and in part because that circuit had no governing precedent regarding the standard of scrutiny for laws discriminating on the basis of sexual orientation. As such, these suits forced the Department of Justice (DOJ) to take a position on an open legal question rather than deferring to existing precedent, as it was able to do in other circuits. Attorney General Eric Holder responded by announcing that DOJ would no longer defend the constitutionality of DOMA's Section 3.[146] The Republican leadership of the House of Representatives stepped into the void created by the administration's decision, but in October 2012, the Second Circuit joined the First in declaring DOMA's federal nonrecognition provisions unconstitutional.[147] In June 2013, the Supreme Court agreed.[148] This landmark victory in *Windsor v. United States* (2013) has already produced additional favorable holdings, and more are likely to follow in the coming years.[149]

Most legal disputes regarding the parental (as opposed to spousal) rights of LGBT persons have involved nonconstitutional questions of family law. But where state governments have maintained policies explicitly discriminating against LGBT parents, organized rights advocates have sometimes mounted state or federal constitutional challenges. In addition to the successful challenges to recently enacted deprivations of LGBT parental rights that I detail above, the most noteworthy such example was a long-running effort to dismantle Florida's statutory ban on adoptions by homosexuals, which dated to the antigay backlash led by Anita Bryant in 1977. In *Cox v. Florida Department of Health & Rehabilitative Services* (Fla. 1995), the state high court rejected a federal constitutional challenge to the statute but left open the possibility of a similar challenge on state constitutional grounds.[150] The plaintiffs failed to pursue this possibility, but after *Lawrence v. Texas* came down in 2003, the state's LGBT rights advocates filed a new federal challenge. Reading *Lawrence* narrowly, a unanimous Eleventh Circuit panel rejected this challenge in January 2004, and the full circuit then divided 6–6 on a request for rehearing.[151] Several years later, the ACLU picked up on the state constitutional issue that had been left open in 1995, and in September 2010, an intermediate appellate panel struck down the law.[152] When state officials declined to appeal, the statute was finally laid to rest.[153]

In sum, policy advocates regularly turn to the courts in an effort to dismantle existing policies that (in the advocates' view) infringe on fundamental legal rights. When elected lawmakers prove unresponsive to calls for legal change, the courts will often appear as an avenue worth exploring. When the time is right—particularly when legal doctrine and public sentiment are both moving in a favorable direction—judges will sometimes heed these calls, issuing decisions that disrupt entrenched policy status quos, sometimes in unpredictable ways.

Using Courts to Clear the Channels of Political Change

In addition to lawsuits seeking immediate and direct policy change, rights advocates often use litigation to assist campaigns for policy change that they are conducting primarily via electoral and legislative channels. Put another way, even when relying on more conventional forms of democratic politics, rights advocates often find themselves drawn into court in an effort to facilitate the success of those democratic campaigns. After all, campaigns for legislative change face a variety of obstacles—many of them rooted in the famously fragmented system of policymaking authority in the United States—and litigation can sometimes prove useful in removing or surmounting these obstacles. Put still another way, rights advocates utilize judicial politics to achieve policy change directly, but they also use it to enable themselves to conduct politics in other fora.

In some cases, policy advocates face legal rules that make it difficult or even impossible to win a desired change via democratic channels. When a state constitutional provision bars state and local legislators from enacting a desired policy, the best available option will sometimes be federal constitutional litigation to remove the state constitutional bar. Likewise, when state and local procedural requirements make it prohibitively difficult to enact a desired policy via ballot initiative or referendum, advocates may call on judges to invalidate or modify those requirements. In other cases, policy advocates face a fragmented field of political authority that complicates the effective implementation of policy changes that they have already won via democratic channels. At both the state and federal levels, executive officials sometimes refuse to implement legislative changes that they oppose. Likewise, federal legislators and executives sometimes interfere with policies enacted at the state level, and state officials sometimes do the same with policies enacted by Congress and the president. In each of these circumstances, policy advocates sometimes call on judges to clear the channels of political change.

When successful, these suits may produce judicial decisions invalidating policies enacted by electorally accountable officials, but they do so in an effort to enable or vindicate alternative policies that were also enacted by electorally accountable officials. As a result, these policy-altering judicial decisions are best understood not as challenges to democratic authority but as interventions on the side of one institution with a legitimate claim to such authority against other institutions that also have such a claim. From the perspective of rights advocates, litigation sometimes represents an effort not to constrain someone else's legislative strategy but to enable and defend their own legislative strategy. Some of the legal disputes that I have already characterized as examples of direct challenges to democratically enacted policies can be reinterpreted along these lines, but this alternative frame brings new legal conflicts into view as well.

Litigating to enable legislative politics

In the former category, recall the Rehnquist Court's 1996 decision in *Romer v. Evans.* LGBT rights advocates have won statutory protections against employment discrimination in twenty-one states, along with similar protections in a number of local jurisdictions.[154] Each of these policy changes was the result of legislative action, but such action would have been constitutionally precluded in at least one state (and probably more) if not for the holding in *Romer.* By persuading the high court to invalidate the Colorado constitutional provision prohibiting such antidiscrimination protections, LGBT rights litigators enabled the enforcement of such protections that had already been democratically enacted in Boulder, Denver, and Aspen. Even more significantly, the successful litigation enabled the Colorado legislature to adopt a statewide gay rights bill a decade later. If not for the *Romer* decision, moreover, opponents of gay rights would have tried to replicate Amendment 2 in other states, and it is likely that the effort to enact antidiscrimination protections via democratic means would have been closed off in a substantial portion of the country.

More recently, SSM advocates in California explicitly sought to avoid litigation in their campaign to expand partnership rights for same-sex couples, but they were eventually drawn into court by the actions of their opponents (and of some wildcat supporters). This conflict dates back to the mid-1990s, when LGBT rights advocates began trying to persuade the state's elected lawmakers to incrementally extend the rights of marriage to gays and lesbians. They adopted this strategy because the California legislature was more supportive of LGBT rights than any other state legislature in the country and because they hoped to avoid the political backlash that had greeted the movement's recent courtroom victory in Hawaii (Cummings and NeJaime 2010). They quickly persuaded the legislature to approve a bill in 1994 that would have created the first statewide domestic partnership registry in the country, but it was vetoed by Republican governor Pete Wilson. The LGBT rights advocates persisted with their legislative and incremental strategy, and five years later, Democratic governor Gray Davis signed the domestic partnership bill into law. This legislative victory prompted SSM opponents to launch a ballot initiative campaign preemptively banning SSM. The state's voters enacted this statutory ban on SSM, known as Proposition 22, in March 2000, but both Davis and his Republican successor continued to sign bills incrementally expanding the legal rights attached to domestic partnerships. Most notably, the California Domestic Partner Rights and Responsibilities Act of 2003 provided that "[r]egistered domestic partners shall have the same rights, protections, and benefits, and shall be subject to the same responsibilities, obligations, and duties under law . . . as are granted to and imposed upon spouses." Having extended all the rights of marriage without the name, the legislature then voted for full marriage equality in 2005 and again in 2007. These bills went too far for Republican governor Arnold Schwarzenegger, who vetoed them.

If SSM advocates had been in full control of the situation, they would have continued with this legislative strategy until SSM had been legalized. In February 2004, however, San Francisco mayor Gavin Newsom unexpectedly directed city officials to begin issuing marriage licenses to same-sex couples. The resulting "winter of love," in which gay and lesbian couples flocked to San Francisco City Hall to marry, prompted an array of legal challenges from SSM opponents, who contested the legality of these marriages. These legal challenges made it inevitable that the state's courts would address the constitutionality of the state's existing marriage laws, so the state's leading LGBT rights advocates finally challenged those laws on state constitutional grounds (Cummings and NeJaime 2010, 1274–85). It was this challenge that led the state high court to legalize SSM in May 2008, which in turn led the state's voters to enact Proposition 8 the following November. From that point forward, the movement's preferred legislative strategy was unavailable because the state constitution now barred recognition of SSM. For SSM advocates, the available options now consisted of (A) state constitutional litigation, which was a long shot because it was hard to see how a court could invalidate a state constitutional amendment on state constitutional grounds; (B) federal constitutional litigation, which was more promising in the abstract but whose fate would be in the hands of a federal judiciary that had moved markedly rightward over the past eight years; and (C) an effort to re-amend the state constitution.

The state's leading LGBT rights advocates tried option A first, but they were not surprised when California's high court ruled against them in *Strauss v. Horton*. At that point, they were leaning toward option C, but Ted Olson and David Boies preemptively launched option B by filing *Perry v. Schwarzenegger*. Faced with the inevitability of a federal judicial ruling on the constitutionality of Proposition 8, the advocacy organizations joined the fight (Cummings and NeJaime 2010, 1298–1304). They helped Olson and Boies persuade a Ninth Circuit panel to invalidate Proposition 8, and when SCOTUS granted certiorari in December 2012, the groups joined Olson and Boies in urging the Court to affirm the Ninth Circuit decision. As I note above, this suit eventually led to the relegalization of SSM in California (though without a ruling on the merits from SCOTUS). If it had not done so, SSM supporters would have attempted to repeal Proposition 8 via a new state constitutional amendment.

In both Colorado and California, then, LGBT rights advocates sought to advance their aims principally via legislative channels, but were drawn into federal court when the state constitutions were amended in an effort to block those legislative advances. Put another way, where legislative institutions and processes of direct democracy have been pitted against one another, gay rights advocates have sometimes engaged in litigation to buttress and defend the particular arena of democratic politics that is currently on their side.

Litigating to call attention to the need for legislation (and perhaps to win some piecemeal protections in the meantime)

In a similar scenario, rights advocates sometimes use litigation to seek temporary or partial policy victories while their broader campaign is proceeding through legislative channels. By dramatizing the issue with sympathetic plaintiffs, these suits can increase pressure on legislative institutions to act. In the meantime, they may also achieve some incremental policy changes on the ground.

Consider an example from the abortion context. In the early 1990s, abortion providers faced a widespread pattern of violent attacks by anti-abortion extremists, including systematic efforts to prevent patients from accessing clinic facilities (Banks 1994). In 1991, for example, Dr. George Tiller's clinic in Wichita, Kansas, was one of the targets of Operation Rescue's "Summer of Mercy," which employed civil disobedience tactics to shut down virtually all abortion services in the city for several weeks. (Operation Rescue was one of the most visible and aggressive antiabortion organizations at the time.) Dr. Tiller's home and horse farm were destroyed by arsonists that year, and in August 1993, he was shot in both arms while leaving his clinic (Belluck 2000; Greenhouse 2000a). Earlier that year, Dr. David Gunn had been murdered in Pensacola, Florida, and the following year, Dr. John Britton and his bodyguard were murdered there as well. The summer of 1994 also witnessed the fire-bombing of a clinic in Falls Church, Virginia, and later in the year, two receptionists were killed and five people were injured in a shooting at two clinics in Brookline, Massachusetts. By David Garrow's count, this wave of terrorist violence "took the lives of three doctors, three other clinic personnel, and one law enforcement officer before dissipating" (2007, 37; see also Hull and Hoffer 2001, 261).[155]

Abortion rights advocates responded with a range of tactics—including direct action of their own, training volunteers to engage in the nonviolent defense of clinic staff and clients against disruptive protesters—but they recognized that the scope of the problem necessitated federal legislative change. They eventually persuaded Congress to enact the Freedom of Access to Clinic Entrances (FACE) Act, and they persuaded some state and local legislatures to enact similar protections. The FACE Act, signed by President Clinton in May 1994, imposed nationwide criminal penalties on anyone who uses force, threats, or "physical obstruction" to "injure, intimidate or interfere with any person" providing or receiving reproductive health services. The bill also authorized clinic employees and clients to sue protesters in federal court for damages and injunctive relief, explicitly empowering federal judges to enjoin protesters from obstructing clinic entrances.

Even before these notable legislative victories, however, abortion providers regularly and repeatedly appealed to state and federal trial courts for injunctions against the organized violence. In doing so, they relied on statutes that had been enacted to target private conspiracies by organizations like the Mafia and the Ku Klux Klan (Hull and Hoffer 2001, 261–63). These legal avenues were far from perfect, but they did provide some piecemeal legal protections while the legislative campaign proceeded. More important, by calling attention to widespread antiabortion violence, they increased the pressure for a legislative solution.

Consider, for example, the Supreme Court's decision in *Bray v. Alexandria Women's Health Clinic* (1993), handed down one week before Bill Clinton was inaugurated. The case was litigated under the Reconstruction-era Ku Klux Klan Act, which authorizes federal suits against persons engaged in a conspiracy to deprive others of the privileges and immunities of national citizenship or the equal protection of the laws. In the years leading up to the Clinton era, several suits relying on this statute had persuaded federal judges to provide some protection to abortion providers and their clients. In 1989, the NOW Legal Defense and Education Fund had gone to court on behalf of a number of clinics in the Washington, DC, metropolitan area, securing an injunction preventing Operation Rescue's members from "physically impeding access to, and egress from, premises that offer and provide legal abortion services and related medical and psychological counseling."[156] In *Bray*, however, the Court vacated the injunction against the DC-area protests, holding that the KKK Act applies only to conspiracies motivated by "racial, or perhaps otherwise class-based, invidiously discriminatory animus." Even assuming that the statute applied to gender as well as race, Justice Scalia held for a five-justice majority that Operation Rescue's conspiracy was not motivated by discriminatory animus against women.[157] This holding did not end all litigation under the KKK Act, but it severely curtailed the utility of such suits, reinforcing the conviction of abortion providers that targeted federal legislation was necessary.[158]

Meanwhile, abortion providers had also litigated a number of cases alleging violations of federal racketeering laws. As far back as 1986, they had filed a complaint in federal district court in Illinois alleging, as SCOTUS later put it, that the leaders of Operation Rescue "were members of a nationwide conspiracy to shut down abortion clinics through a pattern of racketeering activity including extortion in violation of the Hobbs Act." If the clinics could prove this claim, they would be entitled to injunctive relief and treble damages under the federal RICO (Racketeer Influenced and Corrupt Organizations) Act.[159] The trial court dismissed the suit in 1991, and the Seventh Circuit affirmed the following year, but with no federal clinic protection law yet on the books, the abortion providers continued to pursue this avenue.[160] The antiabortion protesters had persuaded the Seventh Circuit that the RICO Act applied only where the racketeering enterprise was motivated by a desire for economic gain, but a unanimous Supreme Court reversed this holding in January 1994.[161] On remand, the trial judge issued a sweeping nationwide injunction prohibiting Operation Rescue from obstructing access to abortion clinics, but this legal avenue would eventually come to naught as well. The justices had second thoughts, and in February 2003, an eight-justice majority vacated the injunction.[162] When a Seventh Circuit panel subsequently held that one of the clinics' claims remained live, SCOTUS intervened with yet another reversal in 2006, this one unanimous.[163]

By this point, however, the significance of the case was muted, both because it had evolved to focus on a series of technical questions regarding the interpretation of federal statutes that had nothing to do with abortion rights and because the 1994 FACE Act had provided new legal tools for the clinics to protect themselves. Viewed from afar, the clinic defense litigation that I survey here does not appear to have had any great policy significance. The main action was in Congress rather than the courts, and most of the suits that were initiated prior to the enactment of the FACE Act were eventually dismissed. Still, many of these suits succeeded in making it more difficult for antiabortion protesters to shut clinics down, with injunctions in place for several years in some cases, and they certainly drew attention to the problem of antiabortion violence, thus contributing to the drive for a congressional response. Indeed, when the FACE Act was introduced in the Senate, the bill included congressional findings noting that prior to the Court's decision in *Bray*, clinic blockades were "frequently restrained and enjoined by Federal courts in actions brought under" the KKK Act, but that the Court's recent decision had left abortion providers without an effective legal remedy.[164] *Congressional Quarterly* subsequently reported that the *Bray* decision was "[a] major spur" to the FACE Act, with pro-choice legislators responding "immediately" to the decision with "plans to push legislation that would undo" its effects.[165]

Litigation initiated by democratically elected policymakers when other policy avenues are closed off

Litigation in the areas of abortion, affirmative action, gay rights, and gun rights often targets policies that had been enacted by democratically elected lawmakers, but given the well-known decentralization of lawmaking authority in the United States, such litigation is often *supported* or even initiated by democratically elected lawmakers as well. Like policy advocates outside of government, policy advocates within government sometimes turn to the courts when other avenues of change are closed off. In doing so, public officials often work closely with nongovernmental allies to maximize the collective resources and expertise that are available to the litigation campaign. Efforts by public officials to encourage private litigation have drawn increasing attention in the scholarly literature, and efforts by public officials to engage in litigation directly have begun to draw some attention as well (Burke 2002; Farhang 2010; Gifford 2010; Mulroy 2012; Pralle 2009).

This chapter has already noted several examples of such litigation. In *Romer v. Evans*, the plaintiffs included not just gay and lesbian Coloradans but also the Boulder Valley School District, the City and County of Denver, and the Cities of Boulder and Aspen, each of which was litigating to defend the legality of antidiscrimination ordinances that they had enacted. Likewise, the lawsuit that persuaded the California Supreme Court to legalize SSM in 2008 was launched not just by the private LGBT rights bar but also by the City and County of San Francisco (Cummings and Ne-Jaime 2010). Massachusetts attorney general Martha Coakley filed one of the Obama-era constitutional challenges to DOMA Section 3; it was not her case that produced the landmark SCOTUS decision in 2013, but her suit helped push the issue through the federal courts on favorable terms. And one of the suits seeking to stop Operation Rescue's clinic blockades was filed by local officials in West Hartford, Connecticut.

With this frame in mind, consider also the series of tort lawsuits filed by local governments against gun manufacturers during the Clinton and Bush eras. These suits were brought by city and county government officials who were eager to regulate the sale and possession of firearms within their jurisdictions. Even where they had broad popular support, they were generally unable to do so on their own, either because such regulations were precluded by state preemption laws or, where the local governments did have authority to act, because their regulations were rendered ineffective by the ease with which criminal enterprises could divert guns from other state and local jurisdictions with looser regulations.

In at least one case, local government leaders went to court with a *Romer*-style suit seeking to invalidate a state preemption law.[166] Elsewhere, with legislative channels closed off or ineffective, mayors and county executives went to court with suits designed to regulate firearms directly or at least to recoup the law enforcement and medical costs incurred by their jurisdictions as a result of gun violence.[167] In an effort to emulate the recently successful wave of litigation against the tobacco industry, these local officials worked closely with leading gun control advocates, particularly from the Brady Center to Prevent Gun Violence and the NAACP, who regularly filed parallel claims on behalf of victims of gun violence (DeConde 2001, 274–75, 282–83; Goss 2006, 197–98; Haltom and McCann 2008; Landau 2000; Lytton 2008, 1843–49). The first of the local government suits was filed by New Orleans in 1998, followed by similar suits on behalf of about thirty other cities and counties over the next few years (Rostron 2005). These local jurisdictions were joined by at least one state government, with New York attorney general Eliot L. Spitzer filing a similar suit, and by the Clinton administration, with Secretary of Housing and Urban Development Andrew Cuomo helping to orchestrate a class-action lawsuit on behalf of the nation's 3,200 public housing authorities (Stout and Perez-Pena 1999).

Collectively, these suits emphasized that the firearms industry's negligent marketing and distribution practices predictably allowed guns to fall into criminal hands, and they sometimes contended that the manufacturers had negligently failed to incorporate adequate safety features in their guns' designs as well. These legal claims were long shots from the beginning, and none of them saw much success in court, in part because of a successful effort by gun manufacturers and their allies to preempt them legislatively.

Consider the fate of several suits filed in New York. In February 1999, a federal jury in Brooklyn awarded $4 million in damages to a victim of gun violence who had sued the manufacturers of the gun.[168] This verdict was reversed on appeal in 2001, but by that time, additional suits had been filed by New York City, Attorney General Spitzer, and the NAACP.[169] The gun manufacturers managed to fight off these suits as well, in one case with help from their allies in Congress. A state trial court dismissed Spitzer's suit in August 2001, and an intermediate appellate court affirmed in June 2003, on the grounds that the state high court had recently reiterated "its present and longstanding posture of denying liability where the causal connection between the alleged business conduct and harm is too tenuous and remote."[170] In federal court, Senior District Judge Jack B. Weinstein dismissed the NAACP suit in July 2003, on the grounds that plaintiffs had failed to demonstrate that they had "suffered harm different in kind from that suffered by the public at large," as required by New York public nuisance law.[171] In the NYC suit, Judge Weinstein scheduled a trial for November 2005, but on October 26 of that year, President Bush signed the Protection of Lawful Commerce in Arms Act (PLCAA), which shielded gun manufacturers from civil liability for actions involving "the criminal or unlawful misuse" of their product by third parties. The act explicitly directed that any such civil actions pending at the time of enactment should be immediately dismissed, but NYC's lawyers argued that the statute was both unconstitutional and inapplicable to their suit. Weinstein delayed the trial and then ruled that the federal law was constitutional but inapplicable, as the suit fell within one of the statute's specified exceptions. As such, he declined to dismiss the case.[172] In April 2008, a divided Second Circuit panel reversed, agreeing with Weinstein that the federal statute was constitutional but disagreeing on the statutory point and dismissing the suit.[173] This case represented one of a number of unsuccessful constitutional challenges to the 2005 immunity law.[174]

Even before this statute had been enacted, similar suits had been dismissed in a number of other jurisdictions—some on the grounds that plaintiffs lacked standing, others because manufacturers were not liable for the unlawful use of their products. In late 2001 and early 2002, for example, Third Circuit panels dismissed suits brought by Camden County, New Jersey, and Philadelphia, Pennsylvania.[175] Around the same time, the California and Connecticut Supreme Courts dismissed suits that had been brought by victims of a 1993 mass shooting and the city of Bridgeport, respectively, and an intermediate appellate court in Florida dismissed a suit brought by Miami-Dade County.[176] In November 2002, a state trial court dismissed a case filed by Wilmington, Delaware, and two years later, the Supreme Court of Illinois did so for a case filed by the City of Chicago.[177]

In a few cases, however, these litigation efforts were showing some progress before the 2005 federal statute was enacted. In a Brady Center case from New Mexico, brought on behalf of the parents of a minor child killed in an accidental shooting, an intermediate appellate court reversed a holding of summary judgment in favor of the defendants in 2001. The state high court denied review later in the year, thus clearing the way for trial.[178] Over the next two years, state high courts in Ohio and Indiana allowed suits filed by the Cities of Cincinnati and Gary to continue as well, as did an intermediate appellate court in New Jersey with a suit filed by the City of Newark.[179] Once the PLCAA was enacted, all of these suits were subject to immediate dismissal, and the prospects of future such suits became much dimmer. Courts sometimes held that a particular claim fell within one of the statute's specified exceptions and hence allowed it to continue,[180] but in other cases, they dismissed suits that had once looked promising. Consider *Ileto v. Glock* (9th Cir. 2003), in which a divided Ninth Circuit panel initially ruled in favor of the victims of a 1999 shooting at a Jewish Community Center in Granada Hills, California, who had sued the manufacturers of the guns that had been used in the incident.[181] This decision sharply divided the full circuit, but its judges voted to deny en banc review in May 2004, and SCOTUS denied certiorari the following January, thus clearing the way for trial.[182] But PLCAA was enacted later that year, leading the trial judge to dismiss the case in March 2006.[183] A divided Ninth Circuit panel affirmed this dismissal, and SCOTUS again declined to hear the case.[184]

The PLCAA's enactment left local government leaders with significantly constrained legal options, but they continued to exploit some avenues that remained available. In May 2006, for example, New York City mayor Michael Bloomberg announced that the city was suing fifteen out-of-state gun dealers, alleging that they knowingly facilitated straw purchases designed to acquire firearms for persons prohibited from buying or possessing them. The City subsequently sued twelve additional out-of-state dealers, and by August 2007, twelve of the twenty-seven defendants had settled, agreeing to modify their sales practices and to have those practices supervised by a court-appointed monitor.[185] When two of the defendants—federally licensed firearms dealers located in South Carolina and Georgia, respectively—withdrew their counsel and declined to participate in the litigation, Judge Weinstein issued a default judgment enjoining them from continuing certain unlawful sales practices.[186] A unanimous Second Circuit panel vacated the injunction two years later, but the district court then reinstated a modified injunction that continued to impose some limits on the dealers' sales practices.[187]

In sum, gun control advocates have long relied primarily on legislative strategies to advance their policy aims, but the urban jurisdictions where those aims have the broadest support have repeatedly been frustrated by the lack of action on the part of state and federal legislators. In this context, advocates both in and out of government began to supplement their legislative strategies with carefully orchestrated litigation in the 1990s. Even if fully successful, these lawsuits would not have obviated the need for legislation, and as it happens, most of them were eventually dismissed. For a time, however, the suits looked like a promising avenue for shifting the dynamics of a policy conflict in which advocates of gun control had been making very little headway. In other words, from the perspective of the mayor of New York or New Orleans, the long-standing failure of Congress and most state legislatures to adequately regulate handguns made a turn to the courts seem worth a try.

Litigating to enforce victories previously won via electoral and legislative campaigns

In still another circumstance, advocates sometimes turn to court in an effort to compel compliance with policy changes that they have already won via legislative channels. In some cases, a regulatory policy explicitly empowers courts to play a role in its enforcement (Burke 2002; Farhang 2010). For example, the 1994 FACE Act authorized federal courts to enjoin antiabortion protests that disrupted clinic operations, and DOJ lawyers sought and obtained several such injunctions in the early years after the act's enactment.[188] In other cases, policy advocates call on courts for help in surmounting continued resistance within government to their prior legislative victories. When advocates win a policy change via ballot initiative, they sometimes have to sue state officials to get them to comply. Likewise when state officials are obstructing a policy change won at the federal level, or vice versa, or when a newly elected administration is trying to ignore or undermine a policy enacted by its predecessor, supporters of a democratically enacted policy change often call on judges to help achieve the policy's effective implementation.

Consider the issue of public funding for abortion. Since 1976, Congress has repeatedly used an annual appropriations rider (known as "the Hyde Amendment") to bar the use of federal Medicaid funding to pay for abortions. After unsuccessfully challenging this provision in federal court, abortion rights advocates sought to repeal or ameliorate it legislatively.[189] During the Clinton era, they persuaded the Democratic Congress to modify the Hyde Amendment so as to authorize Medicaid funding for abortions in cases of rape and incest (as well as cases involving dangers to the pregnant woman's life, which had long been allowed). Acting on this new legislative language in December 1993, the Clinton administration directed state Medicaid officials to start paying for abortions in all three contexts. A number of states resisted these new requirements, relying on their own statutory or constitutional provisions that banned or severely restricted public funding for abortions. Abortion rights advocates responded, in turn, by going to court. In Michigan, for example, state officials relied on a statutory provision, enacted by the state's voters in 1988, that banned public funding for abortion except when necessary to save the pregnant woman's life. The state's Planned Parenthood affiliate went to federal court, seeking an injunction directing the state to comply with the newly modified Hyde Amendment, and in January 1996, a Sixth Circuit panel ruled in the abortion providers' favor.[190] By this point, abortion providers had won similar challenges in the Fifth, Eighth, and Tenth Circuits as well.[191] This conflict was reprised in the Obama era, when several Republican-controlled state legislatures enacted laws purporting to cut off all Medicaid funding to Planned Parenthood. The organization challenged such laws in Arizona, Indiana, and Kansas, and with support from the Obama administration, persuaded the federal courts to enjoin all three of them as inconsistent with federal Medicaid law.[192]

In the gun control context, advocates successfully sued California attorney general Dan Lungren for inadequately enforcing the state's 1989 ban on assault weapons.[193] Several years later, the Brady Center unsuccessfully sought to reprise this suit at the federal level, alleging that the Bureau of Alcohol, Tobacco, and Firearms was inadequately enforcing the 1994 assault weapons ban that had been signed by President Clinton (Goss 2006, 85). Likewise, Attorney General John Ashcroft provoked litigation when he delayed putting into effect a Clinton administration regulation regarding background checks for gun purchases. The regulation called for the Federal Bureau of Investigation (FBI) to preserve background records for ninety days, which FBI officials insisted was necessary to allow them to search for gun purchases by persons using false identification and to audit unauthorized uses of the background check system itself. The Violence Policy Center, a national gun control organization, filed suit to compel Ashcroft to implement the regulation.[194]

In all of these category 3 suits, advocates called on judges to side with one set of democratically accountable officials against another set of such officials who had adopted competing policy positions. A judicial ruling in the advocates' favor could well be characterized as antidemocratic because it would necessarily involve ruling against the democratically accountable officials lined up on the other side. But the same is true in reverse, as a ruling favoring the other side would necessarily involve rejecting the policies supported by the democratically accountable officials lined up with the litigators. As such, our evaluations of the democratic legitimacy of rights-protecting judicial decisions should distinguish between litigation designed to challenge democratic politics and litigation designed to facilitate it. Even when movement organizations set out to pursue their policy aims solely through conventional democratic means, they sometimes discover that litigation is necessary to clear the channels of political change.

*   *   *

Moreover, even if movement organizations foreswore litigation altogether, they would still find themselves drawn into court to defend against lawsuits initiated by their ideological opponents. This chapter makes clear that left-liberal rights advocates routinely engage in litigation on the issues of abortion, affirmative action, gay rights, and gun rights, but even if none of the suits surveyed in this chapter had been filed, policy outcomes in these four issue areas would still have been shaped to a significant degree by courts. All the while that left-liberal advocates were calling on judges to veto new and unwanted restrictions on rights, to disrupt entrenched policy status quos, and to clear the channels of political change, their counterparts on the right were doing the same. It is to these stories that I now turn.

CHAPTER TWO

Rights on the Right

Beginning with Richard M. Nixon's election as president in 1968, the Republican Party successfully pulled American electoral politics to the right for a full generation, a trend that did not begin to reverse until Barack Obama's election forty years later. Throughout this era, conservative advocates both inside and outside the GOP sought to emulate their liberal opponents by building the infrastructure necessary to engage in judicial politics alongside their electoral politics (Teles 2008). This infrastructure did not develop overnight, but once in place, it enabled libertarian and conservative advocates to call on judges to assist their campaigns for policy change via legislative and electoral institutions. Just as the mid-twentieth-century NAACP sought to advance its vision of racial equality by persuading judges to enjoin new legislative restrictions on rights, to dismantle existing such restrictions, and to enable their efforts to change policy legislatively, the Center for Individual Rights (CIR) and a number of allied organizations sought to advance their "color-blind" vision of racial equality in the same three ways. When the University of Texas adopted a new race-conscious admissions policy in 2004, Edward Blum's anti–affirmative action organization, the Project on Fair Representation, orchestrated a legal challenge that eventually made its way to the Supreme Court.[1] By this point, CIR had already litigated several cases designed to dismantle race-conscious admissions policies that had long been in place, with two of those suits producing significant victories.[2] And when Ward Connerly joined with one of CIR's plaintiffs to lead a ballot initiative campaign to ban affirmative action altogether in Michigan, CIR's litigators called on state and federal judges to compel state officials to schedule the initiative for a vote and, once it had been enacted, to comply with its commands.[3]

Using Courts as Veto Points

Many of the category 1 lawsuits that I describe in chapter 1 fit the standard caricature of liberal judicial activism: When liberals lose at the polls, they invariably turn to unaccountable judges in an effort to reverse those defeats. There is some truth to this story, but the same dynamic has played out just as regularly in reverse, with conservatives losing at the polls and then trying their luck in court.

Blocking gun control policies

Consider the issue of gun control. Throughout the Clinton, Bush, and Obama eras, gun rights advocates regularly challenged recently enacted gun control policies in court. Prior to the Clinton era, such litigation had generally been unnecessary, as these advocates had long been successful in blocking legislative action, particularly at the federal level. In the late 1980s, however, this congressionally focused strategy started to break down (Goss 2006, 46–47; Spitzer 2004, 141). In response to rising rates of violent crime in general, and the increasing incidence of notorious mass shootings in particular, Congress became increasingly willing to consider gun control measures. The first President Bush had opposed most such efforts, but in 1993 and 1994, Bill Clinton signed two significant bills into law. In response, the National Rifle Association (NRA) and its allies ratcheted up their political efforts, but they also turned to a court-based rights mobilization strategy that they had long seen as both unnecessary and unlikely to succeed.[4] After all, while the Second Amendment guaranteed "the right of the people to keep and bear arms," its opening clause emphasized this right's close connection to the eighteenth-century citizens' militia, and SCOTUS had never once relied on the amendment to invalidate a legislative regulation of firearms.

The first major gun control measure of the Clinton era was the Brady Bill, enacted in November 1993. Acting in response to widespread calls for a national waiting period on handgun purchases, which would enable the criminal background checks that were necessary to enforce the longstanding prohibition on the purchase of handguns by convicted felons, Congress imposed a five-day waiting period that would remain in effect until 1998, at which point it would be superseded by a computerized system for instant background checks (Goss 2006, 176–79; Pickerill 2004,

103–16; Spitzer 2004, 126). In addition to waiting periods and background checks, the late 1980s and early 1990s witnessed increasing support for an outright ban on semiautomatic assault weapons, and in September 1994, Clinton signed a major crime bill that included a ten-year ban on the sale and possession of nineteen such guns, as well as a variety of copycat weapons that resembled them in specified ways. The Clinton crime bill also included provisions banning firearms possession by persons currently subject to a domestic violence restraining order. During this same period, blue-state legislatures also passed a number of new gun control measures, including bans on assault weapons, prohibitions on handgun possession by children, and declarations of parental liability for shootings by their children (DeConde 2001, 239; Goss 2006, 182; Spitzer 2004, 13).

In the wake of these legislative developments, gun rights advocates turned to the courts to prevent these new restrictions from taking effect, but the first such litigation to receive national attention came in response to a less well-known gun control measure that dated to the Bush era. When Alfonso Lopez Jr. was prosecuted under the 1990 Gun-Free School Zones Act (GFSZA), his lawyers argued that the law exceeded Congress's enumerated powers under Article I. In 1993, a Fifth Circuit panel endorsed this argument, throwing out Lopez's conviction. The decision rested entirely on the limits of congressional authority to regulate interstate commerce, with Circuit Judge William Garwood noting that virtually all federal firearms regulations, dating back nearly sixty years, applied only to guns that had traveled in interstate commerce. In Judge Garwood's view, the GFSZA's prohibition of mere possession of a firearm, whether or not it had traveled across state lines, was both anomalous and constitutionally questionable. (President Bush had made the same point in a signing statement when the bill was enacted.) Lopez's lawyers had not raised any Second Amendment concerns, but in a footnote, Judge Garwood noted that "some applications" of the statute might be problematic on these grounds as well, citing a recent article by Sanford Levinson for the proposition that "this orphan of the Bill of Rights . . . should be taken seriously."[5]

As with the gay rights litigation surveyed in chapter 1, the Clinton-era gun rights disputes reveal the important interaction between movement litigation and wildcat suits in shaping the path of the law. Advocacy organizations carefully plan their own suits, selecting targets that they view as particularly vulnerable and/or strategically important, but nonmovement plaintiffs regularly file additional suits. When these latter suits make headway in the courts, the movement advocates regularly feel compelled to join the fight, whether or not they supported the suits at the outset.

The constitutional challenge in *United States v. Lopez* was filed on behalf of a criminal defendant by his federal public defender. But once the Supreme Court agreed to hear the case, conservative scholars and public interest litigators climbed aboard, filing several amicus briefs in support of Lopez, with two of those briefs raising the Second Amendment issue. (The brief filed by the Pacific Legal Foundation raised the Second Amendment issue as part of a broader federalism argument, and the brief filed by Academics for the Second Amendment raised it directly and at length.) The following year, the Supreme Court affirmed the Fifth Circuit's holding, with Justice Clarence Thomas following Garwood's lead in noting the Second Amendment issue as ripe for further litigation. President Clinton immediately proposed a revised statute, limiting the GFSZA's reach to guns that had crossed state lines or otherwise affected interstate commerce, and Congress enacted this revised statute in 1996. This new law provoked constitutional challenges as well, but the federal courts upheld it, and the Supreme Court did not intervene.[6]

While the *Lopez* litigation was proceeding, the Brady Bill's waiting period provision took effect in February 1994. Until 1998, this provision would require local law enforcement officers to conduct criminal background checks for all would-be gun purchasers in their jurisdictions. Here, the movement advocates did not hesitate, with the NRA orchestrating a lawsuit alleging that this provision represented an unconstitutional federal interference with state and local government autonomy and that, as a result, the entire Brady Bill was invalid (Winkler 2011, 72). Several additional law enforcement officers filed suit on their own, and by April 1995, four federal district judges had invalidated the background check provision, though they all found it severable from the rest of the bill.[7] These decisions relied on *New York v. United States* (1992), in which SCOTUS had held that the Tenth Amendment prohibits the federal government from "commandeering" state officials to enforce federal law. In September 1995, a divided Ninth Circuit panel reversed the holdings in two of these cases, upholding the background check requirements.[8] A Second Circuit panel reached the same conclusion in March 1996, but that same month, a Fifth Circuit panel went the other way.[9]

With the federal courts thus divided, the Supreme Court agreed to hear the Ninth Circuit case. One of the petitioners was Richard Mack, an Arizona sheriff whom the NRA had recently named Law Enforcement

Officer of the Year (DeConde 2001; Siegel 2008). The NRA filed an amicus brief urging the Court to invalidate the Brady Act's background check requirements, as did a number of other supporters of gun rights, including Colorado attorney general Gale Norton on behalf of eight state governments. In June 1997, the Court sided with Mack, Norton, and the NRA, with Justice Antonin Scalia writing for a five-justice conservative majority, and Justice Thomas once again raising the Second Amendment issue in a separate concurrence: "If . . . the Second Amendment is read to confer a personal right to 'keep and bear arms,' a colorable argument exists that the Federal Government's regulatory scheme, at least as it pertains to the purely intrastate sale or possession of firearms, runs afoul of that Amendment's protections. . . . Perhaps, at some future date, this Court will have the opportunity to determine whether Justice Story was correct when he wrote that the right to bear arms 'has justly been considered, as the palladium of the liberties of a republic.' "[10] This holding in *Printz v. United States* (1997) marked the second time in three years that SCOTUS had invalidated a federal gun control law. Most of the justices were moving cautiously in doing so, but Thomas had again signaled the possibility of bolder action to come.[11]

Meanwhile, litigation also proceeded against the federal restrictions on military-style assault weapons. Even before Clinton had signed the 1994 crime bill, federal law had banned the sale and possession of some specific weapons, and these bans had sparked a number of constitutional challenges that were of obvious relevance to the 1994 provisions as well. In 1992, for example, Raymond Rybar Jr. was indicted for violating a 1986 federal ban on the possession of machine guns. He responded by challenging the constitutionality of this ban on both commerce clause and Second Amendment grounds. On the Second Amendment issue, a Third Circuit panel quickly disposed of Rybar's claims on the authority of *United States v. Miller* (1939), which remained the high Court's most recent interpretation of the amendment.[12] On the commerce clause issue, SCOTUS's recent decision in *Lopez* had made the question somewhat tougher, but the panel disposed of this claim too, noting that similar challenges to the 1986 ban had been raised and rejected in the Fifth, Sixth, Seventh, Eighth, Ninth, and Tenth Circuits.[13] In short, the federal appellate courts uniformly declined to extend the holding of *Lopez*, though the judges were not unanimous on this question. The *Rybar* holding was issued by a divided panel, with Circuit Judge Samuel Alito dissenting, and the following year, the Fifth Circuit, sitting en banc, affirmed a similar holding by a vote of 8–8.[14] If the gun rights position in either of these cases had garnered a single additional vote, the 1986 Act would have been invalidated. The resulting conflict in circuits would have made Supreme Court review likely, and the Court's resulting decision would have had significant implications for the constitutionality of the Clinton-era assault weapons ban. For the time being, however, gun rights advocates did not have consistent support from the federal courts.

Litigation against the 1994 assault weapons ban produced similar results. With support from the NRA, firearms manufacturers filed at least two federal constitutional challenges to the ban, but neither was successful. On the commerce clause issue, a DC Circuit panel followed the Third Circuit's analysis of the machine gun law in *Rybar*, holding that the assault weapons ban was a legitimate exercise of the commerce power.[15] When the manufacturers petitioned for rehearing, Circuit Judge David Sentelle argued that the panel's decision "cannot be reconciled with *Lopez*," noting that the 1994 assault weapons ban, "like the parallel firearms act stricken as unconstitutional in *Lopez*, regulates, under purported authority drawn from Congress's power to regulate interstate commerce, activity (or inactivity) that is neither commerce nor interstate."[16] None of Sentelle's colleagues agreed, so the manufacturers then urged SCOTUS to intervene. The Clinton administration opposed certiorari on the grounds that "the nationwide market for firearms renders purely local prohibitions ineffective," and the Court declined to hear the case in October 2000.[17] In a separate case filed in the Sixth Circuit, Federal District Judge Robert H. Cleland rejected a similar commerce clause claim, which the plaintiffs then abandoned on appeal.[18]

By this time, national attention had turned to a constitutional challenge to the Clinton crime bill's ban on firearms possession by persons subject to a domestic violence restraining order. In April 1999, Federal District Judge Sam R. Cummings held this provision facially unconstitutional, endorsing a controversial new reading of the Second Amendment in the process.[19] Federal courts had long held that the amendment guaranteed a collective right of the citizenry to participate in state militias and that it did not protect an individual right to possess and use guns for civilian purposes. State courts had long held that their state constitutional analogues to the Second Amendment did protect such an individual right—in part because the wording of many of those state provisions made their individual rights import clear. But until Cummings's decision in *United States v. Emerson* (N.D. Tex. 1999), this reading had rarely been adopted by judges interpreting the federal provision. SCOTUS had said nothing on the issue since its 1939 *Miller* decision, which appeared to endorse the conventional collective rights understanding, but in recent years, a variety of scholars and gun rights advocates had questioned this long-standing view, and Judge Cummings endorsed the new individual rights model.

When the Fifth Circuit heard the case the following year, it received amicus briefs on behalf of more than fifty organizations, a level of activity that again drew national media attention to the case (Glaberson 2000). In October 2001, the appellate panel joined Judge Cummings in endorsing the individual rights view of the Second Amendment, even while noting that no other circuit had done so. Indeed, the panel cited decisions from the First, Third, Fourth, Sixth, Seventh, Eighth, Ninth, Tenth, and Eleventh Circuits that had adopted the contrary collective rights interpretation.[20] Despite these legal barriers, the panel endorsed the new individual rights view in an eighty-four-page section relying on the text and original understanding of the Second Amendment. (The panel nonetheless reinstated the government's indictment of Emerson, remanding for trial on whether the law was sufficiently narrowly tailored to withstand constitutional scrutiny.) After the Fifth Circuit denied en banc rehearing in November 2001, the high Court was presented with a clear conflict in circuits. The justices denied certiorari the following June, but as other federal courts stuck with their long-standing collective rights interpretation, the Court would have to intervene to resolve the conflict eventually.[21]

If and when it did so, the Court would no longer be pushing against headwinds from the federal executive branch. After George W. Bush succeeded Clinton in the White House in 2001—with John Ashcroft succeeding Janet Reno at the Department of Justice (DOJ)—the federal government's litigation posture in gun rights cases shifted significantly. Following the Fifth Circuit decision in *Emerson*, Attorney General Ashcroft instructed all federal prosecutors that the *Emerson* opinion reflected "the correct understanding of the Second Amendment" and that all future litigation by the department's criminal division should conform to this new understanding (Greenhouse 2002). The following May, in its brief opposing certiorari in *Emerson*, the Office of Solicitor General (OSG) attached Ashcroft's letter and noted the government's shifting view as follows:

> In its brief to the court of appeals, the government argued that the Second
> Amendment protects only such acts of firearm possession as are reasonably

related to the preservation or efficiency of the militia. The current position of the United States, however, is that the Second Amendment more broadly protects the rights of individuals, including persons who are not members of any militia or engaged in active military service or training, to possess and bear their own firearms, subject to reasonable restrictions designed to prevent possession by unfit persons or to restrict the possession of types of firearms that are particularly suited to criminal misuse.[22]

In August 2004, DOJ's Office of Legal Counsel (OLC) formally endorsed this view, with Principal Deputy Assistant Attorney General Steven G. Bradbury issuing a 106-page memorandum concluding that "[t]he Second Amendment secures a right of individuals generally, not a right of States or a right restricted to persons serving in militias."[23]

As of this point, virtually no Second Amendment litigation had actually been successful in court. The winning claims in *Lopez* and *Printz* had relied on Article I and the Tenth Amendment rather than the right to bear arms, and even in *Emerson*, the conviction for possessing a gun while subject to a domestic violence restraining order had eventually been allowed to stand.[24] From 1996 through 2003, Ninth Circuit panels had rejected Second Amendment challenges to a municipal decision to deny a concealed carry permit; to a statewide ban on assault weapons, which the California legislature had enacted in 1989 and strengthened ten years later; and to a county government's prohibition of gun possession on public property, which served to prevent the holding of gun shows at the county fairgrounds.[25] The Second Amendment arguments had not had much better luck in other circuits,[26] and besides *Lopez* and *Printz*, most gun rights litigation relying on other grounds had been unsuccessful as well. In July 2000, a divided DC Circuit panel had rejected the NRA's contention that "the Brady Act requires immediate destruction of personal information [generated during background checks] relating to lawful firearm transactions," upholding a Clinton administration regulation authorizing the temporary retention of such data.[27]

Most state constitutional challenges to recently enacted gun control laws had met a similar fate. Even where state courts acknowledged that their state constitutions protected an individual right to bear arms, they generally held that this right was subject to reasonable regulation, and that the particular regulation at issue was, in fact, reasonable.[28] During the Bush era, gun rights advocates no longer had to worry about new gun control measures at the federal level, but they continued to challenge any state and local regulations that emerged. Slowly but surely, these challenges started to bear fruit. For example, when the San Francisco electorate voted in November 2005 to ban the possession of handguns and the sale of all firearms within the city, the NRA persuaded the state courts to permanently enjoin the measure before it took effect.[29]

By this time, however, the partial victory in *Emerson* had broadened the ambitions of gun rights advocates. If the Second Amendment guaranteed an individual right to possess guns for private, civilian uses, then the legal campaign could plausibly target not just the newer regulations that I emphasize here, but also a wide variety of gun restrictions that had been on the books for many years. This more aggressive litigation, which I examine below, eventually produced landmark Supreme Court victories in *District of Columbia v. Heller* (2008) and *McDonald v. Chicago* (2010). And these victories encouraged additional challenges to newly enacted gun control measures in turn. For example, when the local city councils in Washington, DC, and Chicago responded to *Heller* and *McDonald* by enacting new gun control ordinances to replace those that had been invalidated, gun rights advocates immediately challenged these new laws in court. In the District of Columbia, local lawmakers responded to the Supreme Court's invalidation of their near-total ban on handgun possession by enacting a sweeping new set of handgun registration requirements and by banning assault weapons and large-capacity ammunition clips. Gun rights advocates challenged these new provisions on Second Amendment grounds, but a divided DC Circuit panel rejected the challenge.[30] In Chicago, the city council likewise responded to *McDonald* by immediately enacting a new ordinance that imposed a limit of one handgun per home, required such guns to be kept in the home, continued to ban gun sales within the city, and imposed a number of other restrictions on gun owners. Gun rights advocates immediately filed several federal constitutional challenges to the new law. In one such challenge, a Seventh Circuit panel enjoined a provision banning firing ranges within city limits, a provision that struck gun rights advocates as particularly egregious given that the law required significant firearms training as a condition for receiving a gun permit.[31] When a school shooting in Newtown, Connecticut, prompted a new wave of state gun control laws in 2013, gun rights advocates filed a new wave of Second Amendment challenges.[32]

Blocking gay rights policies

In the LGBT rights context, the litigation that has received the most attention has originated on the left. In other words, the most widely noted gay rights conflicts of the past twenty years have pitted court-based action in favor of gay rights against legislative and electoral actions by opponents of gay rights. On a number of occasions, however, this dynamic has been reversed, with gay rights advocates winning expansions of rights through legislative action and their conservative opponents responding with litigation. These latter suits—many of them initiated or supported by conservative advocacy organizations like the Alliance Defense Fund (ADF), the American Center for Law and Justice (ACLJ), and Liberty Counsel—have drawn far less attention.[33]

For example, when elected officials have acted to expand partnership rights for same-sex couples, conservative opponents have often filed suit. Beginning in the mid-1980s, a number of city and county governments—first in California and then spreading nationwide—enacted policies allowing same-sex couples to formally register their domestic partnerships with the local government. In some cases, the local jurisdictions agreed to extend health insurance and other employment benefits to the domestic partners of their own employees and, less often, to require companies doing business with the city to extend such benefits as well; in other cases, the policies provided no substantive benefits beyond formal government recognition of the relationship. In at least twenty-six different local jurisdictions, the enactment of a domestic partnership policy sparked a legal challenge from gay rights opponents.[34] In most cases, these challenges were argued and/or financed by ADF, ACLJ, or other conservative litigation organizations (Gossett 2009, 166). More recently, the successful adoption of state constitutional amendments banning same-sex marriage (SSM) has sometimes been followed by lawsuits seeking to invalidate local domestic partnership policies that (in the view of SSM opponents) are inconsistent with those amendments.[35]

The expansion of partnership rights by state lawmakers has often sparked similar reactions. In response to the Hawaii Supreme Court's holding in *Baehr v. Lewin* (Haw. 1993), the state legislature enacted a statute extending some rights and benefits of marriage to same-sex couples, whom the law termed "reciprocal beneficiaries." This 1997 statute fell far short of full equality, but it granted gay and lesbian couples more legal rights than they had in any other state at the time. Three years later, Vermont's elected legislators (and Governor Howard Dean) went further, enacting a Civil Union Act that extended all state law rights and benefits of marriage to same-sex couples. Like the Hawaii statute, the Vermont law was enacted in response to a state high court holding—in this case, the landmark decision in *Baker v. Vermont* (Vt. 1999). Beginning in 1999, the California legislature became the first to extend legal recognition to same-sex couples in the absence of a court order, enacting a series of domestic partnership laws that eventually extended all state law rights and benefits of marriage. Over the next fourteen years, the state legislatures of Colorado, Connecticut, Delaware, Illinois, Maine, Maryland, Minnesota, Nevada, New Hampshire, New Jersey, New York, Oregon, Rhode Island, Washington, and Wisconsin expanded the legal rights of same-sex couples as well.[36] In at least seven of these states, conservative opponents of SSM filed legal challenges seeking to block the implementation of these laws.[37]

Likewise when state judges have expanded partnership rights, SSM opponents have sometimes responded by asking federal judges to block such expansions.[38] When state electorates have threatened to expand marriage equality via ballot initiative, SSM opponents have sometimes called on state judges to block those efforts.[39] And when local elected officials have tried to expand partnership rights on their own, SSM opponents have again called on courts to intervene. In 2004, San Francisco mayor Gavin Newsom began issuing marriage licenses to same-sex couples, contending that the state's then-discriminatory marriage laws were unconstitutional and hence that he was duty-bound not to enforce them. Liberty Counsel's lawyers replied by contesting his authority to make that determination, persuading the California Supreme Court to hold that the 4,000 marriage licenses issued by Mayor Newsom to same-sex couples were "void and of no legal effect."[40] When the mayor of New Paltz, New York, followed Newsom's lead, Liberty Counsel joined with other conservative litigation organizations to launch a similar challenge, which yielded similar results.[41] When the mayor of Seattle issued an executive order mandating recognition of lawful SSMs (issued by other states) for employee benefits purposes, the American Family Association's Center for Law & Policy (CLP) challenged this order as inconsistent with state law, though in this case, the challenge was unsuccessful.[42]

These dynamics have not been limited to partnership rights. When state or local jurisdictions have expanded antidiscrimination laws to cover sexual orientation, opponents of gay rights have often responded with legal challenges to these policies as well. After New Jersey added sexual orientation to its antidiscrimination law in 1992, the state branch of the Orthodox Presbyterian Church filed a First Amendment challenge alleging that the statute sought to suppress a disfavored viewpoint (i.e., speech condemning homosexuality). A unanimous Third Circuit panel rejected this claim in October 1996, but four years later, SCOTUS held (in a different case) that the state statute did indeed violate the First Amendment, at least as applied to so-called expressive associations such as the Boy Scouts of America.[43] Similar challenges have been filed against antidiscrimination policies enacted by the legislatures of California, New Mexico, and Oregon, and by local jurisdictions in Kentucky, Maryland, and Texas.[44] Once state and local jurisdictions began extending their antidiscrimination laws to cover gender identity as well as sexual orientation, gay rights opponents called on courts to enjoin these provisions too, and legislative efforts to bar discrimination on the basis of marital status have sometimes sparked such challenges as well.[45]

The same goes for legislative efforts to impose heightened penalties on crimes of violence motivated by antigay animus. Opponents of these laws have repeatedly challenged them on free speech grounds, in part because every defendant convicted under such a law has an incentive to raise every plausible challenge and in part because gay rights opponents sincerely believe that such laws infringe their First Amendment rights. These legal challenges have been part of a broader conflict about the constitutional legitimacy of laws targeting hate crimes. The Supreme Court's decisions in *R.A.V. v. St. Paul* (1992), *Wisconsin v. Mitchell* (1993), and *Apprendi v. New Jersey* (2000), each originating with a racially motivated crime, signaled that penalty enhancement provisions for bias-motivated crimes were constitutional but that the First Amendment required such statutes to be carefully drafted to punish biased acts rather than biased words or thoughts, and that the Sixth Amendment required the fact of biased motive to be proven to a jury beyond a reasonable doubt. Most judicial efforts to apply these distinctions in practice have originated with crimes motivated by racial or religious bias, but antigay hate crimes have produced some notable appellate holdings as well. In 1995, the California Supreme Court unanimously upheld the state's hate crimes law against a First Amendment challenge brought by the perpetrators of a violent antigay assault in San Francisco's Castro District, but three years later, the Minnesota Supreme Court unanimously invalidated a provision of its state's hate crimes law, dismissing charges of felony harassment for disrupting a National Coming Out Day celebration held in a public park.[46]

As with the constitutional challenges to criminal punishments of racially motivated hate crimes, many of these cases have emerged from wildcat litigation, with private or state-provided criminal defense attorneys exploring any available avenue to defend their clients. On some occasions, however, organized opponents of gay rights have actively litigated against statutory bans on antigay violence or harassment. When a local school district in Pennsylvania adopted a policy in 1999 prohibiting verbal or physical harassment on the basis of sexual orientation (among other characteristics), CLP's litigators contended that the policy infringed their clients' First Amendment "right to speak out about the sinful nature and harmful effects of homosexuality."[47] And in 2009 when President Obama signed the first federal statute providing hate crimes protections to LGBT persons, a conservative public interest law firm known as the Thomas More Law Center filed a similar challenge, with the head of the American Family Association's Michigan chapter as lead plaintiff. This challenge to the Matthew Shepard and James Byrd Jr. Hate Crimes Prevention Act was unsuccessful, but in the Pennsylvania case, Third Circuit Judge Samuel Alito wrote for a unanimous panel in enjoining the antiharassment policy.[48]

Blocking abortion rights policies

A similar dynamic has held in the abortion rights context, with conservative opponents of abortion regularly denouncing left-liberal litigation efforts for thwarting the democratic will, but with the conservatives themselves willing to call on courts for help whenever they are losing in the legislative arena. Prior to *Roe v. Wade* (1973), abortion opponents sometimes litigated directly on behalf of the fetal right to life, challenging the legislative decriminalization of abortion on federal constitutional grounds (Garrow 1994, 522; Greenhouse and Siegel 2010, 150–57; Price and Keck 2013). SCOTUS closed off this line of argument in *Roe* by holding that fetuses were not constitutional persons, and since that holding, abortion opponents have relied heavily on legislative strategies for restricting abortion. Even still, they have continued to appeal for judicial assistance in contexts where such appeals seemed likely to help. In particular, where state or federal legislatures have enacted pro-abortion laws, abortion opponents have often sought judicial relief.

During the early years of the Clinton presidency, abortion rights advocates failed to achieve their goal of winning a statutory codification of *Roe*, but they did persuade the Democratic Congress to enact the Freedom of Access to Clinic Entrances (FACE) Act. As I note in chapter 1, this law was a response to an escalating wave of violent attacks by antiabortion extremists, and it provided both federal prosecutors and abortion rights lawyers a variety of legal tools to prevent antiabortion protesters from disrupting clinic operations. Abortion providers had been seeking injunctions against such protests even before the FACE Act was enacted, relying on a variety of existing statutes designed to target private conspiracies, but the new law provided much firmer legal footing for these claims. Abortion opponents responded by filing a series of First Amendment challenges to both the judicial injunctions and the legislative restrictions on their protest activities. Despite vocal support from three members of the Supreme Court, these challenges were mostly unsuccessful, but they did chip away at some of the more sweeping judicial and legislative restrictions, and the effort has not yet run its course.

In the suits that originated prior to the FACE Act, abortion opponents, led by Liberty Counsel's Mathew Staver and ACLJ's Jay Sekulow, argued that neither the RICO (Racketeer Influenced and Corrupt Organizations) Act nor the Ku Klux Klan Act could be applied to enjoin antiabortion protests without infringing on the First Amendment (Hacker 2005). Note, for example, *Madsen v. Women's Health Center* (1994). The case originated when a Florida trial court expanded an existing injunction restricting protests targeting the Aware Woman Center for Choice in Melbourne, Florida. The clinic's staff had requested the expansion after the protesters had "openly cheered" the March 1993 murder of Dr. David Gunn in Pensacola (Rohter 1994). As expanded in April 1993, the injunction imposed a 36-foot buffer zone around the clinic's property line that demonstrators were prohibited from entering; a 300-foot buffer zone around the clinic's property line in which they were prohibited from approaching a patient "unless such person indicates a desire to communicate"; and a 300-foot buffer zone around the homes of clinic staff, in which they were prohibited from protesting in any manner. Represented by Staver, the protesters objected to the injunction on First Amendment grounds in both state and federal court. These efforts produced conflicting decisions from an Eleventh Circuit panel and the Florida Supreme Court in October 1993.[49]

Staver petitioned for certiorari from the state high court judgment, which had held the injunction justified by the state's interest in insuring public safety and protecting the right of women to obtain safe abortions, and SCOTUS granted the petition and consolidated the cases (Hacker 2005, 72–74). Solicitor General Drew Days defended the injunction, and in June 1994, Chief Justice William Rehnquist wrote for a six-justice majority that sought to split the difference between the two sides. The Court struck down the 300-foot ban on approaching patients and the 300-foot buffers around staff residences, but upheld the 36-foot buffer zone around the clinic's entrance and the ban on excessive noise. This was too much for Justice Scalia, who published an angry dissent, joined by Justices Kennedy and Thomas, complaining that the Court's abortion jurisprudence was an "ad hoc nullification machine [that had now claimed] its latest, greatest, and most surprising victim: the First Amendment."[50] The following year, when the Court declined to hear an appeal of a ruling by the New Jersey Supreme Court that kept antiabortion pickets at least 100 feet away from an abortion provider's home, Scalia wrote separately to note that the Court's decision in *Madsen* "has damaged the First Amendment more quickly and more severely than I feared." Scalia characterized the injunction at issue in the New Jersey case as an "unconstitutional prior restraint," but nonetheless voted to deny certiorari because his colleagues were unlikely to revisit the issue "in another case involving the currently disfavored class of anti-abortion protesters."[51]

The following week, the Court declined to hear an appeal from a case that had gone the other way, but in March 1996, the justices entered the fray once again, granting certiorari in *Schenck v. Pro-Choice Network.*[52] The *Schenck* case had originated in 1990, when abortion providers in and around Rochester and Buffalo, New York, sought an injunction against Operation Rescue. Federal district judge Richard J. Arcara subsequently enjoined the antiabortion organization from trespassing on or impeding access to the clinics' property and from demonstrating within 15 feet of any doorway, parking lot entrance, person, or vehicle seeking to enter or exit such property. The court allowed an exception to this 15-foot buffer zone for "conversation[s] of a non-threatening nature by not more than two people with each person or group of persons they are seeking to counsel," but even these conversations would have to cease whenever the persons to whom they were directed indicated that they did not wish to talk. (The antiabortion protesters characterized this activity as "sidewalk counseling," but Judge Arcara found that it often consisted of "harassing, badgering, intimidating and yelling at the patients . . . in order to dissuade them from entering" the clinics.[53]) Represented by Sekulow, the protesters challenged the injunction on First Amendment grounds, and in February 1997, Rehnquist again wrote for a divided Court in upholding some components of the injunction while striking down others. Eight justices sided with Sekulow in holding that the floating buffer zones around people and vehicles entering and leaving the clinics were overbroad and hence unconstitutional, but by the same 6–3 vote as in *Madsen*, the Court upheld the fixed buffer zone around clinic entrances. This latter holding prompted Scalia, joined by Kennedy and Thomas, to complain that the Court was making another "destructive inroad upon First Amendment law."[54]

In this legal context, President Clinton's signing of the FACE Act in 1994 prompted immediate constitutional challenges, raising both First Amendment and *Lopez*-style commerce clause concerns with the act. In constitutional challenges that were initiated by protesters seeking injunctions against the act's enforcement in advance of its application to them, federal courts unanimously upheld the FACE Act against both free speech and commerce clause claims.[55] In cases initiated by the government to enforce the act against clinic blockades, the protesters sometimes raised these same constitutional objections in defense. They convinced one federal appellate panel to modify a FACE Act injunction because it was unconstitutionally overbroad, but these claims were otherwise unsuccessful.[56] In one noteworthy case initiated by providers to enforce the act against threatening speech outside the context of a clinic blockade, a First Amendment claim raised in defense was again unsuccessful, though in this case, the claim sharply divided the Ninth Circuit.[57] All told, seven panels, from six different circuits, rejected constitutional challenges to the statute; five of these holdings were unanimous. The antiabortion protesters petitioned for certiorari in six separate cases, but SCOTUS declined to hear all six.[58]

The high Court never addressed the commerce clause issue, but it did agree to hear Sekulow's First Amendment challenge to a similar clinic-protection statute enacted by the state of Colorado. By this point, ACLJ had successfully challenged two local clinic protection ordinances— enacted in 1993 by Phoenix, Arizona, and Santa Barbara, California, respectively—which required demonstrators who were impeding access to a health-care facility to "withdraw immediately to a distance of at least eight (8) feet away from any person who has requested such withdrawal."[59] In the Colorado case, however, Sekulow was unable to convince the justices that a similar provision, also enacted in 1993, infringed on the First Amendment.[60] Writing for a six-justice majority in *Hill v. Colorado* (2000), Justice John Paul Stevens upheld the statute as a content-neutral regulation of the time, place, and manner of expression. Scalia once again characterized his colleagues' decision as part of the Court's "whatever-it-takes proabortion jurisprudence," and this time, Kennedy read an angry dissent from the bench as well.[61] This anger may in part have reflected his near-absolutist approach to the First Amendment, but like Scalia, he made clear that the case was centrally about abortion politics (Colucci 2009, 61–64; Knowles 2009, 70–74).

The scope and scale of clinic blockades diminished somewhat during the Bush era, but whenever such protests have prompted legislators to come to the clinics' defense, the protesters have continued to call on the courts for protection themselves. Shortly after the SCOTUS decision in *Hill* came down, Massachusetts enacted a clinic protection statute that "was loosely patterned on the Colorado statute" that SCOTUS had upheld.[62] Antiabortion protesters filed an immediate facial challenge, with amicus support from ACLJ, the Family Research Council, Focus on the Family, and Massachusetts Citizens for Life. Relying on *Hill*, a unanimous First Circuit panel rejected the facial challenge in 2001.[63] When the protesters raised an as-applied challenge, a different First Circuit panel rejected that one three years later.[64] Three years after that, the state legislature revised the statute, replacing the Colorado-style floating buffer zone with a 35-foot fixed buffer zone around clinic entrances and driveways. This statute drew yet another First Amendment challenge, with the protesters now represented by ADF, but in July 2009, a unanimous First Circuit panel again sided with the state.[65] The protesters again followed their unsuccessful facial challenge with an as-applied challenge, and the First Circuit again upheld the statute.[66] But while SCOTUS denied certiorari in the 2004 and 2009 holdings, this time the justices took up the case, signaling that the dissenters from *Hill v. Colorado* may now have the additional votes necessary to move in a new direction.[67]

On a related front, when some local jurisdictions began regulating so-called limited-service pregnancy centers—antiabortion organizations that counsel women to continue their pregnancies to term, sometimes providing misleading information about abortion in the process—the pregnancy centers appealed to the First Amendment for relief, with mixed success to date. Federal district judges enjoined such ordinances in New York City and Baltimore, and a divided Fourth Circuit panel affirmed the Baltimore holding, but in July 2013, an en banc panel reversed that holding by an 8–4 vote.[68]

In sum, libertarian and conservative policy advocates, like their left-liberal counterparts, regularly turn to the courts in an effort to reverse their legislative defeats. On the right as well as the left, even if most such efforts are unsuccessful, the courts will often seem a last, best hope that is worth pursuing. Having already lost the policy battle in the legislative arena, it is hard to resist refighting it in the courts.

Using Courts to Dismantle Existing Policies

As with efforts to use the courts as veto points, lawsuits seeking to disrupt entrenched policy status quos have regularly been filed by advocates on the right as well as the left. Such legal challenges sometimes target policies that had been created by judges, but I focus here primarily on challenges to existing policies that had been enacted by electorally accountable legislators or executives.[69] These efforts sometimes emerge from the top down, with calculated decisions by organized rights advocates that evolving patterns of legal doctrine and public opinion have rendered an existing policy newly vulnerable to legal challenge. And they sometimes emerge from the bottom up, with ordinary persons finding lawyers willing to press their case that existing policies violate their legal rights. The suits in this latter category—which I have characterized as wildcat litigation—often appear to be long shots when they are filed, but if and when they make some headway, the organized rights advocates generally climb aboard and seek to take the helm. Again, these dynamics regularly play out on the right as well as the left.

Dismantling legislative restrictions on gun rights

In the gun rights context, criminal defense attorneys repeatedly sought to build on *United States v. Lopez* by challenging the constitutionality of the federal ban on firearms possession by convicted felons, which dated to the federal Gun Control Act of 1968. These efforts were uniformly unsuccessful, given that the felon-in-possession statute, unlike the GFSZA, applied only to guns that had been transported in interstate or foreign commerce. In the nine years following *Lopez*, federal appellate panels issued at least twenty-eight decisions rejecting commerce clause challenges to the felon-in-possession law.[70] All of these holdings were unanimous on this point, though Sixth Circuit Judge Alice M. Batchelder wrote separately in one case to indicate that if not for governing circuit precedent, she would have ruled the other way, and all three members of a Fifth Circuit panel in another case indicated that the issue was due some reconsideration by SCOTUS.[71]

Like *United States v. Lopez*, *United States v. Emerson* (5th Cir. 2001) led to a number of follow-up suits, but here, the organized rights advocates joined the fight. Most notable, within a year and a half of the Fifth Circuit decision in *Emerson*, gun rights advocates had filed two separate constitutional challenges to the District of Columbia's near-total ban on the private possession of handguns. These challenges were initially conceived by attorneys at the Institute for Justice (IJ), one of the nation's leading libertarian public interest law firms. But IJ's leadership, fearing a possible landmark failure at the Supreme Court, declined to support the suit, and NRA officials then tried to talk the IJ lawyers out of filing it. The IJ lawyers ignored this advice, secured private financing, and recruited the Cato Institute's Alan Gura as lead counsel. At that point, the NRA leaders filed a similar suit of their own and tried to gain control of the litigation (Levy 2008; Winkler 2011, 45–63). The NRA suit was dismissed on standing grounds, and when the wildcat suit was allowed to proceed, the NRA and a variety of other gun rights advocacy organizations supported it with amicus briefs.[72] The parallels with two wildcat suits surveyed in chapter 1 are striking. Like *Baehr v. Lewin* and *Hollingsworth v. Perry* (2013), the DC gun rights suit was initiated by ideologically motivated advocates who had some connection to a broader rights-based movement. Like the SSM advocates, the gun rights advocates initiated the suit over the express objections of movement leaders who feared that the litigation would lead to a landmark defeat. And like the leaders of the national gay rights organizations, their gun rights counterparts eventually realized that if they were unable to make the lawsuit go away, their best option was to join in and help it succeed.

The DC handgun ban had been on the books since 1976, but Gura contended that it infringed on the constitutionally protected right to bear arms for purposes of self-defense. Writing for a divided panel, DC Circuit Judge Laurence Silberman noted that the individual rights model that was advanced by plaintiffs and their amici had in recent years been endorsed by the Fifth Circuit, the Department of Justice, several state appellate courts, and liberal constitutional scholar Laurence Tribe.[73] By adding the DC Circuit to this list, Silberman increased the pressure for the Supreme Court to take up the issue.

After the full circuit denied a petition for rehearing (over four dissents) in May 2007, the high Court granted certiorari in November, with the case by this point known as *District of Columbia v. Heller*.[74] The following June, Justice Antonin Scalia wrote for a bare conservative majority in striking down the DC law. After a lengthy discussion of the text, original meaning, and prior judicial interpretations of the Second Amendment, Scalia concluded that "whatever else it leaves to future evaluation, [the amendment] surely elevates above all other interests the right of law-abiding, responsible citizens to use arms in defense of hearth and home."[75] Scalia presented his endorsement of the new individual rights model as a long-awaited return to the original meaning of the amendment, but as Reva Siegel has noted, this ostensibly eighteenth-century vision bore a striking resemblance to the law-and-order Second Amendment forged in the late twentieth-century culture wars. Like Ronald Reagan and Charlton Heston, Scalia read the amendment not as a reflection of "the republican vision of a militia prepared to defend against government tyranny" but as an effort to protect "the law-abiding citizen's ability to defend himself and his family from criminals" (Siegel 2008, 49). Though its practical implications were not fully clear, the *Heller* decision enacted a sea change in constitutional doctrine. As Justice Stevens noted in dissent, "hundreds of judges have relied on the [militia-focused] view of the Amendment" that the high Court had endorsed in *United States v. Miller* (1939). "Even if the textual and historical arguments on both sides of the issue were evenly balanced, respect for the well-settled views of all of our predecessors on this Court, and for the rule of law itself would prevent most jurists from endorsing such a dramatic upheaval in the law."[76]

Gun rights advocates certainly viewed their victory in *Heller* as a momentous one, and they immediately sought to capitalize on it. Just one day after the decision came down, the NRA filed suit against the San Francisco Housing Authority, challenging a policy prohibiting public housing residents from keeping guns in their apartments. The following year, the organization filed a separate challenge to several additional gun-related provisions of San Francisco law, including one that required handguns in the home to be stored in a locked container or disabled with a trigger lock. The 2008 suit persuaded the Housing Authority to cease enforcement of its rule, but the 2009 suit has to date been unsuccessful.[77]

Of even greater significance were two constitutional challenges to Chicago's ban on handgun possession, also filed immediately after *Heller* came down. Chicago's handgun law, which had been on the books since 1983, was broadly similar to the DC law invalidated in *Heller*, but the Chicago suits raised the additional issue of whether and how the Second Amendment applies to state and local governments. At the time that *Heller* was decided, the right to bear arms remained one of the few provisions of the original Bill of Rights that the Supreme Court had not "incorporated" into the Fourteenth Amendment's broad limits on state deprivations of constitutional liberty. As such, federal courts had sometimes rejected constitutional challenges to state and local gun control laws without even reaching the issue of whether the Second Amendment protected an individual or a collective right.[78]

Gun rights advocates hoped to use the Chicago cases to persuade SCOTUS to rectify this failing, but the first circuit to address the issue after *Heller* was the Second, in a case challenging a New York statute prohibiting the possession of a martial arts weapon known as nunchucks. In January 2009, a unanimous panel, including Circuit Judge Sonia Sotomayor, issued a brief per curiam opinion noting that unless and until the high Court reversed its decision in *Presser v. Illinois* (1886), the Second Amendment binds only the federal government.[79] In April, a Ninth Circuit panel became the first to rule the other way, holding in *Nordyke v. King* (9th Cir. 2009) that the Second Amendment applies to state and local governments after all. In an opinion by Circuit Judge Diarmuid F. O'Scannlain, the panel held that

> the right to keep and bear arms is "deeply rooted in this Nation's history and tradition." Colonial revolutionaries, the Founders, and a host of commentators and lawmakers living during the first one hundred years of the Republic all insisted on the fundamental nature of the right. . . . Colonists relied on it to assert and to win their independence, and the victorious Union sought to prevent a recalcitrant South from abridging it less than a century later. The crucial role this deeply rooted right has played in our birth and history compels us to recognize that it is indeed fundamental, that it is necessary to the Anglo-American conception of ordered liberty that we have inherited. We are therefore persuaded that the Due Process Clause of the Fourteenth Amendment incorporates the Second Amendment and applies it against the states and local governments.[80]

This holding presented the Supreme Court with a clear conflict in circuits, but in July, the full circuit voted to rehear the case en banc, thus delaying high Court review for the time being.[81] By that time, the Seventh Circuit had issued a decision in the Chicago cases, which gun rights advocates had seen as their best vehicle all along. Writing for a unanimous panel, Circuit Judge Frank Easterbrook followed the Second Circuit rather than the Ninth, concluding that "[f]ederalism is an older and more deeply rooted tradition than is a right to carry any particular kind of weapon.

How arguments of this kind will affect proposals to 'incorporate' the second amendment are for the Justices rather than a court of appeals" to consider.[82]

The justices were apparently listening, as they granted certiorari in September 2009, prompting a huge outpouring of amicus briefs in support of incorporation. One such brief was filed by Paul Clement on behalf of 251 members of the House and 58 senators, and another was filed by Texas attorney general Greg Abbott on behalf of 38 state governments. Similar briefs filed on the other side—urging the Court to uphold Chicago's handgun ban—represented just 55 members of Congress and 3 state governments. Only among academic scholars did the City of Chicago receive more support than the gun rights advocates. The most widely noted scholars' brief was filed on behalf of 8 leading Fourteenth Amendment scholars, on both the left and the right, in support of the NRA, but these scholars were outnumbered by the more than 60 historians and legal scholars who joined briefs in support of Chicago. The leading national gun control organization, the Brady Center to Prevent Gun Violence, filed a brief in support of neither party, asserting that whether or not the Second Amendment was incorporated against the states, government regulations of the exercise of the right to bear arms should be reviewed under a deferential standard: "Given the harms associated with firearms and the governmental interest in public safety, deference to legislative judgments regarding firearms is appropriate."[83] In June 2010, SCOTUS sided with the majorities in both houses of Congress and among the states, invalidating the Chicago law by the same 5–4 vote as in *Heller*.[84]

In between *Heller* and *McDonald*, the North Carolina Supreme Court had drawn national attention by holding that convicted felons retained their state constitutional right to bear arms, but the federal courts have proven unwilling to go down this road.[85] As I note above, the federal appellate courts have consistently—indeed, unanimously—rejected commerce clause challenges to the federal ban on gun possession by convicted felons. When *Heller* inspired advocates to challenge this law on Second Amendment grounds as well, the appellate courts rejected these challenges too, and SCOTUS declined to intervene.[86] Likewise, when a Seventh Circuit panel upheld a local gun registration ordinance, SCOTUS denied a petition for certiorari.[87] The Seventh Circuit decision came down prior to *McDonald*, but Circuit Judge Diane Wood noted explicitly that the registration law was constitutional whether or not the Second Amendment was incorporated against the states.[88] Since *McDonald*, federal appellate panels have continued to reject Second Amendment challenges to the federal felon-in-possession ban and have likewise rejected challenges to the federal bans on possession of a machine gun, possession of a handgun with obliterated serial numbers, possession of a loaded handgun in a motor vehicle within a national park, possession of a firearm in furtherance of drug trafficking, sale of a firearm to a person under 21, and transportation into a person's state of residence of firearms obtained in another state, as well as the federal bans on gun possession by persons convicted of crimes of domestic violence, persons subject to a domestic violence restraining order, persons convicted of misdemeanors punishable by a sentence exceeding one year, undocumented immigrants, and illegal drug users.[89] Federal appellate panels have likewise rejected Second Amendment challenges to a variety of state requirements for receiving a permit to carry a handgun and to a state statute prohibiting the carrying of weapons in a "place of worship."[90] And state high courts have rejected Second Amendment challenges to a statutory prohibition on carrying of a handgun without a permit, a statutory requirement that handguns stored in the home be kept in a locked container (or equipped with trigger locks), and a public university regulation prohibiting guns on campus.[91] In sum, state and federal courts appear to have moved cautiously in extending *Heller* and *McDonald*'s reach, at least initially. As Allen Rostron (2009, 403–5) has noted, this pattern of decisions is consistent with the experience of the Fifth Circuit between *Emerson* and *Heller*, and of state high courts that recognized a state constitutional right to bear arms prior to *Heller*. In all of these jurisdictions, courts have upheld a wide range of gun control laws as reasonable regulations of the right.

In December 2012, however, a decision from the Seventh Circuit appeared to give new momentum to gun rights advocates' efforts in the courts. In a case litigated by Alan Gura, Circuit Judge Richard Posner held that the right to bear arms for purposes of self-defense extends outside the home, emphasizing that both at the time of the founding and today, the dangers of violent crime were just as great (if not greater) outside the home than within it. As such, the panel struck down Illinois's sweeping statutory ban on carrying guns in public.[92] This decision was issued by a divided panel, and three months later, the full circuit denied the state's request for en banc rehearing by a vote of 6–4.[93] With a wide range of additional gun rights litigation pending at the time of this writing, it is too soon to say whether Posner's opinion signals a newfound willingness of the federal courts to extend *Heller* and *McDonald*'s reach, but it is clear that gun rights advocates like Gura will test this willingness with repeated calls for judges to dismantle existing gun control policies, and it is clear that ordinary criminal defense attorneys will continue to issue additional such calls as well.

Dismantling affirmative action policies

At the outset of the Clinton era, opponents of race-conscious affirmative action faced a wide range of what they considered objectionable policies that had long proven difficult to dislodge. Beginning in the late 1960s and accelerating in the 1970s, local, state, and national government institutions had adopted a variety of policies favoring racial minorities in an effort to compensate for past policies that had disfavored them. Most notable, public school districts had adopted race-conscious student assignment plans in an effort to integrate their schools; public colleges and universities had adopted race-conscious admissions and financial aid policies in an effort to integrate their campuses; public employers had adopted race-conscious hiring and promotion rules in an effort to integrate their workplaces; federal courts and prosecutors had pressured certain categories of private employers to adopt such hiring and promotion rules as well; and a variety of government agencies had implemented a range of preferences to increase the portion of public contracting dollars that went to minority-owned firms. These policies had never been particularly popular, but over the course of the 1970s and 1980s, they had nonetheless become bureaucratically entrenched (Skrentny 1996). Despite repeated efforts, opponents of affirmative action had virtually no success in persuading legislative institutions to repeal such policies or even to limit them in any significant way. These failures spanned all levels of government—local, state, and federal—and they continued even after their partisan allies captured both houses of Congress in 1994 (Skrentny 2001).

Unable to make any headway in the elected branches, color-blind rights advocates relied extensively on litigation, and also on a parallel campaign to curtail affirmative action via ballot initiatives. These efforts were led by two different organizations, located on opposite coasts, but the two often coordinated with one another, and the effort as a whole represented a more or less coherent campaign—waged in the name of color-blind "civil rights"—to win a nationwide ban on affirmative action (Greve 2004).

From the outset, the legal context for this campaign was shaped by the Supreme Court's 1978 decision in *Regents of the University of California v. Bakke,* in which Justice Lewis Powell had successfully defused the conflict (at least for the time being) with a pragmatic compromise (Bybee 2000). Writing only for himself—with four justices to his left and four others to his right—Powell had invalidated the strict racial quota that was then used for admissions to the UC-Davis medical school, but had noted that the more flexible race-conscious admissions policy described in an amicus brief from Harvard University would likely pass constitutional muster. Conservative critics had been seeking to undo this compromise ever since, and by 1989, President Reagan's appointments had given them at least a tentative majority on the Court. That year, SCOTUS invalidated a local government contracting policy in *Richmond v. Croson,* a decision that sparked a new wave of lawsuits brought by white-owned construction firms and other "victims" of affirmative action policies (Sweet 2010). In advancing these challenges, the white-owned firms, white university applicants, and the like were often represented by what Steven Teles (2008) has characterized as the "first generation" of conservative public interest law firms—a loosely affiliated set of regionally based litigation organizations, funded largely by local business interests.

The year after *Croson*, for example, the Denver-based Mountain States Legal Foundation (MSLF) filed suit against the federal Department of Transportation (DOT) on behalf of Adarand Constructors, a small, white-owned firm based in Colorado Springs, objecting to DOT's preferences for minority contractors, which dated to 1979. That same year, the Washington Legal Foundation (WLF) filed suit against the University of Maryland on behalf of Daniel J. Podberesky, a Hispanic student who objected that African Americans alone were eligible for the school's Benjamin Banneker Scholarship program, which likewise had been in place since 1979. The following year, WLF filed a separate suit objecting to the Education Department's continued support of higher education institutions that issued race-exclusive scholarships. The latter suit was dismissed by a DC Circuit panel in 1993, but by that point, a Fourth Circuit panel had held that Podberesky's suit should proceed to trial, serving notice to selective colleges and universities nationwide that their admissions and financial aid policies were legally vulnerable.[94]

Meanwhile, a newer set of conservative litigation organizations had joined the fight. In the spring of 1991, a Georgetown University law student publicized the racial disparities in grades and test scores that he had uncovered while working in the university's admissions office. After Dean Judith Areen denounced his actions and a number of fellow students called for his expulsion, lawyers with the DC-based Center for Individual Rights (CIR) came to his defense. At that point, the school agreed to grant him his degree, while reprimanding him for disclosing the admissions data without authorization (Maguire 1992; Teles 2008, 325). In addition to landing the issue of university admissions practices on the front page of national newspapers, the Georgetown controversy had the significant effect of drawing CIR into the affirmative action conflict, and by 1993, the organization had agreed to join a suit that had been filed against the University of Texas School of Law (UT). With anti–affirmative action students again having obtained confidential admissions data, the president of the National Association of Scholars (NAS) persuaded CIR to join the fray (Teles 2008, 232–37; Greve 2004). (NAS is an organization of faculty dedicated to opposing "political correctness" on campuses nationwide.) Before long, the campaign against race-conscious admissions policies would become CIR's principal preoccupation.

Throughout this period, white public employees—particularly teachers, police officers, and firefighters—filed regular challenges to the racial preferences that were widely used by local governments as well, as did white parents of school-age children with the race-conscious student assignment policies that were widely used by local school districts. In each of the four policy contexts in which affirmative action was widespread— government contracting, public university admissions and financial aid, public employment, and public school assignment policies—some suits proved successful in dislodging policies that legislative institutions had been unwilling to abandon.

In October 1994, for example, a Fourth Circuit panel struck down the University of Maryland's blacks-only scholarship program, and in June 1995, the Supreme Court held that a race-conscious federal contracting policy was subject to strict judicial scrutiny.[95] This latter holding in *Adarand Constructors v. Pena* (1995) represented a significant departure from the Court's last examination of federal contracting policies (in 1980) and from its somewhat more recent examination of federal efforts to promote a diverse range of broadcast programming.[96] Following those older precedents, a unanimous Tenth Circuit panel had upheld the federal contracting policy in February 1994,[97] but SCOTUS was now marking out a new direction, and *Adarand* represented one of the first Supreme Court victories for the nascent conservative public interest law movement. As noted above, the white-owned contracting firm was represented by MSLF, and it received amicus support from WLF, the Equal Opportunity Foundation

(EOF), and the Pacific Legal Foundation (PLF) as well. Also noteworthy, at least in retrospect, is the amicus brief filed by the Associated General Contractors of America, which was authored by John G. Roberts Jr. On behalf of the nation's general contractors, Roberts argued that *Croson's* strict scrutiny should be extended to minority set-asides at the federal level. SCOTUS agreed, and just a decade hence, Roberts would be in a position to extend that holding further as chief justice of the United States.[98]

Still, the conservative victory in *Adarand* was only a partial one. The case provided an opportunity for the Court's five conservative justices to indicate their commitment to constitutional color blindness, but Justice Sandra Day O'Connor sought to limit the force of this commitment. Writing for the Court, she directed federal judges to apply the highest level of scrutiny, but insisted that such scrutiny should not invariably be fatal. In remanding the case to the lower courts, her opinion strongly suggested that the federal government's long-standing contracting policies were unconstitutional, but it did not explicitly say so. As it turned out, litigation continued on this point for years to come.

In March 1996, CIR's lawyers won a major victory when a Fifth Circuit panel struck down the admissions policy at UT's law school, with the appellate judges going so far as to hold that Justice Powell's *Bakke* opinion was no longer good law.[99] This decision in *Hopwood v. Texas* (5th Cir. 1996) drew national media attention, in part because it was the first federal appellate holding in some time to focus directly on the contentious issue of race-conscious university admissions policies and in part because the panel's opinion marked out an aggressively anti–affirmative action shift in federal law (Applebome 1996a). In an effort to increase African American and Latino enrollments, the law school's admissions staff had explicitly considered the race of applicants since the early 1970s. Joined in the case by Theodore (Ted) Olson, a veteran of the Reagan Justice Department who was later named solicitor general by George W. Bush, CIR's lawyers advanced two distinct arguments, and the Fifth Circuit judges endorsed the broader of the two. Olson and his colleagues insisted that UT was not complying with the rules laid down by Justice Powell in *Bakke*, but they also argued that Powell's 1978 opinion had been superseded by *Croson's* subsequent holding that "racial classifications can be justified *only* when used to remedy past discrimination."[100] The implications of this latter argument were far more sweeping, and the Fifth Circuit endorsed it.[101]

Later in the year, an equally sweeping holding from the Third Circuit drew similar national attention. The dispute in *Taxman v. Piscataway Board of Education* (3d Cir. 1996) dated to 1989, when a cash-strapped local school board had decided to lay off a white teacher (Sharon Taxman) rather than a black colleague with equal seniority. The board defended this decision as an effort to preserve faculty diversity, under a policy that had been in place since 1975. But Taxman filed an EEOC (Equal Employment Opportunity Commission) complaint, and the first Bush administration subsequently filed a Title VII suit against the school board. The Clinton administration initially continued the litigation—winning damages on Taxman's behalf in February 1994—but later sought to switch sides, with Assistant Attorney General Deval Patrick arguing that "'faculty diversity' is an appropriate justification for affirmative action under Title VII" and that the school board had lawfully pursued such a goal in this case.[102] Sitting en banc, the Third Circuit rejected this argument in August 1996, holding that affirmative action policies in the employment context were prohibited by Title VII unless they had a remedial purpose. In rejecting the Clinton administration's contention that promoting educational diversity remained a compelling government interest, this decision appeared to be another significant departure from Powell's compromise in *Bakke*.[103]

The Supreme Court declined to hear the *Hopwood* case in July 1996, but granted certiorari in *Taxman* the following June.[104] Fearful that the justices would use the latter case to produce a sweeping negative precedent, a number of civil rights leaders orchestrated a settlement in November 1997, prompting the justices to dismiss the case (Biskupic 1997; Edsall and Fletcher 1997). At this point, the justices largely steered clear of the issue for five years, leaving the federal appellate courts to apply the strict-but-not-necessarily-fatal scrutiny of *Croson* and *Adarand* on their own.[105] Following the high Court's skeptical signals, federal judges invalidated a number of government policies in the employment, student assignment, and university admissions contexts. Other such policies survived judicial scrutiny, but it was clear to public officials everywhere that some of their existing practices were now legally vulnerable.

Consider some examples, beginning with the public employment context. Shortly after *Hopwood* came down, the Fifth Circuit issued another anti–affirmative action decision in *Edwards v. Houston* (5th Cir. 1996), with an en banc panel vacating the consent decree in a long-running employment discrimination suit and allowing a group of white police officers to intervene in the case.[106] Two years later, the Fifth Circuit held that there was insufficient evidence of past discrimination in the Dallas Fire Department to justify its policy of granting racial and gender preferences in promotions.[107] And in 2003, a divided First Circuit panel held that the Boston Fire Department had achieved racial parity and hence that racial preferences in hiring were no longer justified.[108] In a somewhat more complicated employment-related case, the DC Circuit held in 1998 that the Federal Communication Commission's (FCC) 30-year-old equal employment regulations were a constitutionally impermissible effort to force broadcasters to adopt race-conscious affirmative action measures. The Clinton administration argued that the FCC was not requiring broadcasters to adopt racial preferences and hence that *Adarand*'s strict scrutiny did not apply, but a unanimous DC Circuit panel held that the agency's requirements for detailed racially identified hiring records and its imposition of greater regulatory scrutiny on stations where minority employees were underrepresented were enough to bring *Adarand* into play. Under that precedent, Circuit Judge Silberman wrote, "we do not think it matters whether a government hiring program imposes hard quotas, soft quotas, or goals. Any one of these techniques induces an employer to hire with an eye toward meeting the numerical target. As such, they can and surely will result in individuals being granted a preference because of their race."[109] After the full circuit narrowly denied the administration's request for en banc rehearing, the administration then made a tactical decision not to petition for certiorari, fearing that the justices would give Silberman's holding even greater force by affirming it.[110] The administration instead sought to revise the FCC rules to meet Silberman's objections, but in January 2001, the DC Circuit invalidated the new rules on the same grounds.[111]

In other cases, however, state and federal judges continued to allow public employers to make race-conscious employment decisions. In July 1996, just one day after SCOTUS decided not to hear the *Hopwood* case, Circuit Judge Posner wrote for a Seventh Circuit panel in upholding a race-conscious promotions policy for the staff of a prison boot camp. Posner applied *Adarand*'s strict scrutiny but emphasized O'Connor's less-than-fatal understanding of such scrutiny, and unlike his colleagues on the Third and Fifth Circuits, he held that "the rectification of past discrimination is not the only setting in which government officials can lawfully take race into account in making decisions." In the case at hand, well-documented expert testimony demonstrated the penological necessity of integrating the staff that was tasked with guarding a majority-black population of inmates.[112] In 1998, another Seventh Circuit panel upheld a municipal employment policy that authorized the consideration of race in promotion decisions, and a First Circuit panel did likewise. In each case, the judges applied strict scrutiny but found that the policies at issue— from the Chicago Fire Department and the Boston Police Department, respectively—were narrowly tailored remedies for the departments' own past racial discrimination.[113] In the higher education context, the Nevada Supreme Court upheld a race-conscious hiring policy designed to encourage the hiring of minority faculty members at the state's public universities.[114]

Race-conscious government contracting policies met a similar fate; a good number were struck down in court, but the details of the specific policies—and the composition of the appellate panels, a point to which I return in chapter 3—produced occasional decisions upholding such policies as well. In June 1997, a divided DC Circuit panel held that a white-owned defense contractor had standing to challenge the constitutionality of the Small Business Administration's 8(a) contracting policy. This policy was the same one that was at issue in *Adarand*, and like the Department of Transportation, the Pentagon had been presuming that all minority-owned firms and no white-owned firms were eligible for the 8(a) set-aside. The Clinton administration had responded to the suit by withdrawing the particular navy procurement at issue from the 8(a) program, but the appellate panel held that the Dynalantic Corporation's ongoing "lack of opportunity to compete for Defense Department contracts reserved to 8(a) firms" was sufficient to confer standing. Citing a 1993 Supreme Court holding, the panel held that Dynalantic need not "demonstrate that it actually would have won (or will win) the award of a particular contract. Dynalantic's injury is 'the inability to compete on an equal footing in the bidding process, not the loss of a contract.'"[115] Several years later, a Federal Circuit panel likewise reinstated a federal constitutional challenge to a minority set-aside policy that was mandated by the National Defense Authorization Act of 1987, directing the trial court to subject the policy to strict judicial scrutiny.[116]

In other cases, however, federal contracting policies survived this increasingly strict scrutiny. In the *Adarand* case itself, the Clinton administration revised the race-conscious policy at issue and then successfully defended it in court. On remand from the Supreme Court, a Tenth Circuit panel acknowledged that the original version of the policy—the one that Adarand Constructors had first challenged a decade earlier—was unconstitutional, but held that Congress and the Clinton administration had adequately revised it in the interim.[117] Three years later, in another MSLF case, a different Tenth Circuit panel upheld the City of Denver's race-conscious contracting policy as well.[118] Around the same time, a DC Circuit panel upheld a contracting preference for firms owned by Native Americans that Congress had written into its annual Defense Appropriations Acts since 1990.[119]

The story of race-conscious student assignment policies in the public schools during this period was again similar. A number of such policies were invalidated, but in the absence of bright-line rules from SCOTUS, others survived. In 1999 and 2000, for example, the Second, Fourth, and Ninth Circuits each issued decisions upholding race-conscious student assignment policies. In the Ninth Circuit case, the judges rejected a challenge to the admissions policy of a "lab school" run by UCLA's School of Education, holding that the policy served the university's compelling interest in maintaining a research population that mirrored the student population of the state.[120] In the Second Circuit, the trial court had relied on *Hopwood* in holding that remedying past discrimination was the only interest compelling enough to justify race-conscious student assignments, but the appellate panel reversed. Holding that an interdistrict transfer policy in the Rochester, New York, metropolitan area served the compelling government interest of reducing racial isolation in the participating schools, the panel remanded the case for trial to determine whether the policy's racially restrictive eligibility rules were narrowly tailored to promote that interest.[121] The Fourth Circuit decision likewise endorsed the consideration of race in the assignment of students to public schools, in this case in the context of a long-running desegregation dispute. In 1965, a group of African American families in Charlotte, North Carolina, had challenged the local school district for avoiding its affirmative obligation to integrate, a suit that produced a landmark 1971 Supreme Court decision approving race-conscious busing.[122] In 1992, the school district revised its desegregation plan by adding so-called magnet schools, open to students throughout the district but with the seats apportioned on a race-conscious basis. A white student challenged this policy in 1997, and in 1999, the trial court held that the district had achieved unitary status and hence that race-conscious remedies were no longer permissible. It was this decision that the Fourth Circuit panel reversed in November 2000.[123]

These three decisions made clear that race-conscious student assignment policies sometimes continued to hang on, but that they were doing so by a thread. All three decisions noted in the previous paragraph were issued by divided panels, and when the Fourth Circuit agreed to review the Charlotte decision en banc, the magnet school policy again survived by a single judicial vote. In September 2001, the circuit's judges voted 6–5 to uphold the race-conscious policy, with two members of the majority noting that if the policy were newly enacted in 2001, they would have joined their dissenting colleagues in striking it down.[124]

In other cases, anti–affirmative action litigators managed to garner the single additional vote that eluded them in Charlotte. In June 1998, a Ninth Circuit panel held that the student assignment policy used by the San Francisco Unified School District (SFUSD) was subject to strict scrutiny under *Adarand*, a decision that led the school district to abandon the policy.[125] The First Circuit also struck down a race-conscious school assignment plan in 1998, and two separate Fourth Circuit panels did so the following year. The First Circuit decision came in a suit against the prestigious Boston Latin School, with the appellate panel holding that the popular high school could no longer continue reserving seats for racial minorities.[126] The Fourth Circuit decisions came in response to similar constitutional challenges to the student assignment plans in two suburban Washington, DC, school districts, each of which considered race (among other factors) in assigning students to particular schools. As in the higher education cases, the stated justification of these policies was to maintain diverse student bodies that would enhance the education of all students. In response, the Fourth Circuit panels each concluded that SCOTUS had not yet decided whether such diversity amounted to a compelling government interest, but that even if it did, these plans were not narrowly tailored to promoting that interest.[127] In another such case, a Ninth Circuit panel held that the Seattle School District's use of race as a tiebreaker in assigning students to popular public high schools was prohibited by the anti–affirmative action ballot initiative that the state's voters had enacted in 1998.[128]

These student assignment cases were not yet drawing widespread attention, but they reflected the emergence of a broad new litigation front. The Seattle case would continue for another five years, and there were many more like it on the dockets of the federal courts.[129] For the time being, however, it was the university admissions cases that drew the lion's share of national attention. After SCOTUS had decided not to hear the *Hopwood* case (in July 1996), CIR's principal strategy had been to file suit against prestigious public universities in other circuits. If they won, they would expand the geographic range in which affirmative action was outlawed. If they lost, they would create a conflict in circuits that would increase the chances for Supreme Court review. As such, CIR filed suit against the University of Washington (UW) School of Law in March 1997, and before the year was out, it filed two separate suits against the University of Michigan (UM) as well.

At UM, philosophy professor Carl Cohen had been waging a one-man campaign against the university's admissions policies for some time. After publishing an anti–affirmative action book in 1995, he used a Freedom of Information Act request to obtain the university's admissions data. This request revealed a series of grids in which high school grades and standardized test scores were applied differently to white and nonwhite applicants. Cohen published his findings in *Commentary* in June 1996, drawing the attention of several state legislators. After a legislative hearing featuring Cohen's testimony, Republican lawmakers Deborah Whyman and David Jaye held a press conference in May 1997 asking anyone who felt unjustly rejected by UM to contact them. Whyman and Jaye forwarded the names to CIR's lawyers in Washington, DC, and after interviewing several of these potential litigants, the lawyers filed suit on behalf of Jennifer Gratz and Patrick Hamacher in October 1997 (Belkin 1998; Stohr 2005, 36–47). Alleging that UM's main undergraduate college was using race not just as a plus factor but as "one of the predominant factors (along with scores on standardized tests and high school grades) . . . for determining admission," CIR's lawyers emphasized the racially segregated admissions grids and waiting lists that Professor Cohen had uncovered. Two months later, they filed a parallel suit against UM's Law School, this one on behalf of rejected white applicant Barbara Grutter. The Law School's admissions procedures were less rigid than the undergraduate policy, with faculty and staff individually reviewing each applicant's entire file, but from CIR's perspective, the policy was simply a less forthright means to the same end of reserving a specified percentage of seats for applicants from certain favored racial groups.

Meanwhile, a number of other public universities faced similar challenges filed by private counsel. At the University of Texas, the same lawyer who had initiated the *Hopwood* litigation filed a new case on behalf of a white applicant who had been rejected from the university's doctoral program in counseling psychology. Federal District Judge James R. Nowlin held for the university on the grounds that the applicant would have been rejected even under a race-neutral admissions process, but a

Fifth Circuit panel reversed in October 1998, reiterating the *Hopwood* panel's holding that diversity is not a compelling state interest.[130] A year later, the Supreme Court reversed the Fifth Circuit, reinstating the trial court's holding that Francois Daniel Lesage would have been rejected even if the admissions process had been entirely race neutral and hence that he had suffered no legally cognizable injury.[131]

At the University of Georgia (UGA), administrators had modified their undergraduate admissions policy in 1996, moving from a dual-track system for white and nonwhite applicants to one that reviewed most applicants on race-neutral criteria but awarded bonus points to nonwhite applicants who fell near the cutoff line. This change did not succeed in avoiding legal liability. Represented by A. Lee Parks, a crusading anti– affirmative action attorney in Atlanta, several rejected white applicants filed suit in 1997. In two separate rulings in 1999, Federal District Judge B. Avant Edenfield struck down the policy that had been used through 1995 and expressed significant constitutional skepticism toward the post-1995 policy.[132] He rejected the challenge to the latter policy on standing grounds—finding that the applicant at issue had failed to show that the university had subjected his application to the race-conscious stages of the admissions process—but more or less invited the attorneys to find a new plaintiff with stronger credentials. Parks responded by doing just that, and university president Michael F. Adams responded by proclaiming his continued determination to consider race in assembling the student body. With neither side backing down, Edenfield invalidated the university's post-1995 policy in July 2000. Joining a fast-growing group of federal judges, he disparaged Powell's *Bakke* opinion as idiosyncratic and nonbinding and complained that higher education administrators had provided no actual evidence of the educational benefits of racial diversity.[133]

This legal conflict over the merits of educational diversity was increasingly sharp, and by mid-1999, it seemed increasingly likely that it would be resolved in Michigan. CIR's challenge to the University of Washington had quickly been mooted by I-200, the state's 1998 voter-enacted ban on affirmative action.[134] In Michigan, however, both CIR suits continued to move forward, and the university's lawyers raised the stakes by using them to present the strongest case yet in support of Justice Powell's holding that (some) race-conscious admissions policies were justified by the compelling state interest in the educational benefits that flow from a diverse student body.

UM's president, Lee Bollinger, assembled a team of university officials and outside lawyers tasked with documenting the benefits of campus

diversity (Stohr 2005, 39–43). Building on a wide-ranging effort by leaders of the higher education establishment that was already underway,
Bollinger's team commissioned an unprecedented social scientific examination of the educational benefits of a diverse student body. By the time
the *Gratz* and *Grutter* suits proceeded to discovery, UM was ready with
an army of academic experts prepared to testify that the university's affirmative action policies enhanced the quality of education for all students
(Stohr 2005, 79–80).[135] As the cases proceeded, Bollinger also sought to
line up a variety of elite opinion leaders on UM's side. This task was slow
going at first, but in August 1999, former President Gerald Ford (a UM
alumnus) agreed to publish an op-ed in the *New York Times* decrying the
suits against his alma mater (Stohr 2005, 128–30). Around this same time,
Bollinger and Marvin Krislov, UM's general counsel, persuaded the vice
chairman of General Motors and the CEO of Steelcase Inc., an office-
furniture manufacturer, to join the cause. As a result of these efforts, GM
filed an amicus brief supporting the university's policies in July 2000, and
Steelcase led a long group of Fortune 500 companies in filing a similar
such brief in October (Stohr 2005, 137–40). Meanwhile, Bollinger's net-
working was laying the groundwork for another brief that would eventually prove even more significant. Sparked by a conversation with James M.
Cannon, former chairman of the US Naval Academy Board of Visitors,
Bollinger directed Krislov to explore the potential impact of a ban on
affirmative action at the US service academies (Stohr 2005, 140–42).

   These efforts appeared to face a significant headwind in the federal
courts. Federal District Judge Patrick Duggan ruled in UM's favor in
the undergraduate case in December 2000, but Federal District Judge
Bernard Friedman went the other way in the law school case three months
later, and most federal judges seemed to be following Friedman rather
than Duggan.[136] In the UGA cases, for example, unanimous Eleventh
Circuit panels ruled against the university twice in 2001, reinstating one
suit that Judge Edenfield had dismissed on standing grounds and ruling
against the university on the merits in another suit.[137] In the latter case, the
panel held that even if Powell's *Bakke* opinion were legally binding—a
point on which the judges expressed considerable skepticism—the university's policy would still be unconstitutional. In other words, even assuming that educational diversity were a compelling interest, UGA made
such rigid and mechanical use of race, at the expense of other types of
diversity, that its policies could not survive strict scrutiny. This case might
have made it to SCOTUS, but affirmative action advocates universally
thought the Michigan cases were a better vehicle, given the record that

Bollinger's team had assembled on the educational benefits of diversity. Heeding these implications, UGA officials announced in November that they would not appeal the decision and that the university would eliminate all consideration of race in assembling its fall 2002 entering class (Hebel 2001; Laird 2005, 41–43; Schemo 2001b).

At this point, all eyes turned to Michigan. In May 2002, a sharply divided Sixth Circuit reversed Judge Friedman's holding in *Grutter v. Bollinger*, finding that the law school's policy of individualized consideration of applicants' race was constitutionally permissible. Writing for the majority, Chief Judge Boyce Martin emphasized that "the Law School's consideration of race and ethnicity is virtually indistinguishable from the Harvard plan Justice Powell approved" in *Bakke*.[138] CIR's lawyers quickly appealed this holding to SCOTUS. They were eager to have the justices hear the undergraduate case as well, but the Sixth Circuit had not yet issued its decision, with Chief Judge Martin reportedly sitting on his opinion in the hopes that the high Court would act first (Stohr 2005, 214). After all, if Martin was hoping to rule for UM, the undergraduate case was a harder one in which to do so. The university had abandoned the racially segregated admissions grids that Professor Cohen first complained about, replacing them with a system in which African American, Hispanic, and American Indian applicants (along with low-income applicants and recruited athletes) received a 20-point bonus on a 150-point scale. Judge Duggan had upheld this revised policy, relying heavily on the social scientific evidence presented by the university's expert witnesses and amici, but from CIR's perspective, Duggan's holding seemed flatly inconsistent with the skeptical scrutiny demanded by the high Court in its recent decisions. Unwilling to wait for the Sixth Circuit decision to come down, CIR's attorneys filed a petition for certiorari before judgment in *Gratz*—that is, a request that the justices hear the case without waiting for the Sixth Circuit to decide it first. Michigan's attorneys, for their part, urged the justices to deny certiorari in *Grutter*, but they agreed with their adversaries that if SCOTUS were to hear either of the cases, it should hear them both together. In December, the Court announced that it would do just that.[139]

The Bush administration had offered no opinion on either petition, but once the Court placed the cases on its docket, the pressure for the administration to enter the fray intensified. Solicitor General Olson drafted an aggressive attack on *Bakke* for the president's approval, but White House counsel Alberto Gonzales prevailed on the president to take a more

moderate position (Stohr 2005, 235–45). President Bush issued a nationally televised statement on January 15, 2003, that was sharply critical of
Michigan's admissions policies, but the following day, OSG filed briefs
with SCOTUS that called for no significant changes in the law.[140] Indeed,
CIR's lawyers were disappointed by the briefs' insistence that the cases
"require[d] this Court to break no new ground to conclude that respondents' race-based admissions policy is unconstitutional" (Kolbo 2006).
The anti–affirmative action litigators had spent years trying to dismantle
Powell's holding in *Bakke*, but their supposed allies in the Bush administration now appeared to agree with Powell that the pursuit of educational
diversity "is an important and entirely legitimate government objective."
Seizing on the widely noted Top Ten Percent policy that Bush himself
had signed while governor of Texas—under which UT was required to
admit all students who graduated in the top 10 percent of their class from
any high school in the state—the administration's strategy was to endorse
educational diversity as a goal but to insist that race-neutral means for
achieving it were preferable and available. Because UM had failed to
adequately consider such alternatives, the administration insisted that the
Court could and should invalidate the university's existing policies without reconsidering *Bakke*.[141]

Michigan's lawyers responded by contesting as "fantasy" the administration's factual assertion that race-neutral alternatives would work. No
one had yet devised such a policy for use in law school admissions, in
Texas or anywhere else, and even at the undergraduate level, it was far
from clear that the Texas 10 percent plan could work at UM, which admitted students from a national applicant pool. As such, "[t]here is . . . no way
for this Court to reverse the Sixth Circuit's decision without 'breaking . . .
new ground.'" Put another way, Barbara Grutter "cannot prevail unless
the square holding of *Bakke* is overruled, expressly or *sub silentio*."[142]

Perhaps even more significant, the Bush administration's tepid opposition to UM's policies stood in stark contrast to an ever-growing chorus of
elite support for those policies. The Court received amicus briefs supporting UM from long lists of civil rights organizations, educational institutions, and scholarly associations; more than 120 members of Congress; the
governor of Michigan, the mayor of Detroit, and more than sixty other
state and local elected officials; twenty-two state governments; General
Motors and a group of Fortune 500 companies that had now grown to
sixty-five; and twenty-nine former high-ranking officers and civilian leaders of the US Army, Navy, Air Force, and Marine Corps. The sheer

volume of support for UM drew widespread media attention, and the oral arguments later that spring revealed that the justices had been reading what the amici had to say, particularly the retired military leaders.

When the decisions came down in June 2003, Chief Justice Rehnquist wrote for a six-justice majority in *Gratz*, striking down the university's policy for undergraduate admissions, but O'Connor wrote for a separate five-justice majority in *Grutter*, upholding the more flexible race-conscious process used by the university's law school. In doing so, O'Connor garnered a judicial majority for Powell's long-contested endorsement of race-conscious measures to promote educational diversity. Citing two of the briefs filed by higher education officials, O'Connor noted that Powell's 1978 opinion had served ever since "as the touchstone for constitutional analysis of race-conscious admissions policies." For twenty-five years, "[p]ublic and private universities across the Nation have modeled their own admissions programs on Justice Powell's views on permissible race-conscious policies." Regardless of whether Powell's rationale commanded a judicial majority in 1978—a point on which the federal appellate courts had been sharply divided—O'Connor indicated that the Court today endorsed his "view that student body diversity is a compelling state interest that can justify the use of race in university admissions."[143]

In defending this holding, O'Connor relied heavily on the elite consensus in support of affirmative action. Pointing to the findings made by Judge Friedman, the expert testimony included in the trial record, an amicus brief submitted on behalf of three higher education associations, and several recent books, O'Connor endorsed UM's claim that the presence of a racially diverse student body "break[s] down racial stereotypes," improves classroom learning, and "better prepares students for an increasingly diverse workforce and society." Citing the briefs from General Motors and other Fortune 500 companies, she noted that "[t]hese benefits are not theoretical but real, as major American businesses have made clear that the skills needed in today's increasingly global marketplace can only be developed through exposure to widely diverse people, cultures, ideas, and viewpoints." She then cited the military brief for the proposition that "a 'highly qualified, racially diverse officer corps . . . is essential to . . . national security' "; the Bush administration's brief for the proposition "that 'ensuring that public institutions are open and available to all segments of American society, including people of all races and ethnicities, represents a paramount government objective' "; and the brief filed by the Association of American Law Schools for the proposition that "universities, and in particular, law schools, represent the training ground for a large number of our Nation's leaders." As such, "[a]ccess to legal education (and thus the legal profession) must be inclusive of talented and qualified individuals of every race and ethnicity, so that all members of our heterogeneous society may participate in the educational institutions that provide the training and education necessary to succeed in America."[144]

O'Connor's conservative colleagues objected to her opinion at every level. Their fundamental constitutional disagreement rested on O'Connor's insistence that "[n]ot every decision influenced by race is equally objectionable." In contrast, Justice Thomas would have held that "racial discrimination in higher education admissions is categorically prohibited by the equal protection clause."[145] Under Thomas's absolutist vision of the Fourteenth Amendment, O'Connor's arguments about the educational benefits of diversity were constitutionally irrelevant. But Thomas did not stop with a statement of that straightforward principle. In a thirty-page dissenting opinion in *Grutter*, he repeatedly objected to affirmative action policies as patronizing and unjust. Opening with an invocation of Frederick Douglass's 1865 call for the country to leave African Americans free to stand on their own two legs, Thomas insisted that "blacks can achieve in every avenue of American life without the meddling of university administrators." With his own experience at Holy Cross and Yale Universities as an unspoken backdrop, he objected that even deserving blacks were tarred with the stigma of affirmative action, and he called on universities to cease conducting "social experiments on other people's children."[146] In separate dissenting opinions of their own, Rehnquist and Kennedy emphasized that even if educational diversity were a compelling interest, neither of UM's admissions policies was narrowly tailored to promote that interest. With respect to the automatic 20-point racial bonus for undergraduate applicants, Justices O'Connor and Breyer agreed with their more conservative colleagues, producing a 6–3 victory for Jennifer Gratz.

Though CIR had technically won a split decision, higher education officials immediately and unanimously declared the twin holdings to be a significant victory for affirmative action. On the steps of the Court, Bollinger's successor as UM president, Mary Sue Coleman, proclaimed the decisions "a huge victory for all of higher education" (*All Things Considered* 2003). Other university leaders had similar reactions, and even two years later, this remained a widespread sentiment.[147] Most journalistic accounts followed this script as well, with Bloomberg's Greg Stohr speaking for many others when concluding that the day marked "a stunning victory for affirmative action" (2005, 305).

In line with these accounts, the most notable short-term result of the Michigan decisions was that state and federal courts became increasingly willing to uphold race-conscious policies. Just three days after the decisions came down, the Washington Supreme Court held that Seattle's race-conscious school assignment plan did not violate I-200, though this decision focused on state law and did not mention *Gratz* or *Grutter*.[148] Later in the year, a unanimous Eighth Circuit panel joined the Tenth Circuit in upholding the federal Department of Transportation's minority set-aside policies, as modified by a 1999 congressional statute and subsequent DOT regulations. Those regulations provided for contracting preferences for all small businesses owned and controlled by "socially and economically disadvantaged individuals," but they made it easier for firms owned by minorities (and women) to qualify. In the panel's words, "race is made relevant in the program, but it is not a determinative factor." Citing *Gratz* and *Grutter*, the panel found this balance constitutionally acceptable.[149] The following month, the Supreme Court denied certiorari in *Concrete Works of Colorado v. Denver*, thus leaving in place the Tenth Circuit's holding that Denver had shown a compelling interest in remedying discrimination in the construction industry. Scalia and Rehnquist dissented, noting that the Court's refusal to hear the case, together with its decision in *Grutter*, "invites speculation that [*Croson*] has effectively been overruled."[150]

The following year, CIR's first major effort to persuade the federal courts to adopt a strict reading of *Gratz* ended in failure, with its long-running suit against UW providing the vehicle. Appealing the denial of their claim for damages on behalf of their clients—unsuccessful law school applicants from the mid-1990s—CIR general counsel Michael Rosman argued that UW's pre-1998 admissions policy violated the "narrow tailoring" requirement of *Gratz*. But the Ninth Circuit rejected this claim in December 2004, upholding the law school's (no-longer existing) policy and affirming the district court's refusal to award damages.[151] When SCOTUS denied certiorari in October 2005, this case was finally over.

Some holdings went the other way, but most federal judges appeared to be following the high Court's signals from *Grutter*.[152] In January 2006, however, Samuel Alito replaced Justice O'Connor, leading the Court to veer back in a more skeptical direction. The shifting legal fortunes of race-conscious government policy first came into view in the public school student assignment context. As I note above, appellate panels in the First, Fourth, and Ninth Circuits had invalidated race-conscious school assignment policies prior to *Grutter*, though other panels in the Second, Fourth, and Ninth Circuits had upheld such policies. In *Grutter*'s wake, three federal circuits addressed the issue. In cases involving policies in Lynn, Massachusetts; Louisville, Kentucky; and Seattle, Washington, all three courts applied strict scrutiny, but all three upheld the policies, finding that the school districts could continue considering students' race in an effort to prevent the resegregation of schools.[153] In a noteworthy concurring opinion in the Seattle case, Circuit Judge Alex Kozinski argued that such policies should not even be subject to strict scrutiny. Since neither the purpose nor the effect of the Seattle plan was to oppress minorities, to segregate the races, or to give preferences to some races over others, Kozinski insisted that it "carrie[d] none of the baggage the Supreme Court has found objectionable in cases where it has applied strict scrutiny." And while it was "tempting to adopt rules of law that give us the ultimate say on hotly contested political questions," there was "much to be said for returning primacy on matters of educational policy to local officials," and doing so required the courts to adopt a more deferential standard of review.[154] Kozinksi was outvoted on the level of scrutiny to be applied, but federal judges were overwhelmingly of the opinion that race-conscious plans for integrating primary and secondary schools were constitutionally legitimate under *Grutter*.

When the Court denied certiorari in the *Lynn* case in December 2005, the justices signaled that they were satisfied with this status quo, but Alito replaced O'Connor the following month, and the Court then agreed to hear the Louisville and Seattle cases. When these decisions came down in June 2007, Justice Breyer echoed Kozinski's call for judicial deference, but he did so in a sixty-five-page dissenting opinion. A bare conservative majority reversed the Ninth Circuit decision that Kozinski had joined, with Chief Justice Roberts applying strict scrutiny and holding that the local policies at issue neither served a compelling government interest nor were sufficiently narrowly tailored. In what was fast becoming a pattern on his Court, Roberts declined an invitation to expressly overrule the Court's prior decision—in this case, *Grutter*—but nonetheless made clear that he was setting out in a new direction. The most widely noted passage of his opinion in *Parents Involved v. Seattle School District* (2007) was his flat insistence that "[t]he way to stop discrimination on the basis of race is to stop discriminating on the basis of race."[155] Justice Kennedy's separate opinion sought to limit the scope of this holding, but Roberts's opinion for the Court nonetheless marked a sea change in the law.

Two years later, the same five-justice majority held in *Ricci v. DeStefano* (2009) that the New Haven Fire Department could not legitimately discard the results of a civil service exam given to firefighters seeking promotions. This case presented the justices with an unusual conflict between two different lines of doctrine under Title VII—one prohibiting "disparate treatment" (i.e., intentional discrimination) and the other prohibiting practices that had a "disparate impact" on certain groups, whether or not that impact was intentional. When the fire department's test results had been announced, the department's African American firefighters noted the disparate performance of different racial groups and made a colorable threat of a disparate impact suit. This threat prompted the city to discard the test results, and a Second Circuit panel (including Judge Sotomayor) held that because the city, "in refusing to validate the exams, was simply trying to fulfill its obligations under Title VII when confronted with test results that had a disproportionate racial impact, its actions were protected."[156] This 2008 holding appeared consistent with long-standing judicial and executive branch interpretations of the landmark statute, but the full circuit then split 7–6 in a vote to deny rehearing, with a sharp dissent from Circuit Judge Jose Cabranes signaling that the legal issue remained a live one.[157] SCOTUS then granted certiorari, and in June 2009, Justice Kennedy held for the Court that the city's decision to ignore the test results—and hence to deny promotions to those firefighters who had performed well—was itself an impermissible example of racially disparate treatment.[158] In a separate concurring opinion, Scalia suggested that the disparate impact doctrines on which the fire department had relied—and which the federal EEOC had advanced for decades—might themselves be unconstitutional violations of the equal protection clause.

The signals sent by the Roberts Court in *Parents Involved* and *Ricci* are likely to encourage federal judges to once again ramp up their suspicion of race-conscious public employment, contracting, and education policies. It is too soon to assess the scope of any such changes, but their direction seems clear. In the government employment context, a unanimous Second Circuit panel reinstated a suit by white firefighters against a 1980 consent decree in Syracuse, New York, with Circuit Judge Debra Ann Livingston writing separately to note the possibility "that a decree that appeared to meet the relevant constitutional standards as understood in

1980 may fail to satisfy current precedent."[159] In the public school assignment context, a divided Sixth Circuit panel held that the Shelby County, Tennessee, public school system, which had been the subject of school desegregation litigation since 1963, had now achieved so-called unitary status. As such, the panel dissolved all existing judicial orders governing the district, including those involving student assignment and faculty integration. On the issue of faculty diversity, the panel's opinion emphasized that continued enforcement of the district court's mandates would require the district to engage in race-conscious hiring and firing of teachers. Citing Chief Justice Roberts's opinion in *Parents Involved,* the panel held that "[r]ace-based hiring of the sort ordered by the district court violates the Constitution."[160]

As these holdings make clear, the legal landscape has shifted enough to render legally vulnerable a variety of race-conscious policies that have been in place for decades. Even in the higher education context, where admissions officers continue to follow the path marked out by *Grutter,* the signs of legal change are clear. After *Grutter* effectively voided the *Hopwood* decision in 2003, UT reinstated a race-conscious admissions process—supplementing, but not displacing, the existing Top Ten Percent policy. Affirmative action opponents challenged the new policy as inconsistent with *Gratz* and *Grutter,* contending that UT had identified a race-neutral process that succeeded in producing a diverse student body (i.e., the Top Ten Percent plan) and hence that university officials had no legitimate reason to reintroduce the consideration of race. In January 2011, a Fifth Circuit panel sided with the university, holding that UT's decision to reintroduce race-conscious admissions had been "studied, serious, and of high purpose," and that the university was using a "holistic, multi-factor approach, in which race is but one of many considerations," an approach that remained permissible under *Grutter.*[161] This decision was unanimous, but seven judges subsequently voted in favor of en banc rehearing.[162] They were outvoted 9–7, but SCOTUS then granted certiorari, vacated the panel holding, and remanded with instructions for the Fifth Circuit to uphold the policy only if "no workable race-neutral alternatives would produce the educational benefits of diversity." Writing for the Court, Justice Kennedy insisted that "[i]f a 'nonracial approach . . . could promote the substantial interest about as well and at tolerable administrative expense,' then the university may not consider race."[163] This holding will almost certainly lead to policy change at UT, and it may yet force university administrators elsewhere to reevaluate their existing practices.

In sum, policy advocates on the right as well as the left regularly turn to the courts in an effort to dismantle existing policies that (in the advocates' view) infringe on fundamental legal rights. When elected lawmakers prove unresponsive to calls for legal change, the courts will sometimes serve as a battering ram, useful for dislodging the policy status quo. As Gordon Silverstein has emphasized, these judicial interventions can have unpredictable effects, but from the advocates' perspective, litigation may nonetheless appear as the only viable path for forcing reconsideration of existing policies that violate their rights (2009, 245–68).

Using Courts to Clear the Channels of Political Change

Again on the right as well as the left, advocates call on courts not just to change policy directly but also to facilitate campaigns for policy change that the advocates are conducting in other arenas. Given the famously fragmented character of the American policy process, advocates regularly find their legislative campaigns hindered by obstacles that are best surmounted via litigation. As such, calls for advocates to eschew litigation in favor of democratic politics—whether on normative or strategic grounds—are likely to founder on the practical reality that litigation is often necessary to the practice of democratic politics itself.

Litigating to enable legislative politics

In November 2010, right-to-life advocates in Alaska proposed a ballot measure that would have amended state law to "affirm that the natural right to life and body of the unborn child supercedes the statutory right of the mother to consent to the injury or death of her unborn child." In accordance with the state's initiative process, the advocates planned to circulate a petition, gather the requisite number of signatures, and then submit the proposal to the state electorate for an up-or-down vote. In January 2011, however, state officials determined that the proposal was "clearly unconstitutional" and declined to certify the initiative. In an effort to clear the way for their continued pursuit of legislative change, the advocates then went to court, urging the state's judges to allow the state's voters to weigh in on the proposal. A unanimous state high court ruled against the advocates in May 2013.[164]

This dynamic has played out even more regularly in the LGBT rights context. In chapter 1, I survey a number of examples of such category

3 litigation by gay rights advocates; here, I note a number of similar examples by gay rights opponents. As Douglas Reed has noted, these opponents have regularly challenged state legal rules governing the ballot initiative process, with the "legal strategies designed to facilitate and enhance [their] capacity to engage in constitutional mobilization outside of the courtroom" (1999, 916). Reed's account focuses on the activities of the Oregon Citizens Alliance in the 1990s, but the phenomenon has continued in more recent years. When the Oregon legislature enacted new domestic partnership and antidiscrimination laws in 2007, opponents responded with petition drives against both statutes. When the state ruled that they had collected insufficient signatures, the opponents filed a federal constitutional challenge to the state's signature verification process. Likewise, when the Illinois Board of Elections blocked an advisory question that SSM opponents sought to place on the ballot in November 2006, advocates of the ballot measure filed suit. Represented by ADF lawyers in both cases, the gay rights opponents argued that the states' ballot access requirements were so onerous as to violate the federal constitutional guarantees of freedom of speech and equal protection of the laws. These suits were rejected by unanimous panels of the Ninth and Seventh Circuits, respectively.[165]

Most of the major sites of SSM conflict have witnessed a similar mix of direct democracy and litigation, though the precise dynamics have varied from state to state. When the Hawaii Supreme Court threatened to legalize SSM in *Baehr v. Lewin*, opponents organized a ballot measure calling for a constitutional convention to reverse the decision. In November 1996, 163,869 people voted for the measure, and 160,153 voted against, but the state high court subsequently held that, counting abstentions, the measure had actually fallen short of majority support.[166] At that point, supporters of the ballot measure filed a federal constitutional challenge, persuading District Judge David Ezra that the state court had improperly changed the rules of the game after the vote had been held. Judge Ezra ordered a new election, but a Ninth Circuit panel stayed this order pending appeal and then unanimously reversed Judge Ezra's holding in March 1998.[167] Despite this lack of success in court, the state legislature voted to place the constitutional convention measure on the ballot once again, with Governor Ben Cayetano signing the bill in May 1998. The voters decisively rejected the measure the following November, but on the same day, they enacted a separate measure amending the state constitution to provide that "[t]he legislature shall have the power to reserve marriage to opposite-sex couples."

In Massachusetts, SSM opponents likewise sought to amend the state constitution to preempt and then reverse a state high court decision legalizing SSM, and they called on both state and federal judges to facilitate these attempts. In the early 2000s, while *Goodridge v. Department of Public Heath* was pending in the state's courts, SSM opponents petitioned the legislature to foreclose the suit by putting a state constitutional amendment before the voters. In the summer of 2002, the legislature's Democratic leaders adjourned the body without considering the proposal, even though enough signatures had been submitted for it to move forward and even though SSM opponents clearly had sufficient votes within the legislature. At that point, the SSM opponents filed suit, asking the state high court to compel the president of the Senate to reconvene the legislature. The court declined to do so in December 2002.[168]

After *Goodridge* came down, SSM opponents sought to reverse the decision via constitutional amendment, and they again called on the courts to facilitate the effort. They initially sought to amend the constitution via a procedure that required majority support from state legislators, with the two houses meeting jointly as a constitutional convention, in two separate votes, followed by a majority vote of the state electorate. The legislature gave its first required approval in March 2004, and SSM opponents then petitioned the state high court to delay *Goodridge*'s effective date, scheduled for May 17, to allow the amendment process to play out. The court declined to do so, and after SSM supporters picked up several legislative seats that fall, the legislature voted down the proposed amendment the following year.[169]

At that point, the SSM opponents pursued an alternative amendment route—the same one they had used in 2002—which required the submission of 65,825 valid signatures of registered voters, followed by support from 25 percent of the state legislators (i.e., 50 votes), meeting in two successive constitutional conventions, followed by a majority vote of the electorate. The amendment's proponents submitted the required signatures, but in July 2006 and again the following winter, the legislature's Democratic leaders prevented the proposal from coming to a vote. Republican Governor Mitt Romney then filed suit (as a private citizen), alleging that once having received the valid signatures, the convention was constitutionally obligated to hold a vote on the proposed amendment. The year ended with the state high court holding that it lacked authority to order the convention to act, but nonetheless criticizing the convention for "indifference to, or defiance of, its constitutional duties." In the unanimous view of the justices, the convention did indeed have a "constitutional duty to vote, by the yeas and nays, on the merits of all pending initiative amendments before recessing on January 2, 2007."[170] Six days later, the members of the convention did so. Though under no legal compulsion, a number of legislators appeared chastened by the court's rebuke, and 61 voted for the amendment (with 132 against). According to the state's amendment procedures, the proposal needed to gain 50 votes one more time—from a constitutional convention composed of the newly elected legislators in each house—at which point it would have been placed on the ballot for November 2008. In June 2007, however, the measure fell short of 50 votes in the newly seated Convention.

As I note in chapter 1, the SSM conflict in California has likewise involved a complex interaction of litigation, legislation, and direct democracy. SSM opponents have relied most heavily on the latter route, but once again, they have regularly called on the courts to facilitate these efforts. In 2005 and 2006, with SSM opponents planning two separate petition drives for the California ballot, state attorney general Bill Lockyer made their task more difficult by drafting petition language clearly indicating that the initiatives would threaten the state's existing domestic partnership policy. The initiative proponents challenged Lockyer's actions in court, but a state trial judge upheld most of the language he had drafted.[171] With the attorney general's petition language in place, the proponents failed to gain enough signatures to reach the 2006 ballot. Similarly, after the state high court legalized SSM in May 2008, SSM opponents called on the voters to amend the state constitution to reverse the decision. Once their proposal qualified for the ballot as Proposition 8, state attorney general Jerry Brown changed the ballot title and language to emphasize more clearly that the initiative would eliminate the then-existing right of same-sex couples to marry. Proposition 8 proponents challenged these changes in court, again unsuccessfully.[172]

After the voters approved Proposition 8 in November 2008, the measure's proponents filed yet another suit against what they saw as an undue hindrance on their democratic participation, in this case the state's statutory requirement that initiative campaigns release the names of their donors. Represented by ADF lawyers and longtime conservative litigator James Bopp Jr., Proposition 8's proponents argued that "their contributors ha[d] been subject to threats, reprisals, and harassment," and hence that compelled disclosure of their identities would chill their constitutionally protected speech.[173] This suit was unsuccessful, but SSM opponents advanced similar arguments in a variety of contexts, and the courts have sometimes responded favorably.[174] For example, when Ted Olson and David Boies challenged Proposition 8 on federal constitutional grounds, the ballot measure's proponents relied on similar claims in their efforts to resist discovery of their internal campaign documents and to prevent the trial proceedings from being televised. Both of these claims succeeded, with a Ninth Circuit panel holding that compelled disclosure of private campaign documents would unduly discourage the exercise of First Amendment rights and SCOTUS holding that the trial judge in *Perry* had improperly authorized real-time streaming of the trial proceedings on the Internet.[175]

In fact, SCOTUS showed a remarkable interest in this issue during its 2009 term. In addition to the California case, the justices intervened in a similar dispute from Washington, where supporters of Referendum 71 (a failed 2009 effort to repeal the state's domestic partnership law) filed a First Amendment challenge to the state's plan to release copies of the ballot petitions, thus revealing the names of all who had signed them. State officials argued that such release was required by the state's Public Records Act, but supporters of the referendum, again represented by Bopp, contended that this law was unconstitutional, at least as applied to referendum petitions. On Bopp's account, the act's application in this context would discourage state residents from signing petitions, thus chilling political speech. Federal District Judge Benjamin H. Settle enjoined the state from releasing the names in September 2009, but a Ninth Circuit panel vacated the injunction the following month.[176] The referendum's supporters appealed to the Supreme Court, which reinstated the temporary injunction, pending the outcome of the appeal.[177] The Court affirmed the Ninth Circuit the following June, but its early intervention in October had the effect of preventing the state from disclosing the names of petition signers prior to the election.[178]

Having successfully blocked what they saw as a state-imposed barrier to their electoral success in Washington, gay rights opponents filed a similar challenge in Maine, once again represented by Bopp. Here, the state's voters were faced with a November 2009 ballot question calling for a repeal of the marriage equality statute enacted by the state legislature earlier that year. In the weeks leading up to the vote, state election officials investigated the National Organization for Marriage (NOM), a leading supporter of the repeal campaign, for failing to reveal the names of its donors. The state's campaign finance laws imposed extensive reporting requirements on all persons or organizations that solicit or receive contributions or make expenditures of more than $5,000 in a campaign for or against a ballot measure, but Bopp argued that these requirements violated the First Amendment. In August 2011, a unanimous First Circuit panel rejected Bopp's constitutional challenge.[179]

A similar story unfolded in Washington, DC. In 2009, the DC City Council enacted two SSM laws, first extending recognition to SSMs lawfully contracted in other jurisdictions and then authorizing full marriage equality within the district. In response, local opponents of SSM petitioned for a ballot initiative to enact a provision that "[o]nly marriage between a man and a woman is valid or recognized in the District of Columbia." The city's Board of Elections and Ethics excluded the proposal from the ballot on the grounds that DC law prohibits ballot measures that would authorize discrimination as defined by the city's Human Rights Act. Represented by ADF, SSM opponents challenged this ruling in court, but a divided DC Court of Appeals rejected the challenge in July 2010.[180]

Opponents of race-conscious affirmative action have likewise made heavy use of ballot initiatives to advance their policy aims, and they too have regularly called on judges to remove barriers to the electoral success of these initiatives. In January 2005, affirmative action opponents submitted more than 500,000 signatures to state election officials in support of the Michigan Civil Rights Initiative (MCRI), which was modeled on California's Proposition 209. The Michigan secretary of state subsequently ruled that the initiative's proponents had submitted sufficient valid signatures, but after affirmative action supporters raised allegations of fraudulent signature-gathering practices, the state Board of Canvassers declined to certify the initiative for placement on the ballot. The MCRI campaign went to court, and in October 2005, the Michigan Court of Appeals ordered the board to certify the initiative for the November 2006 ballot.[181] The board subsequently did so, and in March 2006, a divided state high court declined to hear an appeal from affirmative action supporters.[182] In November, MCRI was adopted by 58 percent of the state's voters.

As with SSM opponents, affirmative action opponents have litigated not just to gain access to the ballot, but also to force changes in what they see as misleading ballot language drafted by state officials. For example, when color-blind rights advocates sought to replicate their Michigan success in Missouri, Secretary of State Robin Carnahan adopted an official ballot title characterizing their proposed constitutional amendment as a "ban [on] affirmative-action programs designed to eliminate discrimination against, and improve opportunities for, women and minorities in public contracting, employment, and education." Objecting to this language as misleading, the Missouri Civil Rights Initiative campaign persuaded a state trial judge to recharacterize the proposed amendment as a "ban [on] state and local government affirmative action programs that give preferential treatment in public contracting, employment, or education based on race, sex, color, ethnicity, or national origin."[183] Despite this change, the campaign failed to gather sufficient signatures to reach the November 2008 ballot.

Litigating to call attention to the need for legislation (and perhaps to win some piecemeal protections in the meantime)

Rights advocates sometimes use litigation in a more or less explicit effort to draw attention to the need for legislative action. In the direct democracy context, in addition to suits regarding ballot access and ballot language, litigation can contribute to initiative and referendum campaigns by drawing the attention of voters to the issue in the weeks and months preceding the election.

For example, the anti–affirmative action suit against UW—filed by CIR's lawyers in March 1997 and noted in category 2 above—was litigated alongside a parallel effort to ban affirmative action via ballot initiative, and the lead plaintiff in the lawsuit, Katuria Smith, became the leading public face of the initiative campaign. In strictly legal terms, *Smith v. University of Washington* turned out to be relatively insignificant, as the successful ballot initiative effectively mooted CIR's federal constitutional challenge. Despite the formal legal result, however, the litigation was hardly a failure, as it played a crucial role in the initiative proponents' victory at the polls. The state's voter guide for the Washington Civil Rights Initiative (formally known as I–200), included a disputed allegation from columnist Nat Hentoff regarding Smith's chances of admission to UW. According to Hentoff, law school dean Roland Hjorth had publicly acknowledged that Smith would have been admitted if she were black. In October 1998, just weeks before the election, the *Seattle Post-Intelligencer* reported that the initiative's "supporters have made Smith their poster child of reverse discrimination, seizing on her solid academic record and the odds she overcame as evidence that race-based affirmative action is unfair" (Foster and Schubert 1998). And shortly after election day in November, CIR's Michael Greve noted in a letter to supporters that "*Smith v. University of Washington* focused the debate over I-200, the state's popular referendum for official colorblindness. The clear evidence of UW's discriminatory policies, coupled with the school's implausible denials, contributed greatly to I-200's overwhelming popular approval."[184] Similarly, John Carlson, recruited by Ward Connerly to serve as chair of the I-200 campaign, emphasized the significance of the television advertisements, which "told a simple, powerful story of a young woman from rural Washington, Katuria Smith, raised by a single mom in a low income home, who graduated from community college and the University of Washington with honors, only to be rejected by the law school, while more than 90 percent of African Americans who were accepted had lower grades and test scores" (Carlson 1998, 6). A few years later, when a local television journalist asked Carlson how important Smith was to I-200's success, he recalled that "she was very important because she put a human face on the initiative."[185]

In addition to coordinating with simultaneous litigation efforts, ballot initiative campaigners sometimes appealed to narratives constructed by prior litigation efforts as well. In Michigan, CIR's lawsuits were mostly unsuccessful, but they helped spark and support an initiative movement that fared better. In July 2003, just weeks after SCOTUS issued its decisions in *Gratz* and *Grutter,* Connerly traveled to Ann Arbor to launch the MCRI campaign, announcing the effort with CIR's lead plaintiffs, Jennifer Gratz and Barbara Grutter, at his side. Six months later, Gratz announced that she was returning home to Michigan to serve as executive director of the campaign, and from that point on, she was the leading public face of MCRI. As with Katuria Smith and the Washington initiative eight years earlier, Gratz's personal story as a sympathetic victim of discrimination at the hands of an elite liberal university played an important role in the campaign's success. When the state's voters adopted MCRI in November 2006, they outlawed both the race-conscious law school policy that CIR's lawyers had failed to persuade SCOTUS to strike down in *Grutter* and the new race-conscious undergraduate policy that university officials had designed in the wake of *Gratz*. When Connerly subsequently extended his campaign to Colorado, he followed the successful Michigan model by installing a former plaintiff from an anti–affirmative action lawsuit as executive director of the local campaign—in this case, Valery Pech Orr from *Adarand Constructors v. Pena*—though here, the initiative was rejected at the polls.

In sum, color-blind rights advocates have relied on two principal strategies in contesting affirmative action policies, and these strategies have reinforced one another in important ways. The lawsuits have fostered a rights rhetoric that has helped the initiative campaigns win public support. And the initiative campaigns have buttressed a narrative of legislative intransigence that makes judicial intervention seem less objectionable. As Reed has noted, "legal mobilization's strength stems, in part, from its capacity to translate grievances or 'mere' interests into claims of fundamental rights" (1999, 892). Even unsuccessful litigation can foster the successful entrenchment of new understandings of rights by drawing public attention to—and providing a compelling narrative in support of—parallel efforts at legal change conducted via legislative means (McCann 1994, 227–77).

Litigation initiated by democratically elected policymakers when other policy avenues are closed off

On the right as well as the left, democratically accountable lawmakers often find their policies the target of litigation, but they sometimes initiate litigation themselves when other avenues of policy change are closed. The most prominent recent example of this phenomenon on the right was the set of constitutional challenges to the 2010 Affordable Care Act (aka Obamacare) filed by Republican attorneys general and/or governors from twenty-six states.[186] Several of the legal conflicts that I have surveyed in this chapter can be redescribed along these lines, but this frame brings some additional conflicts into focus as well. Massachusetts Governor Mitt Romney filed the suit that persuaded the Democratic leadership of the state legislature to schedule a vote on a pending anti-SSM amendment that they opposed.[187] Local law enforcement officers filed the Tenth Amendment challenges to the Brady Bill that led to *Printz v. United States* (1997). The Second Amendment suit that produced *McDonald v. Chicago* (2010) was filed on behalf of a would-be handgun owner in Chicago, but it was supported by amicus briefs from a majority of the sitting members of both houses of Congress, plus thirty-eight state governments. In suits that I examine below, California governor Pete Wilson challenged several state affirmative action policies that he had been unable to persuade the legislature to repeal, and an Ohio state legislator challenged a public university's domestic partnership policy.[188] And when an Iowa trial court granted a "divorce" to a couple seeking dissolution of a Vermont civil union, ADF lawyers represented a group of state legislators and their allies (including one member of Congress) in filing a petition with the state high court.[189]

In addition to civil suits challenging policies enacted at a different level of government, public officials sometimes use their law enforcement powers to advance their policy agendas directly through the courts. For example, after being elected Kansas attorney general in 2002, Phill Kline immediately opened an investigation of Dr. George Tiller, whose Women's Health Care Services clinic was one of the leading providers of late-term abortions in the country. In 2004, Kline issued a subpoena demanding medical files of sixty of Dr. Tiller's patients, as well as thirty patient files from Planned Parenthood of Kansas and Mid-Missouri (Barstow 2009). Kline indicated that he was investigating suspected violations of the state's late-term abortion law, as well as the statutory requirement for doctors to report evidence of child sexual abuse. The Kansas Supreme Court rejected a motion to quash the subpoena but warned Kline to be careful not to release any information that could be used to identify individual patients.[190] When Kline subsequently made the files available to pro-life medical experts without requiring any pledge of confidentiality, the state high court responded with a sharp rebuke.[191]

Kline was unseated in November 2006, but his Democratic successor, Paul Morrison, continued the investigation, eventually filing criminal charges alleging that Tiller had an improper financial relationship with another doctor who had provided the legally required second opinion authorizing nineteen late-term abortions in 2003. Kline himself had filed such charges shortly before leaving office (in December 2006), but a state trial judge dismissed them and Morrison subsequently refiled them (Associated Press 2006). In March 2009, a jury acquitted Tiller on all counts. Two months later, Scott Roeder, a pro-life activist who had attended much of the trial, shot and killed Tiller inside his church (Barstow 2009).

Meanwhile, after Morrison replaced Kline as state attorney general, the Johnson County Republican Precinct Committee appointed Kline to fill out the remainder of Morrison's term as Johnson County district attorney.[192] In this capacity, Kline initiated another grand jury investigation in October 2007, filing 107 criminal charges against the local Planned Parenthood affiliate, alleging that the clinic performed illegal abortions and falsified documents.[193] His efforts also prompted two separate grand jury investigations initiated by citizen petitions. None of these investigations led to convictions, and Kline himself was voted out of office yet again and subsequently faced state ethics charges for providing misleading information to the grand juries (Fry 2011). But for six years, he had used the power of his two offices in an effort to end the performance of late-term abortions in Kansas. He would have outlawed all such abortions via statute if he had the power to do so (and if such a law were not constitutionally precluded by *Planned Parenthood v. Casey*), but with that option closed off, the prosecutorial powers of state and local government provided an avenue worth pursuing.

Litigating to enforce victories previously won via electoral and legislative campaigns

Finally, on the right as well as the left, advocates sometimes turn to court in an effort to compel compliance with policy change that they have already achieved via legislative means. In particular, conservative opponents of gay rights and affirmative action have regularly filed suits seeking to enforce ballot measures that had previously been enacted by voters. In the gay rights context, after successfully enacting a number of state constitutional amendments that banned not just SSM but also civil unions and other similar legal relationships, SSM opponents filed suit in several states to enjoin enforcement of domestic partnership policies that (in their view) ran afoul of the new amendments. In Michigan, a group of Ann Arbor residents filed a taxpayer suit, represented by the Thomas More Law Center, alleging that the local school district's domestic partnership policy was prohibited by the state's 2004 constitutional amendment banning SSM.[194] In Ohio, a state legislator filed a similar suit against Miami University, alleging that its continued provision of domestic partnership benefits violated the state's anti-SSM amendment, also enacted in 2004.[195] And when the Cleveland city council and the Wisconsin state legislature enacted domestic partnership laws in 2008 and 2009, respectively, ADF lawyers filed similar challenges.[196]

In the affirmative action context, supporters of Connerly's ballot initiative campaigns have likewise turned to litigation to defend their ballot victories against repeal or retrenchment and to compel reluctant administrators to enforce them. Connerly's first and most notable victory was the enactment of Proposition 209 by California voters in November 1996. In the wake of this victory, Connerly founded the American Civil Rights Institute (ACRI), dedicated to carrying the campaign nationwide. ACRI has relied primarily on copying the successful Proposition 209 strategy in other states, but it has regularly engaged in litigation as well. One of its first actions was to join the coalition seeking to fend off a federal constitutional challenge that had been filed by Proposition 209's opponents, and after succeeding in that effort, ACRI subsequently supported several suits seeking to force broad compliance by state agencies with the new constitutional requirement. ACRI's sister organization, the American Civil Rights Foundation (ACRF), served as lead plaintiff in at least two such cases, and Connerly himself did so in a third.[197]

In each of these cases, Connerly and ACRF were represented by the Pacific Legal Foundation (PLF), a California-based public interest law firm that had supported Proposition 209 from the beginning. PLF's lawyers litigated a number of other such cases as well, with their most significant victory coming in *Hi-Voltage Wire Works, Inc. v. City of San Jose* (Cal. 2000), in which the state high court invalidated San Jose's race-conscious contracting policy. In the wake of Proposition 209's enactment, the city had modified the policy to require that general contractors either submit bids that include a sufficient number of minority-owned subcontractors or document their unsuccessful efforts to find such subcontractors. Representing a white-owned contracting firm, PLF's Sharon Browne persuaded the state high court that this modified requirement still amounted to an unlawful racial preference, with Justice Janice Rogers Brown announcing the decision in a sweeping color-blind opinion. Three justices objected to the breadth of Justice Brown's arguments, but the court was unanimous in holding San Jose's policy inconsistent with the recent state constitutional amendment.[198]

The following year, PLF's lawyers won another notable victory, persuading an intermediate appellate court to invalidate affirmative action provisions in five separate state statutes. Relying on the state high court's construction of Proposition 209 in the *Hi-Voltage* case, the court struck down a 1978 law imposing racial goals and timetables on hiring by community colleges, a similar provision of the state's civil service rules, and three statutes mandating preferences for minority-owned businesses in the awarding of state contracts.[199] PLF's litigators have not won every case, but across all three policy arenas covered by Proposition 209—government contracting, public employment, and primary and secondary education— they have sent a clear and repeated message that the continued enforcement of race-conscious policies will be met with a legal challenge.[200]

From one angle, these suits simply represented constitutional challenges to existing legislative restrictions on rights—that is, what I have been calling category 2 suits. But from the perspective of the advocates

who litigated them, they represented not challenges to democratic authority (as embodied by the state legislature or local school boards that had
enacted the contested policies) but efforts to vindicate democratic authority (as embodied by the electorate who had enacted Proposition 209).
This appeal to courts to enforce the rights that affirmative action opponents had earlier succeeded in creating via ballot initiative was reprised
in Michigan when CIR's lawyers successfully intervened on behalf of a
white law school applicant in an ongoing suit regarding the constitutional
legitimacy of Proposal 2.[201]

*   *   *

Left-liberal rights advocates have long relied on courts to advance their
policy aims. In recent years, it has become clear that conservative rights
advocates do so just as regularly. On both the left and the right, policy
advocates turn to litigation when faced with newly enacted, rights-
restricting policies that they were unable to block in the electoral and
legislative arenas. On both the left and the right, policy advocates also
litigate when they think the courts might be willing to dismantle rights-
restricting policies that are already in place. And on both the left and the
right, policy advocates litigate when their own legislative and electoral
campaigns might be aided by some judicial assistance.

In this light, it seems clear that no matter how much political denunciation or scholarly skepticism they face, advocates are not likely to withdraw
from judicial politics altogether. This unlikelihood stems in part from the
fact that litigation is sometimes necessary even to the pursuit of democratic politics; this is the central lesson of my category 3 cases. But it also
stems from the recognition that abandoning the courts would amount to
unilateral disarmament, leaving the judicial field entirely to their ideological opponents. As I will emphasize in chapter 5, courts in the contemporary United States are, for better or worse, inextricably entwined with the
rest of the policy process. In the foreseeable future, there is no prospect
that they will be removed from that process altogether or even that their
role will be substantially scaled back. As such, advocacy organizations
may make strategic decisions about where best to pursue their claims in
particular cases, but they are unlikely to forswear courts (or any other
policymaking institutions) across the board when they know that their
political adversaries will continue to fight on that terrain.

The routine appeal to courts by advocates seeking policy change has sparked significant handwringing about undemocratic judges, but those worries seem justified only if judges regularly respond to these appeals in ways that are broadly unacceptable to the American public. As I will emphasize in chapter 4, such antidemocratic judicial decisions have been far less common than sometimes supposed. The operation of contemporary courts does raise an important normative concern, but it is not the one that is usually articulated. The threat to democratic governance is not that courts are too often protecting rights in the face of public opposition, but that courts might protect some categories of broadly supported rights while failing to protect other such categories. As I emphasize in chapter 3, this concern reflects a fear not simply that courts might act undemocratically, but that they might be captured by partisan coalitions.

PART II

Courts, Democracy, and Policy Change

CHAPTER THREE

Are Judges Umpires?

For the first year of Barack Obama's presidency, congressional Republicans fought tooth and nail to prevent the enactment of a sweeping health-care reform bill. In March 2010, their efforts appeared to end in failure, as President Obama signed the Patient Protection and Affordable Care Act (ACA) into law. But the policy conflict did not end at that point. Rather, it simply shifted to the courts, with opponents both inside and outside of government filing federal constitutional challenges to the law in multiple jurisdictions throughout the country.[1] When these suits first started making their way through the federal courts, judges seemed to be assessing the ACA through the same partisan lens as everyone else. The statute had been enacted with solely Democratic votes in Congress, signed by a Democratic president, and challenged in court by Republican state attorneys general and their ideological allies. In the first five federal court holdings resulting from these challenges, three judges appointed by Democratic president Bill Clinton upheld the law, while two appointed by Republican presidents Ronald Reagan and George W. Bush, respectively, struck it down.[2] If the judicial resolution of these disputes had continued in this vein, with a federal judiciary that had a solid Republican majority eventually disposing of the ACA, Democratic supporters of the act would have complained about what seemed a clear instance of partisan justice.

In the event, however, the federal courts stepped back from the partisan brink. When the initial district court holdings were appealed, two prominent Republican appointees (Circuit Judges Jeffrey Sutton and Laurence Silberman) drafted opinions upholding the ACA, and a third wrote a widely noted op-ed supporting its constitutionality.[3] And when the appellate holdings were appealed in turn, Chief Justice John Roberts drafted an opinion upholding it as well.[4] In doing so, Roberts avoided an outcome that many pundits had predicted—a narrowly divided decision from the Supreme Court, with five Republican justices invalidating the signature domestic policy achievement of a sitting Democratic president, over four Democratic dissents, in the middle of an election year. Indeed, from one angle, Roberts's behavior (like that of Judges Sutton and Silberman before him) appeared to evidence a federal judiciary operating at its best. Partisan advocates will always try to bend the law in their direction, but if our life-tenured judges can be trusted to resist those pulls in favor of an evenhanded resolution of constitutional claims from all sides, then the efforts of the advocates are no cause for concern.

From another angle, some Democratic supporters of the ACA were not so reassured. After all, four of the Court's nine justices had voted to invalidate the entire 900-page statute, on the grounds that a single provision violated a heretofore unheard of limitation on congressional power that had been transparently crafted by the law's political opponents. The controversial statutory provision, which required all Americans to maintain health insurance or to pay a modest annual tax penalty, had been endorsed by a wide variety of conservative policy advocates and Republican congressional leaders in the 1990s, and none of them suggested any constitutional concerns until the policy was endorsed by President Obama (Klein 2012). Not only that, but the four dissenting justices declared the individual mandate unconstitutional in an opinion that borrowed much from the rhetorical denigration that the ACA had suffered for two years at the hands of Tea Party Republicans.[5] From the perspective of Democratic supporters of the ACA, the dissenting opinion issued by Justices Antonin Scalia, Clarence Thomas, Samuel Alito, and Anthony Kennedy was so aggressively hostile to the new health-care law that the decision was far from reassuring about the evenhandedness of our federal courts.

In addition, the opinion by Chief Justice Roberts seemed to side with his Republican allies in many particulars. Even while upholding most of the ACA's central features, Roberts endorsed two key constitutional claims advanced by its critics. First, he held that the individual mandate provision exceeded the scope of congressional authority under the commerce clause. (Roberts nonetheless upheld this provision as a legitimate exercise of congressional taxing powers.) And second, he held that a provision compelling state governments to dramatically expand their Medicaid rolls amounted to an unconstitutionally coercive use of the federal government's spending powers. The first holding endorsed the central claim that had been articulated by conservative lawyers in response to the ACA's enactment, and the second endorsed a line of argument that conservative lawyers had for years advanced against exercises of federal regulatory authority, but that had never yet gained traction on the Court. From this angle, then, it seemed that Roberts was not so much acting as a neutral umpire but playing the long game on behalf of his partisan team.

Judging, Umpiring, and the Rule of Law

Contemporary judges regularly compare themselves to umpires, suggesting that their job is simply to enforce the legal rules as written, without regard to who wins or loses. As Roberts himself put it in his opening statement to the Senate Judiciary Committee in September 2005:

> Judges are like umpires. Umpires don't make the rules, they apply them. The role of an umpire and a judge is critical. They make sure everybody plays by the rules, but it is a limited role. Nobody ever went to a ball game to see the umpire. . . . I have no agenda, but I do have a commitment. If I am confirmed, I will confront every case with an open mind. I will fully and fairly analyze the legal arguments that are presented. I will be open to the considered views of my colleagues on the bench, and I will decide every case based on the record, according to the rule of law, without fear or favor, to the best of my ability, and I will remember that it's my job to call balls and strikes, and not to pitch or bat.[6]

In a subsequent interview with Jeffrey Rosen, conducted at the end of his first term as chief justice, Roberts noted that his model for judging as umpiring would be his greatest predecessor, Chief Justice John Marshall. The principal theme of the interview was Roberts's determination to persuade his colleagues to behave in a less polarized fashion, and his exemplar for this effort was Marshall. Rosen observed that "resist[ing] the politicization of the judiciary [seemed a] daunting task," but that Roberts "view[ed] it . . . as a 'special opportunity,' especially in our intensely polarized age. 'Politics are closely divided,' [Roberts] observed. 'The same with the Congress. There ought to be some sense of some stability, if the government is not going to polarize completely. It's a high priority to keep any kind of partisan divide out of the judiciary as well.' " To succeed in this task, Roberts would have to persuade each of his colleagues (and himself) "to suppress his or her ideological agenda in the interest of achieving consensus and stability" (Rosen 2007).

This is where Marshall comes in, with Roberts emphasizing the great chief justice's "willingness to disappoint his ideological supporters. . . . [E]ven if Marshall had the votes to push the Federalist agenda harder than he did, he thought it 'better to proceed in a way that . . . wasn't going to alienate people on the Court and turn the Court into another battleground.'" Roberts continued: "Marshall could easily have got on the Court and said, 'I'm the last hope of the Federalists—we're out of Congress, we're out of the White House—and I'm going to pursue that agenda here.' And he would have not only damaged the Court but could have smothered it in the cradle. But instead he said, 'No, this is my home now, this is the Court, and we're going to operate as a Court, and that's important to me,' and as a result he made the Court the institution that it has become" (Rosen 2007).

In this version of the Court's founding myth, Marshall heroically established judicial independence in the face of hostile partisan attacks. In the landmark case of *Marbury v. Madison* (1803), Marshall believed that President Thomas Jefferson and Secretary of State James Madison had acted unlawfully in refusing to deliver William Marbury's commission to serve as justice of the peace in the District of Columbia. Marshall nonetheless declined to order Madison to deliver the commission, choosing to husband the Court's power and prestige for another day. From this angle, the Jeffersonian attacks on Marshall and his colleagues look like a primordial threat to an independent judiciary, the early precursor of today's judicial removal campaigns in response to gay rights decisions. After all, President Jefferson and his congressional allies repealed the 1801 Judiciary Act, effectively firing sixteen federal judges to whom the Constitution had guaranteed life tenure. To prevent (or at least delay) the Court from invalidating this repeal, they also abolished the Court's June and December terms, establishing one annual term in February to take their place. They did so in April 1802, which meant that the Court would not meet again until February 1803. Most egregiously of all, they sought to purge the courts of judges who would not bend to their will. In 1803 and 1804, they successfully impeached and removed District Judge John Pickering. They then impeached Justice Samuel Chase, and if they had succeeded in removing him from the high Court, they were planning to target Marshall next. Luckily, Marshall and his colleagues withstood this onslaught and patiently marked out a sphere of independence for the federal courts. Marshall cleverly constructed his *Marbury* holding in a way that made it impossible for the Jeffersonian Republicans to resist or ignore it, and the failure of the Chase impeachment effectively established a congressional norm against using impeachment to remove judges because of disagreement with their rulings from the bench. In other words, Marshall's efforts created a Court that would stand outside of politics, defending long-term constitutional principle in the face of short-term partisan pressures.

With this story in mind, Roberts's performance in the ACA case parallels Marshall's in *Marbury*, in that both leaders sought to preserve the Court's power and independence by declining an opportunity to directly rebuke a president with whom they disagreed. As some observers have noted, however, Roberts's performance in the ACA case recalled another side of Marshall's efforts in *Marbury* too (Epps 2012). Like Roberts, Marshall rebuked the president's actions, even while declining to issue a holding that would require the president to change course. And like Roberts, Marshall appeared to be holding the Court's fire for other, more winnable, battles to come (Toobin 2012, 295–96).

Indeed, when we turn our attention from President Jefferson's partisan attacks on the courts to the judicial actions that prompted those attacks, the implications of the episode for modern debates about polarized judging appear in a different light. After all, the Jeffersonians were responding to the Federalists' flagrant effort to capture the judiciary, an effort that included grossly partisan conduct by federal judges themselves. Put another way, it is true that the Jeffersonians acted in ways that are inconsistent with modern notions of judicial independence, but the same is true of their Federalist opponents. The reason the Jeffersonians attacked the courts was that the Federalists were using the courts so blatantly to promote their own partisan ends.

The facts of this story are well known, but their significance is not always appreciated. As Bruce Ackerman has documented at length, lame-duck president John Adams and his Federalist allies in Congress voted in early 1801 to reduce the size of the Supreme Court from six to five. This statute would have prevented Adams from replacing Oliver Ellsworth, who had recently resigned as chief justice, but the Federalists made sure to delay its enactment until after Marshall had been confirmed for Ellsworth's seat. In other words, the Federalists simultaneously returned the Court's size to six while providing that it would drop to five on the next vacancy, thus depriving the incoming President Jefferson of an opportunity to make an appointment on the next judicial resignation or death. This same statute expanded the jurisdiction of the federal courts and created sixteen new Article III judgeships, which increased the size of the federal judiciary by more than 70 percent. In the waning days of their terms, President Adams and the Federalist Senate then rushed to fill these new judgeships, emphasizing partisan loyalty more than legal expertise in doing so (Ackerman 2005, 116–41).

Meanwhile, prominent Federalist judges had been acting in explicitly partisan ways. Marshall himself worked closely with President Adams in selecting the "midnight judges" for the sixteen new circuit court seats, even after the Senate confirmed him as chief justice on January 27, 1801. If that were not bad enough, Marshall continued to serve as Adams's secretary of state until the conclusion of the president's term on March 3. As a result, the *Marbury* case "required the new chief justice to assess the constitutional implications of his own negligence in failing, as secretary of state, to deliver the commission to" William Marbury. It is hard to argue with Ackerman's characterization of this as a "grotesque" example of "judicial impropriety" (Ackerman 2005, 136). Even more notoriously, Justice Chase had been delivering partisan speeches from the bench, both before and after the 1800 election, and had enthusiastically sentenced his political opponents to jail (under the 1798 Sedition Act) and even to death (in a notorious treason trial). It was for his conduct of these trials that the Jeffersonians impeached him, and while his acquittal in the Senate did indeed establish a norm that partisan members of Congress should not lightly impeach federal judges, the episode also established a norm that federal judges should not use their authority for partisan ends (Whittington 1999, 20–71).

With these founding developments in mind, we might reasonably ask how fully today's judges are adhering to this latter norm. After all, if judges are by and large acting as neutral umpires, then most of the sound and fury over judicial confirmations (in the US Senate) and judicial elections (in most states) is a waste of time. So long as presidents and voters are choosing judges who are honest and qualified, we need not be concerned about the partisan backgrounds of the judges themselves. But if today's judges are instead behaving like Marshall and Chase, then we should be concerned about the potential for a partisan faction to capture the courts and use their judicial powers for partisan ends. As William Blake and others have noted, the image of judging as umpiring tends to convey a falsely formalistic account of umpiring, which in fact involves a fair amount of rule creation as well as rule application (Blake 2012; see also Graber 1999). But even if one adopts a fully realistic conception of both umpiring and judging, the analogy still conveys the useful reminder that both sets of decision makers should make their calls without regard to preexisting sympathies in favor of particular teams.

In this light, it is worth considering whether and to what extent contemporary judges' answers to legal questions regarding abortion, affirmative action, gay rights, and gun rights divide along more or less the same lines as partisan politicians' answers to political questions regarding these issues. To the extent that these divides match up, the outcome of the legal questions will turn principally on which partisan side succeeds at placing more of its appointees on the bench (and blocking more of the opposing side's appointees).

In recent years, a number of scholars have turned their attention to this question of judicial partisanship, with much of that attention focusing on the federal appellate courts. This focus results in part from the fact that these courts resolve far more legal disputes than does the Supreme Court; hence, understanding the degree to which legal outcomes are shaped by partisan considerations requires looking at decision-making dynamics below the high Court level. It also results from the fact that the federal appellate courts provide an almost perfect laboratory for examining the issue because they consist of large groups of Democratic and Republican appointees who are randomly assigned to three-judge panels to hear individual cases (Miles and Sunstein 2008b, 835). Most scholars who have studied decision making by federal appellate judges have used the party of the appointing president as a proxy for judicial ideology in an effort to assess the relative weight of ideological and legal influences on judicial decision making (Epstein, Landes, and Posner 2013, 57, 180; Fischman and Law 2009). In this chapter, I examine partisanship for its own sake in an effort to assess the degree to which our courts have broken down into competing partisan teams.

In one notable study, Cass Sunstein and several co-authors assembled a dataset of more than 6,000 decisions issued by three-judge appellate panels, finding that 52 percent of the votes issued by Democratic judges were liberal, compared to 40 percent of the votes issued by Republican judges (2006, 13). This twelve-point difference seems large enough to raise suspicion that judges are not mere umpires, but Sunstein also found significant evidence that judges are sometimes willing and able to reach agreement across partisan lines. For one thing, the patterns of polarization varied significantly across circuits, with the difference between Democratic and Republican votes ranging from less than ten points on the DC Circuit to twenty-two points on the Sixth Circuit (2006, 111–12).[7]

In addition to testing for the direct effects of judicial partisanship, Sunstein and his colleagues also searched for evidence of panel effects. That is, they investigated whether a judge votes differently depending on the composition of the panel on which he or she is sitting. On the Sixth Circuit, they found minimal evidence of such effects, but on other circuits, the effect was sometimes quite large. Indeed, "in nine of the twelve circuits, a judge's vote is predicted fairly well by the political affiliation of the president who appointed the judge in question [but] it is predicted at least as well by the political affiliation of the president who appointed the two other panel members" (2006, 111). These panel effects appear to indicate that judges are open to persuasion by their colleagues, that norms of collegiality lead them to suppress their own dissenting views, or that the presence of a potential "whistle-blowing" dissenter leads panel majorities to moderate their views (2006, 20–21).[8] Consider the fact that 62 percent of the decisions in Sunstein's dataset that were issued by panels of three Democratic judges (DDD) were liberal, while only 52 percent of the decisions issued by DDR panels were liberal. The Democratic judges have the same degree of control over the outcome in each of these categories, but the presence of a single Republican judge leads to significantly fewer liberal holdings. Likewise, only 36 percent of decisions issued by RRR panels were liberal, but that figure rose to 41 percent for DRR panels (Sunstein et al. 2006, 11–12). As a result, if you compare decisions issued by DDD and RRR panels, judicial polarization looks quite extreme, with a difference of twenty-six points in the frequency of liberal decisions, but for DDR versus DRR panels, the difference is only 11 points.

In another notable recent study, Lee Epstein, William Landes, and Richard Posner have emphasized that ideological considerations play a significantly smaller role on the federal appellate courts than on SCOTUS because of the greater force of legal commitments on the former courts than the latter (2013, 168, 182–83). For example, they find substantial evidence that federal appellate judges appointed by both Democratic and Republican presidents are more likely to issue a conservative decision when they are reviewing a conservative district court holding and more likely to issue a liberal decision when reviewing a liberal district court holding (2013, 191–96; see also Cross 2007, 39–68). In other words, the ideological influences on their decision making are dampened by the legal norm of deference to trial court holdings. A number of scholars have likewise found substantial evidence that both Democratic and Republican appointees usually seek to faithfully implement clear holdings issued by the Supreme Court (Cross 2007, 8; Hall 2011, 16; Johnson 1987; Sunstein et al. 2006, 88).

Despite the evidence of panel effects, deference to trial court decisions, and adherence to Supreme Court precedent, the Sunstein and Epstein/ Landes/Posner studies make clear that there is indeed significant partisan divergence in judicial voting on federal appellate courts, a finding that has been confirmed by a number of additional studies (Cox and Miles 2008; Fischman 2011, forthcoming; Miles and Sunstein 2008a; Revesz 1997; Sunstein and Miles 2009).

In a helpful examination of the nomination and confirmation process for federal appellate judges, Nancy Scherer (2005) traces this judicial polarization to a variety of institutional changes in American politics during the latter half of the twentieth century. In particular, the rise of single-issue interest groups and the increasing polarization of the national political parties shifted the process of federal judicial appointments from a system of partisan patronage to one more focused on ideological and policy goals. This shift was accelerated by the post-1960s willingness of federal judges to tackle a greater range of politically salient issues, which increased the perceived stakes involved in judicial selection.

Scherer argues that no significant partisan polarization occurred on the federal courts until the late 1960s, when appointees of Presidents Lyndon Johnson and Richard Nixon diverged on civil rights. This trend accelerated in subsequent decades, as appointees of Jimmy Carter, Ronald Reagan, George H. W. Bush (GHWB), and Bill Clinton polarized further than their predecessors in civil rights cases and diverged to an even greater extent in abortion cases. On the latter issue, Scherer found that Carter and Clinton appointees were 44 percentage points more likely to issue pro-abortion rights votes than were Nixon, Reagan, and GHWB appointees (2005, 37–42). By contrast, Sunstein and his colleagues examined twenty-three separate legal issues and found abortion to be right in the middle of the pack in terms of polarized voting, with a partisan divide of just sixteen points.[9] The two most polarized issues in their dataset were gay rights and affirmative action, with partisan divides of forty and twenty-eight points, respectively.[10] They did not examine gun rights, but they found that polarized voting appeared quite common in death penalty and Eleventh Amendment cases and in some labor and civil rights disputes as well. In some of these areas (including abortion), they found that patterns of partisan voting by individual judges were not dampened at all by panel effects. In other areas (including affirmative action), they found strong evidence that judicial partisanship was influential, but equally strong evidence for the influence of panel effects. And in still other areas (including criminal appeals), they found virtually no evidence of ideological voting at all, indicating either the constraining force of law or the lack of ideo-logical disagreement between Republican and Democratic judges (2006, 20–21; see also Miles and Sunstein 2008b).

On any issue that is widely litigated over an extended period, appel-late judges are likely to be divided. If they were not divided on the issue, the courts would quickly dispose of it, if it were ever litigated in the first place. But while judges are always likely to be divided, the lines of this division need not track the lines of division among partisan policy mak-ers in other institutions. To the extent that judges do divide along the same lines as other policymakers, then the governing party is more likely to capture the courts and the opposition party more likely to complain that the courts have abandoned their commitment to law. Indeed, it was precisely this concern that shaped the founding American commitment to judicial independence. Under the British Crown, Jefferson famously complained that King George III had "made Judges dependent on his Will alone, for the tenure of their offices, and the amount and payment of their salaries."[11] As such, the framers of the US Constitution provided that federal judges would be appointed for life, with guaranteed salaries. When prominent Anti-Federalists objected that these life-tenured judges would be unaccountable tyrants, Alexander Hamilton replied (in the Federalist #78) that "liberty can have nothing to fear from the judiciary alone, but would have every thing to fear from its union with either of the other departments."

Judges as Partisans

With this concern in mind, I turn now to a consideration of the judicial response to the litigation regarding abortion, affirmative action, gay rights, and gun rights that I surveyed in part I of the book. In the aggregate, I cited 332 federal appellate decisions in chapters I and 2, in which indi-vidual judges cast 1,462 separate votes.[12] Of the votes cast by Democratic judges in these decisions, 84.4 percent were in a liberal direction, com-pared with just 51.5 percent of the votes cast by Republican judges. This difference of 32.9 points seems large enough to suggest significant polar-ization, and while the federal appellate courts are sometimes reversed on appeal, the Supreme Court does not seem to be playing a corrective role, at least on the sort of culture war issues that I examine here. For the forty-six SCOTUS decisions cited in part I, the difference between the portion

TABLE 3.1 **Voting by party on federal appellate courts**

	Ideological direction of votes	
Party of appointing president	Conservative	Liberal
Rep (839 votes)	48.5%	51.5%
Dem (623)	15.6%	84.4%

TABLE 3.2 **Judicial polarization over time**

Time period	Percentage-point difference between Dem and Rep support for liberal position in federal appellate voting
1993–1996 (81 decisions; 308 judicial votes)	27.1
1997–2000 (69; 324)	41.6
2001–2004 (55; 227)	26.9
2005–2008 (40; 200)	45.3
2009–2013 (87; 403)	28.0

of Democratic and Republican votes that were cast in a liberal direction was 36.6 points. If the justices are coded in more conventional ideological terms rather than by party of the appointing president, the SCOTUS figure balloons to 54.0 points.[13]

On the appellate courts, the most striking feature of this polarization is that it is asymmetrical. As table 3.1 makes clear, the votes of Republican judges are almost evenly split between liberal and conservative outcomes, but Democratic judges consistently support liberal results. I return to this point below, but first, consider several other dimensions of the data. For one thing, our assessment of judicial polarization might turn in part on whether it is a long-standing, stable feature of the federal courts or a recently emerging (and perhaps accelerating) institutional defect. Scherer argues that judicial polarization emerged in the late 1960s and has increased since then, but Sunstein's data indicate that the level of polarization held steady from the mid-1980s through the early 2000s, in part because both Democratic and Republican appointees trended more conservative during this time (Scherer 2005; Sunstein et al. 2006, 120). On the culture war issues that I have examined, the partisan divide appears relatively stable. As table 3.2 indicates, polarization on the federal appellate courts has neither consistently increased nor decreased since the beginning of the Clinton era.

Another question worth considering is whether judicial polarization varies across the three categories of legal conflicts that I examined in part 1.

TABLE 3.3 **Judicial polarization across categories of legal disputes**

Type of legal challenge	Percentage-point difference between Dem and Rep support for liberal position
Category 1 cases: Using courts to enjoin newly enacted policies (153 federal appellate decisions; 699 judicial votes)	39.1
Category 2 cases: Using courts to dismantle existing policies (145; 625)	32.3
Category 3 cases: Using courts to support democratic politics (38; 150)	6.1

Note: Four decisions are included in more than one category.

As table 3.3 indicates, federal judges generally unite across party lines when asked to clear the channels of political change, but when asked to enjoin a newly enacted policy or to dismantle an existing one, Democratic and Republican judges regularly part ways. The difference between Democratic and Republican votes in category 3 cases is only 6.1 points; the corresponding figures for categories 1 and 2 are 39.1 and 32.3 points, respectively. In other words, judges appear to act more like partisans when the constitutional issue before them focuses directly on a key culture war concern and less like partisans when called on to police the process by which such culture war concerns will be addressed, even if those latter decisions might have a substantial impact on ultimate outcomes.

Aside from the category 3 cases, these aggregate data seem to reveal significant partisan divides in the federal judiciary. To get a sense of what these divides mean in practice, consider several of the legal conflicts that I reviewed in part 1. When I surveyed these conflicts in chapters 1 and 2, I refrained from noting the partisan backgrounds of the judges involved, but in a number of cases, that information seems clearly relevant. Recall, for example, the affirmative action disputes involving the University of Michigan (UM). In late 2000 and early 2001, Federal District Judge Patrick Duggan upheld UM's undergraduate admissions policy, while his colleague Bernard Friedman struck down UM's law school admissions policy.[14] The odd thing about these twin results was that the law school policy was, by all accounts, more constitutionally legitimate than the undergraduate policy, not less so. After all, the undergraduate college automatically awarded 20 points (on a 150-point scale) to all African American, Hispanic, and American Indian applicants, while the law school conducted a holistic review of every applicant, considering race as one factor among many in seeking to assemble a diverse student body. Duggan and Friedman had both been appointed by President Reagan, but when their holdings were appealed, the Sixth Circuit's eleven active judges were widely expected to divide on partisan lines. When the appeals were filed, the circuit had a 6–5 Democratic majority, but by the time the arguments took place in December 2001, two of the circuit's Republican appointees had taken senior status, giving Democrats a 6–3 edge among the remaining active judges. The following April, with the Michigan decisions still pending, Senator Edward Kennedy received a staff memo recommending that the Judiciary Committee hold off on confirming any of President Bush's pending Sixth Circuit nominees until the decisions came down. The recommendation reportedly originated with Elaine Jones of the NAACP Legal Defense Fund (Stohr 2005, 313–14).

The predictions of a closely divided circuit proved accurate in May 2002, when the judges voted 5–4 to uphold the law school admissions policy in *Grutter v. Bollinger* (while issuing no decision on the undergraduate policy). The majority consisted of five Democratic appointees; the dissenting coalition consisted of three Republican appointees and one Democrat. Writing for the majority, Chief Judge Boyce Martin (a Carter appointee) held that Justice Powell's educational diversity analysis from *University of California v. Bakke* (1978) remained legally binding and hence that the law school's flexible consideration of race in pursuit of this goal remained permissible. In dissent, Circuit Judge Danny Boggs (a Reagan appointee) replied that "[t]his case involves a straightforward instance of racial discrimination by a state institution." Emphasizing the university's concession that Barbara Grutter would have been admitted if she were black, Boggs insisted that "the framers of the Fourteenth Amendment decided that our government should abstain from social engineering through explicit racial classifications."[15]

In addition to advancing this familiar substantive argument, Judge Boggs attached a "procedural appendix" in which he accused Chief Judge Martin of manipulating the circuit's scheduling procedures to affect the outcome of the case. One of his allegations was that Martin had concealed CIR's petition for initial hearing en banc from his colleagues for six months, during which time Circuit Judges Alan Norris and Richard Suhrheinrich (both appointees of George H. W. Bush) had taken senior status, thus rendering them ineligible to serve on the en banc panel (and creating the two vacancies that Senator Kennedy tried to prevent President Bush from filling). In separate concurring opinions, Circuit

Judges Karen Nelson Moore and Eric L. Clay (both Clinton appointees) sought to explain this purported irregularity and responded to Boggs's other specific charges as well. They also objected to Boggs's unusual public airing of such internal court procedures. In Judge Moore's words, "Judge Boggs's opinion marks a new low point in the history of the Sixth Circuit. It will irreparably damage the already strained working relationships among the judges of this court, and . . . [will] serve to undermine public confidence in our ability to perform our important role in American democracy."[16] Despite the explanations offered by Moore and Clay, Boggs's unusual dissent sparked an even more unusual congressional investigation of the circuit's panel assignment practices. Within six weeks of the Sixth Circuit decision, US representative F. James Sensenbrenner, Republican chair of the House Judiciary Committee (HJC), had written to Chief Judge Martin requesting documents related to his handling of the case. By the time the investigation concluded, the HJC had "subpoenaed masses of records and conducted multiple interviews under threat of subpoena with judges and court staff" (Peterson 2005, 18). Meanwhile, in January 2003, a conservative watchdog organization filed a formal complaint with the circuit raising the same concerns. The complaint went first to Chief Judge Martin, who recused himself, and then to Judge Boggs, the senior associate judge, who did likewise. It was assigned next to Judge Alice Batchelder, a George H. W. Bush appointee and the one judge who had joined Boggs's procedural appendix. Batchelder chose not to recuse herself, and in May 2003, with the *Gratz* and *Grutter* cases then pending at the Supreme Court, she issued a report accusing Martin of misconduct.[17] Batchelder's report prompted a reply from Senior Circuit Judge Damon J. Keith (a Carter appointee), joined by four colleagues (all fellow Democrats), calling the allegations "totally unjustified and unwarranted" (Lane 2003).

In sum, in the most high-profile case heard by the circuit in at least a generation, the court found itself narrowly divided, largely on partisan lines, with the judges on each side adopting positions closely associated with important members of their partisan coalition and with significant allegations that standard procedures were manipulated to influence the result. To make matters worse, this was not the first procedural dispute that had marred the federal courts' handling of the Michigan cases (Stohr 2005, 95–100). Nor was it the first time that the Sixth Circuit's judges had broken into open conflict with one another, hurling not just legal arguments but allegations of procedural impropriety. Indeed, as the *Washington Post* reported at the time, "open feuding between Republican and Democratic appointees had become standard procedure at the 6th Circuit" (Lane 2003).

Recall also the circuit's 1999 decision regarding Tennessee's statutory requirement that minors receive parental consent before having an abortion. After a divided panel upheld the law, over a sharp dissent from Judge Keith, the circuit's judges split down the middle on whether to rehear the case en banc, with the seven Democratic appointees voting in favor and the seven Republicans against. When the court denied rehearing by virtue of this equally divided vote, Judge Keith dissented. In doing so, he identified by name the seven judges who had voted on each side and complained that as a senior circuit judge—that is, having gone into semiretirement—he was not allowed to participate in the vote. In response, Boggs and Batchelder wrote separately to chastise Judge Keith for commenting on internal court procedures. Boggs complained that Keith had "breach[ed] the long-standing custom of this court that actions by a member of the court with respect to petitions for rehearing of en banc are matters of internal court procedure and are not made public by other judges." Batchelder added that Keith's "own purposes may be furthered by publicly impugning the integrity of his colleagues," but "[c]ollegiality, cooperation and the court's decision-making process clearly are not." Leveling the same accusation against Keith that Moore would level against Boggs three years later in *Grutter*, Batchelder accused her colleague of undermining "public confidence in the judicial system and in this court."[18]

In between the abortion and affirmative action cases, several similar conflicts fractured the circuit. Perhaps most notable was a 2001 death penalty holding in which Judge Boggs objected that his colleagues were engaged in "lawless action" and that henceforward, death-sentenced prisoners "could file a hot dog menu, and the en banc court might use that as a legal basis to stay their execution."[19] When Senior Circuit Judge Nathaniel Jones (a Carter appointee) responded by explaining the en banc procedures that had been followed—including the extraordinary efforts made by Chief Judge Martin to poll the circuit's active judges while he was in Washington, DC, on the day of the 9/11 attacks—Boggs amended his dissent to characterize these procedures as "virtually criminal" and to note that "[t]his type of secret undocumented decision-making by exclusive in-groups is the way decisions are made in totalitarian countries, not usually in the United States." Most inflammatory of all, he denounced Jones's account as "simply a lie."[20] Jones was one of the circuit's four African American judges; the other three—Keith, Clay, and R. Guy Cole Jr. (a

Clinton appointee)—responded with a letter criticizing Boggs's treatment of their colleague as "patronizing and condescending" (Lane 2001). These events took place less than three months before the circuit heard oral arguments in *Gratz* and *Grutter*, and similar conflicts have continued to divide the Sixth Circuit's judges since the *Grutter* episode.[21]

When the dispute over affirmative action in Michigan returned to the circuit in another legal context, the partisan divide surfaced yet again. In July 2011, a divided panel invalidated Proposal 2, the statewide ban on affirmative action that had been enacted by voters in 2006. The decision was issued by two Clinton appointees, with a George W. Bush (GWB) appointee in dissent.[22] On rehearing, the full circuit affirmed the panel holding by a vote of 8–7.[23] The eight-judge majority consisted of seven Democrats and one Republican. (The latter was a judge who had initially been nominated by Clinton and later renominated by GWB as part of a partisan deal to move some of his nominees through the Senate, so it may be more accurate to characterize the eight-judge majority as wholly Democratic.) The seven-judge dissenting bloc consisted entirely of Republican appointees. These dissenting judges confined their critique to legal arguments, but they did not mince words, with three GWB appointees denouncing the en banc panel's holding as flatly inconsistent with law and logic.[24]

The open acrimony on the Sixth Circuit may be unusual, but on all four issues that I survey in part 1, federal judges across the country have sometimes divided along partisan lines. On the abortion issue, I have already noted the Sixth Circuit's polarized handling of Tennessee's parental consent statute in the late 1990s. When Virginia enacted a parental notice requirement around the same time, the issue divided the Fourth Circuit on similar lines. Representing Planned Parenthood, Simon Heller of the Center for Reproductive Law and Policy persuaded a federal district judge to enjoin the 1997 Virginia law before it took effect, but Circuit Judge J. Michael Luttig (a GHWB appointee) quickly stayed that injunction.[25] Planned Parenthood appealed Luttig's holding to the full circuit, and in October 1997, the circuit voted 7–5 to leave Luttig's stay in place, with seven Nixon, Reagan, or Bush appointees in the majority and four Democrats and a Ford appointee in dissent.[26] By the time the circuit issued its ruling on the merits in August 1998, the Ford appointee had retired and one of the other Republican appointees had died, leaving the circuit's ten remaining judges fully polarized on partisan lines. Luttig wrote for the six Republicans in holding that the statute was constitutional under any reasonable interpretation of its provisions. Clinton appointee M.

Blane Michael agreed that Planned Parenthood's facial challenge must fail for the moment, but wrote separately for the four Democrats to indicate that, once construed by Virginia's courts, the statute may well prove unconstitutional.[27]

Likewise, when state legislatures began outlawing "partial-birth abortion" in the mid-1990s, abortion providers immediately challenged these laws, and these challenges quickly polarized the federal courts. In 1997, 1998, and 1999, Republican-appointed appellate judges voted 8–4 to uphold state bans on partial-birth abortion, while their Democratic colleagues voted 0–6.[28]

In the affirmative action context, nothing rivals the Sixth Circuit's deep divide in the various Michigan cases, but the issue has polarized judges on other circuits as well. Recall, for example, the long-running conflict between the Clinton administration and the DC Circuit regarding the legitimacy of the FCC's equal employment regulations. When affirmative action opponents argued that these regulations represented an unconstitutional effort to force broadcasters to adopt race-conscious affirmative action measures, a DC Circuit panel consisting of Reagan appointees Laurence Silberman, David Sentelle, and Stephen Williams unanimously agreed.[29] When the Clinton administration petitioned for en banc rehearing, the full circuit split on partisan lines, with its six Republican appointees voting to deny the petition over four Democratic dissents.[30] When the FCC revised its regulations in an effort to meet the judges' objections, another all-GOP panel invalidated the new rules on the same grounds.[31]

The Clinton administration ran into trouble with Republican appointees on the Third Circuit as well. In *Taxman v. Piscataway Board of Education* (3d Cir. 1996), the administration argued that " 'faculty diversity' is an appropriate justification for affirmative action under Title VII" and that the local school board had lawfully pursued such a goal when it chose to lay off a white teacher rather than a black colleague with equal seniority. The Third Circuit rejected this argument, with eight Reagan-Bush appointees (including Samuel Alito) holding that affirmative action policies in the employment context were prohibited by Title VII unless they had a remedial purpose.[32] Two Republican appointees joined two Democrats in dissent.

More recently, when the University of Texas reinstated race-conscious admissions after the Supreme Court's holding in *Grutter* came down, a Fifth Circuit panel consisting of Carter, Reagan, and GHWB appointees unanimously upheld the new policy, but the Bush appointee (Circuit Judge Emilio M. Garza) wrote separately to issue an explicit call for SCOTUS to reverse *Grutter*, which he characterized as "a digression in the course of constitutional law," a "misstep," an "erroneous path," and a "detour from constitutional first principles."[33] When the plaintiffs petitioned for rehearing, the Circuit's GOP appointees voted 7–4 in favor of the petition, but all five Democratic appointees went the other way, producing a 9–7 vote against rehearing.[34] As I note in chapter 2, SCOTUS then vacated the panel holding and remanded with instructions that seem likely to produce a ruling against UT.[35]

Examples of polarized judicial voting abound in the gay rights context too. In one of the most closely watched disputes over gays in the military during the early Clinton years, a unanimous DC Circuit panel ruled in favor of Joseph Steffan, who had been dismissed from the US Naval Academy shortly before graduating.[36] The panel consisted of Chief Judge Abner Mikva and Circuit Judges Harry Edwards and Patricia Wald, but these three Carter appointees were subsequently outvoted by their seven Republican colleagues, who reversed the panel decision in November 1994.[37] Twenty years later, in a legal climate that was in many ways more hospitable to gay rights, with the Supreme Court having issued its landmark decisions in *Romer v. Evans* (1996) and *Lawrence v. Texas* (2003), federal appellate judges remained divided on the issue, though signs of some cross-party voting were emerging. Consider *Lofton v. Secretary of the Department of Children and Family Services* (11th Cir. 2004), in which gay rights advocates argued that Florida's explicit ban on adoptions by homosexuals was unconstitutional under *Lawrence*. Reading the high Court precedent narrowly, a unanimous Eleventh Circuit panel rejected this challenge in January 2004, and the full circuit then divided 6–6 on a request for en banc rehearing.[38] Three judges voted across partisan lines here—one Democrat and two Republicans—but the other nine judges voted according to type. Particularly galling to gay rights advocates was that one of the six votes against rehearing was cast by Circuit Judge William Pryor, who was then serving on a recess appointment from GWB. Without life tenure, there was no way to know whether Pryor's vote reflected his sincere reading of the law or his desire to curry favor with the administration.

The gun rights issue has likewise witnessed some examples in which appellate judges were fully or at least largely polarized on partisan lines. When the Third Circuit rejected a commerce clause challenge to the 1986 federal ban on possession of machine guns, the decision was issued by two Democratic appointees over a dissent from Samuel Alito.[39] When a Ninth Circuit panel ruled in favor of the victims of a 1999 shooting at a

Jewish Community Center in Granada Hills, California, who had sued the manufacturers of the guns that had been used in the incident, the decision was issued by two Clinton appointees, with Reagan appointee Cynthia Holcomb Hall in dissent.[40] When the defendants petitioned for en banc rehearing, the circuit's ten active Republican judges voted 7–3 in favor of the request, but their seventeen Democratic colleagues voted 2–15.[41] When the case that would become *District of Columbia v. Heller* (2008) first reached the DC Circuit, Reagan appointee Laurence Silberman and GWB appointee Thomas Griffith held that the Second Amendment protected an individual right to bear arms and that this right was unduly infringed by the District of Columbia's near-total ban on handgun possession.[42] Their Republican colleague Karen LeCraft Henderson refused to join this holding, arguing in dissent that the text of the Second Amendment— with its explicit declaration that the right to bear arms is "necessary to the security of a free State"—does not apply to the District of Columbia at all. When the district's lawyers petitioned for en banc rehearing, six Republican appointees voted to deny the petition, with three Democrats and one Republican in dissent.[43] When the Seventh Circuit held that the right to bear arms for purposes of self-defense extends outside the home, the decision was issued by two Republican judges with a Democratic colleague in dissent; when the state of Illinois petitioned for rehearing, six Republican judges voted to deny the petition, over a dissenting opinion from one fellow Republican and three Democrats.[44]

If this sort of partisan divide is widespread across the federal judiciary, it hardly seems accurate to describe judges as neutral umpires. Imagine a baseball season in which the umpires were divided into competing camps, based on their preexisting loyalties to their hometown teams, with members of different camps regularly adopting markedly different interpretations of the rules. Of course, the examples above may not be representative. As Chief Justice Roberts has suggested, it may be that occasional instances of judicial polarization draw outsized attention, while everyone ignores the more common examples of judicial bipartisanship (Rosen 2007).

Judges as Umpires

As I note above, federal judges tend, in the aggregate, to divide on partisan lines. But in evaluating the significance of the partisan gaps presented in tables 3.1, 3.2, and 3.3, it is not altogether clear what our baseline should be. If we expect judges to be nonpartisan umpires, then any non-zero difference between the aggregate votes of Democratic and Republican judges would seem to indicate a troubling pattern of polarization. But if we expect judges to be partisan zealots, then any difference below 100 percent would seem to indicate some measure of neutral umpiring (Miles and Sunstein 2008b, 843–44).

One possibility is to compare judicial voting patterns to those of ordinary voters. In the states that allow lawmaking via ballot initiatives and referenda, voters are regularly asked to weigh in on the same culture war issues that judges confront. Where exit polls are conducted, we have data on support for these ballot measures by voters of different parties. Consider the widely noted anti-SSM initiatives that appeared on state ballots in the wake of *Baker v. Vermont* (Vt. 1999) and *Goodridge v. Department of Public Health* (Mass. 2003). I have found state-level exit poll data for twenty of these initiatives, and the average difference between support from Republicans and support from Democrats was 35.7 percentage points.[45] I have also found exit polls for three other state-wide ballot measures related to LGBT rights, for three anti–affirmative action initiatives, and for five abortion-related ballot measures.[46] Taken together, the mean partisan gap in support for the thirty-one state-level ballot measures noted here was 36.2 points, just slightly higher than the corresponding gap of 35.6 points for all category 1 and 2 decisions issued by federal appellate courts (or 32.9 points, if category 3 decisions are included). In short, voters and judges are more or less equally polarized on partisan lines, despite the fact that the voters are being asked to express a policy preference and the judges are ostensibly being asked to apply existing legal rules. If I exclude the gun rights decisions issued by federal appellate courts (because I have not found exit polls for any ballot measures on the issue of gun rights), then the judges appear *more* polarized than the voters, with a partisan gap of 43.4 percentage points.

But perhaps a better baseline would be to compare judges with elected legislators who are making policy on the same issues. After all, the US House and Senate consider legislation dealing with abortion, affirmative action, gay rights, and gun rights almost as regularly as the federal appellate courts consider lawsuits dealing with such issues. I identified 231 significant pieces of such legislation that came to recorded votes from 1993 through 2012, and coded these votes by party.[47] The results are presented in table 3.4, and from this angle, judicial polarization does not look so bad. If judges were simply behaving as legislators, their votes would diverge

TABLE 3.4 **Polarization across institutions**

Institution	Percentage-point difference between Dem and Rep support for liberal position
US House (134 roll call votes; 56,296 individual votes)	65.2
US Senate (97 roll call votes; 9,423 individual votes)	63.7
SCOTUS (46 decisions; 411 individual votes)	36.6
Federal appellate courts (332 decisions; 1,462 individual votes)	32.9

TABLE 3.5 **Judicial and congressional polarization by issue**

Issue	Percentage-point difference between Dem and Rep support for liberal position . . .	
	On federal appellate courts	In Congress
Affirmative action (288 judicial votes; 1,951 congressional votes)	54.9	77.7
Abortion (417; 37,765)	39.2	69.2
Gay rights (290; 9,160)	39.0	64.5
Gun rights (467; 16,843)	12.7	54.6
Total (1,462; 65,719)	32.9	64.9

along partisan lines far more sharply than they actually do. This holds true across all four issues that I have examined, as indicated by table 3.5.

This juxtaposition with Congress helps make sense of the asymmetrical character of the judicial polarization that I noted earlier. On the federal appellate courts, the votes of Republican judges (on the four issues I have studied) are almost evenly split between liberal and conservative outcomes, while Democratic judges consistently support liberal results. On the Democratic side, this pattern holds true across all four issues. As table 3.6 indicates, Democratic judges vote in ways that are strikingly similar to Democratic legislators; indeed, on three of the four issues, the judges support liberal results more consistently than the legislators do. By contrast, Republican judges vote like Republican legislators only on the affirmative action issue. In gay rights and abortion cases, as table 3.7 makes clear, Republican judges support conservative results more than half the time, but still far less consistently than their partisan allies in Congress. On gun rights, the behavior of Republican judges does not resemble conservative legislating at all.

These patterns are likely due to the constraining force of legal doctrine or, to put the same point a different way, to the institutionally motivated behavior of federal judges (Keck 2007b). Indeed, the cases detailed in

TABLE 3.6 **Democratic support for liberal position, on the courts and in Congress**

	Support for liberal position by Democratic . . .	
Issue	Appointees on federal appellate courts	Members of Congress
Gun rights (186 Dem votes on appellate courts; 8,282 Dem votes in Congress)	88.2%	73.9%
Abortion (169; 18,323)	87.6%	80.2%
Gay rights (143; 4,750)	81.8%	73.0%
Affirmative action (125; 921)	77.6%	92.6%
Total (623; 32,276)	84.4%	77.9%

TABLE 3.7 **Republican support for conservative position, on the courts and in Congress**

	Support for conservative position by Republican . . .	
Issue	Appointees on federal appellate courts	Members of Congress
Affirmative action (163 Rep votes on appellate courts; 1,030 Rep votes in Congress)	77.3%	85.1%
Gay rights (147; 4,410)	57.1%	91.5%
Abortion (248; 19,442)	51.6%	89.0%
Gun rights (281; 8,561)	24.6%	80.7%
Total (839; 33,443)	48.5%	87.1%

part 1 of the book include a number of examples in which judges seem to have approached divisive culture war issues differently than have members of Congress. In particular, judges regularly join across party lines in responding to clear legal signals from SCOTUS, in rejecting extreme legal claims, and in forging doctrinal compromises.

Given the low probability that any particular federal appellate holding will be reversed by the Supreme Court, judicial politics scholars have long explored the possibility that lower court judges might ignore or defy high Court precedent. As I note above, however, most such studies have found that appellate judges generally adhere to such precedent pretty faithfully (Cross 2007, 8; Hall 2011, 16; Johnson 1987; Sunstein et al. 2006, 88). In chapters 1 and 2, I review several sets of decisions that illustrate this claim. In the abortion context, for example, the high Court's reaffirmation of *Roe v. Wade* in 1992 prompted at least some Republican judges to reject sweeping legislative bans that they otherwise might have upheld.[48] Twenty years later, when a number of state legislatures sought to ban all abortions

after twenty weeks' gestation—that is, several weeks prior to the constitutional line of fetal viability that SCOTUS had long drawn—the first
such law to face the federal appellate courts was enjoined by a panel consisting of two Republican appointees and one Democrat and then invalidated by an altogether different panel consisting of two Democrats and
one Republican.[49] Both holdings were unanimous. Likewise, when South
Dakota enacted a parental notification law without the judicial bypass
option required by Supreme Court precedent, an Eighth Circuit panel
that included two Reagan appointees unanimously struck it down.[50]

This sort of pattern is clearest in the context of partial-birth abortion.
As I note above, the first wave of challenges to such laws quickly polarized
the federal courts, but once SCOTUS entered the fray—striking down
Nebraska's partial-birth ban in June 2000—Democratic and Republican
judges alike followed the high Court's lead. Less than a month after the
Court's decision in *Stenberg v. Carhart* (*Carhart I*) (2000), the Third
Circuit invalidated New Jersey's 1997 partial-birth law, with Circuit Judge
Alito concurring separately to note that this statute was virtually identical
to the Nebraska law and hence that it could not stand under *Carhart I*.[51]
Two days later, Fourth Circuit Judge Luttig (like Alito, a GHWB appointee) reached the same conclusion regarding Virginia's law. Luttig noted
that prior to *Carhart I*, he had judged the Virginia statute to be consistent
with *Casey*, but that in *Carhart I*'s wake, he had no choice but to strike it
down.[52] Three days after Luttig issued his opinion, a Sixth Circuit panel
reached the same judgment with respect to Kentucky's partial-birth ban,
and a couple weeks after that, a Fifth Circuit panel did the same with
Louisiana's law.[53] In early 2001, a First Circuit panel struck down Rhode
Island's law, as did an en banc Seventh Circuit panel for the Illinois and
Wisconsin laws.[54] A few years later, an Eighth Circuit panel struck down
Missouri's partial-birth abortion ban as well.[55] All of these decisions were
unanimous.

When President George W. Bush signed a federal ban in 2003 that was
very similar to these unconstitutional state laws, the courts responded
in similar fashion. In three separate constitutional challenges filed by
abortion rights advocates, federal appellate panels held that the federal
act imposed an undue burden under *Casey* and *Carhart I*. On the Ninth
Circuit, the holding came from a unanimous panel of three Democratic
judges.[56] An Eighth Circuit panel was also unanimous, and this one consisted of two Reagan-GHWB appointees and one Democrat.[57] On the
Second Circuit, Clinton appointee Chester J. Straub would have upheld

the federal ban, but he was outvoted by one fellow Democrat and one Republican, with the Republican appointee (John M. Walker Jr.) noting his duty to follow *Carhart I* no matter how "personally distasteful" he found the result.[58] Federal district judges had invalidated the statute in all three cases as well, so all told, eleven of the first twelve federal judges to rule on the federal ban voted to strike it down. At the appellate level, Republican appointees supported this result by a vote of 3–0, while their Democratic colleagues did so by a vote of 5–1.

Of course, this sort of lower court responsiveness to shifts in Supreme Court doctrine is not inevitable. When Alito replaced Sandra Day O'Connor and the high Court reversed course on the partial-birth issue, some federal judges followed the new signals, but this time, bipartisan consensus did not return. Consider the long-running legal and political conflict over Virginia's partial-birth law. After the Fourth Circuit invalidated the state's first statutory ban under *Carhart I*—in the July 2000 Luttig opinion noted above—the legislature enacted a revised statute closely modeled on the 2003 federal law. In June 2005, a divided Fourth Circuit panel struck down this revised law, with two Clinton appointees in the majority and a GHWB appointee in dissent.[59] The full circuit denied a request for rehearing later that year, but SCOTUS vacated the decision after *Gonzales v. Carhart* (*Carhart II*) (2007) came down.[60] On remand, the original Fourth Circuit panel struck down the law again, by the same polarized vote, but in June 2009, an en banc panel reversed, with six Republican appointees outvoting the circuit's five Democrats.[61]

The Virginia litigation makes clear that judicial polarization is sometimes robust enough to withstand relevant shifts in the law, particularly when the legal signals are less than fully clear. After all, when SCOTUS upheld the federal partial-birth ban in *Carhart II*, it did so while purporting to leave *Carhart I* on the books. Since the two decisions are in significant tension with one another, it is no surprise that some federal judges adhered to *Carhart II* less strictly than others. The earlier examples from Alito, Luttig, and Walker indicate that judges are sometimes willing to set aside their own commitments when their legal duty is clear, but when that duty is clouded by conflicting precedents and hair-splitting opinions from SCOTUS, judges may feel more freedom to pursue ideologically driven changes in the law.

In the gun rights context, the legal status quo at the beginning of the Clinton era included virtually no precedents of any kind that seemed to authorize the judicial invalidation of gun control policies. This quickly started to change, but in each of the landmark SCOTUS decisions striking down such policies, the justices provided a clear indication of the limited reach of the doctrinal revisions that they were contemplating. In *United States v. Lopez* (1995), the Court held that the Gun-Free School Zones Act (GFSZA) exceeded the scope of congressional authority under the commerce clause but, in doing so, contrasted this statute with the federal ban on gun possession by convicted felons, noting that the latter, but not the former, applied only to firearms that had traveled in (or otherwise affected) interstate commerce.[62] When Congress responded by amending the GFSZA to add such a jurisdictional element, a bipartisan Eighth Circuit panel unanimously upheld the revised law, and SCOTUS declined to hear the case.[63] And when criminal defense lawyers raised repeated commerce clause challenges to the felon-in-possession law, the federal appellate courts repeatedly and unanimously rejected such challenges. In the twenty-eight such cases cited in chapter 2, GOP appointees cast fifty-four votes to uphold the law, and Democratic appointees cast thirty to do likewise. There were no dissents.[64]

Likewise in *District of Columbia v. Heller*, the Court held that Washington, DC's handgun ban violated the right to bear arms, but Justice Scalia's opinion for the Court noted that the holding should not "be taken to cast doubt on longstanding prohibitions on the possession of firearms by felons and the mentally ill, or laws forbidding the carrying of firearms in sensitive places such as schools and government buildings, or laws imposing conditions and qualifications on the commercial sale of arms."[65] In ten post-*Heller* decisions addressing the compatibility of the felon-in-possession ban with the newly invigorated Second Amendment, twenty-one GOP judges and nine Democrats ruled unanimously that the ban remained constitutional. In one of these holdings, Tenth Circuit Judge Timothy M. Tymkovich (a GWB appointee) wrote separately to complain about this result—wondering aloud "whether Second Amendment law would have been better served if the regulations *Heller* addressed in dicta had been left to later cases"—but he nonetheless joined his colleagues in following the clear legal signals that SCOTUS had sent.[66] In the thirty-seven other post-*Heller* Second Amendment holdings cited in chapter 2, GOP appointees were somewhat more willing to enforce the high Court holding beyond its immediate legal context, but this willingness remained the exception rather than the rule, with Republican judges casting twenty-four votes in favor of a Second Amendment claim in these cases, but sixty-eight votes against. The corresponding tally for Democratic judges was

5–49. These tallies include multiple holdings addressing the same statutes, with the criminal defense context creating a more or less permanent
incentive for litigating constitutional claims, even when their prospects of
success are limited. These repeated long-shot claims by ordinary criminal
defense attorneys have produced the relatively nonpolarized pattern in
the aggregate data on gun rights, though as I note above—citing *Moore
v. Madigan* (7th Cir. 2012), litigated by Alan Gura in an effort to extend
Heller's reach—at least one key challenge has divided federal appellate
judges on partisan lines.

In the gay rights context, the judicial response has been shaped by two
legal signals from SCOTUS whose specific contours were opaque but
whose general direction was clear. In both *Romer v. Evans* and *Lawrence
v. Texas*, the high Court invalidated antigay policies without clearly speci-
fying a standard of review for assessing the constitutionality of other such
policies. Still, the two decisions made clear that the federal Constitution
provided some substantive protection to gay and lesbian rights—a fact
that had been far from evident since *Bowers v. Hardwick* (1986)—and a
significant number of federal judges seem to have gotten the message. In
part 1 of the book, I cite seven federal appellate decisions on LGBT rights
issued prior to *Romer*. Judges were sharply polarized in these cases, with
Republican appointees supporting liberal results only 12.5 percent of the
time, compared to 78.6 percent for Democratic appointees. In the forty-
seven such decisions issued since *Romer,* the Democratic figure rose at the
margins (to 82.2 percent), and the Republican figure rose dramatically (to
48.8 percent), thereby cutting the partisan gap in half. In this light, the
Court's decision in *United States v. Windsor* (2013) seems likely to reduce
the gap still further.

In the affirmative action context, where judicial polarization has been
most consistent (and most symmetrical), the votes of Democratic and
Republican judges alike have sometimes shifted in response to doctrinal
changes initiated by the Supreme Court, but only where the import of
those changes has been sufficiently clear. In *Adarand Constructors v. Pena*
(1995), the Court held for the first time that all race-conscious affirmative
action policies are subject to strict judicial scrutiny, but Justice Scalia was
unable to find five votes for his view that all such policies were inherently
unconstitutional. As a result, federal appellate judges were left to apply
a precedent indicating that race-conscious policies were constitutionally suspect but might nonetheless be legitimate if they served ends that
were sufficiently compelling. In the face of this legal ambiguity, the judges
polarized. For example, in twelve post-*Adarand* decisions regarding the

constitutionality of race-conscious student assignment plans for primary and secondary schools, Republican-appointed judges supported the constitutional challengers by a 16–4 vote, while the Democratic tally was 7–17.

But the legal landscape shifted again with *Grutter v. Bollinger* (2003), in which SCOTUS held for the first time that a race-conscious affirmative action plan survived strict scrutiny. In *Grutter*'s wake, three federal circuits addressed the issue of race-conscious student assignment plans, in cases involving public school policies in Lynn, Massachusetts; Louisville, Kentucky; and Seattle, Washington, respectively. Following the high Court's lead, all three courts upheld the policies under the strict-but-not-necessarily-fatal scrutiny called for by *Grutter*.[67] Judicial polarization did not disappear, but both Democratic and Republican judges moved toward greater support for the controversial policies, with Republicans now evenly divided, 5–5, and their Democratic colleagues voting 1–8.[68] As I note in chapter 2, the Roberts Court's shifting signals in *Parents Involved v. Seattle School District* (2007), *Ricci v. DeStefano* (2009), and *Fisher v. University of Texas* (2013) are likely to encourage federal judges to once again ramp up their suspicion of race-conscious policies, but with *Grutter* still on the books as well, the scope of such change is hard to predict.

In addition to reaching across party lines in an effort to faithfully implement clear legal signals from SCOTUS, judges regularly reach unanimity (or near-unanimity) in rejecting extreme legal claims, from both the left and the right. The judicial holdings that I survey in part 1 include multiple examples of broad judicial agreement that the most far-reaching legal arguments advanced by advocates on each side were beyond the pale.

In the gay rights context, for example, federal judges have repeatedly rebuffed the long-shot efforts of SSM opponents to haul state constitutional disputes into federal court. When the Hawaii Supreme Court held in March 1997 that the state constitution required nonvotes on a ballot measure to be counted as no-votes, and hence that a call for a state constitutional convention had been narrowly rejected, SSM opponents filed a federal constitutional challenge, alleging that the state courts had improperly changed the rules of the game after the vote had been held. In March 1998, a bipartisan Ninth Circuit panel unanimously rejected this challenge, and SCOTUS denied certiorari the following year.[69] Likewise, federal judges united across party lines to reject Liberty Counsel's last-ditch effort to prevent the Massachusetts high court's 2003 *Goodridge* decision from taking effect. Represented by Liberty Counsel's Mat Staver, the vice president of the Catholic Action League in Boston sought a permanent injunction against the implementation of *Goodridge* on the grounds that the state high court had usurped the powers of the state legislature, thus violating the federal constitutional declaration that "[t]he United States shall guarantee to every State in this Union a Republican Form of Government." Given the 150-year-old tradition holding the guarantee clause nonjusticiable, it was no surprise that this claim was unanimously rejected by a Nixon-appointed district judge and a bipartisan First Circuit panel, and that the Supreme Court declined to intervene.[70] In Oregon, when gay rights opponents challenged the state's long-standing procedures for verifying petition signatures—with ADF lawyers advancing a long-shot First Amendment claim and an even longer-shot, *Bush v. Gore*–inspired equal protection claim—their challenge was unanimously rejected by a GWB-appointed district judge and a bipartisan Ninth Circuit panel.[71]

State appellate judges have likewise reached unanimity in rejecting a number of extreme legal claims advanced by SSM opponents. When the Vermont legislature enacted the nation's first Civil Union Law in 2000, SSM opponents responded by arguing that the vote should be nullified because fourteen members of the legislative majority had violated a House Rule providing that "members shall not be permitted to vote upon any question in which they are immediately or directly interested." Their alleged violation was that they had participated in a low-stakes betting pool to guess the number of yeas and nays on the Civil Union Bill. The plaintiffs alleged further that the representatives' participation in the pool amounted to a violation of the state constitutional provision "that no member of the General Assembly may 'receive any fee or reward' for bringing forward or advocating any bill," as well as the state statutory ban on lotteries. The state high court unanimously dismissed these claims in 2001.[72]

In Massachusetts, SSM opponents repeatedly sought to amend the state constitution to ban SSM—first in an effort to preempt what they feared would be a judicial defeat in *Goodridge* and then in an effort to overturn that decision. Under the state constitution's cumbersome amendment procedures, they were unable to do so without some support from the state legislature, but the legislature's Democratic leaders repeatedly declined to act on their proposals. The SSM opponents repeatedly asked the state high court to compel the legislative leaders to schedule a vote, but the court declined to do so in December 2002, April 2004, and again in December 2006.[73] The state justices were narrowly divided in *Goodridge* itself, but all three of these decisions were unanimous.[74]

Notably, state appellate judges have repeatedly reached unanimity (or near-unanimity) in rejecting extreme legal claims advanced by SSM *supporters* as well. Though state high court justices in Massachusetts and California have been denounced as judicial activists for legalizing SSM, these same justices have rebuffed SSM advocates when their claims reached too far. In Massachusetts, while SSM opponents were trying to amend the state constitution, both before and after *Goodridge*, SSM advocates twice asked the state high court to enjoin election officials from putting the proposed amendments before the voters. The court twice declined, each time unanimously.[75] In California, SSM supporters like-wise called on the state high court to block a ballot measure designed to reverse the court's own decision legalizing SSM, but the court declined to do so, without dissent, and Proposition 8 appeared on the ballot in November 2008.[76] Once the initiative was enacted, SSM supporters then filed another long-shot legal challenge, this time asking the high court to invalidate the newly enacted state constitutional amendment as an ille-gitimate constitutional revision. Though the court had legalized SSM by a 4–3 vote just one year prior, it now ruled 6–1 that the voters had law-fully reversed that decision.[77] Similarly, when San Francisco Mayor Gavin Newsom attempted to revise the state's marriage laws on his own, the state justices held that he had no authority to do so.[78] This decision was unanimous and was joined by all four of the justices who would them-selves legalize SSM four years hence.

On the abortion issue, as with gay rights, the basic legal conflict is a polarizing one, but judges have nonetheless been able to unite in reject-ing some of the more extreme legal claims advanced by advocates on each side. For more than a generation, the central rhetorical trope used by opponents of legal abortion has been the fetal "right to life," but virtu-ally no judges anywhere have held that fetuses actually have such a legal right, in part because of the clear legal signals sent by SCOTUS on this point.[79] Likewise, when right-to-life advocates sought to reopen the *Roe v. Wade* litigation thirty years after its conclusion—representing the origi-nal "Jane Roe" (aka Norma McCorvey), who had now come to oppose the landmark decision—federal judges had little difficulty dismissing the claim as mooted by the passage of time. This conclusion was reached by a GWB-appointed district judge and an all-GOP Fifth Circuit panel, and SCOTUS declined to hear the case.[80]

From the other side, consider the litigation involving Medicaid funding for abortion that I survey in chapter 1. During the Clinton era, a number of states resisted the federal mandate that Medicaid cover the costs of abortion in cases of rape and incest (as authorized by the newly modified Hyde Amendment), and during the Obama era, a number of states sought to ban public funding of Planned Parenthood, even for non-abortion-related health services. In both contexts, abortion providers filed suit, and while the issue of abortion funding tends to polarize elected legislators, the particular legal question faced by the courts in these cases was straightforward. In seventy roll call votes from 1993 through 2012 on whether the federal government should pay for abortions (for Medicaid recipients, government employees, federal prisoners, and so on), the gap between Democratic and Republican support for such funding was 70.1 points. But in seven appellate decisions on whether states were free to ignore the requirements of federal Medicaid law, Democratic and Republican judges alike were unanimous that the answer was no.[81]

In the gun rights context, I have already noted the unanimous rejection by federal appellate courts of constitutional challenges to the federal felon-in-possession law, on both commerce clause and Second Amendment grounds. On the other side, the long-shot efforts of local governments to regulate firearms via tort litigation met a similar fate. In the four federal appellate holdings in suits initiated by local government officials that I cite in chapter 1, Republican judges ruled against the local governments 6–0, and their Democratic colleagues did so 5–1.[82]

In the affirmative action context, judges have regularly diverged on party lines—indeed, in both Congress and the federal appellate courts, it is the most polarized of the four issues I have examined—but the Supreme Court has at least partly dampened this polarization by rejecting some of the most far-reaching claims advanced by advocates. In particular, affirmative action opponents have sometimes argued that the Constitution prohibits racial preferences without exception (or perhaps with de minimis exceptions), and affirmative action supporters have sometimes argued that race-conscious policies are constitutionally required (or at least that they cannot constitutionally be repealed). The Supreme Court has repeatedly rejected the former claim and has signaled that it is likely to reject the latter. On the anti–affirmative action side, the Court's strictest color-blind holding to date is *Parents Involved v. Seattle School District*, in which Chief Justice Roberts declared that "the way to stop discrimination on the basis of race is to stop discriminating on the basis of race."[83] But that line appeared in a section of the opinion endorsed by only four members of the Court, as Justice Kennedy joined two fellow Republican appointees and the Court's two Democrats in maintaining that at least some race-conscious government actions remained permissible. The Court declined another opportunity to impose a per se ban on race-conscious affirmative action in *Fisher v. University of Texas*. On the pro-affirmative action side, the Ninth Circuit has twice rejected claims that California's ban on affirmative action is unconstitutional, holding that no matter how close the question of whether states are constitutionally *permitted* to employ affirmative action, it is clear that they are not constitutionally *required* to do so.[84] Affirmative action supporters persuaded the Sixth Circuit to go the other way in the sharply polarized en banc holding regarding Michigan's Proposal 2 that I note above, but SCOTUS agreed to hear the state's appeal, and the justices will almost certainly reverse the Sixth Circuit and reinstate the ban.[85]

An additional lesson of the Court's affirmative action holdings for the judicial umpiring debate is that judges are sometimes able to craft centrist legal compromises that split the difference between the constitutional worldviews of the two parties (Perry and Powe 2004). Indeed, on all four issues that I have examined, the Supreme Court's landmark legal holdings of the past twenty years fit this description. In *Gratz v. Bollinger* (2003) and *Grutter v. Bollinger*, the Court held that the University of Michigan was constitutionally precluded from granting a twenty-point bonus to all applications from underrepresented minorities but was permitted to give such applications a more flexible boost in the admissions process. In *Planned Parenthood v. Casey* (1992), the Court held that states are prohibited from banning abortion altogether but that they remain free to impose a range of restrictions that fall short of such a ban. In *Carhart I* and *II*, the Court followed up by holding that some statutory bans on partial-birth abortion go too far in burdening women's constitutional rights but that other such bans are constitutionally legitimate. In *Romer v. Evans*, the Court invalidated for the first time a state law that discriminated on the basis of sexual orientation, but it did so in an opinion that had few clear implications for other such discriminatory laws. The Court issued a more expansive opinion in *Lawrence v. Texas*, but it did so only after most states had already repealed their criminal sodomy laws, and even here, the Court avoided declaring that such laws infringed on a "fundamental right." In *District of Columbia v. Heller*, the Court invalidated a gun control law on Second Amendment grounds for the first time, but its opinion indicated that most other gun control policies remained constitutionally legitimate.

In light of these decisions, it is clear that coding judicial votes in binary fashion—as either liberal or conservative—may obscure some significant efforts by judges to mark out a middle ground. As such, my aggregate numbers on polarization may tend to overstate the phenomenon. Indeed, some scholars have suggested in recent years that courts are the least polarized and most centrist policymaking institutions in the contemporary United States (Rosen 2006). As H. W. Perry and Lucas Powe (2004) have noted, the contemporary Democratic and Republican parties have adopted radically different understandings of the Constitution, but the controlling justices on the Supreme Court have endorsed neither of them. This tendency toward judicial centrism results at least in part from the fact that people who are successfully nominated and confirmed for federal judgeships generally have more moderate views (at least on certain issues) than other partisan elites (Graber 2006a, 687–95; Perry and Powe 2004, 694).

But parallel examples of judicial compromise have emerged from state high courts as well. As courts of last resort, these institutions are similar to SCOTUS (and different from the federal appellate courts) in having broad authority to craft essentially any constitutional doctrine they choose. And like SCOTUS, the state high courts have sometimes used this authority to craft doctrines that split the difference between competing advocates. Years before *District of Columbia v. Heller*, the Ohio and Connecticut Supreme Courts held that their state constitutions protected the right of individuals to bear arms, but that this right was subject to reasonable regulation and that state and local legislative bodies remained free to ban the possession and sale of assault weapons.[86] Likewise, shortly before *McDonald v. Chicago* (2010), the Washington Supreme Court held that the individual right to bear arms was incorporated and applied to the states by the Fourteenth Amendment (and was secured by the Washington Constitution as well), but that the state remained free to ban the possession of firearms by juveniles.[87]

Or recall *Baker v. Vermont*, in which the Vermont Supreme Court helped redirect what had been a sharply polarized national debate over SSM by inventing a compromise position that would prove to have significant popular support. Writing for the court, Chief Justice Jeffrey Amestoy held that the common benefits clause of the Vermont Constitution required the state to extend all state law rights of marriage to same-sex couples, but that it was up to state lawmakers whether to do so under the marriage laws or under a newly created institution. The state legislature responded by enacting the nation's first Civil Union law. The Vermont judges borrowed this idea from a report issued by the Hawaii Commission on Sexual Orientation and the Law, which had been created in the wake of *Baehr v. Lewin* (Haw. 1993), and from scholarly treatments of registered partnership laws in Denmark and Norway, and they advanced this compromise despite a sharp dissenting opinion accusing them of abandoning their duty to vindicate legal rights.[88] When the marriage equality issue reached the New Jersey Supreme Court in 2006, the New Jersey justices were likewise unanimous that the state must extend the rights of marriage to same-sex couples, and likewise divided on whether it must allow SSM itself. Here, four of the seven followed their Vermont colleagues in adopting the compromise path.[89]

Notably, these efforts at judicial compromise sometimes succeed in bridging partisan divides. Legislative debates over marriage equality and gun control tend to be polarized, with most Democratic legislators supporting such policies and most Republicans opposing them, but it is not inevitable that these divisions are reproduced in court. Indeed, the landmark SSM holdings in California, Iowa, and Massachusetts were each authored by a justice who had been appointed by a Republican governor. The Connecticut SSM holding was authored by a justice appointed by Independent governor Lowell Weicker. In Vermont, Chief Justice Amestoy had been appointed by a Democratic governor but had himself been elected seven times as the state's Republican attorney general. In New Jersey, the 2006 civil union holding was authored by a justice who had been appointed by Democratic governor James E. McGreevey, but the three justices who held out for full marriage equality had all been appointed by Republican governor Christine Todd Whitman. In the state gun rights cases, the judicial majority in Ohio consisted of two Democrats and three Republicans, while the Connecticut holding was issued by two justices who had been appointed by Democratic governors and three who had been appointed by Governor Weicker. In Washington, the state justices voted 9–0 that the Second Amendment applies to state as well as federal legislation and 8–1 that the state was nonetheless free to ban gun possession by juveniles.

These voting coalitions should be interpreted with caution, given the widely varying judicial selection procedures across states. In Ohio and Washington, Supreme Court justices are elected in nonpartisan elections, but in Ohio, both major parties regularly nominate candidates for the open seats. In New Jersey and Vermont, justices are selected by gubernatorial appointment, but in New Jersey, most governors have adhered to a long-standing norm of maintaining partisan balance on the court. As such, Republican governors have regularly appointed registered Democrats and vice versa. On the court that decided *Lewis v. Harris* (N.J. 2006), only one of Governor Whitman's four appointees was a registered Republican.

Still, whichever way you slice it, a court consisting of four Republican appointees and three Democratic appointees—or a court consisting of four registered Democrats, two Republicans, and an Independent—held unanimously that New Jersey must extend the rights of marriage to same-sex couples. Overall, state justices appointed by Democrats have been more likely than their Republican colleagues to support expanded marriage rights for same-sex couples, but the difference is not as stark as might be expected. In Massachusetts and California, the judicial majorities that legalized SSM each included three Republican appointees; in Iowa, there were two; and in Connecticut, there was one, plus three judges who had been appointed by Governor Weicker. All told, twelve state high court justices appointed by Republican governors have voted to endorse full marriage equality, one other has endorsed the compromise civil union position, and fourteen have voted against legal recognition for same-sex couples. On the Democratic side, sixteen justices have supported full equality, eight others have supported civil unions, and ten have voted against legal recognition of any kind. In the aggregate, the partisan gap between the votes of Democratic and Republican justices in all 124 state high court decisions cited in part 1 is just 11.1 points.[90] Juxtaposed with the much larger gaps reported in table 3.4, this figure suggests that some judges remain capable of reaching across party lines even in these polarized times, and that some judicial institutions remain capable of forging broadly acceptable compromises as well.

*   *   *

This institutional capacity is still present, but the data I have presented in this chapter suggest troubling signs of deterioration. The question for defenders of state and federal courts in the years to come is whether these institutions can continue to withstand the ever-escalating pressures of partisan polarization. And the question for judges is whether they are doing all they can to ensure that their institutions are worth defending. As judicial history since *Marbury* has made clear, judicial partisanship invites political attacks. Political attacks may come in the absence of judicial partisanship too, but for judges to credibly argue that such attacks are unwarranted, they need to keep their own house in order. Put another way, the long-standing judicial complaint about media accounts of judicial partisanship is misdirected. Federal judges have long objected to press reports suggesting that their performance is politicized, and indeed they tend to object even to straightforward depictions of judges as members of relatively consistent voting coalitions (Edwards 1985; Rosen 2007; Walker 2007). But surely the solution to polarized judging is not for the press to pretend it does not exist, but for judges themselves to vote in less polarized ways.

In sum, the story of the ACA's fate in the federal courts turns out to illustrate a broader pattern. The courts have maintained some willingness to act on dimensions other than partisanship, but this independence remains under significant strain. During the period I have examined, 1993 to 2013, the Republican Party has repeatedly been on the verge of capturing firm control of the federal judiciary, only to have those courts pulled back to a position of rough balance before their victory was complete. At the outset of the Clinton era, more than 60 percent of sitting federal judges had been appointed by Republican presidents (Goldman 1993). Clinton's two terms in office reduced this supermajority to a bare 51 percent, but George W. Bush's two terms brought it back to 60 percent eight years later (Goldman, Slotnick, Gryski, and Schiavoni 2005; Goldman, Slotnick, and Schiavoni 2011). President Obama cut this figure to 52.7 percent during his first term, and by the end of his second, we can expect the return of a modest Democratic majority.[91] Even then, despite Democrats having won the popular vote in five of the last six presidential elections, the Republican Party will remain in close striking distance of majority control of the federal courts.

Given this pattern of partisan imbalance, any signs of partisan judging are likely to encourage the GOP to continue and even escalate its fight to win firm control of the courts. These efforts, in turn, are likely to inspire Democrats to resist what appears to them to be an illegitimate power grab. In the midst of such partisan combat, it will be up to the judges themselves to abstain from the fight. They need not be perfect umpires, but they do need to continue marking out bipartisan readings of the law with some regularity. The claim of impersonal judging has always been a fiction, at least in part. But as E. P. Thompson noted long ago with respect to the rule of law, judges can maintain the fiction of impartiality only by actually being impartial, at least some of the time (1975, 262–63). As Keith Bybee has observed more recently, "[j]udges must visibly appear to play the role of neutral umpire, for it is by maintaining appearances of impartiality that judges reinforce their claim of actually being impartial and worthy of receiving public support" (2011, 314).

CHAPTER FOUR

Are Judges Tyrants?

As I note in the previous chapter, federal judicial nominees regularly describe the job for which they are nominated as a modest one. Umpiring is important to the game of baseball, but as John Roberts noted in 2005, "[n]obody ever went to a ball game to see the umpire."[1] So also with judging. It is vitally important to the fair and efficient operation of our political and economic systems; to note just one example, a central achievement of modern democratic state-building was to enable private contract disputes to be resolved by a neutral third party rather than a contest of force. But like umpiring, judging best takes place in the background rather than at the center of public attention.

Partisan elected officials sometimes echo this narrative, but only when describing judges who share their partisan affiliation or ideological preferences. When describing judges and judicial nominees with whom they disagree, partisan officials tell a very different story. When the Senate Judiciary Committee held hearings in January 2006 on President George W. Bush's nomination of Samuel Alito as associate justice of the United States, Democratic senator Charles Schumer observed that Alito's record on the Third Circuit, where he had sat for fifteen years, revealed a remarkably consistent pattern of conservative votes. Recalling the image that Roberts had deployed so successfully the year before, Senator Schumer noted that "[i]f the record showed that an umpire repeatedly called 95 percent of pitches strikes when one team's players were up and repeatedly called 95 percent of pitches balls when the other team's players were up, one would naturally ask whether the umpire was being impartial and fair." Referring to *United States v. Rybar* (3d Cir. 1996)—a case I examined in chapter 2, in which Judge Alito had voted to strike down the federal ban on possession of machine guns—Schumer asked the nominee whether he still held "these cramped views of congressional power" and whether he would continue to "engage in judicial activism to find ways to strike down laws that the American people want their elected representatives to pass and that the Constitution authorizes." These questions, of course, were rhetorical, as Schumer reminded the nominee that "[t]he court is not a legislature, free to substitute its own judgment for that of elected bodies."[2]

Three years later, when President Barack Obama nominated Sonia Sotomayor to join Justice Alito on the Court, Republican senator Jeff Sessions pursued a similar line of attack. Characterizing the nomination as a dangerous step toward "a Brave New World where words have no true meaning and judges are free to decide what facts they choose to see," Sessions complained that "[i]n this world, . . . [w]e have seen federal judges force their own political and social agenda on the nation, dictating that the words 'under God' be removed from the Pledge of Allegiance and barring students from . . . even silent prayer in schools." Just as Schumer had complained about conservative judges' reliance on "cramped views of congressional power" to invalidate gun control laws, Sessions complained about liberal judges' reliance on "foreign laws, world opinion, and a United Nations resolution" to invalidate capital punishment laws. The upshot was the same; Senator Sessions, like Senator Schumer, objected that policy was being made by "unelected judges."[3]

This sort of attack on judicial power has such a long and storied history in American politics—and is so widespread in contemporary political discourse—that providing additional examples hardly seems necessary. For more than a generation, Republican presidential candidates have regularly invoked the specter of activist judges on the campaign trail (Keck 2004; McMahon 2011; Stephenson 1999, 163–217). In 2000, George W. Bush warned voters that his Democratic opponent, Al Gore, would appoint "liberal activist justices who will use their bench to subvert the legislature," and in his State of the Union Address four years later, he objected that "[a]ctivist judges . . . have begun redefining marriage by court order, without regard for the will of the people and their elected representatives. On an issue of such great consequence, the people's voice must be heard."[4] Eight years after that, when a Ninth Circuit panel struck down California's Proposition 8, Republican presidential candidate Mitt Romney sounded the same theme:

> Today, unelected judges cast aside the will of the people of California who voted to protect traditional marriage. This decision does not end this fight, and I expect it to go to the Supreme Court. That prospect underscores the vital importance of this election and the movement to preserve our values. I believe

marriage is between a man and a woman and, as president, I will protect tra-
ditional marriage and appoint judges who interpret the Constitution as it is
written and not according to their own politics and prejudices. (Sargent 2012)

This line of criticism has become so widespread that it is sometimes
adopted by judges themselves. When describing their own decisions, they
generally stick to the umpiring image described in chapter 3, but when
describing their colleagues' decisions, judges sometimes invoke images of
judicial activism or even judicial tyranny. This stance remains more common on the right than the left, but the balance has been shifting for a number of years, and if the Roberts Court continues to strike down campaign
finance regulations, voting rights laws, gun control policies, and affirmative action measures, liberal critics of judicial review are likely to catch
up to their conservative counterparts. To note just one recent example,
Justice Ruth Bader Ginsburg used an interview with the *New York Times*
to denounce the Court's decision in *Shelby County v. Holder* (2013) as
"stunning in terms of activism" (Liptak 2013).

My goal in this chapter is to assess the degree to which this sort of complaint about undemocratic judging accurately characterizes the public's
assessment of rights-protecting judicial decisions. If the judicial defense
of rights is inherently undemocratic, then there is indeed a substantial
amount of illegitimate judicial activism in the contemporary United States.
In part 1 of the book, I cited 111 separate decisions issued by federal appellate courts that are best characterized as rights protecting, from the
perspective of the party seeking judicial intervention. I also cited 55 such
decisions issued by state high courts and 22 issued by SCOTUS. These figures appear to indicate that judicial activism is a regular occurrence, but
as with the raw numbers indicating patterns of polarized judicial voting,
it is difficult to evaluate them without providing some significant context.

For one thing, it is worth emphasizing that most rights-based lawsuits
continue to be unsuccessful. On both the left and the right, advocates
ask judges to reverse democratically enacted policies far more often than
judges actually do so. While I identified 111 decisions in which federal
appellate courts endorsed and defended a rights claim, I identified 221 in
which they declined to do so. In other words, these courts ruled favorably
on only 33.4 percent of the rights claims that they heard. On SCOTUS
and the state high courts, the corresponding figures are 47.8 and 43.7 percent, respectively. These numbers do not paint a picture of judges eager
to reach out and impose their will; in fact, the aggregate pattern is more

consistent with a general judicial reluctance to do so. Moreover, many of the allegedly activist judicial decisions that drew the loudest complaints were subsequently reversed on appeal. When a DC Circuit panel struck down the pre-Clinton policy banning military service by homosexuals in *Steffan v. Aspin* (D.C. Cir. 1993), the three judges on the panel might well have been acting undemocratically, and their decision is included in my list of 111 potential candidates for activist decisions by federal appellate courts.[5] But this activism had little practical impact, as the full circuit reversed the holding just one year later.[6]

In addition, some of these rights-protecting decisions are better understood as efforts to facilitate democratic politics than to hinder it. Seventeen of the 111 rights-protecting decisions issued by federal appellate courts were category 3 holdings; these 17 are best understood as efforts to remove barriers to legislative change or to facilitate the implementation of policies already won via legislative change. For example, 7 of the 17 represented successful efforts by abortion providers to compel state governments to adhere to the terms of federal Medicaid law. None of the 17 posed direct challenges between judicial and democratic authority.[7] Excluding these category 3 holdings, I am left with 94 decisions issued by federal appellate courts that seem good candidates for activist judging—that is, 94 category 1 and 2 decisions in which a federal appellate court enjoined a newly enacted policy or struck down an existing one. From state high courts, there are 46 additional such decisions, and from SCOTUS, 18 more.

But these aggregate numbers mask a fair amount of repetition within the system. If a dozen state legislatures enacted flatly unconstitutional statutes—prohibiting, say, public criticism of the US president—and if a combination of state and federal courts subsequently enjoined all twelve of them, it would not be wrong to say that judges had thwarted the democratic will twelve times, but it would seem more accurate to say that the courts had identified a single unconstitutional policy and had prevented all state governments from enacting or enforcing that policy.

If we count substantially similar policies only once, and if we include only judicial decisions that have survived all subsequent appeals, chapters 1 and 2 identified thirty-three distinct public policies that were potentially thwarted by rights-protecting judicial decisions. In some cases, a single type of policy was enacted and invalidated in multiple jurisdictions, but there are just thirty-three policy types whose enforcement was blocked by judges.

Finally, it is worth reiterating that these invalidations of democratically enacted policies have been called for (and issued by) political and legal actors from across the ideological spectrum. Of the 94 rights-protecting decisions issued in category 1 and 2 cases by federal appellate courts, 52.1 percent are best characterized as liberal decisions, while the other 47.9 percent were conservative. On state high courts, rights-protecting tendencies leaned more heavily leftward, but on SCOTUS, they leaned the other way; 78.3 percent of the rights-protecting category 1 and 2 holdings issued by state high courts were liberal decisions, but just 33.3 percent of those issued by SCOTUS. The judicial federalism literature suggests that these latter two figures are likely related; with SCOTUS trending rightward in recent decades, state courts became a more attractive venue for rights advocates on the left (Brennan 1977; Price 2013). But taking the performance of US courts as a whole, it seems clear that if judges are thwarting the democratic will, they are doing so on behalf of both liberal and conservative ends. This bipartisan character of contemporary judicial activism is illustrated by the list of thirty-three invalidated policies— sixteen on the right and seventeen on the left—in tables 4.1 and 4.2.

TABLE 4.1 **Conservative policies invalidated in court, 1993–2013**

Issue area	Invalidated policy
Abortion	Criminal bans on abortion in AR, LA, ND, NV, OK, UT
	Criminal bans on post-20 week abortions in AZ, GA
	Criminal bans on partial-birth abortions in AR, AZ, FL, IA, IL, KY, LA, MI, MO, NE, NJ, OH, RI, VA, WI
	Informed consent/waiting period requirements in DE, MT, NC, OK, SD, TN
	Parental involvement requirements in AK, AZ, CA, CO, FL, ID, LA, MA, MT, NJ, SD
	Requirement that abortions be performed by physicians in MT
	Restrictions on public funding of abortion in AK, AZ, MN, NM, WV
Affirmative action	Anti–affirmative action initiative in MI, MO
Gay rights	Antigay initiatives that repeal and/or prohibit the enactment of antidiscrimination laws in CO, FL, MD
	Criminal bans on consensual sodomy in AR, GA, MA, MD, MN, MO, MT, TN, TX
	Bans on SSM in CA, CT, IA, MA
	Failure to extend state law rights of marriage to same-sex couples in NJ, VT
	Defense of Marriage Act (federal nonrecognition provision)
	Failure to provide domestic partnership benefits to public employees in AK, AZ, MT, NH, OR
	Restrictions on LGBT parenting rights in AR, FL, OK
Gun rights	Prohibition on doctors discussing gun safety with patients in FL

TABLE 4.2 **Liberal policies invalidated in court, 1993–2013**

Issue area	Invalidated policy
Abortion	Local clinic defense laws in AZ, CA, OH, PA
	Local regulation of limited-service pregnancy centers in NY
Affirmative action	Race-exclusive scholarship program in MD
	Race-conscious university admissions policies in GA, MI, TX
	Race-conscious public employment policies in CA, CT, MA, NJ, TN, TX, and at the FCC
	Race-conscious government contracting policies in CA, WA, and at DoD
	Race-conscious student assignment policies in CA, KY, MA, MD, TN, VA, WA
Gay rights	Local domestic partnership ordinances in FL, GA, MA, MI, MN, PA, VA
	Prohibition of antigay discrimination (as applied to Boy Scouts of America) in NJ
	Prohibitions of antigay violence or harassment in MN, PA
Gun rights	Gun-Free School Zones Act (GFSZA)
	Brady Bill's temporary background check provisions
	Local bans on possessing handguns in CA, DC, IL
	State bans on carrying firearms in IL, WI
	Local ban on assault weapons in OH
	Ban on gun possession by convicted felons in NC
	Bans on gun shows or firing ranges in CA, IL

These thirty-three invalidated policies represent the full universe of potentially countermajoritarian exercises of judicial review that I have identified. In any given case, however, the extent to which a rights-protecting judicial decision is incompatible with the popular will is an empirical question (Barnum 1985). For one thing, any given exercise of judicial review might preclude less policymaking authority than sometimes supposed. Even leaving aside instances of successful efforts at non-compliance—a story I take up in chapter 5—many rights-protecting judicial decisions by their own terms leave elected legislatures with significant room to engage in continued policymaking on the question at hand. In the abortion context, for example, the Supreme Court has repeatedly held that states are free to require some form of parental involvement before a minor can have an abortion but that such statutes must include a judicial bypass option. Following these holdings, federal courts have occasionally invalidated parental involvement mandates that lacked adequate bypass procedures—invalidations that are reflected in table 4.1—but these decisions have left democratic majorities free to continue mandating parental involvement in most circumstances.

Moreover, even when exercises of judicial review are broader in scope, it is often far from clear that they have thwarted any identifiable public will. After all, legislative institutions in the contemporary United States are often less than fully responsive to public sentiment, so some of the thirty-three policies that courts have invalidated may not have been popular to begin with. Put another way, some of the judicial decisions invalidating these policies are likely to have had broad public support. Consider, for example, the Don't Ask, Don't Tell (DADT) policy signed by President Clinton in November 1993. Federal District Judge Virginia A. Phillips permanently enjoined the policy in October 2010, but it does not appear in table 4.1 because Congress repealed the policy two months later, and the Ninth Circuit then vacated Judge Phillips's holding.[8] But if the legislative change had never happened (and if the judicial invalidation had survived on appeal), the courts and not Congress would have been on the side of popular majorities. In 1993, during the legislative debate prompted by Clinton's pledge to allow gays and lesbians to serve openly in the military, national public opinion polls revealed that 40 to 47 percent of the public supported Clinton's initial position.[9] After Clinton accepted a legislative compromise that allowed gays and lesbians to serve only if they successfully maintained absolute secrecy regarding their sexual orientation, public support for allowing them to serve openly began to increase. Indeed, from June 1994 through September 2011, national polls reported majority support for this position almost without exception, with that support exceeding 75 percent in multiple polls.[10] When Congress fails to repeal a rights-restricting policy despite clear and unambiguous evidence of majoritarian opposition to the policy, stretching over a decade or more, it would seem that judges who strike the policy down should be praised rather than denounced on democratic legitimacy grounds.

Likewise, when a rights-protecting judicial decision is immediately ratified by the White House and both houses of Congress, it is hard to characterize the decision as fundamentally undemocratic. Indeed, when appellate judges consider issuing a rights-protecting decision, they often have reliable signals that the decision will draw support from important democratic actors. As Scott Barclay has noted, all but one of the landmark state high court decisions legalizing same-sex marriage (SSM) came in states where the statutory ban on SSM had been superseded by more recent legislative expressions of support for gay and lesbian relationships. Those more recent legislative enactments fell short of full marriage equality, but they likely signaled to the state justices that support for the older bans on SSM was declining. Iowa is the only state to date in which "a state's highest court acted in direct contradiction to the most recent expression of legislative preference" regarding same-sex relationships (Barclay 2010, 122). In similar fashion, when SCOTUS invalidated gun control laws on Second Amendment grounds in *District of Columbia v. Heller* (2008) and *McDonald v. Chicago* (2010), the justices had received amicus briefs signed by a majority of sitting members of both houses of Congress, urging them to do just that. On affirmative action, Neal Devins has emphasized the remarkable array of amicus briefs indicating elite support for the continued practice of race-conscious admissions, characterizing the justices' 2003 decisions in the two University of Michigan cases as "a picture-perfect reflection of the social and political forces beating against" the Court (2003, 377–78).

If rights-protecting judicial decisions sometimes follow rather than buck democratic sentiment, then we need to investigate the supposed antidemocratic character of such decisions more carefully. After all, as Lisa Hilbink (2008) has noted, judicial institutions are not inherently any less capable of serving a function of democratic representation than are legislative or executive institutions. In the US context, prominent scholars have long noted that many of the Supreme Court's most famous (or notorious) rights-protecting decisions had broad public support, with some scholars suggesting that the Court will issue such decisions *only* when such support is present (Dahl 1957; Klarman 2004, 2005; Rosen 2006). Even if the latter claim is overstated, Mark Graber (1993) is surely correct that when elected institutions produce nonmajoritarian outcomes, the exercise of judicial review is not necessarily countermajoritarian.

In this light, consider three conditions under which democratically enacted policies might lack democratic support, in which case the judicial invalidation of those policies cannot be assumed to be countermajoritarian. First, state legislatures sometimes enact policies that are responsive to local democratic majorities but opposed by national democratic majorities. In the abstract, there is no reason to suppose that an elected state legislature would be more likely to reflect national public opinion than would a panel of federal judges appointed by the president and confirmed by the Senate. Indeed, the existing literature suggests that one of the most important functions of federal judicial review is to enforce national sentiment against local outliers (Barnum 1985, 654; Klarman 1996; Powe 2000; Whittington 2007, 105–20). Think, for example, of a federal judicial decision invalidating a sweeping restriction on abortion rights enacted by a red-state legislature or a sweeping restriction on gun rights enacted by a blue-state legislature. Second, both state and federal legislatures sometimes enact policies that are responsive to one wing of a polarized electorate—or even to nonelectoral special interests—rather than to the median voter. And third, both state and federal legislatures sometimes enact policies that had democratic support at the time, but then leave those policies on the books long after such support has disappeared. Given the fragmented character of the American policymaking process, supporters of a policy are often able to prevent its repeal even when their numbers have dwindled significantly below 50 percent. At the federal level, for example, a repeal bill could have the support of voting majorities in both houses of Congress but still be filibustered by 41 senators or vetoed by the president.

When any of these three conditions holds, a court's exercise of judicial review may move the policy status quo closer to public sentiment. For example, while *Roe v. Wade* and its progeny are often denounced as leading examples of unaccountable judicial activism, public opinion polls have revealed consistent popular support for the abortion rights that have been protected by those decisions. From April 1989 through December 2012, Gallup conducted fourteen national polls that mentioned *Roe v. Wade* by name and asked whether it should be overturned or maintained; 51 to 68 percent of respondents indicated support for the landmark decision, with just 25 to 39 percent expressing opposition. For all seventy-three such national polls that I have identified (including the fourteen from Gallup), the corresponding ranges are 45 to 68 percent and 21 to 43 percent, respectively. This public support for *Roe v. Wade* has been remarkably stable over a period of several decades. As Samantha Luks and Michael Salamone have noted, drawing on a wide range of existing studies, "[s]olid majorities want the Court to uphold *Roe v. Wade* and are in favor of abortion rights in the abstract," though it is also true that "substantial majorities favor procedural and other restrictions, including waiting periods, parental consent, spousal notification, and bans on 'partial-birth' abortion" (2008, 101; see also Jelen and Wilcox 2003, 490–91). As such, Jeffrey Rosen expressed a widespread scholarly assessment when he characterized the Rehnquist Court's decision in *Planned Parenthood v. Casey* (1992)—reaffirming *Roe* but simultaneously upholding most provisions of Pennsylvania's restrictive abortion law—as "precisely calibrated to reflect the public's policy views" (2006, 99).

Roe itself may have gone somewhat further (toward "abortion on demand") than the public was willing to support, but Scott Lemieux makes a strong case that the decision "was closer to the majority of the

public than the state [legislatures] were" at the time. *Roe* is often criticized for preempting legislative progress in liberalizing abortion laws, but
Lemieux makes clear that the wave of legislative reform in the late 1960s
and early 1970s was relatively modest and had stopped far short of the
median voter's support for legal abortion. At the time *Roe* was decided,
86 percent of the public favored a maternal health exception to criminal
bans on abortion, 79 percent favored a rape exception, and 57 percent
favored decriminalization altogether. Despite this public sentiment, thirty-
three states either prohibited abortion without exception or permitted it
only when necessary to save the pregnant woman's life. Only four states
had decriminalized abortion altogether; only thirteen others allowed abortion when necessary to protect the pregnant woman's health; and only one
other allowed it in cases of rape. In short, pre-*Roe* abortion laws reflected
the ability of "a determined [and] well-organized minority [to] prevail[]
over a more diffuse majority" (Lemieux 2004, 222–24; see also Greenhouse and Siegel 2011). The Court's 1973 invalidation of these existing
laws altered public policy in the direction of majoritarian sentiment.

Indeed, it was precisely this legislative unresponsiveness that led abortion rights advocates to court in the first place (Lemieux 2004, 225–29).
Keith Whittington (2007, 124–34) and Emily Zackin (2008) have documented a similar dynamic in other contexts, and the contemporary LGBT
rights movement has likewise made heavy use of litigation in part because
legislative institutions persistently ignored their claims for so long. Gays
and lesbians have faced substantial prejudice and discrimination at the
hands of democratic majorities, but even where the public has supported
gay rights, legislative institutions have been remarkably unresponsive.
As I note above, national democratic majorities opposed DADT for
sixteen years before Congress repealed it. In an even more extreme example, national democratic majorities have agreed for more than thirty-
five years—at least since Gallup began asking the question in 1977—that
"homosexuals should . . . have equal rights in terms of job opportunities," but Congress has repeatedly failed to enact the Employment Non-
Discrimination Act (Egan and Sherrill 2005; Mezey 2007, 179–80, 221–22).
LGBT rights advocates have had more success combating employment
discrimination at the state level, but even there, the legislative progress
has substantially lagged public opinion (Lax and Phillips 2009, 373).

In this context, state and federal judges have repeatedly been willing to
entertain rights claims whose broad popular support has failed to produce
legislative change. On the issue of relationship recognition, for example,

LGBT rights advocates had made very little progress in state or federal legislative institutions prior to their contemporary litigation campaign. Several local gay rights organizations were lobbying for statewide domestic partnership policies in the early 1990s, but these policies were quite limited in scope, and their advocates were having very little success. The DC City Council voted to create a domestic partnership registry in 1992, but Congress blocked the bill from taking effect for another ten years. The California legislature voted to create a similar registry in 1994, but Governor Pete Wilson vetoed the bill, and it would be another five years before his Democratic successor signed it into law. Legislation to extend domestic partnership benefits to federal employees has been introduced in Congress every year since 1997 but has made virtually no progress. In 1999, 2000, and again in 2001, the Massachusetts Senate passed a bill to extend such benefits to state employees, but House Speaker Thomas Finneran repeatedly blocked the bill. In opinion polls, popular majorities have long supported limited legal and economic benefits for same-sex partners, but even in the blue states, elected lawmakers failed to enact such benefits until judges began prodding them to do so (Keck 2009).

Likewise, throughout the 1990s, state and federal legislatures were almost uniformly unwilling to curtail existing race-conscious affirmative action policies, despite substantial evidence of public opposition to such policies. The federal courts issued a series of decisions doing what legislatures were unwilling to do, and a strong case can be made that the unelected judges reflected public sentiment better than did the elected legislators. As Paul Frymer (2008, 133) has put it, much judicial activism occurs in areas of legislative inattentiveness, and as Michael Paris (2010, 187–223) has emphasized, judicial politics and democratic politics sometimes push in the same direction. Stated differently, judicial politics is sometimes an avenue of democratic politics rather than an alternative to it. In this light, I devote the remainder of this chapter to assessing whether, when, and how much the exercises of judicial review summarized in tables 4.1 and 4.2 have run counter to public sentiment.

Following the Public

Of the thirty-three policies listed in tables 4.1 and 4.2, eleven appear to have lacked support from popular majorities before, during, and after their invalidation. In each of these eleven cases, judges invalidated policies without threatening any identifiable majority will; in most of them, it seems likely that the rights-protecting judicial decisions were more popular than the rights-infringing policies.

For example, during the early years of the Clinton era, the federal courts invalidated near-total bans on abortion that had been enacted by Louisiana and Utah in 1991.[11] Two decades later, state courts in Nevada and Oklahoma invalidated proposed initiatives that would have extended legal personhood to fetuses, and federal judges in North Dakota and Arkansas invalidated statutory bans on all abortions after six and twelve weeks' gestation, respectively.[12] The operative effect of the proposed Nevada and Oklahoma laws was unclear, but the intent of their advocates was to ban abortion altogether, presumably with no exceptions except when necessary to save the pregnant woman's life. The statutes from Arkansas, Louisiana, and Utah provided explicit such exceptions for threats to maternal life. Arkansas's statute also provided an exception for cases of "medical emergency," as did North Dakota's, and Utah's provided an exception in cases posing "grave" threats to the pregnant woman's health. In all of these states, the statutes would have banned some abortions that doctors judged necessary to promote and protect the health of their patients. The Arkansas, Louisiana, and Utah statutes provided exceptions for cases where the pregnancy resulted from rape or incest, but the North Dakota law did not, and only the Utah law provided an exception for cases in which the child would be born with significant birth defects.

These statutes may have been popular in certain states, but nationally, they almost certainly lacked majority support. When pollsters specify exceptions for cases of rape, incest, and threats to the pregnant woman's life, the median respondent sometimes supports abortion bans, but responses vary significantly with question wording.[13] These polls suggest that popular majorities might be willing to support abortion bans that lack maternal health exceptions, but when asked explicitly about this issue—that is, whether abortion should be banned even for pregnancies that pose threats to women's health—only small minorities say yes. The General Social Survey (GSS), conducted by the University of Chicago's National Opinion Research Center, has long asked whether it should "be possible for a pregnant woman to obtain a legal abortion if the woman's own health is seriously endangered by the pregnancy." On twenty-seven occasions from 1972 to 2012, support for banning abortions in such cases ranged from 7 to 14 percent. Likewise, in the years leading up to the judicial invalidations of the Louisiana and Utah laws, Gallup reported that just 14 to 17 percent of respondents supported banning abortion in cases where the pregnant woman's health was threatened. On four occasions from 1996 to 2011, Gallup divided the issue into separate questions regarding dangers to the woman's mental and physical health; 27 to 35 percent of respondents supported banning abortion in the former case, but just 11 to 17 percent in the latter. These polls appear to indicate that the laws that were invalidated in Arkansas, Louisiana, Nevada, North Dakota, Oklahoma, and perhaps Utah lacked democratic support.

GSS and Gallup have likewise reported that only small minorities of the American public support abortion bans in cases of pregnancy resulting from rape. These polls provide additional evidence that the proposed personhood amendments from Nevada and Oklahoma and the statutory ban on post-six-week abortions in North Dakota lacked national popular support. On seventeen occasions from 1972 to 1991, GSS asked whether "it should be possible for a pregnant woman to obtain a legal abortion if she became pregnant as a result of rape"; 10 to 20 percent of respondents said no. On ten occasions from 1992 to 2012, the range was 15 to 24 percent. A long list of other polls have found similar results, with a May 2003 Gallup poll reporting that even during the third trimester, only 39 percent of respondents were willing to ban abortions in cases of rape. If this latter poll is accurate, then the Louisiana and Utah laws lacked public support on this ground too, as they allowed abortions in cases of rape only during earlier stages of pregnancy.

These data are summarized in the top line of table 4.3, along with similar data regarding public support for legal abortion in cases of severe fetal defects. Taken together, they make clear that over decades of national polling, sweeping legislative bans on abortion have failed to garner majority support. As such, the judicial invalidation of such bans would seem to be a vindication of, rather than a threat to, the democratic will.

Another set of judicially invalidated laws that have lacked broad popular support is the antigay initiatives invalidated by SCOTUS in 1996 and by the high courts of Florida and Maryland in 1994 and 2008, respectively.[14] The Colorado Amendment was democratically enacted, and the Florida and Maryland measures might well have been likewise if they had come to a vote, but these measures did not (and do not) appear to have the support of democratic majorities nationally. As I note above, Gallup has long asked whether "homosexuals should or should not have equal rights in terms of job opportunities." On three occasions from 1989 to

TABLE 4.3 **Judicially invalidated policies that lacked public support**

Invalidated policy	Years of invalidation	National public support for the invalidated policy . . .		
		For five years prior to invalidation	During years of invalidation	Subsequent to years of invalidation
Criminal bans on abortion in AR, LA, ND, NV, OK, UT	1992–2013	7–17% (7 polls regarding pregnancies that threaten woman's health)	8–17% (14)	Unknown
		9–23% (11 polls regarding pregnancies resulting from rape)	11–24% (27)	Unknown
		16–22% (10 polls regarding cases of severe fetal defects)	17–46% (26)	Unknown
Antigay initiatives that repeal and/or prohibit the enactment of antidiscrimination laws in CO, FL, MD	1994–2008	13–18% (5)	8–30% (18)	18–36% (5)
Prohibition of antigay discrimination (as applied to Boy Scouts of America) in NJ	2000	Unknown	31–36% (2)	Unknown
Restrictions on LGBT parenting rights in AR, FL, OK	2006–2011	44–48% (4)	35–52% (14)	36–42% (4)
Failure to provide domestic partnership benefits to public employees in AK, AZ, MT, NH, OR	1997–2011	Unknown	23–40% (8)	20% (1)
Criminal bans on consensual sodomy in AR, GA, MA, MD, MN, MO, MT, TN, TX	1996–2003	32–54% (7)	33–49% (14)	31–49% (16)
Local bans on possessing handguns in CA, DC, IL	2008–2010	30–37% (8)	13–45% (6)	10–32% (8)
Race-conscious university admissions policies in GA, MI, TX	1996–2003	17–24% (3)	11–39% (13)	23–29% (5)
Race-conscious public employment policies in CA, CT, MA, NJ, TN, TX, and at FCC	1996–2009	14–51% (19)	14–35% (13)	19% (1)
Race-conscious government contracting policies in CA, WA, and at DOD	2000–2008	31–48% (3)	Unknown	Unknown
Race-conscious student assignment policies in CA, KY, MA, MD, TN, VA, WA	1998–2009	11–13% (2)	15–29% (5)	Unknown

1993, the portion of respondents opposing such rights ranged from 13 to 18 percent and appeared to be declining over time. On eleven occasions from 1994 to 2008—that is, during the period of invalidation—the range was just 8 to 13 percent. In April 1997, a Tarrance Group Poll reported that only 25 percent of respondents opposed the Employment Non-Discrimination Act (ENDA), which "would extend civil rights and prevent job discrimination against gays and lesbians." And in 2000 and 2005, Princeton Survey Research Associates (PSRA) reported 20 percent and then 30 percent opposition to "laws to protect gays and lesbians from prejudice and discrimination in job opportunities." More recently, CBS reported in May 2010 that 36 percent of respondents believed it was no longer "necessary to have laws to protect gays and lesbians from discrimination in housing and employment," but a July 2011 Human Rights Campaign (HRC) Survey reported just 18 percent opposition to laws "[p]rotecting gay, lesbian, bisexual, and transgender people from discrimination in employment, housing, and public accommodations."

While the public supports laws protecting gays and lesbians from discrimination, it also appears—or, at least, it appeared in 2000—to support exempting the Boy Scouts of America (BSA) from such laws. As a result, when SCOTUS held that New Jersey's antidiscrimination law could not constitutionally be applied to the BSA, it did not appear to thwart any identifiable majority will.[15] The data here are limited, but just a few days before the SCOTUS decision came down, Gallup/CNN/USA Today (USAT) reported that 31 percent of respondents "think the Boy Scouts of America should . . . be required to allow openly gay adults to serve as Boy Scout leaders," with 64 percent in disagreement. A few days after the decision came down, PSRA/Newsweek reported 36 percent opposition to the high Court's decision, with 56 percent of respondents agreeing with the Court "that The Boy Scouts of America have a constitutional right to block gay men from becoming troop leaders." Several more recent polls suggest that the public's views may have begun to shift on this issue, but these polls have focused on the desirability of the BSA's discriminatory policies without asking directly whether the organization should be required to alter those policies.[16]

In the relationship recognition context, the landmark marriage equality holdings from Massachusetts, Connecticut, California, and Iowa represented judicial invalidations of policies that had popular support at the time, but the decisions protecting LGBT parenting rights in Arkansas, Florida, and Oklahoma invalidated policies that did not (and do not) have such support.[17] Statutory restrictions on adoptions by gay parents were once popular—and may yet be popular in Arkansas, Florida, and Oklahoma—but by the time the courts started striking them down, their support nationally appears to have dipped below the median. In twelve national polls conducted during the Clinton era, 47 to 70 percent of respondents expressed opposition to adoption rights for gays and lesbians; these rights were opposed by a plurality of respondents in all twelve polls and by an absolute majority in eight of them. But in twenty-two such polls conducted from 2001 to 2013, the corresponding range was just 35 to 52 percent, with LGBT adoption rights opposed by a plurality only four times and by a majority only once. In one additional poll assessing support for gay parenting rights outside the adoption context, PSRA / Newsweek reported in December 2008 that only 19 percent of respondents opposed such rights.

Likewise, when judges ordered state or local governments in Alaska, Arizona, Montana, New Hampshire, and Oregon to extend domestic partnership benefits to public employees, they invalidated laws that appear to have had no more than 40 percent national support, and perhaps significantly less than that.[18] Eight national polls from 1997 to 2011 (the period of invalidation) assessed public support for health insurance and other employee benefits for gay and lesbian partners without mentioning SSM or otherwise suggesting that the same-sex partners would have rights and benefits equivalent to those of opposite-sex spouses. Opposition to such benefits ranged from 23 to 40 percent and appeared to be decreasing over time. In one more recent poll, Gallup/USAT reported in November 2012 that just 20 percent of respondents opposed such benefits. As such, when judges have expanded LGBT partnership rights at the margins, they do not seem to have thwarted the democratic will.

The story is similar with criminal bans on consensual sodomy. From 1996 to 2002, LGBT rights advocates persuaded state courts in Arkansas, Georgia, Maryland, Massachusetts, Minnesota, Missouri, Montana, and Tennessee to invalidate such bans, and in 2003, they persuaded SCOTUS to invalidate Texas's law (and, by implication, all remaining such laws).[19] All of these statutes had been democratically enacted, but by the time they were invalidated, none of them had national democratic support. In September 1991, Gallup reported that 54 percent of respondents thought "homosexual relations between consenting adults . . . should not be legal," but that figure dropped to 44 percent the following year and never again reached a majority. During the period when a number of state courts were striking these laws down (i.e., 1996–2002), Gallup reported 42 to 47 percent support for the bans. In the most recent polls before *Lawrence v. Texas* (2003), 35 to 37 percent of the public held this view. This number increased following the decision, peaking at 49 percent in January 2004, but then declined again, reaching a new low of 31 percent in May 2012.[20] Multiple polls conducted by ABC/WaPo, CBS/NYT, the Los Angeles Times (LAT), Quinnipiac, and Time/CNN have reported similar results; the aggregate ranges are indicated in table 4.3.

Many judicial decisions protecting rights on the right have likewise invalidated policies that lacked democratic support. In addition to the successful suit by the BSA noted above, several gun rights and affirmative action holdings fit this description. In the gun rights context, I recounted in chapter 2 three instances in which judges invalidated local bans on handgun possession.[21] The two most prominent of these decisions have drawn significant fire for their allegedly countermajoritarian character, but it seems odd to characterize them as antidemocratic when the laws they invalidated were broadly unpopular (Posner 2008a; Wilkinson 2009). Gallup has long asked whether "there should or should not be a law that would ban the possession of handguns, except by the police and other authorized persons." The only time such a ban received majority support was in 1959. Since 1980, such support has not exceeded 43 percent. In the five years leading up to *District of Columbia v. Heller* (2008), it did not exceed 36 percent. In the most recent poll before the decision, it was 30 percent. In five polls conducted since *Heller* came down, it has not exceeded 29 percent. Polls conducted by ABC/WaPo, CBS/NYT, CNN/Opinion Research Corporation (ORC), and Pew have reported somewhat higher numbers on occasion, but from 2003 to 2013, only one of twenty-two national polls reported support greater than 38 percent. In short, long-standing and consistent evidence indicates that the judges in *Heller*, *McDonald*, and the like invalidated laws that lack the support of national majorities.

Many of the race-conscious affirmative action policies that have been invalidated in court have likewise lacked public support. On this issue, question-wording effects have made the data notoriously difficult to interpret, with popular majorities regularly expressing support for "affirmative action" but opposition to "racial preferences" (Le and Citrin 2008, 165; Steeh and Krysan 1996, 129–30). But when pollsters have asked directly about the specific sorts of policies that have been invalidated in court, the median response for most such policies has been negative.

Consider the example of race-conscious university admissions. From 1996 to 2003, federal courts invalidated admissions policies at the flagship public universities in Texas, Georgia, and Michigan.[22] In the years leading up to these decisions, popular majorities were sometimes willing to express support for the vague concept of affirmative action, but in three national polls asking directly whether universities should give preference to minority applicants, only 17 to 24 percent of respondents said yes.[23] The pace of polling picked up during the period of judicial invalidation, and the results remained similar. In thirteen national polls from 1996 to 2003, 11 to 39 percent of respondents offered support for race-conscious admissions policies. Most of these polls were conducted in early 2003, while the Michigan cases were pending at SCOTUS. In five more recent polls, support has remained within this range, with Gallup reporting three times that 23 to 28 percent of respondents indicated that "an applicant's racial and ethnic background should be considered to help promote diversity on college campuses, even if that means admitting some minority students who otherwise would not be admitted"; 67 to 70 percent of respondents instead indicated that "[a]pplicants should be admitted solely on the basis of merit, even if that results in few minority students being admitted." When judges have invalidated policies reflecting the former description, they do not appear to have thwarted any identifiable democratic will.

So also with the race-conscious government employment policies invalidated by state and federal courts from 1996 to 2009.[24] National polls have only rarely asked about support for race-conscious hiring and promotion decisions by *government* employers, but they have regularly asked about support for such race-conscious employment decisions more generally. In the five years preceding the judicial invalidations, for example, CBS/NYT conducted ten polls asking respondents whether they "believe that where there has been job discrimination against blacks in the past, preference in hiring or promotion should be given to blacks today." Support for such policies hit 49 percent in January 1992, but otherwise fell between 20 and 39 percent. During this same period, PSRA/Newsweek reported 51 percent support for racial preferences in hiring to ensure that "a local police force . . . will have the same racial makeup as its community," but ANES and GSS reported just 14–16 percent support for the proposition that "because of past discrimination, blacks should be given preferences in hiring and promotion."

While the courts were invalidating such policies, from 1996 to 2009, support for race-conscious hiring and promotion decisions remained a minority view. On seven occasions during this period, GSS asked respondents whether they were "for or against preferential hiring and promotion of blacks"; support never exceeded 18 percent. ABC and Gallup/CNN/USAT reported support below 20 percent as well, while CBS/NYT and Quinnipiac reported somewhat higher levels, though never exceeding 35 percent. The June 2009 Quinnipiac poll sought to distinguish the public's views on racial preferences in "government jobs" and "jobs in private companies," reporting 25 percent and 21 percent support, respectively. This poll was conducted while *Ricci v. DeStefano* (2009) was pending at SCOTUS, and also included a question describing the case and asking respondents whether the Court should "order the city to promote the . . . white and . . . Hispanic firefighters who scored high enough for promotion"; 71 percent of respondents said yes, with just 19 percent supporting the city's decision to discard the test results "because no blacks scored high enough to qualify for promotion." A similar poll from CNN/ORC reported 31 percent support for the city. Since the *Ricci* decision came down, GSS has again reported 19 percent support for "preferential hiring and promotion of blacks."

In addition to the data noted so far, a number of national polls have regularly asked about support for racial preferences in education and employment, without distinguishing the two contexts. Responses vary significantly with question wording, and support for racial preferences sometimes comes in a bit higher than it does for the separate questions on education and employment. But even in these questions, such support remains a minority position. In nine national polls from 1991 to 1995, support ranged from 15 to 46 percent; in eight such polls from 1996 to 2009, it ranged from 5 to 46 percent.[25]

With regard to race-conscious government contracting policies, national polling has been sparse, but the available data suggest that affirmative action is no more popular in this context than in the areas of education or employment.[26] In three polls conducted in 1995, while *Adarand Constructors v. Pena* (1995) was drawing national attention to the issue, AP, NBC/WSJ, and PSRA/Newsweek reported 31 to 48 percent support for policies that require setting aside a certain percentage of government contracts for minority-owned firms or "that give minority-owned businesses a better chance than other businesses at winning contracts." So also with race-conscious student assignment plans in the public schools: The polling data are limited but nonetheless suggest that the policies facing judicial scrutiny have lacked broad public support.[27] In seven national polls from 1993 to 2009, 11 to 29 percent of respondents expressed support for the use of race-conscious criteria to assign children somewhere other than their neighborhood school.

Leading the Public

In addition to striking down policies that lack national democratic support, judges sometimes invalidate policies that are supported by popular majorities at the time but whose support is on a downward trajectory and subsequently dips below 50 percent. In these cases, the courts may be out in front of the public, but they are moving in the same direction. As David Barnum has put it, judges sometimes follow the trend if not the distribution of public opinion (1985, 659).

In *Podberesky v. Kirwan* (4th Cir. 1994), for example, a Fourth Circuit panel invalidated a blacks-only scholarship program at the University of Maryland. Perhaps surprisingly, the limited polling available at the time revealed significant support for such policies. In February 1990, GSS reported that 73 percent of respondents favored "[p]roviding special college scholarships for black children who maintain good grades," and the following year, LAT reported an identical percentage who approved "of allowing colleges and universities to reserve some scholarships for minority students." (In a separate question, 67 percent also approved of reserving some scholarships for white students.) In March 1995, however, just five months after *Podberesky* came down, NBC/WSJ reported just 19 percent support for "college scholarship programs available only to black or minority students." Given that this language directly tracked the actual policy at issue in the case, it seems likely that public support for such policies was on the wane at the time the Fourth Circuit decision came down. The other likely possibility is that the two poll results from 1990 and 1991 were anomalous, and that public support for race-exclusive scholarships was never particularly strong. Either way, it seems likely that there was no stable majority sentiment that was thwarted by the Fourth Circuit decision.

The same description holds for the two cases cited in chapter 2 in which judges invalidated state bans on carrying firearms in public.[28] During the five years prior to these holdings, NORC's National Gun Policy Survey asked on three occasions whether "public places, such as stores, movie theaters and restaurants, should allow or prohibit people from carrying concealed weapons on their premises"; 76 to 83 percent of respondents favored prohibition. During this same period, however, two national polls reported just 49 to 50 percent support for "a law requiring a nationwide ban on people carrying a concealed weapon." During the period of invalidation (2003–2012), three similar polls reported 42 to 48 percent support for a nationwide ban, and in January 2013, CBS/NYT reported support of just 32 percent. In short, these judicial holdings imposed constitutional limits on policies that may once have had national democratic support, but that appear to have lost that support more recently.

The best examples of this phenomenon are the landmark SSM holdings recounted in chapter 1. From 2003 to 2009, state high courts invalidated discriminatory marriage laws in California, Connecticut, Iowa, and Massachusetts, and when California voters reenacted such a law in 2008, Federal District Judge Vaughn Walker invalidated it in 2010.[29] Three years later, SCOTUS let this latter decision stand and, in a separate case, invalidated a key provision of the federal Defense of Marriage Act (DOMA).[30] In the four state court holdings, the judges invalidated discriminatory laws that had clear majority support at the time. In the five years preceding the 2003 decision in *Goodridge v. Department of Public Health* (Mass. 2003), seven national polls reported 51 to 64 percent support for limiting civil marriage to opposite-sex couples. During the period of state court invalidation, the pace of polling picked up considerably, and the vast majority of these polls continued to indicate democratic support for existing discriminatory marriage laws. In 74 national polls from 2003 to 2009, these laws were supported by a plurality of respondents seventy-one times (and by an absolute majority in sixty-seven of those cases). In 2010, when Judge Walker invalidated Proposition 8, seven of nine national polls continued to indicate plurality support for bans on SSM. But in the years since these invalidations of state marriage laws, the pattern has shifted. In 41 national polls from 2011 to 2013, the invalidated laws received plurality support only once. Thus, by the time SCOTUS held that the federal government must recognize lawful SSMs from the states that authorize them, the justices had public opinion on their side. In sixteen national polls conducted in 2013, support for DOMA did not exceed 44 percent. The aggregate ranges for all relevant polls are indicated in table 4.4.[31]

When the Vermont and New Jersey Supreme Courts ordered state officials to provide same-sex couples with the rights of marriage but not the name, the pattern of public support was similar. When the first of these rulings came down in 1999, with the Vermont court holding that the state's

TABLE 4.4 **Judicially invalidated policies that had public support at the time of invalidation, but have since lost that support**

Invalidated policy	Years of invalidation	National public support for invalidated policy . . .		
		For five years prior to invalidation	During years of invalidation	Subsequent to years of invalidation
Race-exclusive scholarship program in MD	1994	73% (2 polls)	Unknown	19% (1)
State bans on carrying firearms in IL, WI	2003–2012	49–83% (11)	42–48% (3)	32% (1)
Bans on SSM in CA, CT, IA, MA	2003–2010	51–64% (7)	40–70% (83)	36–47% (41)
Defense of Marriage Act (federal nonrecognition provision)	2013	34–57% (59)	34–44% (16)	Unknown
Failure to extend state law rights of marriage to same-sex couples in NJ, VT	1999–2006	Unknown	32–58% (53)	25–46% (37)

long-standing failure to provide legal recognition to same-sex couples violated state constitutional equality principles, the state justices invalidated a law that had the support of roughly half the country. By the time the New Jersey justices issued a similar decision in 2006, public support for the invalidated law was shakier. Since that time, such support has fallen well below the median.

Because the civil union concept was new, no national polls on the issue were conducted prior to the Vermont decision, but less than a year after the decision, Gallup reported that 54 percent of respondents opposed a "law that would allow homosexual couples to legally form civil unions, giving them some of the legal rights of married couples." In thirty such polls from 1999 to 2006, the range of respondents opposing such laws was 34 to 58 percent. Twenty-three additional polls during this period provided respondents with three options: full marriage equality, civil unions or domestic partnerships that provided the rights of marriage without the name, or no legal recognition for same-sex couples. In these polls, 32 to 45 percent indicated support for no legal recognition. In thirty-seven national polls conducted from 2007 to 2013—twelve asking directly about civil unions, plus twenty-five 3-option polls—the corresponding range was 25 to 46 percent, but the no-legal-recognition position exceeded 40 percent in only four of the thirty-seven instances.

In sum, when six state high courts issued rulings expanding the legal rights of same-sex couples, they were out in front of a national public that was moving in the same direction. By the time federal judges began following this path, they appeared to have national majority support. Prior to the initial judicial interventions in Vermont and Massachusetts, popular majorities supported state and federal bans on SSM and (by a narrower margin) state and federal refusals to grant same-sex couples the rights of marriage without the name. But in both cases, that support was decreasing at the time and has since dropped below 50 percent. Whether these facts legitimize the judicial decisions is a difficult question, but there is no evidence that the decisions prevented the fulfillment of a stable pattern of majoritarian preferences. Indeed, they may well have facilitated the fulfillment of an emerging such pattern.

Thwarting the Public

While many rights-protecting judicial decisions are best understood as following or leading the public will, other such decisions may be said to thwart that will. Of the thirty-three policies listed in tables 4.1 and 4.2, the judicial invalidation of seventeen of them might well fit this latter description. This count includes four policies for which I have found no directly relevant national polling data, but erring on the side of coding democratically enacted statutes as popular, I assume for the moment that each of these policies had national democratic support.

The countermajoritarian difficulty is presented in starkest form when judges invalidate a federal statute, but this remains an infrequent occurrence. Throughout most of its history, the Supreme Court has issued fewer than two such decisions per year.[32] On the issues of abortion, affirmative action, gay rights, and gun rights, only four federal statutes have been invalidated over the past twenty years. The Supreme Court struck down the federal nonrecognition provision of DOMA, the GFSZA, and the background check provisions of the Brady Bill, and a Federal Circuit panel invalidated a minority set-aside policy that was mandated by the National Defense Authorization Act of 1987.[33] The judges were following the public in the minority set-aside case and leading the public in the SSM cases (or indeed following the public by the time SCOTUS's decision came down). But in the two gun rights holdings, they may well have been thwarting the public. In the Brady Bill case, the evidence of public support for the invalidated policy seems clear. While the bill was pending in August 1993, a Time/CNN/Yankelovich poll reported 92 percent support for "requiring a five-day waiting period before anyone can buy a gun to allow time to check a buyer's background." After President Clinton signed the bill in November, Gallup reported that 79 to 87 percent of respondents supported "[t]he Brady Bill, which requires a five-day waiting period on the purchase of all guns in order to determine whether the prospective buyer has been convicted of a felony."[34] This support appeared to hold over time, as a Gallup/CNN/USAT poll reported 84 percent support in June 1997, just three days before SCOTUS issued its decision in *Printz*. In twenty-six national polls since then, 65 to 96 percent of respondents supported mandatory background checks. These data are summarized in the top line of table 4.5.

I have found no direct polling evidence regarding public support for the GFSZA, but this policy may have been broadly popular as well. In April 1993, a Harvard School of Public Health survey reported that 62 percent of respondents believed "that the widespread availability of guns and the resulting violence have . . . made children [they] know more concerned about their safety in school." And in June 1998, an American Association of University Women survey reported that 84 percent of female registered voters believed that the federal government should play a strong role in "helping to guarantee that schools are safe from violence, guns, and drugs." Erring on the side of coding democratically enacted statutes as popular, I include the GFSZA in table 4.5.[35]

Some state and local gun control laws that have been invalidated have also had broad public support. For example, when a Sixth Circuit panel held that a local ban on assault weapons was unconstitutionally vague, the invalidated law almost certainly had the support of national popular majorities.[36] In thirty-three polls from 1993 to 1997, legislative bans on "assault weapons," "semiautomatic assault guns," "semiautomatic military-style rifles," or the like received majority support in all cases but one. In fifty-eight such polls from 1999 to 2013, the legislative bans received majority support fifty times. Likewise, when the North Carolina Supreme Court held that the state could not constitutionally deny convicted felons the right to bear arms, the judges appear to have acted against the national democratic will.[37] The data are more limited here, but three polls from 2008 to 2012 reveal 88 to 92 percent support for "[p]reventing certain people, such as convicted felons or people with mental health problems, from owning guns." Polling has been even more

TABLE 4.5 **Judicially invalidated policies that had (or may have had) public support at the time of invalidation and have since maintained that support**

Invalidated policy	Years of invalidation	National public support for the invalidated policy . . .		
		For five years prior to invalidation	During years of invalidation	Subsequent to years of invalidation
Brady Bill's temporary background check provisions	1997	79–92% (7 polls)	84% (1)	65–96% (26)
GFSZA	1995	Unknown	Unknown	Unknown
Local ban on assault weapons in OH	1998	48–83% (33)	Unknown	43–82% (58)
Ban on gun possession by convicted felons in NC	2009	88% (1)	Unknown	91–92% (2)
Bans on gun shows or firing ranges in CA, IL	1997–2011	Unknown	51% (1)	Unknown
Prohibition on doctors discussing gun safety with patients in FL	2012	Unknown	Unknown	Unknown
Informed consent/waiting period requirements in . . .	DE, MT (1999–2003)	74–79% (3)	78% (1)	66–71% (4)
	SD, TN (2000–2011)	Unknown	Unknown	Unknown
	NC, OK (2010–2011)	Unknown	50% (1)	Unknown
Requirement that abortions be performed by physicians in MT	1999	Unknown	Unknown	Unknown
Local regulation of limited-service pregnancy centers in NY	2011	Unknown	Unknown	Unknown
Parental involvement requirements in AK, AZ, CA, CO, FL, ID, LA, MA, MT, NJ, SD	1995–2007	57–80% (15)	69–80% (15)	71–76% (3)
Criminal bans on partial-birth abortions in AR, AZ, FL, IA, IL, KY, LA, MI, MO, NE, NJ, OH, RI, VA, WI	1997–2007	57–71% (2)	46–77% (32)	64% (1)
Criminal bans on post-20-week abortions in AZ, GA	2012–2013	71% (1)	48–66% (3)	Unknown
Restrictions on public funding of abortion in AK, AZ, MN, NM, WV	1993–2002	42–73% (13)	44–55% (5)	50–72% (8)
Local clinic defense laws in AZ, CA, OH, PA	1995–2009	Unknown	83% (1)	Unknown
Local domestic partnership ordinances in FL, GA, MA, MI, MN, PA, VA	1995–2008	Unknown	53–73% (7)	68–77% (2)
Prohibitions of antigay violence or harassment in MN, PA	1998–2001	Unknown	56–76% (6)	67–74% (4)
Anti–affirmative action initiative in MI, MO	2009–2012	40–82% (2)	55–64% (3)	80% (1)

limited with regard to support for local bans on gun shows or firing ranges of the sort struck down in Santa Clara, California, and Chicago, Illinois, but PSRA/Newsweek reported in August 1999 that 51 percent of respondents favored "banning gun shows where people often buy and sell guns without much supervision or regulation."[38] No polls have assessed national support for the 2011 Florida statute prohibiting doctors from discussing firearms safety with their patients, which was enjoined on free speech grounds in 2012, but in the absence of evidence to the contrary, I code this law as reflecting the national popular will as well.[39]

In the abortion context, popular majorities have long and consistently maintained that abortion should be legal but restricted in a variety of ways (Luks and Salamone 2008, 101). As a result, most of the state statutory regulations that have been challenged in court appear to have broad public support. Most such regulations have survived these challenges, but when courts have intervened, they have likely been doing so against the will of national democratic majorities. For example, judges in Delaware and Montana have enjoined informed consent statutes that required patients to visit an abortion provider, receive certain state-mandated information, and then wait an additional twenty-four hours before having the abortion; in Tennessee and South Dakota, judges have enjoined similar laws that required waits of forty-eight and seventy-two hours, respectively.[40] And in North Carolina and Oklahoma, judges have enjoined statutes requiring that women be shown an ultrasound image of the fetus before undergoing an abortion.[41] Polling has been limited, but the available data indicate democratic support for at least some of these provisions. The Delaware and Montana statutes almost certainly had such support. In eight national polls regarding mandatory twenty-four-hour waiting periods from 1994 to 2011, 66 to 79 percent of respondents supported such requirements. (Four additional polls reported 86 to 88 percent support for laws requiring providers to inform patients about certain risks of and/or alternatives to abortion before performing the procedure.) Support for the ultrasound requirements in North Carolina and Oklahoma appears significantly lower but still, perhaps, a bare majority of the public. In the one relevant poll that I have identified, Gallup reported in July 2011 that 50 percent of respondents favored "a law requiring women seeking an abortion to be shown an ultrasound image of her fetus at least 24 hours before the procedure," with just 46 percent opposed. Support for the Tennessee and South Dakota laws is unknown, as I have found no polling on two- or three-day waiting periods. The same goes for Montana's requirement that abortions be performed by doctors, invalidated by the state high court in 1999, and—with the political dynamics running in the opposite direction—for the local ordinance regulating so-called limited-service pregnancy centers that was enjoined in 2011.[42]

In a similar pattern, most state laws requiring some form of parental involvement before a minor can have an abortion have been upheld, but when the courts have struck down such laws, they may well have acted against the wishes of national majorities. State and federal judges have invalidated eleven such laws for lacking maternal health exceptions, lacking adequate "judicial bypass" provisions, or violating state constitutional privacy rights, with all eleven of these decisions coming between 1995 and 2007.[43] The statutory details vary from state to state, but parental involvement requirements in general appear to have broad and stable public support. During the five years preceding the judicial invalidations, fifteen national polls reported 57 to 80 percent support for such laws. During and after the period of invalidation, eighteen additional polls reported 69 to 80 percent support. These levels might drop if respondents were told that the hypothetical laws lacked maternal health exceptions and/or judicial bypass provisions, but it seems clear that at least some of these judicial decisions have invalidated policies that have broad public support.

Likewise with the fifteen state statutory bans on partial-birth abortion that were enjoined by federal courts, beginning in 1997.[44] This line of decisions persisted only until 2007—when SCOTUS reversed course in *Gonzales v. Carhart* (*Carhart II*) (2007)—but while they lasted, these holdings clearly had the effect of thwarting the democratic will. In two national polls preceding the judicial invalidations, Gallup reported 57 to 71 percent support for "a law which would make illegal the use of an abortion procedure conducted in the last three months of pregnancy known as 'partial birth abortions,' except in cases necessary to save the life of the mother." The pace of polling picked up considerably during the period of invalidation, and most such polls continued to indicate majority support for these legislative bans. In thirty-two national polls from 1997 to 2007, support fell below 50 percent just three times and never below 46 percent. In one more recent poll, Gallup reported in July 2011 that support stood at 64 percent.

In a new but related set of legal disputes that emerged during President Obama's first term, state and federal courts invalidated two state statutory bans on all abortions after twenty weeks' gestation.[45] Prompted by the US House of Representatives' approval of similar legislation, two national polls asked directly about such restrictions in 2013. ABC/WaPo reported that 66 percent of respondents indicated that abortion should be banned after twenty weeks, banned after fewer weeks, or banned altogether. In response to a question with significantly different wording, United Technologies/National Journal reported just 48 percent support, though this figure still represented a plurality of respondents. In table 4.5, I also include results from two polls conducted by Gallup in 2011 and 2012, in which 64 to 71 percent of respondents indicated that "abortion should generally be . . . illegal during . . . the second three months of pregnancy."

Support for bans on public funding of abortion has been somewhat lower, but has usually exceeded 50 percent as well. In the late 1970s and early 1980s, abortion rights advocates failed to persuade the federal courts to invalidate such restrictions on federal constitutional grounds, but from 1993 to 2002, they persuaded the high courts of Alaska, Arizona, Minnesota, New Mexico, and West Virginia to do so on state constitutional grounds.[46] During the five years leading up to these judicial invalidations, thirteen national polls reported 42 to 73 percent support for banning public funding of abortion. These levels remained almost identical during and after the period of invalidation, with thirteen national polls reporting 44 to 72 percent support. Taken together, twenty-three of these twenty-six polls reported plurality support for this position.

Likely also popular, based on the limited available polling data, were the local clinic defense laws invalidated on First Amendment grounds from 1995 to 2009.[47] I have found only one national poll asking directly about such policies, with Gallup reporting 83 percent support (in June 2000) for state laws "requir[ing] protestors at abortion clinics to stay a specified distance away from the facility at which they are demonstrating." Several additional polls have asked questions that are indirectly relevant to the issue, and they appear to confirm this high level of support.[48]

In the gay rights context, conservative rights advocates have regularly called on courts to invalidate recently enacted policies that they had been unable to block in the legislative arena. Most such efforts have been unsuccessful, but when judges have heeded these calls, they have generally done so in the face of majoritarian opposition. From 1995 to 2008, state appellate courts invalidated local domestic partnership policies in Florida, Georgia, Massachusetts, Michigan, Minnesota, Pennsylvania, and Virginia.[49] As I note above—in the context of a polar opposite set of judicial holdings *mandating* the provision of domestic partnership benefits for state employees—a consistent and growing national majority supports such benefits policies. As such, the judicial decisions invalidating or curtailing these policies have clearly been countermajoritarian. During and after the period of invalidation, nine national polls have reported 53 to 77 percent support for "providing health insurance coverage to gay partners" or the like.[50]

Likewise, when the Minnesota Supreme Court struck down a provision of its state's hate crimes law in 1998, and when a Third Circuit panel invalidated a local school district's prohibition on antigay bullying in 2001, public support was on the side of the invalidated policies rather than the judges.[51] Less than a year after the Minnesota decision came down, NBC/WSJ reported that 61 percent of respondents thought it was "a good idea . . . to expand hate crime laws to include crimes committed on the basis of the victim's sexual orientation," and CNN/Time reported that 76 percent of respondents favored a federal law that would mandate "increased penalties . . . for people who commit crimes against homosexuals out of prejudice against them." All told, nine national polls have reported 56 to 76 percent support for such policies, and one additional poll has reported 73 percent support for "passing a law to prohibit bullying and harassment against minority groups in schools, including gay, lesbian, bisexual, and transgender students or the children of gay, lesbian or transgender parents."

Finally, when the Missouri courts blocked a proposed anti–affirmative action initiative in 2009 and when the Sixth Circuit invalidated Michigan's Proposal 2 three years later, the judges almost certainly acted against the wishes of national majorities.[52] The Michigan initiative had been enacted by 57.9 percent of the state's voters, and similar initiatives in six other states each received at least 49.2 percent of the vote; all but one were enacted, with Colorado's 2008 measure falling just short. National polling on affirmative action has been limited in recent years, but a June 2009 Quinnipiac poll asked expressly whether "affirmative action programs that give preferences to blacks and other minorities in hiring, promotions and college admissions should be continued, or . . . abolished"; 55 percent of respondents favored abolition. In response to two additional questions in the same poll, 61 percent of respondents indicated opposition to "affirmative action programs that give preferences to blacks in hiring, promotions, and college admissions [in order to increase diversity]," and 64 percent opposed such preferences for Hispanics. More recently, Gallup reported in April 2013 that 80 percent of respondents would "vote against . . . a law which would allow your state to give preferences in job hiring and school admission on the basis of race."

Broad or Narrow, Not Just Up or Down

In sum, I have identified just seventeen judicially invalidated policies—on the subjects of abortion, affirmative action, gay rights, and gun rights—that may well have been popular before, during, and after their invalidation. But this list of seventeen policies overstates the quantum of democratically illegitimate judging, as the scope of the invalidating decisions was often quite limited in space or time. With respect to most of these policies, courts have invalidated them in some state or local jurisdictions but have left lawmakers in the rest of the country free to continue pursuing them. In some cases, state courts have adopted constitutional standards that are tighter than their federal counterparts; in others, state or federal courts have invalidated a particular policy in its most extreme form, while leaving milder versions of that policy in place elsewhere. Likewise, courts have sometimes invalidated a particular set of policies for a time but later reconsidered those decisions, allowing elected lawmakers to enact the desired policies once again. As such, in evaluating exercises of judicial review, we need to attend not just to the fate of the particular statute at issue but also to the breadth of the holding laying that statute to rest.

In the abortion context, for example, the Supreme Court's holding in *Stenberg v. Carhart* appeared to prevent state legislatures nationwide from enacting or enforcing statutory bans on partial-birth abortion. But the decision was issued by a 5–4 vote, and one member of the five-justice majority wrote separately to indicate that if the statute had been more carefully drafted, "the question presented would be quite different than the one we face today." Indeed, Justice Sandra Day O'Connor continued, "a ban on partial-birth abortion that only proscribed the D&X method of abortion and that included an exception to preserve the life and health of the mother would be constitutional."[53] O'Connor cited three existing state bans that in her view passed constitutional muster, and since her vote was necessary to the Court's majority, it seems clear that the constitutional holding left continued room for state legislatures to act on the issue. Even if that signal were not clear in 2000, moreover, it became clear when SCOTUS upheld a federal ban on partial-birth abortion seven years later. The earlier holdings had been countermajoritarian, but *Gonzales v. Carhart* (2007) brought the courts back in line with the democratic will. While thirteen state bans continue to be enjoined under *Carhart I* and its progeny, the federal ban is in effect nationwide.[54]

In a somewhat different story, Montana and Tennessee are precluded (by state court decisions) from imposing mandatory waiting periods on women seeking abortions, but the other forty-eight states remain free to impose such requirements. The only such laws to be struck down in federal court—not counting decisions that were subsequently reversed— were from Delaware (where the law lacked a maternal health exception) and South Dakota (where its seventy-two-hour waiting period was the longest in the country). The latter decision remains pending on appeal, as does a 2011 decision enjoining North Carolina's ultrasound law. Even if both of these decisions ultimately survive, state legislatures will remain free to impose one-day waiting periods and a range of informed consent requirements. Given this doctrinal landscape, it is no surprise that thirty-five states have mandatory counseling requirements on the books and that twenty-six of them link these requirements to a specified waiting period.[55]

With respect to parental involvement requirements, a handful of state courts have invalidated such laws, but federal courts have done so only where the laws were unusually strict.[56] As a result, most states remain free to enact such laws in various forms, and thirty-nine are currently in effect.[57] The same goes for state statutory requirements that abortions be performed by physicians (as opposed to physicians' assistants or other health-care workers). The Montana Supreme Court invalidated such a law on state constitutional grounds in 1999, but SCOTUS had already rejected a federal constitutional challenge to the law, so the other forty-nine states remain free to enact similar requirements.[58] Thirty-nine of them have done so.[59] A similar story holds for statutory restrictions on public funding of abortion. In chapter 1, I cite five cases in which state high courts invalidated such restrictions on state constitutional grounds, but these courts did so only after SCOTUS had declined to do so on federal constitutional grounds. As such, the remaining states are free to maintain such restrictions, and thirty-three of them currently do so.[60] Likewise, the fact that federal appellate courts invalidated four local ordinances limiting antiabortion protests is surely outweighed by the fact that those same courts uniformly upheld the federal FACE Act.

In the gay rights context, the Minnesota Supreme Court struck down the state's statutory prohibition on antigay hate crimes, but the federal government and thirty states currently maintain similar such laws, and the courts have upheld these laws when challenged.[61] The same goes for anti-bullying laws that explicitly protect gay students. When a Third Circuit panel invalidated such a policy in 2001, it precluded a single school district from enforcing it, but most such districts remain free to do so; indeed, six-teen states currently maintain such policies statewide.[62] State courts have also invalidated a number of local domestic partnership laws, but in most of the country, local governments remain free to enact such policies. If and when Congress and the White House decide to extend domestic part-nership benefits to federal employees, no legal barrier stands in their way.

Courts have occasionally invalidated gun control policies that have popular support, but again, the scope of these invalidations has been quite limited. The North Carolina Supreme Court held that convicted felons retain their state constitutional right to bear arms, but as I note in chap-ter 2, the federal courts have repeatedly rejected constitutional challenges to the federal felon-in-possession ban. Likewise, the Wisconsin Supreme Court held that the state's concealed weapons ban could not constitution-ally be applied to a grocery store owner who kept a handgun on the prem-ises for self-defense. But the court left this statute on the books even in Wisconsin—indicating that it was constitutionally enforceable in some contexts—and the decision had no effect on similar concealed weapons bans elsewhere in the country. The Seventh Circuit invalidated Illinois's statutory ban on carrying guns in public, but given the unusually sweeping nature of that ban, state governments will likely remain free to impose restrictions on concealed carrying even if this holding survives on appeal.[63]

The only gun control policies that were constitutionally precluded nationwide were the GFSZA and the Brady Bill's provision requiring local law enforcement officers to conduct background checks on would-be firearms purchasers. Even here, however, judges left other policymakers with substantial room to maneuver. In the latter case, SCOTUS invali-dated a temporary provision that was set to soon expire, while leaving in place the federal system of instant background checks that superseded it. In the former case, SCOTUS invalidated the federal ban on gun posses-sion in schools because the regulated activity lacked any substantial con-nection to interstate commerce; when Congress reenacted the law with a provision indicating that it applied only to guns that had traveled in interstate commerce, the federal courts upheld it.[64]

In sum, state and federal judges have invalidated seventeen demo-cratically enacted policies that may well have been supported by popular majorities. But in six of these cases, the policies were invalidated at the state or local level while similar policies were upheld at the federal level.[65] With the federal policies in effect nationwide, the policy significance of the state and local laws is significantly diminished. In six additional cases, state or local policies have been invalidated in some jurisdictions but upheld in others. This fact does not make the invalidating decisions any less countermajoritarian, but it does narrow their significance. Judges have prevented legislators in some cities and states from expanding domestic partnership benefits; from imposing waiting periods, parental involvement mandates, or physician-only requirements on abortion; from regulating limited-service pregnancy centers; and from banning affirmative action, but legislators in most cities and states remain free to do these things. In two other cases, judges have invalidated policies on which we have virtually no public opinion data and that have not been widely copied by other lawmakers. In these cases—involving local bans on gun shows or firing ranges and a state ban on doctors discussing gun safety with their patients—there is no evidence that the judges thwarted any significant national public will, though it is possible that the individual judicial decisions were countermajoritarian.

That leaves just three policies whose judicial invalidation may well have thwarted the national democratic will, but even here, the judges' word was hardly the final story. State and federal courts have invalidated two statutory bans on abortion after twenty weeks' gestation, but litigation on the issue remains pending, and state and federal legislators continue their efforts to enact similar laws. The Supreme Court invalidated the GFSZA and a provision of the Brady Bill, but as I have already noted, the practical scope of these holdings was limited.

*   *   *

The narrow reach of most exercises of judicial review—together with the fact that the courts' broader assertions of power are sometimes successfully resisted—has led some scholars to conclude that courts are a relatively insignificant feature of the American policy and political landscape. That conclusion is unsupported by the evidence, in my view, and I challenge it in chapter 5. But the burden of this chapter has been simply to show that exercises of judicial review often have broad public support.

One reason for this broad support is that, across all four issues that I have examined, judges have regularly refused to give rights advocates everything they wanted. Abortion rights advocates want abortion on demand, LGBT rights advocates want full marriage equality, color-blind rights advocates want a strict ban on race-conscious affirmative action policies, and gun rights advocates want an unfettered right to carry any kind of firearm anywhere they want. None of these demands have been supported by national democratic majorities, with the exception of full marriage equality from 2011 to the present. But with only occasional exceptions, none of these things were ordered by courts either. On the whole, what courts have actually ordered has been respect for a more modest set of rights claims. Abortion can be restricted in a variety of ways, but may not simply be outlawed. Same-sex couples should have some legal rights, but not necessarily full equality. Racial quotas are unconstitutional, but more flexible race-conscious policies are allowed. And gun rights are protected, but legislatures remain free to impose commonsense restrictions on who can carry them, what kinds of guns they can carry, and where they can bring them. These more modest rights claims all have broad public support.

CHAPTER FIVE

Are Judges Sideshows?

Judges regularly describe themselves as neutral legal umpires but sometimes describe their colleagues as unaccountable tyrants. Partisan officials echo both stories, depending on whether they are describing allied or opposing judges. Scholars often tell a third story, in which judges are neither to be praised nor feared. Indeed, on this scholarly account, much of the political conflict over judicial decisions is a waste of time. Because the vast majority of such decisions are consistent with the public will, they ordinarily do not make much difference. We have no reason to fear that judges are arbitrarily imposing their own preferences on the country, but neither should we expect them to heroically defend constitutional principles against hostile democratic majorities. The lesson of a wide range of scholarly literature on courts in the United States (and elsewhere) is that judges will rarely try to do either of these things, and that when they do try, they will rarely succeed.

Much of this literature can be traced to an influential 1957 article by Robert Dahl, which contended that the Supreme Court almost never challenges policies supported by the national governing coalition. After all, the justices themselves are usually members of that coalition and thus share its key priorities. Dahl emphasized that the Court had only rarely invalidated federal statutes and that when it had done so, the statutes themselves were usually either outdated or trivial; in other words, the invalidated laws almost never reflected important priorities of the then-governing coalition. Building on Dahl's seminal account, Howard Gillman (2002, 2006), Mark Graber (1993), Michael Klarman (2004), Terri Peretti (1999), and Keith Whittington (2007) have argued that most exercises of judicial review—even those that appear countermajoritarian at first glance—are consistent with the preferences of the governing coalition, or at least the preferences of an important faction within that coalition.

In a related story, Barry Friedman (2009) and Jeffrey Rosen (2006) have argued that most high Court decisions—across the full range of issues and the full scope of the Court's history—are consistent with national public opinion.

As a corollary, a number of leading scholars have argued that on the rare occasions when judicial decisions do depart from the public will, they tend to be ineffective or counterproductive. Perhaps most notably, Gerald Rosenberg has long argued that rights-protecting judicial decisions tend to be simply ignored. In a widely cited 1991 book, Rosenberg dubbed the Supreme Court a "hollow hope," insisting that even its most celebrated decisions have been inconsequential. Emphasizing that judges are usually unwilling and almost always unable to impose unpopular rights on the nation at large, Rosenberg pointed to *Brown v. Board of Education* (1954) as the prime example of a rights-protecting decision that was effectively ignored by other policymakers. Rosenberg acknowledged that it was possible for courts to produce significant social change, particularly when there was "ample legal precedent" for such change, when such change had significant support among both lawmakers and the public, and when these supporters had an available set of market mechanisms or other incentives for facilitating compliance with the courts' decisions (1991, 30–36). He granted that when these conditions are present, rights-protecting decisions *might* prove consequential, but he insisted that in actual practice, they rarely do so.

In a subsequent edition of the book, Rosenberg clarified that such rights-protecting decisions tend to be inconsequential *at best*; indeed, in many cases, they actually prove counterproductive. Here, he turned his attention from *Brown* to the modern same-sex marriage (SSM) decisions, extensively documenting the conservative countermobilization that followed the LGBT rights movement's state high court victories in Hawaii, Vermont, and Massachusetts (2008, 339–419). While the Court's mandate in *Brown* had simply been ignored, having no appreciable effect on the actual progress of school desegregation, the state courts' decisions in *Baehr v. Lewin* (Haw. 1993), *Baker v. Vermont* (Vt. 1999), and *Goodridge v. Department of Public Health* (Mass. 2003) actually made things worse, provoking a concerted political backlash that produced regressive policy changes throughout the country.

This backlash argument has been developed most fully by Michael Klarman, who has long argued that Rosenberg underplayed the significance of *Brown*. On Klarman's account, the decision was far from inconsequential, but its impact was equally far from what the judges (and the

NAACP litigators) intended. Indeed, the chief impact of the landmark decision was to exacerbate the racist rhetoric and segregationist policies that characterized southern politics at the time. In this version of the story, *Brown* sparked massive resistance, polarizing southern racial politics and undermining the efforts of white moderates. As a result, when southern blacks turned to direct action protest in the early 1960s, they were met with increasing violence. Because it was northern revulsion at Bull Connor's fire hoses and police dogs that led to the 1964 Civil Rights Act, Klarman sometimes suggests that the *Brown* litigation ultimately produced progress on civil rights (2004, 385, 441–42; see also 1994). At other times, however, he emphasizes that racial liberalism was gradually but steadily advancing before the Court clumsily intervened, sparking a resurgence of white supremacy and thus undermining the very cause the justices were hoping to promote (2004, 442, 464–65).

Like Rosenberg, Klarman has applied this backlash narrative to the contemporary SSM context as well, insisting that the Massachusetts high court's landmark 2003 decision met a fate similar to that which followed virtually every other effort by judges to defend a rights claim that lacked popular support: "The most significant short-term consequence of *Goodridge*, as with *Brown*, may have been the political backlash that it inspired. By outpacing public opinion on issues of social reform, such rulings mobilize opponents, undercut moderates, and retard the cause they purport to advance" (2005, 482).[1]

As with the umpire and tyrant narratives, this narrative of judges as sideshows captures part of the story. It is true, as I show in chapter 4, that even the most controversial judicial decisions often have substantial public support. It is likewise true that judicial decisions sometimes provoke substantial political resistance. But it does not follow from either of these facts that judicial decisions are inconsequential or counterproductive. To the contrary, both popular and unpopular judicial decisions regularly have significant effects on policy, in both intended and unintended directions.

Even if judges *never* acted against the wishes of popular majorities—a claim that is not supported by the evidence in chapter 4—their decisions might still have significant independent effects on policy outcomes. Put another way, there are a variety of conditions under which majoritarian judicial decisions may alter the policy status quo. On issues characterized by sectional polarization, federal courts will sometimes enforce national sentiment against local outliers (Klarman 1996). On issues characterized by legislative unresponsiveness, state and federal courts will sometimes invalidate statutes that contemporary democratic majorities do not support (Klarman 1997). And on issues characterized by multiple democratically legitimate alternatives, court decisions will sometimes change the ultimate outcome by reversing the relevant veto points (Silverstein 2009, 145).

When judges do act against the wishes of popular majorities, further avenues of judicial influence are opened. Even when such decisions provoke substantial political resistance, they often launch or redirect policy trajectories in consequential ways. Under some conditions, judges are able to withstand the resistance and maintain rights-protecting doctrines that lack popular support. Under other conditions, rights-protecting decisions are successfully curtailed at the margins but continue to impose meaningful constraints on policies emerging from other institutions. And even when rights-protecting decisions are fully reversed, they sometimes foster the development of movements and the articulation of rights claims in ways that vindicate the original decision over time (McCann 1994).

This complex array of causal paths makes it difficult to evaluate the policy impact of particular judicial decisions or of judicial institutions in general. Rosenberg and Klarman are surely correct that rights-protecting judicial decisions are rarely the final word; indeed, this finding has been endorsed by a wide range of research. Robert Post and Reva Siegel have questioned the excessive scholarly focus on the backlash phenomenon, but they too have emphasized that most controversial judicial decisions are not final in any meaningful sense. In the abortion context, Post and Siegel note that while *Roe v. Wade* (1973) is often criticized for foreclosing democratic deliberation on the issue, it in fact "seem[s] to have increased political engagement rather than diminished it" (2007, 398). Susan Burgess (1992) and Neal Devins (1996) have likewise documented repeated efforts by Congress to respond to the Court's abortion rights decisions and to influence the direction of future such decisions. In a broader analysis of congressional responses to Supreme Court invalidations of federal statutes, Mitch Pickerill has demonstrated that roughly half of such decisions issued from 1954 to 1997 were followed by "congressional attempts to save the underlying statutory policy" (2004, 42; see also Blackstone 2013). As Gordon Silverstein notes, "judicial rulings are [often] only the start of a complex iterated game, a game of leap-frog in which one decision serves as the jumping-off point for the next. These are games in which a judicial decision responds to legislative choices, and the next round of legislative choices is built on that legal ruling, leading to yet another round of legal rulings and legislative actions" (2009, 2; see also 128–51). Jeb Barnes and Mark C. Miller put it this way: "[N]o branch of government has the final say on the meaning of federal statutes or the U.S. Constitution. Instead, policymaking is best understood as an ongoing, interbranch dialogue" (2004, 11; see also Shapiro 1964).

Writing from a somewhat different tradition, Michael McCann has drawn on his long-running examination of legal mobilization by left-liberal political movements to point out that rather than settling political conflicts, Supreme Court rulings more "often serve to encourage or generate further litigation on public issues." On McCann's account, the high Court often serves as a catalyst, shaping the legal agendas, opportunities, and resources of political movements with its key decisions: "When the Court acts on a particular disputed issue, it can at once elevate the salience of that issue in the public agenda, privilege some parties who have perceived interests in the issue, create new opportunities for such parties to mobilize around causes, and provide symbolic resources for those mobilization efforts in various venues" (1999, 71). Writing from a still different tradition, Charles H. Franklin and Liane C. Kosaki have noted that "[w]hen the Court rules on politically controversial cases, it may establish the law of the land, but it does not put an end to debate. It neither converts the opposition nor ends the controversy. A satisfactory theory of Supreme Court impact must recognize that Court decisions do not necessarily bring about agreement and may instead sow the seeds of dissension" (1989, 753–54; but see Hanley, Salamone, and Wright 2012).

In sum, rights-protecting judicial decisions are part and parcel of broader, ongoing policy debates and political conflicts. As such, any understanding of their ultimate significance must grapple with the range of responses that they provoke on the part of other policymakers. The scholarly tradition of "judicial impact" research has emphasized the on-the-ground significance of rights-protecting judicial decisions: Did *Roe* lead rates of legal abortion to go up? Did *Goodridge* lead more same-sex couples to gain access to health insurance? Did *Hopwood v. University of Texas* (5th Cir. 1996) and *Gratz v. Bollinger* (2003) lead to fewer African Americans attending selective universities? Did *District of Columbia v. Heller* (2008) and *McDonald v. Chicago* (2010) lead gun violence in Washington, DC, and Chicago to increase, decrease, or stay the same? Answering such questions requires careful data gathering and analysis, but it also requires attending to the varying paths of policy contestation that intervene between the judicial decisions in question and their long-term policy impacts.

Drawing on the universe of rights-protecting judicial decisions detailed in part 1 of the book, this chapter describes four responses to such decisions that have recurred with some regularity: resistance, compliance, compromise, and innovation. In actual practice, the lines between these categories tend to blur, but the categories represent ideal types that may help illuminate the complex set of real-world reactions to controversial judicial decisions. Policymakers sometimes respond to such decisions by trying to minimize their influence or prevent them from taking effect altogether. At other times, they fully comply with such decisions, either because they agree with them or because they conclude that resistance would be futile. At still other times, policymakers meet the judges half way, trying to preserve some parts of an invalidated policy, while accepting the courts' preclusion of other parts. And finally, they sometimes respond to judicial disruptions of the policy status quo by crafting novel policies that serve some of their initial goals while also pushing the policy conversation in new and unanticipated directions. Taken together, the lesson of these four sets of reactions to controversial judicial decisions is that courts are inextricably entwined with the rest of the policy process. At least on the issues of abortion, affirmative action, gay rights, and gun rights, policy outcomes at any given point are likely to be the result of a long-running set of political conflicts taking place across multiple institutions.

Resistance

As I note above, Rosenberg has long emphasized that judicial institutions generally lack the capacity to enforce compliance with their holdings. In his seminal analysis of the implementation of *Brown*, he noted that for ten years following the landmark 1954 decision, "virtually *nothing happened*"; that is, very few African American children in the South actually started attending integrated schools (2008, 52, emphasis in original). This sort of noncompliance is often taken as evidence that controversial judicial decisions are inconsequential, but this reading tends to draw our attention away from the profound policy and political consequences, even if unintended, that sometimes result from unpopular or polarizing judicial decisions. As Klarman has argued at some length, what followed *Brown* was not "nothing," but rather an escalating pattern of active resistance (2004, 344–442). On Klarman's account, far from being irrelevant to subsequent events, the decision was counterproductive, at least in the short term.

Quite a number of rights-protecting judicial decisions in the areas of abortion, affirmative action, gay rights, and gun rights have provoked such a political backlash. This phenomenon has been most widely noted in the LGBT rights context, where rights advocates have won a steady stream of remarkable courtroom victories over the past twenty years. Most notably, a number of state and then federal judges invalidated bans on criminal sodomy and expanded the legal rights of same-sex couples. The sodomy decisions were met with broad compliance, as I detail below, but some of the marriage holdings provoked widespread resistance.

Students of both judicial institutions and LGBT rights have emphasized that the marriage equality movement's initial legal victories were regularly followed by legislative backlash (D'Emilio 2007; Klarman 2005; Mucciaroni 2008; Rimmerman 2002; Rosenberg 2008). The Hawaii Supreme Court's 1993 decision in *Baehr* sparked immediate and widespread legislative efforts to constrain or reverse its effect. The Utah legislature was the first to act, clarifying its own rules for marriage eligibility just months after the decision came down and prohibiting the recognition of out-of-state SSMs two years later. As a number of states considered similar measures, Congress enacted the Defense of Marriage Act (DOMA) in 1996, declaring that the federal government would not recognize SSMs and that each state was free to refuse such recognition as well. When the Alaska courts entered the fray, the Alaska legislature responded first by enacting a statutory prohibition on SSM and then by scheduling a citizens' referendum on whether to place the ban in the state constitution. Hawaii's legislators likewise proposed a state constitutional amendment that would authorize the legislature to limit marriage to opposite-sex couples, and in November 1998, the voters enacted these amendments in both states.

By the time this nationwide legislative reaction to the judicial decisions had run its course, forty-four state legislatures and thirty-two state electorates had voted to ban SSM, some of them more than once.[2] The policy result, as of October 2013, was thirty-five states with legal bans on SSM.[3] Twenty-nine of those thirty-five have enshrined the bans in their state constitutions, and nineteen of those twenty-nine constitutional provisions include language that appears to ban not just SSMs but also civil unions, domestic partnerships, and any other form of legal recognition for same-sex couples.[4] As I have noted elsewhere, some states moved in the opposite direction during this same period, with elected lawmakers voting to expand the legal rights of same-sex couples, but it is clear that the courtroom victories of SSM advocates sparked substantial legislative resistance nationwide (Keck 2009).

In addition to reversing the relevant policies directly, SSM opponents also responded to their courtroom defeats by trying to elect conservative legislators, executives, and judges who would then be in a position to restrict the further expansion of SSM. After *Baker v. Vermont* led the Vermont legislature to enact the nation's first civil union law in April 2000, SSM opponents mobilized their supporters in the statewide elections that fall. As William Eskridge has noted, those elections were "conducted in significant part as a referendum on civil unions, with [Republican gubernatorial nominee Ruth] Dwyer vigorously assailing [Democratic governor Howard Dean] and his party for their support of the new institution" (2002, 81). Taking the primary and general election results together, sixteen incumbent legislators who supported the civil union bill were voted out of office (Pinello 2006, 33; Robinson 2001). These results were not enough to reverse the policy—Democratic supporters of the Civil Union Act maintained control of the state senate and the governor's mansion—but they surely signaled a note of caution to legislators elsewhere who were considering the Vermont law as a model.

Likewise, a number of scholars have emphasized that the largest wave of anti-SSM ballot initiatives (in the wake of the 2003 *Goodridge* decision) may have had broader electoral consequences. In particular, Klarman and Rosenberg each argue that the presence of such amendments on eleven state ballots in November 2004 helped draw religious conservatives to the polls and thereby contributed to President George W. Bush's reelection and to the GOP's pickup of four additional seats in the US Senate. Since President Bush and the Republican Senate subsequently named John Roberts and Samuel Alito to the Supreme Court, Klarman suggests that SSM litigators may bear responsibility for entrenching a conservative judicial majority as well (2005, 468; see also Rosenberg 2008, 369–82). The empirical claim that the Republican Party's 2004 electoral victories are attributable to the presence of anti-SSM initiatives on the ballots of battleground states is the subject of significant dispute among political scientists, but Klarman and Rosenberg make a strong case that national Republican operatives intentionally encouraged the placement of these measures on the ballot in key states, and this effort may have contributed to President Bush's victories in Ohio and Iowa and to GOP Senate victories in Kentucky, Oklahoma, and South Dakota.[5]

A few years later, when the Iowa legislature declined to support a state constitutional amendment to reverse the state high court's holding in *Varnum v. Brien* (Iowa 2009), SSM opponents launched an effort to remove the justices responsible for the holding. Three of those justices were subject to retention elections in November 2010, and a heated campaign financed largely by the National Organization for Marriage, the American Family Association, and other anti-SSM organizations persuaded the voters to unseat all three of them (Sulzberger 2010).

Judicial decisions protecting abortion rights have also provoked considerable resistance by both popular movements and elected policymakers. Where the decisions were issued by state courts on state constitutional grounds, abortion rights opponents have sometimes sought to reverse the courts via state constitutional amendment, just as gay rights opponents have done in the SSM context. Consider, for example, the long-running legal and political conflict regarding parental involvement requirements for minors seeking abortions in Florida. The conflict dates to 1989, when the state high court struck down a statutory parental consent requirement on state constitutional grounds.[6] Ten years later, Governor Jeb Bush signed a bill requiring parental notification rather than consent, but in 2003, the state high court struck this law down as well.[7] The state's voters responded in November 2004 by adopting a state constitutional amendment authorizing the legislature to require parental notification, and the legislature reenacted such a requirement in 2005. Abortion providers filed a federal constitutional challenge to this 2005 statute, but that challenge was unsuccessful.[8] Likewise, when the Tennessee high court declared a state constitutional right to abortion that was broader than the corresponding federal constitutional right, opponents responded with a long-running effort to amend the state constitution to reverse the decision.[9] The amendment was approved by the state legislature in May 2011 and is scheduled to appear on the November 2014 ballot.

Federal judicial decisions protecting abortion rights on federal constitutional grounds have also sparked widespread resistance, but here the prospects of reversal by constitutional amendment are slim. The Republican Party has been formally committed to such an effort since 1980—when its national platform first declared the party's support for adding a "right to life" amendment to the federal Constitution—but the party's principal strategy for resisting federal abortion rights jurisprudence has been to reconstruct the federal courts. Following this strategy, Republican presidents since Ronald Reagan have repeatedly criticized *Roe v. Wade* and pledged to appoint federal judges who will overturn it.[10]

This judicial appointment strategy has been facilitated by the repeated enactment of state legislation (and occasional enactment of federal legislation) seeking to push at the limits of existing federal constitutional law. Elected legislators—particularly but not solely in the red states—have repeatedly sought to limit abortion access as much as federal courts will allow, and the reconstructed federal judiciary has responded by gradually relaxing the constitutional strictures over time. Periodically, lawmakers have intentionally restricted abortion access *more* than the federal judiciary would allow, in the hopes of provoking judicial reconsideration of *Roe* itself.

In the wake of *Planned Parenthood v. Casey* (1992), most new abortion legislation represented state efforts to copy, and incrementally expand on, the Pennsylvania abortion restrictions that the Supreme Court had upheld in its June 1992 decision. In the two years prior to this decision, three state or territorial legislatures had enacted near-total bans on abortion, but in *Casey*'s wake, even red-state legislatures retreated to the kinds of narrower restrictions on abortion that Pennsylvania had successfully defended. In Utah, for example, just two years after enacting a near-total ban, the legislature enacted an informed consent and twenty-four-hour waiting period requirement that was closely modeled on the Pennsylvania law. Within a few years of the *Casey* decision, Idaho, Indiana, Kansas, Louisiana, Michigan, Montana, Nebraska, North Dakota, Ohio, South Carolina, and South Dakota had followed suit. These statutes required abortion providers to provide their clients with certain state-mandated information about fetal development, alternatives to abortion, and the like, and required the clients to then wait a specified period of time before they could undergo the procedure. A number of states also followed Pennsylvania in requiring minors to obtain parental consent before having an abortion; other states required parental notification but not consent. During the Clinton era, no states enacted abortion laws that were clearly unconstitutional under Supreme Court precedent—neither near-total bans on abortion like the Texas law that the Court had struck down in *Roe* nor spousal notification requirements like the Pennsylvania law that the Court had struck down in *Casey* (Devins 2009).

As such, the state legislative response to *Casey* was formally compliant, but nonetheless part of a broader pattern of resistance to the high Court's holdings. Most of these laws were designed both to limit abortion as much as possible within existing constitutional constraints and to provide the federal courts an opportunity to reconsider those constraints. These twin motivations characterized not only the Clinton-era laws modeled on Pennsylvania's, but also the Clinton- and Bush-era bans on partial-birth abortion and a range of highly restrictive legislation enacted during Bush's second term and Barack Obama's first.

In particular, Bush's reelection in 2004 renewed hopes of a reconstituted high Court that would be willing to reconsider *Roe,* and state legislatures responded by enacting a new wave of restrictions. Along with the Florida law noted above, Arkansas, Georgia, Idaho, Oklahoma, South Dakota, and Texas enacted new parental notification or consent requirements in 2005, while Missouri became the first state to prohibit adults from helping minors cross state lines to avoid such a requirement. In addition, Arkansas, Georgia, Indiana, Louisiana, Minnesota, Oklahoma, and South Dakota enacted new informed consent requirements, including provisions that abortion providers must offer patients the opportunity to view an ultrasound image of the fetus, inform them about fetal capacity to feel pain, or (in South Dakota's case) inform them that "the abortion will terminate the life of a whole, separate, unique living human being." South Dakota also enacted a so-called trigger law, providing that abortion would be immediately banned in the event that *Roe* is overturned. The following year, the state went even further, enacting a near-total ban that purported to take effect immediately. This law marked the first such ban enacted by a state legislature since 1991. Louisiana enacted a trigger law of its own in 2006, and Oklahoma, Tennessee, and Utah tightened their parental consent requirements that year as well. Oklahoma also expanded its informed consent requirements—adding provisions regarding both fetal pain and ultrasound images—and Michigan enacted an ultrasound requirement as well.

The state legislatures were further emboldened when Bush successfully appointed Roberts and Alito in 2005 and 2006, respectively, and when this newly reconstituted Court upheld the federal ban on partial-birth abortion in April 2007. Even before this decision in *Gonzales v. Carhart* (*Carhart II*), Mississippi had enacted a trigger law in 2007 and both Mississippi and Idaho had tightened their parental consent and informed consent requirements. In the months following the decision, Louisiana enacted a new partial-birth law, closely modeled on the federal ban; North Dakota enacted a trigger law; Arkansas, Georgia, Louisiana, and Oklahoma tightened their informed consent requirements; and Oklahoma tightened its parental consent requirement. In 2008, Ohio, South Carolina, and South Dakota added ultrasound provisions to their informed consent requirements, and Oklahoma tightened its existing provision, going so far as to require abortion providers to conduct an ultrasound prior to every abortion, to situate the monitor such that the patient can view the image, and to describe various specified elements of the fetal anatomy while doing so. When the Oklahoma Supreme Court invalidated the omnibus abortion statute that contained these provisions, the legislature responded by reenacting the ultrasound provision as a stand-alone bill in 2010.[11] In addition to Oklahoma, Obama's first term witnessed newly restrictive legislation in Alabama, Alaska, Arizona, Arkansas, Florida, Georgia, Idaho, Indiana, Iowa, Kansas, Louisiana, Michigan, Mississippi, Missouri, Montana, Nebraska, New Hampshire, North Carolina, North Dakota, Ohio, Pennsylvania, South Carolina, South Dakota, Tennessee, Texas, Utah, Virginia, West Virginia, and Wisconsin.[12]

Most of these states enacted multiple restrictive laws during this period, with nine of them going so far as to ban abortion altogether after twenty weeks' gestation, on the (disputed) grounds of fetal capacity to feel pain. Texas passed a similar law in 2013, and two additional states pushed the envelope even further that year, with Arkansas banning abortion after twelve weeks' gestation and North Dakota banning it after a fetal heartbeat is detected, typically around six weeks. All twelve of these statutes (along with a post-twenty-week ban that has long been on the books in North Carolina) are clearly unconstitutional under existing doctrine, as they each ban some pre-viability abortions. Also noteworthy are the unprecedented seventy-two-hour waiting period requirements enacted by South Dakota and Utah in 2011 and 2012, respectively. The constitutional status of these statutes is less clear, but they will certainly make it more difficult for some women to obtain abortions and will thereby provide federal judges an opportunity to expand the range of such hindrances that are constitutionally permitted.

The courtroom victories of *conservative* litigators have sometimes been met with similar resistance. For example, in response to judicial decisions defending the rights of white "victims" of affirmative action, there has been a fair amount of subterranean resistance on the part of university administrators and other government officials (Graber 2006a, 696–700; Lipson 2007; Sweet 2010). In some cases, this pattern is better characterized as one of compromise, with public university officials responding to their courtroom defeats with public statements of opposition but ultimately modifying their policies in ways that they hope will pass judicial muster. Still, there are a number of instances in which higher education

officials and their allies in the Clinton administration responded to anti–
affirmative action judicial decisions by pushing back pretty hard.

In February 1995, President Clinton responded to several pending lawsuits, as well as an ongoing campaign to ban affirmative action by state
constitutional amendment in California, by calling for a review of all federal affirmative action programs. After the Supreme Court struck down a
federal contracting set-aside policy in *Adarand Constructors v. Pena* later
that year, the Department of Justice (DOJ) released an Office of Legal
Counsel memorandum emphasizing the limited reach of the Court's holding and instructing federal agencies that no immediate changes in policy
were necessary. A few weeks after that, President Clinton himself delivered a forty-five-minute speech at the National Archives to announce the
results of his review. In doing so, he ordered some notable changes to
federal policy, particularly in the contracting context, but the bulk of his
speech was a ringing endorsement of existing practice—what the editors
of the *New York Times* characterized as a "near-evangelical" defense of
affirmative action (Editors 1995).

Following the president's lead, administration lawyers and policy
makers continued to resist the ongoing judicial dismantling of affirmative action, particularly in the higher education context. For example,
when a Fifth Circuit panel invalidated a race-conscious admissions policy
in *Hopwood v. University of Texas* (5th Cir. 1996), Associate Attorney
General John Schmidt publicly criticized the decision and raised the possibility that DOJ would support the state's appeal to the Supreme Court
(Applebome 1996b). Nearly simultaneously, the federal Department of
Education released the results of a long-running investigation of affirmative action practices at UC Berkeley. In striking contrast with the
Fifth Circuit's holding, the department's Office for Civil Rights (OCR)
endorsed Berkeley's continued use of race in admissions decisions. Two
months after *Hopwood* came down, Solicitor General Drew S. Days III
acted on Schmidt's promise by filing a brief supporting UT's appeal. Days
argued explicitly that the goal of educational diversity provided a compelling justification for race-conscious government action. This argument
had the advantage of finding some daylight between the university admissions and government contracting contexts—a task made necessary by
SCOTUS's holding in *Adarand* the year before—but the Fifth Circuit
panel had explicitly rejected the argument, so the administration's oppo-
sitional stance was clear.

As the conflict escalated in subsequent years, affirmative action supporters continued to appeal to the Clinton administration for help. Early

in 1997, the Universities of California and Texas each reported a sharp drop in the number of undergraduate applications received from African American and Hispanic students. In March, OCR responded by threatening public universities in Texas with the loss of federal funds if they allowed their campuses to resegregate. Assistant Secretary Norma Cantu's letter indicated that despite *Hopwood,* Texas universities remained free to consider race in their admissions decisions; indeed, they were obligated to do so, to the extent necessary to remedy past and present discrimination. This stance sparked sharp criticism from Republican Senator Phil Gramm and Acting Solicitor General Walter Dellinger, among others, and OCR reversed itself in April. By this point, the *New York Times* was reporting partial admissions figures for UT's fall 1997 entering classes, and it appeared that there would be a significant drop in African American and Hispanic enrollments at both the undergraduate and law school levels (Applebome 1997). Affirmative action supporters were also urging OCR to scrutinize the admissions process in California, with the Mexican American Legal Defense and Educational Fund (MALDEF) filing a complaint in March contending that the allegedly race-blind admissions process then underway at Boalt Law School was actually operating to favor white applicants. The complaint emphasized the university's reliance on standardized test scores, its adjustment of undergraduate GPAs based on the perceived quality of the institution, and its favorable consideration of a wide variety of "challenging or enriching life experiences" but not the overcoming of racial obstacles. In the view of MALDEF's lawyers, each of these factors had a discriminatory impact on minority applicants. In response to the complaint, OCR opened an investigation of law school admissions practices at UC Berkeley, UC Davis, and UCLA (Guerrero 2002, 101–3). In June 1997, President Clinton used his commencement address at UC San Diego to offer a vigorous defense of race-conscious admissions policies. Pointing to the recently released admissions figures for the fall 1997 incoming classes at UC law schools, Clinton declared that "we must not resegregate higher education."

Also noteworthy was Clinton's June 1997 nomination of Bill Lann Lee, director of the Western Regional Office of the NAACP Legal Defense and Educational Fund, to serve as assistant attorney general for civil rights. When the Republican Senate surprised the administration with its sharp opposition to Lee's confirmation—with the opposition focused almost entirely on Lee's support for affirmative action—the White House held firm, with Clinton sidestepping the Senate by appointing Lee on an acting basis in December 1997. Lee served in this capacity until August

2000, when Clinton removed Lee's acting title with a recess appointment, which ran through the end of Clinton's term in January 2001. By this time, under Lee's leadership, the Civil Rights Division had filed numerous amicus briefs supporting the continued constitutionality of well-crafted race-conscious policies, particularly in the education context. In 1998, 1999, and 2000, it did so in three separate Fourth Circuit cases involving student assignment policies in the public schools—from Arlington County, Virginia; Montgomery County, Maryland; and Charlotte, North Carolina, respectively.[13] Touting the educational benefits of racial diversity, these briefs cited empirical evidence that would soon prove relevant in the higher education context as well. In 1999, DOJ filed briefs defending the admissions policies in use at the Universities of Michigan (UM) and Washington (UW), and the following year, it did so for the University of Georgia. In each of these briefs, Lee advanced the administration's position that Justice Powell's 1978 holding in *University of California v. Bakke* remained good law, and hence that educational diversity was a compelling government interest. This position was eventually endorsed by the Supreme Court in *Grutter v. Bollinger* (2003), but during the Clinton years, it was at odds with a clear doctrinal trend toward a color-blind reading of the Fourteenth Amendment.[14]

In the gun rights context, there have been fewer rights-protecting judicial decisions to date, and hence fewer opportunities for resistance to such decisions on the part of other policymakers. Still, examples can be found. When Federal District Judge Colleen Kollar-Kotelly invalidated the lame-duck Bush administration's December 2008 decision to allow the carrying of concealed weapons in national parks, the Obama administration chose not to appeal, but within two months, gun rights advocates in Congress had succeeded in reinstating the policy legislatively.[15] Likewise, when local government officials launched the wave of tort suits against firearms manufacturers that I describe in chapter 1, gun rights advocates persuaded thirty-six state legislatures to preempt these lawsuits with legislation stripping local jurisdictions of authority to bring such suits.[16] They then persuaded Congress to enact the Protection of Lawful Commerce in Arms Act, which shielded firearms manufacturers from liability for the unlawful use of their products.

In sum, it seems clear that controversial, rights-protecting judicial decisions sometimes provoke countermobilization by opponents and resistance by other policymakers. But the same is true for controversial rights-protecting *legislative* decisions. As Post and Siegel have put it with respect to the abortion conflict, "some degree of conflict may be an inevitable consequence of vindicating constitutional rights, whether rights are secured by legislation or adjudication" (2007, 377, 390; see also Cummings 2013, 199–202; Eskridge 2013, 296–99; Fontana and Braman 2012). Likewise, Scott Lemieux asks us to imagine a federal statute enacted in January 1973 legalizing abortion nationwide. Is there any good reason to think that the pro-life movement's reaction to this policy change would have been any different than its reaction to *Roe v. Wade*? Indeed, we do not even need to resort to counterfactual speculation. As Lemieux points out, the early legislative victories of the pro-choice movement at the state level prompted an extensive pro-life backlash (Lemieux 2004, 218–19; see also Garrow 1999, 840–41; Greenhouse and Siegel 2011, 2046–71; Post and Siegel 2007, 407–24).

This dynamic is even clearer in the LGBT rights context, where religious conservatives have repeatedly used citizen lawmaking procedures to repeal gay rights policies that had been enacted by elected legislators, just as they have done with gay rights policies enacted by judges (Andersen 2005, 149; Mezey 2007, 31–32). When the California Supreme Court legalized SSM in May 2008, the state's voters reversed that holding by enacting Proposition 8 later in the year. But when Maine's legislature legalized SSM in May 2009, the same thing happened, with the voters repealing the policy before the year was out. Legislative expansions of partnership rights in both Washington State and Washington, DC, in 2009 likewise provoked citizen-initiated repeal efforts, though the former was defeated at the polls and the latter was blocked by the courts. In California, moreover, Scott Cummings and Douglas NeJaime's (2010) careful case study makes clear that similar resistance would have been likely if Governor Arnold Schwarzenegger had signed (rather than vetoed) either of the two SSM bills that came across his desk in 2005 and 2006. In other words, the story line in California is not that the public resisted the *court-ordered* legalization of SSM but that it resisted the legalization of SSM, pure and simple.

This sort of conservative countermobilization in response to legislative expansions of gay rights has a long history. As early as 1977, Anita Bryant made national headlines with her campaign to repeal an antidiscrimination ordinance that had been enacted in Dade County, Florida. The popular singer and advertising icon spearheaded a populist backlash that produced not only a local referendum repealing the ordinance but also a state statute imposing a blanket prohibition on adoptions by homosexuals. Signed by the governor just one day after the Dade County referendum, this statute represented a significant retrogression in parental rights for gays and lesbians in Florida (Rimmerman 2002, 127–29). The Bryant campaign quickly sparked similar efforts in other jurisdictions, and once gay rights advocates started winning legislative victories more often, their conservative opponents repeatedly responded with this sort of electoral pushback (Keck 2009, 179–81).

In short, all victories by rights advocates tend to spark legal and political countermobilization, regardless of whether the victories occurred through legislative, executive, or judicial channels. Each such victory is a defeat for opponents of the particular rights claim at issue, and as Lemieux has noted, "defeats in the legislature, just as surely as defeats in the courts, are likely to generate opposition when issues remain contested" (Lemieux 2004, 244). In any long-running political and legal conflict, "[o]pposition is [likely to be] constant and sophisticated, so that there is never a clear 'win,' only moves that are certain to be countered" (Cummings and NeJaime 2010, 1329). As a rule, "judicial policy-making should . . . be expected to produce no more and no less countermobilization than commensurate policy-making by the political branches" (Lemieux 2004, 178; see also Fontana and Braman 2012).

Compliance

While some controversial rights-protecting judicial decisions are met with resistance, others are met with compliance, sometimes even on the part of policymakers who themselves disagree with the decision in question (Kapiszewski and Taylor 2013, 806). As Matthew Hall has shown, such compliance is particularly likely when the judicial decision has broad public support or when it can be implemented by judges themselves, without requiring affirmative steps by other government officials. In other words, when rights-protecting judicial decisions are popular, they are often met with broad compliance, even in cases where the judges have ordered sweeping policy change (Hall 2011, 28–37, 97–126; see also Paris 2010, 159–215). And when rights-protecting judicial decisions can be effectively implemented by judicial institutions acting alone, they are generally complied with, even if they lack such public support (Hall 2011, 38–96).

Regarding the latter phenomenon, consider that when a court of last resort invalidates a criminal statute on constitutional grounds, it is very difficult for law enforcement officials to continue enforcing that statute. If they continue arresting and indicting people for violating the disputed law, the courts will quickly dismiss the indictments. Given the well-entrenched norm of judicial finality in settling individual legal disputes, such decisions are likely to be effective whether or not the public (and their elected representatives) agree with them.[17] For example, state officials have complied with all of the state and federal court holdings invalidating criminal bans on consensual sodomy. They have sometimes appealed such holdings, but once all appeals were exhausted, they have complied. In some instances, they have chosen to comply even when further avenues of appeal remained open.[18] In the gun rights context, when SCOTUS invalidated local handgun bans in *Heller* and *McDonald*, the cities' lawmakers responded by enacting new gun control measures—a point I take up below—but the cities' law enforcement agencies did not continue to prosecute people under the old laws. Likewise, SCOTUS's invalidation of the Gun-Free School Zones Act (GFSZA) in *United States v. Lopez* (1995) led Congress to revise the statute to meet the Court's constitutional objections, but in the meantime, DOJ stopped prosecuting people under the original statute (Hall 2011, 93).

Some controversial judicial decisions cannot be implemented by judges themselves, requiring instead that other policymakers take affirmative steps to change existing policies, appropriate funds, and the like. Hall demonstrates that even these decisions can be successful, provided that they have significant public support, and Michael Paris has emphasized that such support can sometimes be fostered by the same legal mobilization efforts that produced the judicial decision itself (Hall 2011, 97–126; Paris 2010, 165–90).

In this light, consider once again the SSM cases. While much has been made of the nationwide legislative resistance to judicial decisions expanding the rights of same-sex couples, the vast majority of such decisions have been met with full compliance by the relevant policy makers. When the Vermont and New Jersey high courts ordered the extension to same-sex couples of all state law rights of marriage, the state legislatures each responded by enacting civil unions law. When the California high court legalized SSM itself in 2008, the decision garnered immediate support from the state's entire political establishment (though it was subsequently overturned by a citizen-led initiative at the polls). When the Connecticut Supreme Court legalized SSM that same year, the legislature quickly codified the decision, by votes of 100–44 in the House and 28–7 in the Senate, and the bill was signed by Republican governor Jodi Rell. The *Goodridge* and *Varnum* decisions provoked greater resistance in Massachusetts and Iowa, respectively, but in each case, state officials ultimately complied with the courts' mandates. As Scott Lemieux and George Lovell have noted, even when legislative majorities want to override a judicial decision, the judges will sometimes have enough support in the relevant legislative bodies to effectively veto such efforts (2010, 222–23).

In some cases, state officials have chosen to comply with decisions expanding LGBT partnership rights even before the courts have reached final judgments. For example, when an intermediate appellate court ordered Oregon to extend domestic partnership benefits to state employees in 1998, state officials chose to comply rather than appeal.[19] When an intermediate appellate court in New York ordered a public community college to recognize SSMs lawfully contracted in other jurisdictions, Governor David Paterson responded by directing all state agencies to comply.[20] When an intermediate appellate court in Florida struck down the state's statutory ban on adoptions by homosexuals, State Attorney General Bill McCollum decided not to appeal.[21] And when Federal District Judge Vaughn Walker invalidated California's Proposition 8, state officials likewise chose not to appeal; the nonstate parties who had successfully intervened in the case did appeal, but when SCOTUS held that they lacked standing to do so, state officials authorized the resumption of SSMs within two days.[22]

A similar dynamic has sometimes prevailed at the federal level. When constitutional challenges to the US military's Don't Ask, Don't Tell policy started making headway in 2009 and 2010, the lawsuits provided a significant impetus for Congress to prioritize a long-stalled repeal bill. After Secretary of Defense Robert Gates testified in December 2010 that the only options on the table were congressional repeal or judicial invalidation, and that the former was preferable to the latter, Congress finally repealed the policy (Bumiller 2010b). When constitutional challenges to Section 3 of the Defense of Marriage Act made similar headway, Attorney General Eric Holder declared that the Obama administration would no longer defend the statute in court and urged Congress to repeal it.[23] When SCOTUS endorsed the administration's position in *United States v. Windsor* (2013), federal officials quickly extended benefits eligibility to same-sex spouses of federal employees and began recognizing SSMs for immigration purposes (Gordon 2013; Peters 2013).

As I note in chapter 2, opponents of gay rights have turned to the courts as well, and policymakers have complied with some of their courtroom victories too. On four occasions from 1995 to 2000, SSM opponents persuaded state high courts to invalidate local domestic partnership policies. Gay rights advocates eventually reversed this result in one case, and in two others, same-sex couples subsequently gained access to state benefits via the legalization of SSM, but in Arlington County, Virginia, the judicial holding remains in effect, continuing to bar local officials from extending domestic partnership benefits to their employees.[24] And even in the other local jurisdictions, the decisions were complied with until reversed or mooted by subsequent legal developments.[25]

Many rights-protecting judicial decisions in the affirmative action context have likewise been met with compliance, even if sometimes grudging or reluctant. University administrators have been almost uniformly opposed to decisions invalidating race-conscious admissions, financial aid, and hiring policies, and when faced with such decisions, they have usually pursued all available courtroom appeals. Both during and after these appeals, however, they have generally complied with all relevant court orders, even when doing so has required significant changes to existing policy.[26] Indeed, when the legal tea leaves looked bad enough, they have sometimes engaged in preemptive compliance, modifying legally vulnerable policies in the face of pending or anticipated litigation.

When Lee Bollinger became dean of the UM School of Law in 1987, he quickly launched a review of the school's admissions policies, in part because of his concern that the existing policies were inconsistent with the Supreme Court's governing decision in *Bakke* (Stohr 2005, 13–17). This review eventually led the law school to abandon a "special admissions program" with a "goal" or "target" of enrolling a class that was 10 to 12 percent "Black, Chicano, Native American, and mainland Puerto Rican," and with applications from these groups reviewed by a separate admissions committee that included minority student representatives. In its place, Bollinger installed a new preference for applicants whose

> perspective or experiences . . . will contribute to the diverse student body that we hope to assemble. The applicant may for example be a member of a minority group whose experiences are likely to be different from those of most students, may be likely to make a unique contribution to the bar, or may have had a successful career as a concert pianist or may speak five languages.[27]

When Bollinger became UM's president in 1997, he initiated a similar review of the school's undergraduate admissions policies. On this occasion, the threat of a lawsuit was even clearer, as Professor Carl Cohen launched a public attack on the policy three weeks into Bollinger's term, and Cohen's allies in the state legislature were openly discussing the possibility of legal action. The suits on behalf of Jennifer Gratz and Barbara Grutter were filed later that year, and a few months after that, Bollinger announced that the university was abandoning the controversial policy under which Gratz had been rejected (Bell 1997; Stohr 2005, 33–35, 49–50). Bollinger had initiated these changes before the lawsuits were filed, but they were clearly a response to the shifting legal environment in general and the visible threat of a lawsuit in particular.

By this point, a small wave of anti–affirmative action lawsuits had prompted similar changes on campuses across the country. For example, after the Fourth Circuit invalidated a blacks-only scholarship program at the University of Maryland in 1994, a number of universities within the circuit began to modify their own such programs.[28] In September 1995, the University of Virginia (UVA) announced that it was opening its University Achievement Awards program to underprivileged students of all races (Lederman 1996c). In July 1997, the University of North Carolina began reviewing its scholarship programs for compliance with the Fourth Circuit holding, and when Molly C. Broad took office as the university's president later in the year, she extended the review to include admissions and hiring practices as well, directing the chancellors of each of her campuses to ensure that all race-based policies complied with "evolving legal standards" (Lederman 1997b). That same year, an OCR investigation prompted Northern Virginia Community College to abandon two race-exclusive scholarship programs and open two others to students of all races, on the grounds that the existing policies were inconsistent with *Podberesky v. Kirwan* (4th Cir. 1994) (Healy 1997b; Lederman 1997a).

Likewise, the filing of the *Hopwood* suit in 1993 prompted preemptive policy changes at the UT School of Law, with the chair of the school's admissions committee later testifying that "when one gets sued in federal court it catches one's attention."[29] When the Fifth Circuit ruled against the university in 1996, the state's flagship public universities responded by freezing all admissions activity, and the state commissioner of higher education subsequently ordered the dismantling of a statewide minority scholarship program (Lederman 1996a). When the Fifth Circuit agreed to stay its holding pending appeal, the universities and the commissioner reversed course, resuming race-conscious admissions and financial aid decisions while the state asked the Supreme Court to review the decision (Lederman 1996b). When SCOTUS denied that petition, the state education officials reversed course again, with UT's law school adopting a race-neutral admissions process that led its first-year enrollment of African American students to drop by 86 percent.[30] Beyond the admissions sphere, UT also discontinued its Target of Opportunity program, which was designed to aid the recruitment of minority professors. The program had helped to double the number of black and Hispanic faculty members on campus since its inception in 1987, but university administrators ended it in 1998 on the advice of legal counsel (Selingo 1999a).

In 1997, a federal lawsuit prompted the University of Illinois at Chicago to rescind a policy that let most minority students register for classes before most white students, and the following year, the University of Minnesota (UMN) changed a policy that allowed minority students from out of state to pay in-state tuition (Haworth 1998; Healy 1997a). Reporting on the pending change at UMN, the *Chronicle of Higher Education* quoted the university system's general counsel, who attributed the shift to the "significant changes in the federal legal landscape . . . in the past five years. . . . Just as the law evolves, so do our policies have to account for the stricter legal standards that are clearly on the horizon in the affirmative-action area" (Haworth 1998). In March 1998, the *Chronicle* likewise reported that the University of Georgia (UGA) would abandon a race-exclusive graduate fellowship program, with the university's president observing that "[w]e are continuing to search for creative remedies that meet the law" (Schmidt 1998). Later that year, the *Chronicle* reported on a survey of fifty-eight institutions, eleven of which had recently ended graduate financial aid programs that targeted minorities (Rolnick 1998).

The following year, the University of Wisconsin announced that while it was redoubling efforts to improve minority recruitment, it was dropping numerical enrollment goals by race that had been in place since the late 1980s (Selingo 1999b). UVA began reviewing its admissions policies that year as well, with the shifting legal environment again playing a prominent role in the decision. The Center for Individual Rights (CIR) had drawn attention to UVA's policies with a series of campus newspaper advertisements, and the Fourth Circuit had recently struck down a race-conscious student assignment policy in a public kindergarten program. In October 1999, the *Chronicle* quoted a member of the university's Board of Visitors, indicating that a committee appointed to review the situation "had reached the 'fairly inescapable' conclusion that the university's current policies would not pass muster" in the courts (Schmidt and Healy 1999). The board's president reiterated this concern in a subsequent account, by which time the university had already ended its practice of awarding extra points to African American applicants (Schmidt 1999a, 1999b).

When a federal district court invalidated UGA's undergraduate admissions policy in July 2000, university administrators appealed to the Eleventh Circuit but announced that they were discontinuing their race-conscious practices in the meantime (Guerrero 2002, 186). When an Eleventh Circuit panel affirmed this holding the following year, the university's leaders decided not to appeal at all, announcing that they would eliminate the use of race for the university's fall 2002 entering class (Hebel 2001; Laird 2005, 41–43; Schemo 2001b).[31] They made this decision as part of a strategic calculation that the pending cases from UM provided a better vehicle for defending affirmative action in the Supreme Court, but strategic or not, they complied with the legal judgments against the university, and the university witnessed a significant change in policy as a result. In 2003, Virginia Tech's Board of Visitors went so far as to repeal the university's affirmative action policies altogether (along with its anti-discrimination protections for gays and lesbians). This decision resulted from pressure from Virginia Attorney General Jerry Kilgore, who had threatened the trustees with personal liability if they maintained unconstitutional policies. After a widespread outcry on campus and criticism from Governor Mark Warner, the governing board reversed the decision in April 2003 (Bartlett and Rooney 2003; Winter 2003).

By this time, CIR and its allies were making a strong public push for colleges to eliminate all race-exclusive scholarship and mentoring programs. Roger Clegg's Center for Equal Opportunity (CEO) and Ward Connerly's American Civil Rights Institute (ACRI) had opened this campaign with a February 2001 letter to the Massachusetts Institute of Technology (MIT), objecting to two summer math and science programs that had been limited to African American, Hispanic, and Native American students since their inception in 1969 and 1973. When MIT declined to make changes, CEO and ACRI filed a complaint with the federal Department of Education, and in February 2003, with CIR's Michigan cases now pending at SCOTUS, MIT announced that it would open the programs to students of all races. Princeton University officials responded to similar pressure by announcing similar changes, and the *Chronicle* quoted officials at both universities attributing the changes to fear of legal liability (Schmidt and Young 2003). In May 2003, Clegg reported that fifteen universities had already responded to letters from his organization by agreeing to alter their race-exclusive policies (Blum and

Clegg 2003). Even if this number was inflated, it seems clear that some universities were responding to the open threats of government investigations and lawsuits (Golden 2003; Winter 2003).

This sort of pressure increased in the wake of the high Court's 2003 decisions in the Michigan cases. The Court's *Gratz* decision made clear that large universities, with high volumes of applications to process, could no longer use mechanical formulas that automatically awarded points on the basis of race. In response, UM officials quickly adopted a more flexible policy that was designed to meet the Court's constitutional concerns, and before the year was out, several other selective universities had followed suit (Hall 2011, 113–17; Schmidt 2003b, 2003c, 2003d). It soon became clear, moreover, that *Gratz*'s impact would reach beyond the specific sort of admissions policies that were at issue in the case. Affirmative action opponents worked hard to reinforce this impression. Writing in the *Chronicle*, CIR's Curt Levey (2003) advised college and university officials that they "would do well to cut the celebration short and begin planning now for the eventual phaseout of race-based admissions." Reading *Grutter* narrowly and *Gratz* broadly, Levey warned trustees and other decision makers that if they did not change existing policies, "the decisions will . . . be a road map for bitter and costly litigation." He proceeded to list a number of specific practices that colleges should avoid, including the "[r]eintroduction of race-based admissions by a state that successfully used race-neutral policies to promote diversity." This last warning was a shot across the bow of UT, which was already contemplating such a reintroduction. UT officials ignored the warning, but at Texas A&M, President Robert Gates announced in late 2003 that his university would maintain the race-neutral policies that had been in place since *Hopwood*. And even at UT, campus officials indicated that they would not resume the race-exclusive scholarship programs that had been in place prior to *Hopwood* (Golden 2003).

One reason for *Gratz*'s broad impact was that the courts now had the support of the federal executive branch. Throughout George W. Bush's first term, affirmative action opponents had complained about the administration's lack of commitment to the color-blind cause (Greve 2004). The administration responded by appointing critics of affirmative action to a number of key posts (Selingo 2005). As a result, while *Gratz*'s rules were not crystal clear, the relevant federal agencies were increasingly determined to enforce them strictly. This support expanded the range of credible threats that affirmative action opponents could issue. In September

2003, CEO filed a complaint with OCR, alleging that an African American scholarship program at Washington University in St. Louis was unconstitutional under *Gratz,* and it followed up with similar complaints against several other universities. Writing in *Trusteeship Magazine* that fall, Yale University's general counsel urged her professional colleagues to review all such programs for compliance with *Gratz*, and before 2003 was over, Amherst, Mount Holyoke, and Williams Colleges, and Carnegie Mellon and Indiana Universities had announced that they were opening minority scholarship programs or recruitment events to applicants of all races (Golden 2003; Robinson 2003; Schmidt 2004a). Soon thereafter, the Andrew W. Mellon Foundation and the National Institutes of Health announced that they were doing likewise with several major fellowship programs, and the Law and Society Association announced that it was canceling a National Science Foundation–funded fellowship program for minority students (Schmidt 2004a, 2005a). In April 2004, having reviewed CEO's complaint and met with OCR administrators, Washington University officials announced that they were opening the John B. Ervin Scholars Program to applicants of all races (Schmidt 2004b).

Where universities resisted informal pressure to change their policies, the Bush administration proved willing to bring suit. In November 2005, Acting Assistant Attorney General Bradley J. Schlozman notified Southern Illinois University of an impending lawsuit regarding several race-exclusive fellowship programs. This action marked the first such formal allegation filed by DOJ in the wake of *Gratz*, and the university responded by entering a consent decree in February 2006, agreeing to modify the relevant programs (*Chronicle* 2006; Schmidt 2005b).

With the ability to make credible threats of OCR investigations and DOJ lawsuits, affirmative action opponents were able to force significant policy concessions. By February 2006, Clegg was claiming that more than one hundred colleges had made "voluntary" changes in response to his organization's efforts, and the *Chronicle* was independently reporting recent changes made by Cal Tech, St. Louis and Tufts Universities, and the state universities of Delaware, New Jersey, and New York, in addition to the examples already noted (Schmidt 2006). Meanwhile, CIR's litigators also continued to make use of private (as opposed to government) lawsuits. When UM officials responded to a November 2006 state constitutional ban on affirmative action with continued resistance (or at least delay), CIR filed suit on behalf of a rejected white law school applicant in January 2007. When university officials responded by accelerating their move toward race-neutral admissions policies, CIR's lawyers dropped the suit (Schmidt 2007a). Around the same time, Virginia Commonwealth University settled another suit filed by CIR, with university officials agreeing to open a summer journalism program to white students (Schmidt 2007b).

Local government officials sometimes responded to anti–affirmative action lawsuits in the employment and contracting contexts with preemptive compliance as well. The best-known example is *Taxman v. Piscataway Board of Education* (3d Cir. 1996), in which the Third Circuit held that a local school district could not lawfully make race-based layoff decisions in an effort to preserve faculty diversity. The district successfully petitioned for certiorari, but given the facts of the case—a race-based layoff, with the entire burden of the disputed policy falling on one particular white teacher—advocates of affirmative action arranged a settlement to avoid what seemed a likely defeat at the high court. With national civil rights organizations agreeing to pay about 70 percent of the back pay and attorney's fees that Sharon Taxman sought, the school board agreed to pay the rest and drop its appeal (Biskupic 1997; Edsall and Fletcher 1997). A few years earlier, when SCOTUS had agreed to hear a challenge to Jacksonville, Florida's minority set-aside policy, the city responded by repealing the ordinance in question and replacing it with a new policy that was more narrowly drawn in several respects.[32]

On gun rights, there have been only a handful of rights-protecting judicial decisions to date. As I note above, the Supreme Court's decisions in *Lopez, Heller*, and *McDonald* were all met with compliance from the relevant law enforcement officials (even while local and federal lawmakers tried to circumvent the decisions as much as they could). In addition, at least two post-*Heller* suits have been met with preemptive compliance. In 2009, the San Francisco Housing Authority settled a National Rifle Association suit by agreeing to cease enforcement of a 2005 rule that prohibited the otherwise legal possession of firearms in public housing units.[33] And in 2011, anticipating that a pending challenge to the city's ban on firing ranges would be successful, the Chicago City Council (and Mayor Rahm Emanuel) repealed the ban on the very same day that the Seventh Circuit enjoined the city from enforcing it.[34]

In the abortion context, most of the rights-protecting judicial decisions I have surveyed have involved the invalidation of state criminal statutes. As such, state officials have had little choice but to comply, even while they were often resisting the courts' orders in other ways. On occasion, states have dropped their resistance altogether and fully complied with the letter and spirit of a judicial holding against them. For example, after SCOTUS rejected a facial constitutional challenge to New Hampshire's parental consent law in 2006, while reiterating that the law could not be enforced absent an exception for maternal health, the state could have added a health exception to the statute, or it could simply have allowed the courts to enjoin the statute's application to situations in which the pregnant minor's health was threatened.[35] Instead, the state legislature repealed the law altogether. And when a newly constituted state legislature reenacted the law several years later, it included a (narrowly drawn) exception for threats to maternal health.

Compromise

In addition to resisting or complying with an actual or expected judicial decision, legislators also have the option of seeking to split the difference. In this way, by pushing the policy envelope, ambitious litigation can sometimes clear space for legislative progress in its wake. Just as southern state legislatures often responded to the NAACP's mid-twentieth-century desegregation suits by increasing funding for black schools, northeastern and western state legislatures often responded to late twentieth- and early twenty-first-century SSM suits by extending some legal rights and benefits to same-sex couples. The Hawaii Supreme Court's 1993 decision in *Baehr* led directly to the state's 1997 Reciprocal Beneficiaries Act, which fell far short of full equality but nonetheless granted gay and lesbian couples more legal rights than anywhere else in the nation at the time. (Thirteen years later, when Hawaii LGBT rights advocates challenged this law as falling short of state constitutional equality requirements, the state legislature preemptively complied by enacting a civil union law.) The state legislatures of Connecticut, New Jersey, New Mexico, and New York have likewise expanded partnership rights while a lawsuit seeking such rights was pending in their state's courts.[36]

In Vermont, I have characterized the legislative enactment of a civil union law as an act of compliance rather than compromise because the action was compelled by the state high court. But even here, it is worth remembering that the judges left open the possibility of either civil unions or full marriage equality, thereby allowing the legislators to say that they had chosen the moderate path. In this regard, court decisions sometimes enable elected lawmakers to declare support for policies that they once opposed. The operation of this causal mechanism does not require the judges to persuade or enlighten legislators who were once opposed or blinded, though William Eskridge (2002) and Dan Pinello (2006) have documented several instances in which that appears to have occurred. As Rosenberg has noted, the mechanism simply requires judges to provide political cover for legislators to publicly declare their support for a policy that they previously considered too great a political liability (2008, 34–35).

Moreover, once the compromise policies had been developed in states that were being sued, they then spread to states that did not face immediate litigation. With local SSM advocates following an explicitly legislative strategy, California incrementally extended all state-law rights of marriage to registered domestic partners before the state's first marriage equality suit was filed (Cummings and NeJaime 2010). State legislatures in Colorado, Illinois, Maine, Maryland, Nevada, Oregon, Washington, and Wisconsin likewise extended some legal rights to same-sex couples either before a SSM suit had been filed or after such a suit had reached an unsuccessful conclusion. None of these legislative acts were compelled by court order, but they were surely made easier by the SSM lawsuits that had transformed these once-radical domestic partnership and civil union policies into moderate compromises.[37]

In a different dynamic, some litigation victories have been met with technical compliance, but with lawmakers trying to preserve as much of their original policy as the courts seem likely to allow. When the Georgia Supreme Court invalidated Atlanta's domestic partnership policy in 1995, local lawmakers enacted a modified policy that responded to the Court's concerns, and the Court upheld it two years later.[38] Likewise, when SCOTUS invalidated the GFSZA in *Lopez*, Congress reenacted the law with a jurisdictional provision limiting its application to guns that had traveled in interstate commerce. As I note above, this revised statute survived constitutional challenge.[39]

When the Supreme Court struck down the District of Columbia's near-total ban on handgun possession in *Heller*, the DC City Council quickly responded with a law allowing the registration of a single handgun by any person "for use in self-defense within that person's home," but requiring the gun to be stored in the home, unloaded and either disassembled or locked, except "while it is being used to protect against a reasonably perceived threat of immediate harm to a person within the registrant's home." The council also preserved the district's existing ban on semiautomatic handguns and other assault weapons. After significant pushback from gun rights supporters in Congress, the council relaxed these restrictions further, first with a temporary measure enacted in September 2008 and then with a regular ordinance in February 2009. The new laws allowed the possession of semiautomatic handguns; authorized the registration of more than one handgun, though still only one per month; and permitted registered guns to be kept assembled and loaded in the home. But these new laws also extended the waiting period for handgun purchases to ten days, tightened the ban on assault weapons (other than semiautomatic handguns), banned the possession of high-capacity clips that allow semiautomatic handguns to fire multiple rounds without reloading, and required tougher training and background checks for applicants for gun permits (Rostron 2009, 399). These new laws sparked a constitutional challenge as well—from the same plaintiff and the same litigators as in *Heller*—but that challenge has been unsuccessful.[40]

Chicago was one of the few local jurisdictions with a handgun ban similar to the District of Columbia's, and on the day after *Heller* came down, gun rights advocates filed a Second Amendment challenge to this one as well. Chicago's lawyers sought to defend the long-standing ban by arguing that the constitutional right to bear arms did not apply to state and local governments. Once SCOTUS rejected this claim, Chicago officials responded just as their DC counterparts had. In other words, they revised their local ordinances to meet the letter of the Court's holding while still retaining as much of their antigun policy as they could. Four days after *McDonald* came down, the Chicago City Council enacted a new ordinance that imposed a limit of one handgun per home, required such guns to be kept in the home, and continued to ban gun sales within the city. The law also imposed an extensive system of registration and training requirements for gun owners. As expected, gun rights advocates immediately filed several constitutional challenges to this new law, and these new challenges led to still further compromise by the city's lawmakers.[41]

On the affirmative action issue, the Clinton administration resisted scaling back race-conscious policies in the areas of university admissions and financial aid, even when such retrenchment was ordered by the federal courts, but outside the higher education context, the administration's response is better characterized as a story of compromise. In the area of government contracting, for example, there are some examples of full compliance and other examples of determined resistance, but the overall pattern is one in which the federal executive branch sought to modify existing race-conscious policies enough to satisfy the federal courts while still maintaining some form of preference for minority-owned contractors.[42]

After all, when President Clinton announced the results of his review of federal affirmative action policies in the summer of 1995, he famously summed up his qualified support with the phrase, "mend it, don't end it." On the mending front, he initiated several notable changes to existing federal contracting policies. Over the next two years, the Defense Department suspended its so-called rule of two, which had operated since 1987 to limit some contract bidding to small businesses that are categorized as disadvantaged (*New York Times* 1995); the Federal Communications Commission (FCC) changed its policy for giving bidding discounts to firms owned by minorities and women in the auction of wireless telephone licenses, announcing that all small companies would henceforward be eligible for the preferences (Andrews 1995); the Small Business Administration proposed changes to its 8(a) contracting program, offering to expand the definition of eligible "socially disadvantaged" contractors to include more white-owned companies; the administration announced a three-year moratorium on any new set-aside programs (Holmes 1996a); and DOJ issued guidelines encouraging race-neutral efforts to enable disadvantaged businesses to win federal contracts (while also reducing the moratorium on new set-asides to two years) (Holmes 1996b). In March 1998, the *New York Times* reported that the ongoing review had led the administration to alter or eliminate seventeen affirmative action programs (Holmes 1998). Three months later, the administration announced that henceforward, the federal government would provide a 10 percent bidding preference to disadvantaged firms in industries where the federal government had been underutilizing such firms (Rosenbaum 1998). To determine the eligible industries, the White House tasked the Commerce Department with conducting a series of industry-specific (and in some cases, region-specific) disparity studies to determine when (and where) contracting preferences were still necessary.

These efforts by the federal executive to mark out continued space for affirmative action in the midst of an ever-constricting legal environment were supported by DOJ's litigation efforts. Even while defending affirmative action in the school assignment and university admissions contexts, DOJ lawyers acknowledged that the Third Circuit's widely noted anti–affirmative action decision in *Taxman* may have been correct. They did so in a strategic effort to persuade SCOTUS not to hear the case and then, when the justices ignored that recommendation, to persuade them to affirm the holding on narrow grounds.[43] Two years later, when the DC Circuit declined to review a 1998 panel decision holding that the FCC's long-standing equal employment regulations were a constitutionally impermissible effort to force broadcasters to adopt race-conscious hiring measures, the Clinton administration made a tactical decision not to appeal to the Supreme Court; in January 2000, the FCC announced a revised set of less stringent diversity requirements.[44] Likewise, when the *Adarand* litigation continued on remand, administration lawyers persuaded the Tenth Circuit to uphold most of the set-aside policies at issue. The panel did, however, invalidate the Department of Transportation's Subcontractor Compensation Clause program, which involved the automatic use of financial incentives to encourage the award of subcontracts to disadvantaged business enterprises. Here, the administration chose to discontinue the program rather than appeal.[45]

To a significant extent, this compromise strategy continued when George W. Bush replaced Clinton in the White House. When a DC Circuit panel struck down the revised affirmative action rules that had been issued by the FCC, the Bush administration petitioned for en banc review.[46] When that failed, Bush's chairman of the FCC, Michael Powell, said he was disappointed and that he would seek to write new rules encouraging television and radio companies to recruit more women and minorities (Bloomberg News 2001). Similarly, when the Supreme Court agreed to revisit the *Adarand* case to consider whether the Tenth Circuit had erred in upholding most of the revised DOT regulations, Solicitor General Ted Olson filed a brief that took essentially the same position as his predecessor. According to Olson's brief, the federal government's revised set-aside policy "promotes the compelling interest in assuring that public dollars, drawn from the tax contributions of all citizens, do not serve to finance the evil of private prejudice."[47]

In the higher education context, as I note above, university officials resisted the judicial dismantling of affirmative action in many ways, while also complying with particular holdings when they seemed to have little choice. In some cases, this "compliance" consisted of meeting the judges halfway, as when the University of Maryland responded to the Fourth Circuit's invalidation of a blacks-only scholarship program (in *Podberesky v. Kirwan*) by combining the program with a merit scholarship competition open to all students and allowing racial diversity to be one factor among many in making future awards.[48] Likewise, when the Wisconsin

Department of Public Instruction responded to pressure from OCR by agreeing to open its Minority Precollege Scholarship Program to all needy students, state officials continued to maintain that race could be considered in the application process (Schmidt 2004c). At UGA, administrators attempted a similar compromise by preemptively modifying their undergraduate admissions policy in 1996, moving from a dual-track system for white and nonwhite applicants to one that reviewed most applicants on race-neutral criteria but awarded bonus points to nonwhite applicants who fell near the cutoff line.[49] The First Circuit's 1999 decision in a public school assignment case likewise prompted the University of Massachusetts to announce significant changes to its race-conscious admissions practices, reducing but not eliminating the weight given to race (Healy 1999; Selingo 2000a).

In similar fashion, public school officials have generally complied with judicial decisions invalidating their race-conscious student assignment policies, but in some cases, this response has involved abiding by the courts' specific mandates while still preserving as much of the underlying policy as possible.[50] In Berkeley, California, a 2003 suit from the Pacific Legal Foundation (PLF) prompted public school officials to abandon consideration of the race of individual students, which the district had used in the school assignment process in various ways since 1968. In its place, however, the district began using the racial and economic composition of residential neighborhoods to classify students, structuring the student assignment process to ensure that all schools included students from a diverse set of neighborhoods. This policy survived a legal challenge from PLF.[51] When SCOTUS invalidated race-conscious student assignment policies from Seattle and Louisville in *Parents Involved v. Seattle School District* (2007), Louisville officials responded by adopting a policy modeled on Berkeley's. As in Berkeley, the policy remains race conscious but does not consider the race of individual students. It, too, has withstood legal challenge, though it has sparked significant political controversy locally.[52]

Innovation

The policy changes in Berkeley and Louisville have been part of a broader national move toward socioeconomic diversity rather than racial diversity as the key measure of whether public schools are adequately integrated

(Barnes 2010; Bazelon 2008; Brown 2010; Winerip 2011). From one angle, it makes sense to characterize these shifts as a story of policy compromise. After all, public school officials in both Berkeley and Louisville responded to courtroom defeats by crafting a policy that would preserve as much racial diversity as they could get away with; in each of these districts, the revised policies even remain race conscious. Elsewhere, however, the turn toward socioeconomic diversity has displaced rather than supplemented a focus on racial diversity, and these changes might be better understood as a pattern of policy innovation, sparked by the judicial disruption of the policy status quo.

In addition to resistance, compliance, or compromise, then, it seems clear that legislative and executive officials sometimes respond to policy-altering judicial decisions with more radical policy changes. In other words, legal challenges to existing policies sometimes clear space for the consideration of policy options that had not previously been articulated (or that had been articulated but largely ignored). Even temporary legal victories can have this effect, provoking significant policy experimentation before they are undone.

In the SSM context, for example, the judicial disruption of the status quo has prompted a slow but steady proliferation of state-recognized legal categories for *opposite*-sex relationships. The explicit goal of the SSM lawsuits was to achieve marriage equality for same-sex couples, but as these suits produced judicial holdings demanding a legislative response—and as those legislative responses spread even to states not facing judicial mandates—legislators sometimes tinkered with the legal recognition of straight as well as gay relationships. When California legislators enacted the first statewide domestic partnership registry in 1999, they designed the new legal category primarily with same-sex couples in mind, but they also made it open to opposite-sex couples where one or both partners were sixty-two or older. (Some such couples had been avoiding marriage because of undesirable tax, inheritance, or Social Security consequences, but nonetheless desired a formal state acknowledgment of their relationship.) When the New Jersey legislature enacted a domestic partnership law in 2004, it adopted similar eligibility rules, and when the Maine legislature did so that same year, it opened the new status to all opposite-sex couples, regardless of age.[53] In 2007, the Washington legislature followed California and New Jersey in allowing elderly opposite-sex couples to register as state-recognized domestic partners, and in 2009, the Colorado and Nevada legislatures followed Maine in allowing all opposite-sex couples to do so. Like Maine, Colorado extended only a limited set of rights to such relationships, but Nevada extended all state law rights of marriage to both same-sex and opposite-sex couples who chose to enter registered domestic partnerships. When Hawaii and Illinois legislators enacted civil union laws in 2011, they followed Nevada's lead. None of these statutes were compelled by court order, and none of the litigators in the leading SSM lawsuits openly sought to expand the available categories under which heterosexual couples could gain access to state-recognized rights and responsibilities. But it seems clear that the lawsuits disrupted the status quo in ways that opened the policy agenda to new ideas.

In the abortion context, the federal courts' continued refusal to allow state legislatures to criminalize abortion altogether has prompted repeated instances of policy innovation by pro-life advocates. Before the Ohio legislature banned so-called partial-birth abortion in 1995, very few people had ever heard of the procedure. But by the end of the Clinton era, twenty-nine additional states had joined Ohio in enacting such bans (Devins 2009, 1344). From one angle, this wave of legal change can be understood as a form of legislative resistance to the high Court's holdings. This characterization is even more apt for the 2003 federal ban, which was enacted three years after the Court had invalidated a similar state law from Nebraska. But these laws can also be understood as examples of policy innovation, with judicial holdings on abortion rights prompting continued experimentation on the part of those who opposed the holdings. The same is true for more recent waves of state legislation requiring abortion providers to display ultrasound images of the fetus, to amplify the fetal heartbeat, and/or to convey disputed and potentially misleading information about the risks of abortion before conducting the procedure. Likewise for the recent state laws banning abortion altogether after a specified period of gestation on the disputed grounds of fetal capacity to feel pain.

Perhaps the best example of policy innovation resulting from rights-protecting judicial decisions is the shifting landscape of public university admissions practices since the mid-1990s. CIR's litigation campaign (along with ACRI's parallel ballot initiative campaigns) targeted a well-entrenched policy consensus at selective colleges and universities. At virtually all such schools in the early 1990s, admissions decisions were made on the basis of a combination of academic merit and diversity factors. At most such schools, the vast majority of admissions decisions could be explained by reference to three factors: high school grades, standardized test scores, and race. The stated justification for these policies, again virtually everywhere, was that racially diverse student bodies enhanced the educational process for all students (Lipson 2007).

When the federal courts began disrupting this consensus, college and university administrators responded by experimenting with a wide range of admissions and financial aid policies in an effort to maintain racially diverse student bodies without explicitly considering race. The most notable example of such experimentation took place in Texas in the wake of the Fifth Circuit decision in *Hopwood*. With race-conscious admissions policies having been forbidden by the court, state senator Gonzalo Barrientos called for a task force consisting of professors, students, civil rights advocates, and state legislative aides to explore possible alternatives (Montejano 1998). On the task force's recommendation, the state legislature subsequently adopted a policy guaranteeing admission to the state's flagship public university (and all other public colleges) for every student who graduates in the top 10 percent of her high school class. Given the racial segregation of Texas high schools, the policy's advocates hoped that it would preserve a significant degree of racial diversity at Texas universities.

The Texas Top Ten Percent plan is sometimes characterized as an example of resistance on the part of university administrators who were determined to achieve racial diversity at any cost. In fact, however, while UT administrators were leading defenders of the old race-conscious policy, they objected to the 10 percent plan from the start and repeatedly tried to weaken it once it was in place. It was enacted by a novel coalition of urban and rural legislators, and signed by Republican governor George W. Bush. Affirmative action opponents were likewise divided over the new policy, with some characterizing it as transparent subterfuge, but others praising it as a salutary race-neutral effort to maintain a diverse student body. The policy has been successful in many ways, but because it substantially reduced the discretion of university administrators in selecting their own student bodies, it never would have been adopted (or even considered) if the courts had not disrupted the entrenched policy status quo.

Once adopted, however, the new policy became every bit as entrenched as the old one. Its supporters have touted its success in returning UT to pre-*Hopwood* levels of racial diversity, though the scope of this success remains subject to some dispute.[54] Even more important, the 10 percent policy has fostered appreciation for a conception of educational diversity somewhat different from the one that had been reflected in the pre-*Hopwood* status quo. In particular, it has produced greater representation of poor Texans of all races, and from all communities, at UT's flagship campus (Kahlenberg 2012, 30–31). As such, it has had political supporters in every corner of the state. For twelve years, these supporters were able to fend off UT's repeated attempts to weaken the policy, and even when legislators eventually agreed to modify it, they did not go as far as UT officials had hoped.[55] As Marta Tienda and Teresa A. Sullivan (2009) have noted, the 10 percent policy effectively created a new entitlement, and like all such entitlements, its beneficiaries immediately became a constituency that would resist any subsequent efforts to rescind their benefits, even if fiscal and demographic changes rendered the entitlement problematic.

The post-*Hopwood* policy debates illustrate the potential significance of court decisions that shift the relevant veto points in a fragmented policy process. Prior to *Hopwood*, universities and their advocates never would have allowed the 10 percent policy to be enacted, even if someone had thought of it. But *Hopwood* created a legislative vacuum that was filled by the new policy, and the universities and their advocates then lacked the political muscle to repeal it. Even after SCOTUS effectively took *Hopwood* off the books in 2003, with the *Grutter* decision reauthorizing the use of narrowly tailored race-conscious admissions policies, the universities had insufficient power to dislodge the 10 percent plan (though UT did reintroduce a race-conscious component to supplement it). In short, the *Hopwood* decision created a wholly new policy and political landscape.

Not only that, but the policy innovation subsequently spread to other states, with several adopting policies explicitly modeled on the Texas 10 percent plan. In California, the 1995 decision by the UC Regents to eliminate affirmative action—followed by the 1996 enactment of Proposition 209—forced UC administrators to experiment with race-neutral means for achieving diversity. As in Texas, these responses took shape in a context in which the elimination of race-conscious admissions policies had led to plummeting African American enrollments at the flagship public university campuses (Kahlenberg 2012, 36–38). In March 1999, the UC regents tried to address this problem by adopting their own version of the Texas 10 percent policy, in this case providing that all California high school students graduating in the top 4 percent of their class would be guaranteed admission to the UC system. Unlike the Texas policy, however, California's top 4 percent plan did not guarantee students admission to the campus of their choice. The Texas policy was the only plan anyone had come up with for achieving racial diversity with race-neutral means, but it did so only by sacrificing selectivity, at least as defined by most university admissions officials. But UC's plan was developed by university regents rather than the state legislature, and UC administrators were intent on pursuing racial diversity, academic selectivity, and color blindness simultaneously, a task that proved virtually impossible to accomplish.

Likewise in Florida, with Ward Connerly seeking to reprise his successful ballot initiatives from California and Washington, Governor Jeb Bush sought to preempt the effort by banning affirmative action via executive order (Weissert 1999). In its place, he proposed the One Florida plan, subsequently adopted by the state university regents and the state legislature, which guaranteed university admission to all students graduating in the top 20 percent of their high school class. As in California, this policy did not provide that students could attend the campuses of their choice, but the University of Florida subsequently announced that it would guarantee admission to the top 5 percent of every high school class (*Chronicle* 2002; Selingo 1999c).

In addition to these percentage plans in their various forms, higher education leaders explored a range of other ideas for maintaining racially diverse campuses. One possibility that was often floated was to replace racial preferences with preferences based on economic class, with a 1996 book by Richard Kahlenberg drawing particular attention to the idea. Over the next few years, two prominent studies suggested that this option was unlikely to work, but despite these concerns, the very real fear that racial preferences would soon be outlawed led many supporters of affirmative action to consider class preferences.[56] As with the Texas 10 percent policy, the advocates did so primarily as a contingency plan at first, but once on the table, the new policy option proved to have some staying power (Gose 2005; Hoover 2013). With increased attention came further research, with William Bowen and others reiterating that low-income preferences would not by themselves achieve adequate racial diversity, but finding other grounds on which such preferences might nonetheless be a good idea. In a 2005 book, Bowen and his coauthors found that while many higher education leaders purported to be committed to economic diversity, admissions data at selective universities indicated that low-income and first-generation students were currently receiving no preferences; in fact, it appeared that the preferences were running the other way, with universities giving a small boost to wealthy applicants as compared to poor applicants with comparable qualifications (Bowen, Kurzweil, and Tobin 2005). In 2004, Bowen had given a series of lectures at UVA calling for selective universities to grant explicit preferences to low-income applicants, and in 2005, Richard C. Atkinson, former president of the UC system, echoed this call in a lecture at UM. By 2007, when Senator (and presidential candidate) Barack Obama was asked about race-conscious affirmative action, he responded by noting that it should become "a diminishing tool for us to achieve racial equality in this society" and suggesting that preferences for the poor and for first-generation college students might be better (Zeleny 2007; see also Kahlenberg 2012, 11–25).

In similar fashion, the legal disruption of the policy status quo led some selective colleges and universities to reconsider the weight given to standardized test scores. There had always been a few selective institutions that did not require applicants to submit such scores, but the post-*Hopwood* period of policy experimentation witnessed additional movement in this direction. After all, the Texas 10 percent policy had the effect of admitting most of UT's student body without looking at test scores at all—high school grade-point average was all that mattered for these students—and it soon became clear that the 10 percent students were outperforming their classmates, despite their lower average SAT scores (Glater 2004). Building on such evidence, affirmative action advocates themselves went to court in California, contending that UC's race-neutral admissions policies, which placed a great deal of weight on AP classes and SAT scores, had a discriminatory impact on minority applicants. They advanced these allegations in *Rios v. Regents of the University of California,* filed by the NAACP, MALDEF, and a number of other civil rights organizations in February 1999.

Meanwhile, MALDEF attorneys worked with their allies in the Clinton administration to draw attention to the issue. In the summer of 1999, OCR proposed rules discouraging universities from overrelying on any standardized tests on which scores differed significantly across racial groups. OCR subsequently toned down the proposed rules in response to criticism, but the issue was clearly on the national agenda by this point, and UC President Atkinson drew new attention to it in February 2001 by suggesting that he might discontinue the university's reliance on SAT scores in undergraduate admissions decisions (Schemo 2001a).

At UC, the idea had originated with a fall 1997 report from the university's Latino Eligibility Task Force, which had been tasked with exploring race-neutral alternatives for maintaining Latino enrollments (Selingo

1997). Atkinson ultimately backed down on dropping the SAT, but not before the College Board had responded by negotiating significant modifications to the test (Laird 2005, 201–5). Meanwhile, the UC regents continued to explore other options, adopting a new "comprehensive review" policy in 2001, under which all applicants would be evaluated holistically, with attention to both their academic merits and any special talents or experiences with adversity that they had demonstrated (Selingo 2001). (Under the previous policy, more than half of the class had been admitted on academic criteria alone.) Among other advantages, this change allowed the UC system to settle the *Rios* suit, with the NAACP and its allies agreeing that, by reducing the weight given to measures on which minority applicants tended to underperform, the universities had ameliorated the previous policy's discriminatory impact on such applicants (Equal Justice Society 2004, 64; Miksch 2008).

When UC's flagship campuses—Berkeley and UCLA—experienced continued difficulties with minority recruitment, the system's leaders continued to experiment (Schmidt 2007c). In February 2009, the regents adopted yet another new undergraduate admissions policy, retaining the SAT I requirement but dropping the required SAT subject tests, and reducing still further the number of applicants who would be automatically admitted or excluded solely on the basis of numbers. As a result, the change would expand the flexibility of university administrators to construct a class based on their holistic review of individual applications (Keller and Hoover 2009; Schmidt 2009).

Similar experimentation took place elsewhere. In June 2000, Mount Holyoke College announced that it was dropping the SATs, with the Mellon Foundation supporting a multiyear study of the impact of the change (Wilgoren 2000a). When the University of Massachusetts adopted a new admissions policy that same year, it simultaneously reduced the weight given to both race and SAT scores (Selingo 2000a). When SCOTUS outlawed the mechanical use of race in admissions decisions in *Gratz v. Bollinger*, UMass responded by moving further in the direction of comprehensive review, as did the University of Michigan and Ohio State University (Schmidt 2003d). More recently, Wake Forest University dropped the SAT as an admissions requirement in 2008, as did DePaul University in 2011 (Hoover 2011). As I note above, the Supreme Court's Michigan decisions led to a reconsideration of the post-*Hopwood* policy settlement in Texas as well. At the flagship UT campus in Austin, university leaders moved quickly to return to race-conscious admissions, using such procedures alongside the 10 percent policy that was mandated by state legislation (which helps explain the leaders' ever more insistent calls for the legislature to cap the number of students admitted under the 10 percent policy) (Arenson 2003). At Texas A&M, President Gates announced that the school would maintain its race-neutral policies, but when this announcement sparked a minor flare-up over A&M's so-called legacy preference for children of alumni, Gates then announced that the legacy policy would be dropped. The flagship state universities in California and Georgia dropped legacy preferences during this period as well (Kahlenberg 2012, 25–27, 34, 49). In at least one state, the experimentation with reduced emphasis on standardized tests extended to admissions processes for graduate and professional schools as well. In June 2001, the Texas legislature enacted a statute prohibiting such schools (at the state's public universities) from rejecting applicants solely on the basis of test scores (Wertheimer 2002). The Supreme Court's decision in *Fisher v. University of Texas* (2013) is likely to spark additional such experimentation by university officials (Hoover 2013).

Beyond actual changes in university admissions practices, judicial decisions imposing limits on race-conscious affirmative action also prompted changes in the stated justifications for those practices. It was the Court's decision in *Bakke* that first prompted most colleges and universities to shift from backward-looking compensatory grounds to forward-looking diversity grounds (Menand 2003), and this shift was further entrenched after the Court's decision in *Grutter* twenty-five years later. O'Connor's *Grutter* opinion endorsed the pedagogical conception of diversity that Powell had emphasized in *Bakke*, and it also adopted a rubric of "democratic legitimacy," emphasizing "the importance to our society of having elite educational institutions be visibly integrated" (Lehman 2004, 92). As Jeffrey Lehman and others have noted, this broader justification emerged in large part because CIR's litigation pushed UM to better articulate—and thus to rethink—the justifications for its own policies (Lehman 2004; Lewis 2004).

These developments are sometimes described as a process of preserving a preexisting policy under a new rationale (Menand 2003), but the evolving rationales have tended to influence the operational details of the policies in turn. Consider, for example, the shifting categories of eligible beneficiaries of race-conscious admissions policies over time. As Daniel Lipson and John Skrentny have pointed out, affirmative action policies in the early 1990s generally covered all racial minority groups recognized by the federal government. As the diversity rationale took hold in *Bakke*'s wake, however, the key concept became underrepresentation, which would not necessarily lead to the inclusion of all official minorities. In particular, as Asian American underrepresentation disappeared on many campuses, a number of universities dropped Asian Americans as beneficiaries, though some retained eligibility for Filipino Americans or other specific subgroups (Lipson 2008; Skrentny 2002).

In sum, the late twentieth and early twenty-first centuries witnessed significant changes in university admissions and financial aid policies. Some of these changes were the direct result of litigation or other forms of rights mobilization (such as Connerly's ballot initiative campaigns). Even more were the indirect result of such efforts, which effectively disrupted a well-entrenched policy status quo. These policy innovations were particularly significant because elected legislatures had for so long been unwilling to engage the issue. As with SSM, the litigators (and some sympathetic judges) were able to force a long-neglected issue onto the agenda of other policymakers. The ultimate policy outcomes were unpredictable, but they were far different than they would have been in the absence of judicial action.

*   *   *

In the leading study of congressional responses to Supreme Court invalidations of federal statutes, Mitch Pickerill (2004) emphasizes that judges and legislators frequently care about different things. In particular, judges are often focused on technical questions of legality while legislators care only about the underlying policy objective and the political benefits that they perceive in pursuing that objective. As such, it is not uncommon for Congress to fully comply with a judicial decision invalidating a statute while at the same time preserving much of the disputed policy. If Congress is able to modify the statute in ways that meet the Court's constitutional concerns, then it will often do so, as when it reenacted the GFSZA with a jurisdictional requirement that limits the law's reach to guns that have traveled in interstate commerce.

As I indicated at the outset of this chapter, the categories of resistance, compliance, compromise, and innovation are overlapping. Under certain conditions, legislators and other government officials can simultaneously resist a judicial decision, comply with it, and craft a revised policy that preserves some but not all elements of the predecision status quo.[57] As such, when faced with a rights-protecting judicial decision, lawmakers almost always have a range of policy responses available to them. Far from calling an end to political deliberation and debate, the judicial decrees are mere moments in an ongoing policy process.

This lack of finality complicates any effort to evaluate the policy impact of litigation campaigns. That impact turns not just on the presence or absence of immediate compliance with court orders, but on a long-running set of interactions among lawyers, judges, and other policymakers. The lack of finality likewise complicates our effort to evaluate the democratic legitimacy of rights-protecting judicial decisions. If such decisions are not best understood as externally imposed limits on democratic politics but serve instead as modes of interaction with (or engagement in) such politics, then the legitimacy question should turn not on whether unelected policymakers are playing any role in the process, but instead on whether the interaction of judicial and legislative institutions is producing policy outcomes that are tolerably responsive to the democratic will. It is to these two issues that I now turn.

Judicial Politics in Polarized Times

In public political discourse, denunciations of activist judges often come across as shrill and uninformed, but these arguments dovetail with a long-standing strain of scholarly commentary insisting that rights-protecting judicial decisions are incompatible with democratic governance. In modern constitutional scholarship, this tradition traces its roots to Alexander Bickel's 1962 observation that judicial review is a "deviant institution in the American democracy" (1986 [1962], 18). Bickel ultimately concluded that judicial review was, in some circumstances, democratically defensible, but more recently, Jeremy Waldron has objected that "rights-based judicial review is inappropriate for reasonably democratic societies whose main problem is not that their legislative institutions are dysfunctional but that their members disagree about rights." In Waldron's view, "[o]rdinary legislative procedures" allow democratic citizens to resolve conflicts over rights "in a responsible and deliberative fashion." As such, "an additional layer of final review by courts adds little to the process except a rather insulting form of disenfranchisement and a legalistic obfuscation of the moral issues at stake in our disagreements about rights" (2006, 1406). In the United States, he complains, "the people or their representatives in state and federal legislatures can address . . . questions [of rights] if they like, but they have no certainty that their decisions will prevail. If someone who disagrees with the legislative resolution decides to bring the matter before a court, the view that finally prevails will be that of the judges" (2006, 1350).

In sharp contrast, an altogether different body of scholarly literature has contended that exercises of judicial review are often popular and rarely final. Keith Whittington and others have long argued that judicial supremacy has more often been "established by political invitation [than] by judicial putsch" (Whittington 2007, 294; see also Graber 1993; Wasby 1981, 212–16). Electorally accountable legislators and executives regularly and repeatedly invite judges to resolve divisive policy conflicts, and the judicial responses to these invitations often have broad public support. Likewise, Michael Klarman (2004) and Gerald Rosenberg (1991) have long argued that rights-protecting judicial decisions lacking such support tend to be ignored or successfully resisted. Even if Klarman and Rosenberg pay undue attention to these responses as compared to other possibilities—notably compliance, compromise, and innovation—it seems clear that controversial rights-protecting judicial decisions are rarely final in any meaningful sense. If these accounts of judicial review's actual operation in practice are accurate, then Waldron is tilting at windmills. If, on the contrary, there is something to Waldron's supposition that rights-protecting judicial decisions frustrate the realization of the democratic will, then the regime politics and judicial impact scholars may be underplaying the potential policy significance of such decisions.

On my reading of the recent record of abortion, affirmative action, gay rights, and gun rights conflicts in US courts, neither of these existing accounts—nor the story of judges as umpires—captures precisely the role that courts have been playing. As such, our ongoing conversations about the significance and legitimacy of judicial power may be advanced by a modest reframing of each line of inquiry.

Where Would We Be without Courts?

In the scholarly literature, studies of "judicial impact" have long sought to isolate the policy effects of a single landmark judicial decision (or of a tightly knit group of decisions). These studies have uncovered a wide range of such effects, but have most often been framed as a search for noncompliance. Over several decades now, judicial impact scholars have made clear that just because a court has ordered X, we should not assume that X has come to pass (Becker and Feeley 1973; Rosenberg 1991; Sweet 2010). A separate and distinct group of scholars, working in the "legal mobilization" tradition, has long approached the question from the perspective of advocates rather than judges. Rather than asking whether a judicial decision was effectively implemented, these scholars have asked whether a group of legal advocates has achieved their policy and political aims. This literature has taught us a great deal as well, including the fact that courtroom victories often have important radiating effects, even when they are not effectively implemented, and that even courtroom defeats can sometimes aid the cause by garnering media attention, rallying supporters, provoking new rights claims, and the like (Andersen 2005; McCann 1994; Paris 2010; Scheingold 2004). These studies have called attention to multiple instances in which litigation appears to have had a significant causal impact, but they have usually focused more systematically on litigation's social movement effects than on its policy effects. In other words, they have focused on whether and how litigation has brought new members or resources to a particular movement or transformed the ideological commitments of the movement and its members over time. As a result, while each of these literatures has something to say about the significance of rights-protecting judicial decisions, their scholarly adherents have often talked past one another.[1]

For those of us who are interested in the long-term policy impact of litigation, it may be possible to draw from both of these literatures (and from the story I have told in this book) to better frame our future inquiries. For one thing, we should carefully distinguish between two variations on the question. Some scholarly investigations are efforts to discover whether litigation *works*; others are efforts to discover whether litigation *matters*. These inquiries are obviously related, but they point in somewhat different directions.

If our interest is whether litigation works, from the advocates' perspective, then we would be wise to spell out the policy goals of a given set of advocates at time A, trace the historical process in which they pursued such goals via litigation and other political strategies, assess the policy outcomes at time B, and then evaluate, as best we can, how those outcomes would have differed if the advocates in question had refrained from litigating. Here, it is worth reiterating that rights-based litigation is rampant on the right as well as the left. This observation is increasingly commonplace in the literature and is often mobilized to undercut the perpetual conservative complaint about activist judges. (If conservative judges are just as activist as liberal judges, then surely the complaint rings hollow.) But the observation is significant for another reason as well, in that it undercuts a widespread scholarly complaint about social movement litigation. The choice faced by movement advocates is not whether to fight for their policy priorities in court or through elected legislatures. The choice, rather, is whether these issues will be brought to court, and hence legally framed, by themselves or by their adversaries. Put another way, in a world of constant litigation by friend and foe, the choice faced by advocates is not whether the courts should be involved, but whether they should hear your claims before deciding your fate. Put still another way, the strategic question from the advocates' perspective is one of unilateral disarmament.

Like it or not, litigation is here to stay. The question of interest is whether a given set of advocates is doing better in the current world, where they and their opponents regularly appeal to both legislative and judicial institutions, than they would be doing in a hypothetical world where both sides are appealing to legislative institutions but only their opponents are appealing to courts as well. If abortion rights advocates had refrained from litigating *Roe v. Wade,* the result would not have been a judge-free haven of democratic deliberation. On the contrary, if and when the advocates made any headway in the state legislatures, their opponents would have challenged some of those victories in court. And if state and federal judges were presented with litigation on behalf of a fetal right to life, with no countervailing litigation on behalf of women's right to choose, abortion law might well have developed in a different direction. Rather than a harmonious legislative debate, unencumbered by judicial interference, we might have witnessed the judicial protection of fetal rights (Price and Keck 2013).

In addition to the possibility of litigation by opponents, rights advocates are also aware of the ever-present possibility of wildcat litigation by their allies and sympathizers. If reproductive rights advocates had held off on litigating *Roe*, and if their pro-life opponents had failed to make headway with their fetal rights claims in the courts, any pregnant woman with a lawyer might still have decided to press the issue in court on her own. At that point, as with the marriage equality litigation in Hawaii and the gun rights litigation in Washington, DC, the decision faced by movement advocates is whether to ignore the ongoing litigation or to join in and help it succeed. Either way, the courts will be involved.

If our interest is not just whether (and how) litigation *works* but whether (and how) it *matters*, then our inquiry needs to shift still further. Whether a particular group of advocates got what it wanted—and we will commonly find that the advocates achieved some goals but failed to achieve others—it will often be true that lawyers and judges reshaped political development and policy outcomes in fundamental ways. Thus, in addition to searching for the success or failure of litigation in achieving ex ante goals, we need also to be on the lookout for a range of potential unintended consequences. As Gordon Silverstein (2009) has emphasized, even if an appeal to courts makes strategic sense for particular policy advocates in the short term, that decision might have a variety of negative consequences in the long term, both for the advocates themselves and for the public interest. Here again, I would frame the question somewhat differently than it has often been asked. In rare cases of truly landmark appellate decisions—think *Brown v. Board of Education*—it may be worthwhile to investigate the impact of a single judicial holding. More often, it will make sense to track the impact of a long series of lawsuits and judicial decisions over time. (Silverstein's 2009 book is a model in this regard.) Indeed, even in the case of landmark holdings like *Brown*, the long-term impact of the decision will turn in part on the outcome of the follow-up litigation that comes in its wake. In addition, rather than trying to isolate the independent effects of separate policymaking institutions acting in the same field, it may make more sense to compare the actual policy change that emerged from the interaction of judicial, legislative, and administrative lawmaking with the counterfactual policy change that we might expect to have emerged from a system of legislative and administrative institutions acting alone.

On at least three of the four issues that I have examined in this book, the policy landscape today would be substantially different in the absence of independent judges and rights advocates determined to appeal to those judges. On two of the four issues, advocates successfully used courts to disrupt an entrenched policy consensus that legislative institutions had shown little inclination to upset. In particular, LGBT rights advocates used litigation, in conjunction with parallel legislative, electoral, and protest strategies, to achieve a remarkable degree of policy change over the past two decades (Eskridge 2013). They did so despite repeated popular backlashes to their courtroom victories and despite inconsistent support (at best) from elected lawmakers. One of the most interesting things about this story is that litigation has proven necessary both where the public is hostile to gay rights (as with same-sex marriage [SSM] in the early 1990s) and where the public is supportive (as with sodomy decriminalization in the late 1990s or access to military service more recently). Likewise, movement advocates have found it necessary to litigate not just against their adversaries (red-state legislatures, the Bush administration) but against their friends as well (blue-state legislatures, the Clinton and Obama administrations).

At the dawn of the Clinton era, only eleven states had hate crimes protections for gays and lesbians, and none had them for transgender persons; only seven states had employment discrimination laws that covered sexual orientation, and none of them covered gender identity; no states provided any legal rights to same-sex couples; twenty-three states still criminalized consensual sodomy; and federal law barred gays and lesbians from openly serving in the US military. By August 2013, thirty states had hate crimes protections for gays and lesbians, with fifteen of them covering transgender persons as well.[2] More important, federal protections now exist for both groups nationwide, since President Obama signed the Matthew Shepard and James Byrd Jr. Hate Crimes Prevention Act in 2009. For employment discrimination, Congress has yet to act, but the state numbers are twenty-one for sexual orientation and seventeen for gender identity—up from seven and zero, respectively.[3] On partnership rights, thirteen states have full marriage equality, and SSMs from these states are now recognized by the federal government; six others extend all state law rights of marriage without the name; and one other extends some state law rights of marriage.[4] Sodomy has been decriminalized nationwide, and Don't Ask, Don't Tell (DADT) has been repealed. Many of these policy changes were the direct result of litigation. Others followed indirectly, but no less clearly, as when Congress repealed DADT while constitutional challenges to the policy were making headway in the federal courts. And even where the connection is less clear, all of these changes took place in the shadow of litigation. Every state legislator in the country who cast a vote on any of these policy questions was aware that his or her state's existing discriminatory policies were a magnet for litigation.

Klarman and Rosenberg are correct that many courtroom victories for gay rights have provoked a significant backlash, but as I emphasize in chapter 5, other such decisions have been widely accepted, and even the most controversial ones have often survived the furor. In sum, the lesson here is that rights-based litigation campaigns can sometimes push policy forward even when they spark substantial countermobilization.

On affirmative action, the principal litigators have been on the right, not the left, but they have likewise used courts to disrupt a policy status quo that was firmly entrenched at the outset. As with the gay rights advocates, anti–affirmative action litigators had public support for many of the claims they were pursuing, but they turned to the courts because elected lawmakers of both parties were largely unresponsive to this public sentiment. Their litigation efforts have produced sweeping changes in constitutional doctrine, and these doctrinal developments have modestly reshaped the policy terrain, with a significant possibility of further such changes to come. With regard to constitutional doctrine, the Roberts Court's decision in *Parents Involved v. Seattle School District* (2007) cemented a long-term shift from a doctrinal landscape in which race-conscious student assignment plans were always constitutionally permissible and sometimes constitutionally required to one in which such plans were never constitutionally required and usually constitutionally prohibited (Siegel 2006, 841–43). With regard to policy, the principal goal of color-blind rights advocates from the beginning was to win a nationwide ban on race-conscious affirmative action. The advocates fell one vote short in *Grutter v. Bollinger* (2003), but on a variety of other occasions before, after, and indeed at the same time as this defeat, they prevailed on federal judges to impose constitutional limits on race-conscious policies. Taken together, these lawsuits succeeded in cabining such policies to a significant degree, and they succeeded in this regard despite limited support from legislative institutions at either the state or federal level.

The lawsuit filed by the Center for Individual Rights (CIR) on behalf of Cheryl Hopwood effectively outlawed race-conscious affirmative action in the three states that make up the Fifth Circuit from 1996 to 2003. As I detail in chapter 5, this legal victory provoked substantial policy experimentation before it was undone—experimentation that left the terrain of college and university admissions practices significantly altered. It also laid the groundwork for a subsequent legal victory in *Fisher v. University of Texas* (2013), and this latter decision had nationwide effect. In addition to *Parents Involved* and *Fisher*, affirmative action opponents also persuaded the Supreme Court to limit the constitutionally permissible scope of affirmative action in *Adarand Constructors v. Pena* (1995) and *Gratz v. Bollinger* (2003). These holdings led other policymakers to abandon or alter a number of existing policies, as did federal appellate holdings in cases like *Podberesky v. Kirwan* (4th Cir. 1994) and *Taxman v. Piscataway Board of Education* (3d Cir. 1996). The litigation campaign had a variety of broader radiating effects on policy change as well. In particular, it drew public attention to—and provided a compelling narrative in support of—a parallel campaign of rights mobilization outside of court. Appealing to deeply rooted constitutional principles of equal treatment, Ward Connerly and his allies regularly sought to defend the rights of sympathetic "victims" of affirmative action against infringement at the hands of elite, liberal universities. In doing so, they repeatedly built their successful ballot initiative campaigns on foundations laid by CIR's lawsuits. As I note in chapter 2, the leading public face of the 1998 campaign for the Washington Civil Rights Initiative was Katuria Smith, the lead plaintiff in CIR's then-pending suit against the University of Washington. Eight years later, the leading public face of the campaign for the Michigan Civil Rights Initiative was Jennifer Gratz, the lead plaintiff in CIR's recently concluded suit against the University of Michigan. Thus, the litigation campaign has directly imposed significant constitutional constraints on race-conscious affirmative action policies nationwide, and it has also facilitated the imposition of even stricter limits—indeed, out-right bans—in particular states.[5]

Taken as a whole, this litigation campaign has measurably altered the policy landscape from the Clinton era to the present. Consider the fate of several representative policies that were in place in the early 1990s. In Birmingham, Alabama, the local fire department had adhered to a one-to-one promotions schedule for white and black firefighters since 1981.[6] In Piscataway, New Jersey, the local school board had maintained a race-conscious employment policy since 1975, under which most employment decisions would be made on the basis of candidate qualifications, but "when candidates appear to be of equal qualification, candidates meeting the criteria of the affirmative action program will be recommended."[7] In Lynn, Massachusetts, the school board had employed a student assign-ment policy since 1989 under which parents were entitled to request that their child be assigned somewhere other than their neighborhood school, but in most circumstances, such a transfer request would be denied if it would have the effect of increasing the racial imbalance in either school.[8] In the government contracting context, federal law had since the late 1970s required that most federal contracts offer additional compensation if the contractor hired subcontractors that were certified as small businesses controlled by "socially and economically disadvantaged individuals." The law specified further that "Black Americans, Hispanic Americans, Native Americans, Asian Pacific Americans, and other minorities" shall be pre-sumed to be socially and economically disadvantaged.[9]

In the university admissions context, the University of Texas School of Law maintained a policy under which African American and Mexican American applicants were presumptively admitted if they had a "Texas Index" score (calculated on the basis of applicants' LSAT scores and undergraduate grade-point averages) of 189 or higher; they were pre-sumptively denied if their Texas Index score was 179 or lower. For applicants who fell in between these two cut points, admissions officers had the discretion to admit them on the basis of individual merit. All other applicants—whites, Asian Americans, non–Mexican Latinos, and so on—went through a similar process, but the cut points were 199 and 192, respectively. As such, the presumptive denial score for white applicants was higher than the presumptive admit score for African American and Mexican American applicants. In addition, admissions officers "color-coded" individual applicant files by race, delegated review of applications from African Americans and Mexican Americans to a separate committee, and maintained racially segregated waiting lists.[10] Meanwhile, the University of Maryland at College Park offered the Benjamin Banneker Scholarship, which provided full financial support for four years of study and which, from its inception in 1979, had been open only to African American students.[11]

All of these policies were exemplars of widespread practices in the early 1990s.[12] Today, none of them exist. Some have been replaced by policies designed to get the same results and withstand judicial scrutiny, but even so, the policy landscape has shifted significantly and is likely to shift still further in the wake of the Supreme Court's decision in *Fisher*. The lesson here is that rights-based legal campaigns can sometimes achieve significant policy change even in the absence of consistent judicial support. The federal courts have been broadly responsive to the color-blind rights claims advanced by CIR's litigators but have repeatedly sought to moderate the reach of those claims. Because of this moderation, the courts have been somewhat to the left of the median voter on this issue, but other government institutions have generally been even less responsive. Indeed, elected legislators from both parties have done their best to avoid the issue altogether. Executive branch officials from both parties have tried to maintain the policies that courts have upheld (and sometimes those that courts have struck down), and they have tried to do so with as little public deliberation as possible. Where significant deliberation has occurred, it has usually been because courts demanded it, as when President Clinton responded to the *Adarand* decision with "mend it, don't end it" or when the leaders of the University of Michigan responded to CIR's lawsuits with a sustained public defense of student-body diversity on pedagogical grounds. In sum, in the absence of decisions like *Adarand, Gratz, Parents Involved,* and *Fisher*, it is unlikely that the landscape of race-conscious contracting, employment, and education policies would have changed as much as it did.

The story is somewhat different in the abortion context, where the primary goal of the litigators has been to defend rather than disrupt the policy status quo. Ever since *Roe v. Wade*, these litigators have been using the courts to try to prevent state and federal legislators from making abortions more difficult to obtain. These efforts have been decreasingly successful over time—as an ever-more-conservative federal bench became ever-more deferential to state and federal regulations of abortion—but the courts remain willing to draw some lines even today. It is far from a ringing success story, but the advocates have repeatedly used courts as a veto point to limit the scope of rights retrogression at the hands of pro-life legislators.

As I note in chapter 1, state legislatures have periodically challenged SCOTUS by enacting near-total bans on abortion that are clearly unconstitutional under existing doctrine. If the Court were to overturn *Roe*, it seems likely that some of these states would take the opportunity to ban abortion. Indeed, Louisiana, Mississippi, North Dakota, and South Dakota have enacted statutes providing that abortion bans will automatically take effect if and when *Roe* is overturned. In addition, twelve states still have their pre-*Roe* abortion bans on the books, and eight have laws providing that their intent is to ban abortion to the maximum extent permitted by the federal courts.[13] There is some overlap among these three categories, but taken together, twenty states maintain statutory bans on abortion that they may attempt to enforce if and when the federal courts clear the way. In a counterfactual world without courts, abortion rights advocates would surely win legislative repeal of some of these policies— after all, a judicial withdrawal from the field would instantly transform the policies from symbolic legislative protests to high-stakes regulations of personal and private behavior—but it seems likely that some of them would survive.

Even if few states actually banned abortion altogether, it is beyond question that in a world without courts, multiple states would impose tighter restrictions on abortion access than they do now. As I note in chapter 4, courts over the past twenty years have enjoined two state statutes banning post-twenty-week abortions, four waiting period laws, two mandatory ultrasound requirements, and eleven parental involvement mandates for minors seeking abortions. In the latter category, most of these states have successfully revised their laws in ways that have satisfied judicial scrutiny—indeed, thirty-nine states have parental notification or consent requirements that are currently operational—but none of these states are allowed to enforce these requirements unless they provide a judicial bypass option.[14] If not for the SCOTUS holdings mandating such a procedure, many of these thirty-nine states would likely have dropped it. Likewise, a number of states would, in the absence of courts, enforce bans on public funding of abortion that are stricter than those that they currently maintain.[15]

All told, despite an increasingly hostile judiciary, abortion rights advocates have managed to maintain enough of *Roe*'s constitutional doctrine to defend the status quo of legal abortion. Pro-life advocates have persuaded a number of state legislatures (and occasionally Congress) to curtail abortion rights in a variety of ways, but they would have pushed policy still further in this direction if not for the resistance of state and federal judges. The lesson here is that rights-based litigation can sometimes hold policy stable in the face of substantial pressure for regression.

The gun rights context puts the significance of independent courts (and rights advocates) in still another light. Since the dawn of the Roberts Court, gun rights advocates have won a sea change in constitutional doctrine, but the practical policy impact of this doctrinal change has so far been limited. The Supreme Court's endorsement of the right to bear arms began only in 2008, so the policy impact of these lawsuits may continue to unfold for years to come. Still, it seems clear that the main story line here is that gun rights advocates do not need litigation very much because they do not lose in the legislative arena very often.

In most of the country, firearms possession is thinly regulated at best. Only seven states have statutory bans on the possession of certain military-style assault weapons, with just two others banning possession of such weapons by juveniles.[16] The federal government banned such weapons for ten years, but in 2004, the Republican Congress allowed the Clinton-era assault weapons law to expire. Federal law continues to require a background check for purchasers of handguns or long guns from any federally licensed firearms dealer—a key provision of the 1993 Brady Bill—but the requirement is riddled with loopholes, and even after a notorious school shooting in Newtown, Connecticut, President Obama was unable to persuade Congress to tighten these gaps. Some states have sought to do so on their own, but they have been a distinct minority. The federal requirement does not apply to most purchases made at gun shows or to other private sales by individuals who are not federally licensed dealers. Only five states have mandated universal background checks, with four others mandating them for purchases at gun shows.[17] Only ten have imposed waiting periods (ranging from twenty-four hours to fourteen days) to allow time for a more thorough background check before some or all firearms purchases are authorized.[18] More generally, only thirteen states require a state-issued license or permit for the purchase or possession of a handgun; only one requires gun owners to register all firearms with state or local law enforcement agencies, with five others requiring registration for some types of guns; only six ban the carrying of unconcealed handguns in public, with just thirteen others requiring a license or permit to do so; and none ban the carrying of concealed firearms.[19]

Taken as a whole, this landscape of state gun control policy is the end result of a twenty-year period of state legislative inattention at best, and hostility at worst. The number of states with statutory bans on assault weapons is the same today as it was in 1993; during this same period, the number of states with mandatory waiting periods dropped from nineteen to ten; with license or permit requirements, from fifteen to thirteen; and with bans on concealed carry, from eleven to zero.[20] With the exception of bans on concealed carry, these policies have broad popular support, but gun rights advocates have nonetheless been able to prevent most state legislatures (and Congress) from enacting them. In high-crime urban areas, local lawmakers are generally more likely to enact such policies, but gun rights advocates have persuaded forty-two states to preempt "all, or substantially all, aspects of local firearms . . . regulation."[21] (As I note in chapter 5, they have also persuaded thirty-six states and Congress to enact laws preempting local government *lawsuits* against firearms manufacturers.[22]) On the rare occasions when state or federal lawmakers have enacted gun control policies (or when local lawmakers have enacted policies that are not preempted), gun rights advocates have often gone to court. Since 1995, these legal challenges have sometimes been successful, and since 2008, this rate of success has picked up. Given these recent successes, the rate of such litigation is likely to continue to increase, but as compared to the LGBT rights context, litigation has so far played a more supplemental role on this issue.

In sum, in the absence of independent judges and mobilized rights advocates, the policy landscape on abortion, affirmative action, and gay rights would be substantially different today, and the policy landscape on gun rights would likely differ at the margins. From the advocates' perspective, litigation does not always work, but under a variety of conditions it may serve as a valuable tool, particularly since the strategic dilemma they face is one of unilateral disarmament. From the policy analysts' perspective, the outcomes are literally incomprehensible without attending to the role played by lawyers and judges in a series of ongoing—indeed, never-ending—policy conflicts. Why do thirteen states currently allow same-sex couples to legally marry, a number that will certainly have increased by the time this book is published, and why do seven allow some *opposite-sex* couples to join in a state-recognized union other than marriage? Why have selective colleges and universities very nearly abandoned the obviously efficient practice of presumptively admitting or rejecting most of their applicants on the basis of grades and standardized test scores; indeed, why have some ceased relying on standardized test scores altogether? Why do women who become pregnant as a result of rape or incest have a right to legal abortion and, if they are eligible for Medicaid, the right to state funding of that abortion? Why are residents of Chicago entitled to possess and carry concealed handguns, and why are firing ranges allowed to operate within the city? None of these questions are answerable without attending to the interaction of judicial, legislative, and administrative institutions over a period of many years.

Are Courts Illegitimate?

Popular denunciations of "activist judges" generally rest on some combination of three claims: (1) that the judges are deciding things that should be decided democratically; (2) that they are doing so on the basis of political preferences that are at odds with those of most ordinary citizens; and (3) that the people have no recourse for correcting these decisions. Scholarly critics of judicial power generally present the argument in more nuanced form, but in both versions, the account is often directed against a theoretical version of judicial review that does not much exist in actual practice (Doherty and Pevnick 2014, 94–96).

Consider the three central complaints, in reverse order. Popular denunciations of courts have long made use of rhetoric implying that judges are all powerful; that is surely the central message conveyed by calling them "tyrants." In sometimes less-colorful language, scholarly critics have regularly echoed the claim that judicial review is objectionable in part because it is final. In his canonical critique of "countermajoritarian" courts, Bickel observed that judicial review "is the power to apply and construe the Constitution, in matters of the greatest moment, against the wishes of a legislative majority, which is, in turn, powerless to affect the judicial decision" (1986, 20). More recently, Waldron has likewise objected that allowing the "final determination" of conflicts about rights to be made by judges amounts to a systematic disenfranchisement of democratic majorities (1999, 15; 2006, 1350, 1406).

The observation that rights-protecting judicial decisions are objectionable in part because of their finality has sometimes been echoed by judges themselves. In the abortion context, Justice Antonin Scalia has complained that before *Roe v. Wade*, "political compromise was possible," but "*Roe*'s mandate for abortion on demand destroyed the compromises of the past, rendered compromise impossible for the future, and required the entire issue to be resolved uniformly, at the national level." As such, he denounced the Court for "foreclosing all democratic outlet for the deep passions this issue arouses, [for] banishing the issue from the political forum that gives all participants, even the losers, the satisfaction of a fair hearing and an honest fight."[23] Some years later, Scalia reiterated that the problem with an open-ended interpretation of the due process clause is that "the people's ponderings do not matter, since whatever the people decide, courts have the last word."[24]

One problem with these critiques of activist judging is that "reports of the finality of judicial decisions are greatly exaggerated" (Lovell and Lemieux 2006, 109–10). As Barry Friedman has noted, the finality of judicial declarations of constitutional rights would indeed complicate any effort to defend their democratic legitimacy—if it were true: "If what happened next, after the judiciary pronounced the meaning of the Constitution, is that we all fell to obeisance and the question were not raised again, if we followed the Court's pronouncement in hushed murmurs, we would have a formidable problem on our hands" (2004, 1290). In fact, however, rights-protecting decisions more often provoke continued conflict than obeisance, and this continued conflict influences ultimate policy outcomes. In short, judges do not have the last word after all. As Friedman puts it, "What happens next . . . is that after all is said and done, if the fight is fought and pursued with focus, and attracts enough adherents, the law changes. *Roe* becomes *Casey*. *Bowers* becomes *Romer* and then *Lawrence*. *Brown* becomes *Croson*, then *Adarand*, and then *Grutter* and *Gratz*" (2004, 1293). If actual rights-protecting judicial decisions provoke a wide range of responses on the part of other policymakers, it is misleading to characterize such decisions as calling an end to democratic deliberation and debate.

Of course, if judges are erecting hurdles to the realization of the popular will, one might object on democratic grounds even if the hurdles are surmountable. In a democratic political system, why should popular majorities have to jump so high to enact their will? This question brings me to the second claim in the case against judicial power—the claim that rights-protecting judicial decisions too often rest on political preferences that are at odds with those of most ordinary citizens. As Fourth Circuit Judge J. Harvie Wilkinson III has put it (quoting Blackstone), "[t]he result of judges-as-legislators . . . is 'equity without law,' where rules come from nothing but each judge's varying sentiments," and as Scalia has long emphasized, judges' sentiments are sometimes far from representative.[25] As I demonstrate in chapter 4, however, most rights-based limits imposed by US courts are not only surmountable but also popular.

Here, it is worth reiterating that in evaluating the democratic responsiveness of courts, the question of interest is not whether judicial institutions are democratically responsive in the abstract, nor even whether they are more or less responsive than legislative institutions. The question, rather, is whether our actual system, in which policy emerges from the interaction of courts, legislatures, and executives, is more or less democratically responsive than a hypothetical system of legislative and executive institutions acting alone would be (Doherty and Pevnick 2014). Of course, this sort of counterfactual claim is difficult to assess, but on all four issues that I have examined in this book, the actual patterns of policy change have been the product of long-running interactions among legislative, executive, and judicial institutions, and in none of the four cases do these patterns seem dramatically at odds with democratic preferences. Pushing the point further, it seems likely in all four cases that in the absence of independent courts and mobilized rights advocates, the patterns of policy change would have been *more* at odds with such preferences, at least at the national level.

Consider some examples. In the absence of judges and litigators, there would likely be few, if any, states in which SSM was currently legal. A small number of states might have robust domestic partnership or civil union policies, but even that is highly speculative, as real-world state legislatures enacted such policies only after state courts pushed the envelope by threatening to legalize SSM. The DADT policy might still be on the books, as would at least a dozen state sodomy laws. Some states would currently be enforcing near-total bans on abortion, and many others would be enforcing highly restrictive regulations that go further than national majorities have been willing to support. In the affirmative action context, race-conscious considerations would be a widespread and largely formulaic feature of university admissions and financial aid decisions and would play a more prominent role than they now do in public school assignment, government contracting, and public employment decisions as well. In the gun rights arena, the policy landscape would not look very different than it does today, but in the absence of independent courts and mobilized rights advocates, several large cities would still be enforcing handgun bans that lack national support. In all four contexts, then, it is at least plausible to claim that litigation has rendered the policy process more democratically responsive than it otherwise would have been. This claim is not provable, but at the very least, it undercuts strongly worded denunciations of judges and litigators for thwarting the democratic will.

Which brings me, finally, to the first claim often advanced against judicial review: that electorally unaccountable judges are deciding things that should be decided democratically. Even when judges issue decisions that the public supports, those decisions might still be considered democratically illegitimate on the grounds that they were made by actors who are not accountable to the people. After all, kings and czars might sometimes enact policies that the public likes, but that does not make their enactment any more democratic. Judge Wilkinson, for example, has described the "true casualty" of both *Roe v. Wade* and *District of Columbia v. Heller* (2008) as "the right of the American people to decide the laws by which they shall be governed" (2009, 275). This claim is fundamentally a normative one, which no amount of empirical investigation can rebut, but if our normative evaluations of courts are going to help us render judgment on what actual courts do—as opposed to what idealized courts might do— then those evaluations will have to treat judicial institutions as part and parcel of the American democratic process rather than as alien invaders seeking to limit that process from on high (Shapiro 1964, 45; Wasby 1981, 213).

As a historical matter, judicial review is as much a constituent feature of constitutional democracy as any other institution. In the context of national transitions to democracy, fair courts tend to be a focus of popular demand every bit as much as fair elections, and while the actual impact of constitutional courts on democratic governance varies significantly across time and space, it is by no means accurate to say that constitutional politics is necessarily destructive of, or even opposed to, democratic politics (Hilbink 2008). In the contemporary American context, rights-based litigation is better understood as a form of democratic politics than as an effort to subvert such politics.[26] It has long been a prominent mode of political mobilization and contestation, and it is today used by individual citizens and organized interests across the political spectrum. It is regularly deployed by advocates on both the left and right, both when they are in power and when they are out of power. In other words, its use is not reserved for situations where advocates have lost in the electoral arena and are seeking to undermine or reverse that democratic judgment. Rights advocates litigate against their partisan friends as well as their enemies, both when they are winning in other arenas and when they are losing. After all, their legislative and executive allies are regularly pulled in multiple directions and often appreciate the political cover that is provided by a judicial command to do something desirable but controversial (Rosenberg 2008, 34–35; Wasby 1981, 213).

For advocates, litigation sometimes succeeds and sometimes fails, and its prospects do not differ in the abstract from any other strategies for policy change. For the public, litigation sometimes hinders the democratic responsiveness of government, but just as often promotes such responsiveness. Again, its effects vary in practice across a full range of possibilities but do not differ in the abstract from the range of effects that follow efforts to change policy via electoral campaigning, legislative lobbying, or social protest.

On my reading of the recent history of litigation and judicial decision making on abortion, affirmative action, gay rights, and gun rights, the most significant normative concern with regard to contemporary courts is not countermajoritarianism but partisan capture. Put another way, the key legitimacy question is not the frequency or scope of judicial review but its bipartisan deployment. During periods of significant partisan polarization, when a single partisan coalition captures the courts, we are likely to witness a rash of decisions that are unpopular and that might reasonably be considered democratically illegitimate. In the absence of significant constraints, partisan judges are likely to overreach, protecting expansive conceptions of the legal rights that are supported by their coalition, while ignoring legitimate rights claims advanced by their partisan and ideological opponents. But there are two potential correctives to this situation. One is to urge judges to exercise their power with greater restraint and, if necessary, to impose external limits that mandate such restraint. But a second possibility is to win back some political balance in the courts and for these newly balanced courts to protect rights that are advanced by interests across the political spectrum.

Those who are preoccupied with the legitimacy of judicial power generally advocate bipartisan judicial restraint as the antidote; in other words, they urge judges of all stripes to refrain from exercising judicial review. But if our interest is improving the courts that we have—rather than designing a set of idealized courts—then bipartisan judicial activism would be more feasible, more popular, and normatively preferable.

Calls for judicial restraint are almost never heeded by actual judges, even when the calls were issued by those judges themselves before they joined the bench. Once seated, after all, they are inclined to use their new-found powers for some desirable end, and even if they were inclined to do so cautiously, they would face the dilemma of unilateral disarmament. From the perspective of a federal judge appointed by George W. Bush, if her liberal colleagues are using their power to protect abortion rights, then why would she give up her power to protect gun rights? For bipartisan judicial restraint to take hold, the vast majority of judges would have to refrain from exercising their own authority; most are unwilling to do so, particularly if they have no guarantee that their ideological opponents will follow. Bipartisan judicial activism is more feasible because it can take hold even if every individual judge is engaged only in partisan activism. So long as the courts are politically balanced, the judiciary as a whole can protect both abortion rights and gun rights even if few individual judges believe that both such rights should be protected.

Bipartisan judicial activism is also more popular than bipartisan restraint, provided that judges temper their activism with some degree of "judicial minimalism" (Sunstein 1999). On all four issues that I have examined in this book, the public has been broadly supportive of the principal rights claim at issue—legal abortion, equal treatment for gays and lesbians, color-blind governmental decision making, and the right to bear arms in self-defense. In each of the four cases, the leading rights advocates have generally called for a more robust vision of the particular rights claim than the public has been willing to support, and in each case, the advocates have sometimes persuaded judges to enforce the rights claim in this robust form, at which point the judges have been out in front of the public. If the courts had continued on the paths laid out by the rights advocates, then we might justifiably complain that the courts were standing in the way of the democratic will. In each case, however, the courts stepped back from the brink, adopting a more modest reading of the relevant rights claim that preserved room for continued legislative and executive lawmaking on the issue.

As Mark Graber has emphasized, constitutional theory cannot resolve polarized political conflicts, but constitutional courts may be able to do so, provided that they do not pursue constitutional justice at all costs. Since polarized constitutional controversies do not generally yield clearly correct answers, we should emphasize the ways in which "[c]onstitutional institutions foster social peace by privileging policies that most citizens will tolerate." On this account, "[j]udicial review is constitutionally desirable . . . because justices often reach centrist decisions on matters that badly divide national legislatures" (2006b, 245–49; see also Perry and Powe 2004). As Martin Shapiro has long noted, the basic conflict-resolution function of judicial institutions creates a strong incentive for judges to seek compromise solutions, and as Terri Peretti has put it with regard to the US Supreme Court in particular, "the justices are and should be regarded as politicians who share in the difficult but noble task of political leadership, in generating consensual solutions to the often vexing and contentious issues of the day" (Shapiro 1981; Peretti 1999, 254).

A great many modestly framed rights claims have unambiguous public support. Most fundamentally, popular majorities have regularly and repeatedly rejected the proposition that courts should stop protecting rights altogether. Given the clear public support for certain basic principles of individual liberty and equal treatment—and given the obvious centrality of such principles to any reasonable conception of democratic governance—bipartisan judicial activism is the best obtainable vision of the judicial role. Nobody will be happy with it because virtually all political actors will regularly face rights-protecting judicial decisions with which they profoundly disagree. But a substantial majority of the public will be able to live with it because all of them will find that the courts regularly protect rights that they hold dear.

Coding Procedures for Polarization Analysis

In the text and notes of chapters 1 and 2 I cite several hundred decisions issued by state or federal courts on the issues of abortion, affirmative action, gay rights, and gun rights from January 1993 through August 2013. For the polarization analysis presented in chapter 3, I coded all such decisions that were issued by the Supreme Court of the United States, a federal appellate court, or a state high court. These decisions are listed in appendix B (available at http://press.uchicago.edu/sites/keck/).

The list includes all decisions from chapters 1 and 2 that had close legal and/or political connections to the issues noted above. For example, it includes *Hill v. Colorado* (2000) and *Doe v. Reed* (2010), which were formally First Amendment free speech holdings but which emerged out of legal and political conflicts regarding abortion and domestic partnerships, respectively. The list excludes decisions involving unrelated issues that are cited in the text simply to illustrate some general point about law and courts. For example, it excludes *National Federation of Independent Businesses v. Sebelius* (2012), in which the Supreme Court upheld most provisions of the Affordable Care Act, and which is cited in chapter 2 to illustrate that elected officials sometimes pursue litigation when other avenues of policy change are closed off.

For the federal appellate courts, I coded the party of the appointing president for judges who participated in all decisions issued by three-judge panels and most decisions issued by en banc panels. In the latter category, the published opinions sometimes indicate individual judges' votes by name and, at other times, provide enough detail to allow a reconstruction of individual judges' votes; where neither of these conditions holds, I left the cases uncoded. For the SCOTUS holdings, I coded the party of the appointing president for all justices. I also coded the justices in conventional ideological terms, with Samuel Alito, Anthony Kennedy, Sandra Day O'Connor, William Rehnquist, John Roberts, Antonin Scalia, Clarence Thomas, and Byron White coded conservative, and Harry Blackmun, Stephen Breyer, Ruth Bader Ginsburg, Elena Kagan, Sonia Sotomayor, David Souter, and John Paul Stevens coded liberal. For the state high court decisions, I coded all votes cast by justices who were either elected in a partisan election or appointed by a Democratic or Republican governor. I excluded votes cast by justices who were elected via nonpartisan election or appointed by an independent or third-party governor. All state high court decisions cited in part 1 included at least one judicial vote that was coded. Some states rely primarily on nonpartisan elections to staff their high courts, but they each have provisions for gubernatorial appointments under certain circumstances, and for all cited decisions that issued from such states, at least one of the participating justices had joined the court via such a partisan mechanism.

For holdings from all courts, I included cases resting on nonsubstantive grounds whenever the substantive policy implications of those holdings were clear; for example, a holding dismissing a rights claim on standing grounds is coded as an anti-rights decision. I included denials of certiorari and denials of rehearing whenever those procedural decisions included recorded dissents.

In almost all cases, I coded the ideological direction and the rights-protecting character of the judicial holdings from the perspective of the party who initiated the litigation. For example, if anti–affirmative action litigators persuaded a court to invalidate a race-conscious affirmative action policy, I coded that holding as conservative and rights protecting. In a small number of cases, I coded the holdings from the perspective not of the party who initiated the litigation but the party who had appealed to the court in question. For example, when abortion providers in upstate New York persuaded a federal district judge to enjoin disruptive pro-life protest activities, I would have coded that holding (if I were coding trial court decisions) as a liberal, rights-protecting, category 3 holding. But when the pro-life protesters persuaded a Second Circuit panel to vacate that injunction on First Amendment grounds, I coded that decision as a conservative, rights-protecting, category 1 holding.

Finally, I coded all congressional votes on the issues of abortion, affirmative action, gay rights, and gun rights from 1993 through 2012. Here, I relied on *Congressional Quarterly*'s annual *CQ Almanac*, which provides a comprehensive survey of federal legislative developments. For each bill, I coded no more than one roll call vote from each house for each year. In each case, I used the vote that *CQ Almanac* identified as most significant to the final outcome on the issue of interest. For example, if there was a vote to enact a bill, followed by a presidential veto and then a failed override vote, I coded the override vote. Likewise, if there was a close vote on cloture followed by a more lopsided vote to enact, I coded the cloture vote rather than the vote on final passage. If there was a successful vote to amend an appropriations bill to add, say, an abortion-funding restriction, followed by a vote to enact the appropriations bill, I coded the vote on the amendment. These roll call votes are itemized in appendix C (available at http://press.uchicago.edu/sites/keck/).

Notes

Introduction

1. Confirmation Hearing on the Nomination of John G. Roberts Jr. to be Chief Justice of the United States, 109th Cong., 1st Sess. (September 12–15, 2005), 55.

2. Confirmation Hearing on the Nomination of Hon. Sonia Sotomayor to be an Associate Justice of the Supreme Court of the US, 111th Cong., 1st Sess. (July 13–16, 2009), 59, 66–67, 70, 78–79.

3. Confirmation Hearing on the Nomination of Samuel A. Alito Jr. to be an Associate Justice of the Supreme Court of the US, 109th Cong., 2d Sess. (January 9–13, 2006), 28–30, 403–5, 408–10.

4. Confirmation Hearing of Sotomayor, 3, 24–25, 56, 69, 77–78.

5. Confirmation Hearing of Alito, 12, 26–27, 38, 348–50.

6. Confirmation Hearing of Sotomayor, 8, 26, 140–42, 426–27, 452–54.

7. Republican appointees made up a majority of active federal judges without interruption from January 2005 through August 2013. Indeed, with only a brief interruption between 2001 and 2005—when the GOP portion of the federal judiciary dipped to 49 percent—Republican appointees have held such a majority since 1988. I collected the 2013 numbers from the Federal Judicial Center's Biographical Directory of Federal Judges, available at http://www.fjc.gov/history/home.nsf/page/judges.html. For the earlier numbers, see Goldman (1989); Goldman et al. (2005, 270).

8. For two recent examples, see United States v. Windsor, 133 S. Ct. 2675, 2697–98 (2013) (Scalia, J., dissenting), and Shelby County v. Holder, 133 S. Ct. 2612, 2648 (2013) (Ginsburg, J., dissenting).

9. In October 2009, President Obama signed the Matthew Shepard and James Byrd Jr. Hate Crimes Prevention Act, which extended existing federal hate crimes laws to cover sexual orientation and gender identity. In December 2010, he signed a bill repealing the Don't Ask, Don't Tell policy, thereby allowing gays and lesbians to serve openly in the US military. In May 2012, he declared his support for same-sex

marriage in a televised interview with ABC News, available at http://abcnews
.go.com/Politics/transcript-robin-roberts-abc-news-interview-president-obama
/story?id=16316043#.UbHuFcqwV8E.

10. Perry v. Schwarzenegger, 704 F. Supp. 2d 921 (N.D. Cal. 2010).

11. Planned Parenthood v. Casey, 505 U.S. 833 (1992).

12. I use the term "wildcat litigation" to evoke the concept of a wildcat strike—a
labor action that is initiated by rank-and-file workers without the support of
national union leaders. Scholars of social movement litigation have long noted the
phenomenon (e.g., Wasby 1984, 112–15) but have not, to my knowledge, given it a
name or adequately explored its implications for constitutional politics.

13. I survey this existing literature in more detail in chapter 5, but readers who
are looking for some leading examples might start, on the left, with Gerald Rosenberg's account of mid-twentieth-century civil rights litigation and late twentieth-
and early twenty-first-century LGBT rights litigation (2008, 39–172, 339–429) or
Michael McCann's account of the gender-based pay equity movement (1994); and
on the right, with Steven Teles's account of the Reagan-era rise of the conservative
legal movement (2008) or Kevin den Dulk's account of evangelical cause lawyering
(2008). For one recent study that does examine the use of courts on both sides of
the aisle, see Silverstein (2009).

14. As some readers will recognize, the reference here is to Rosenberg's landmark 1991 book, *The Hollow Hope: Can Courts Bring about Social Change?*,
which I take up more fully in chapter 5.

Chapter One

1. Consider, for example, the suits that persuaded the Warren Court to enjoin
recently enacted school assignment policies in Griffin v. County School Board of
Prince Edward County, 377 U.S. 218 (1964), and Green v. County School Board of
New Kent County, 391 U.S. 430 (1968).

2. The paradigm case here is Brown v. Board of Education, 347 U.S. 483 (1954).

3. Consider, for example, NAACP v. Alabama, 357 U.S. 449 (1958), in which
the organization's lawyers persuaded the Warren Court to prevent Alabama from
forcing a state affiliate to turn over its membership lists, and Bell v. Maryland, 378
U.S. 226 (1964), in which they persuaded the Court to vacate the state trespass
convictions of several sit-in demonstrators in Maryland.

4. For illustrative examples from state and federal court, each of which I examine
below, consider Department of Human Services & Child Welfare Agency Review
Board v. Howard, 238 S.W.3d 1 (Ark. 2006), and Citizens for Equal Protection v.
Bruning, 455 F.3d 859 (8th Cir. 2006). Throughout the text, I use "red states" to
refer collectively to those states that typically supported Republican presidential
candidates in the late twentieth and early twenty-first centuries, and "blue states"
to refer to their Democratic counterparts.

5. On sodomy decriminalization, consider Commonwealth v. Wasson, 842 S.W.2d 487 (Ky. 1992), and Lawrence v. Texas, 539 U.S. 558 (2003). On marriage equality, consider Goodridge v. Department of Public Health, 440 Mass. 309 (Mass. 2003), and United States v. Windsor, 133 S. Ct. 2675 (2013).

6. The paradigm case here is Romer v. Evans, 517 U.S. 620 (1996).

7. Sojourner T v. Edwards, 974 F.2d 27 (5th Cir. 1992), *cert. denied*, 507 U.S. 972 (1993); Jane L. v. Bangerter, 61 F.3d 1493 (10th Cir. 1995), *rev'd*, Leavitt v. Jane L., 518 U.S. 137 (1996), *on remand*, 102 F.3d 1112 (10th Cir. 1996), *cert. denied*, Leavitt v. Jane L., 520 U.S. 1274 (1997). See also Guam Society of Obstetricians & Gynecologists v. Ada, 962 F.2d 1366 (9th Cir.), *cert. denied*, 506 U.S. 1011 (1992).

8. Women's Medical Professional Corp. v. Voinovich, 130 F.3d 187 (6th Cir. 1997); Richmond Medical Center v. Gilmore, 183 F.3d 303 (4th Cir. 1998). The 1995 Ohio statute also banned all postviability abortions. The Sixth Circuit holding invalidated this provision as well, and on this point, Justice Thomas, joined by Chief Justice Rehnquist and Justice Scalia, urged the high Court to intervene. Voinovich v. Women's Medical Professional Corp., 523 U.S. 1036 (1998).

9. Carhart v. Stenberg, 192 F.3d 1142 (8th Cir. 1999); Planned Parenthood of Greater Iowa, Inc. v. Miller, 195 F.3d 386 (8th Cir. 1999); Little Rock Family Planning Services v. Jegley, 192 F.3d 794 (8th Cir. 1999); Hope Clinic v. Ryan, 195 F.3d 857 (7th Cir. 1999). During this same period, federal district courts enjoined partial birth bans from Arizona, Florida, Louisiana, and Michigan. Planned Parenthood of Southern Arizona, Inc. v. Woods, 982 F. Supp. 1369, 1378 (D. Ariz. 1997); A Choice for Women v. Butterworth, 54 F. Supp. 2d 1148 (S.D. Fla. 1998); Causeway Medical Suite v. Foster, 43 F. Supp. 2d 604 (E.D. La. 1999); Evans v. Kelley, 977 F. Supp. 1283 (E.D. Mich. 1997).

10. Hope Clinic v. Ryan, 195 F.3d 857, 876, 878, 880–81 (7th Cir. 1999). The following month, the circuit's judges again split sharply, with the five judges from the original majority voting to deny the abortion providers' request for a stay. The four dissenters picked up a fifth vote from newly seated Circuit Judge Ann Claire Williams, but by virtue of an equally divided vote, the panel denied the stay. Hope Clinic v. Ryan, 197 F.3d 876 (7th Cir. 1999).

11. Brief for the US as Amicus Curiae in support of Respondent, Stenberg v. Carhart (March 29, 2000), 5–7.

12. Stenberg v. Carhart, 530 U.S. 914 (2000).

13. Ibid., 979.

14. Joined by Rehnquist and Scalia, Thomas published a lengthy dissent arguing that the Nebraska law did not impose an undue burden as defined by *Casey*. He prefaced this discussion by reiterating his view that "the *Casey* joint opinion was constructed by its authors out of whole cloth, . . . that it has no origins in or relationship to the Constitution and is, consequently, as illegitimate as the standard it purported to replace." Chief Justice Rehnquist and Justice Scalia each wrote separately to reiterate that *Casey* was "wrongly decided" and "must be overruled." Ibid., 952, 956, 982.

15. Planned Parenthood v. Farmer, 220 F.3d 127 (3d Cir. 2000); Richmond Medical Center v. Gilmore, 224 F.3d 337 (4th Cir. 2000); Eubanks v. Stengel, 224 F.3d 576 (6th Cir. 2000); Causeway Medical Suite v. Foster, 221 F.3d 811 (5th Cir. 2000); Rhode Island Medical Society v. Whitehouse, 239 F.3d 104 (1st Cir. 2001); Hope Clinic v. Ryan, 249 F.3d 603 (7th Cir. 2001); Reproductive Health Services of Planned Parenthood of the St. Louis Region, Inc. v. Nixon, 429 F.3d 803 (8th Cir. 2005).

16. Women's Medical Professional Corp. v. Taft, 114 F. Supp. 2d 664 (S.D. Ohio 2000), rev'd, 353 F.3d 436 (6th Cir. 2003).

17. Brief for the US as Amicus Curiae Supporting Reversal, Women's Medical Professional Corp. v. Taft (6th Cir. 2003), February 2002.

18. In Utah, the federal district court issued a preliminary injunction in June 2004 but lifted that injunction shortly after *Carhart II* came down three years later. Utah Women's Clinic v. Walker, No. 2:04CV00408 PGC (D. Utah May 31, 2007). A trial court likewise struck down the Michigan law, and here, the law swept so broadly that a unanimous Sixth Circuit panel affirmed the decision even after *Carhart II*. Northland Family Planning Clinic, Inc. v. Cox, 487 F.3d 323 (6th Cir. 2007). In Virginia, a divided Fourth Circuit panel struck down the law in June 2005. The full circuit denied a request for en banc rehearing later that year, but SCOTUS vacated the decision after *Carhart II* came down. On remand, the original Fourth Circuit panel struck down the law again, by the same divided vote as its original holding, but in June 2009, an en banc panel reversed. Richmond Medical Center for Women v. Hicks, 409 F.3d 619, *reh'g en banc denied*, 422 F.3d 160 (4th Cir. 2005), *vacated and remanded*, Herring v. Richmond Medical Center for Women, 550 U.S. 901 (2007), *aff'd*, Richmond Medical Center for Women v. Herring, 527 F.3d 128 (4th Cir. 2008), *rev'd en banc*, 570 F.3d 165 (4th Cir. 2009).

19. Isaacson v. Horne, 716 F.3d 1213 (9th Cir. 2013); Edwards v. Beck, 2013 U.S. Dist. LEXIS 75277 (E.D. Ark. 2013); Lathrop v. Deal, Civil Action No. 2012-cv-224423 (Super. Ct. Fulton Cty., Ga., December 21, 2012); MKB Management Corp. v. Burdick, 2013 U.S. Dist. LEXIS 102620 (D.N.D. 2013).

20. In re Initiative Petition No. 395, 286 P.3d 637 (Okla. 2012).

21. In 2010, for example, the ACLU persuaded a Nevada trial judge that a proposed fetal personhood initiative violated the state's requirement that ballot measures be limited to a single subject. The initiative proponents appealed to the state high court, but the justices unanimously dismissed the appeal as moot, on the grounds that the targeted election date had now passed. Personhood Nevada v. Bristol, 245 P.3d 572 (Nev. 2010).

22. Casey v. Planned Parenthood, 14 F.3d 848 (3d Cir. 1994); Planned Parenthood v. Casey, 510 U.S. 1309 (1994) (Souter, J., in chambers).

23. Barnes v. Moore, 970 F.2d 12 (5th Cir. 1992).

24. Fargo Women's Health Organization v. Schafer, 507 U.S. 1013, 1014 (1993).

25. Fargo Women's Health Organization v. Schafer, 18 F.3d 526 (8th Cir. 1994).

The Eighth Circuit panel was unanimous in vacating the stay pending appeal, but Circuit Judge Theodore McMillian reserved judgment on the merits in a one-sentence concurrence. Note also Utah Women's Clinic v. Leavitt, 844 F. Supp. 1482 (D. Utah 1994), in which Federal District Judge Dee Benson rejected a constitutional challenge to Utah's 1993 informed consent law.

26. The South Dakota case was Planned Parenthood v. Miller, 63 F.3d 1452, 1467 (8th Cir. 1995).

27. A Woman's Choice—East Side Women's Clinic v. Newman, 904 F. Supp. 1434 (S.D. Ind. 1995); 132 F. Supp. 2d 1150 (S.D. Ind. 2001).

28. A Woman's Choice—East Side Women's Clinic v. Newman, 305 F.3d 684 (7th Cir. 2002).

29. Karlin v. Foust, 975 F. Supp. 1177 (W.D. Wis. 1997).

30. Karlin v. Foust, 188 F.3d 446, *en banc reh'g denied*, 198 F.3d 620 (7th Cir. 1999).

31. In a thorough survey of the case law, Linda J. Wharton, Susan Frietsche, and Kathryn Kolbert (2006, 357–67) identified only two limited exceptions to this pattern—that is, two cases in which federal district judges had enjoined some or all applications of an informed consent/waiting period statute. See Summit Medical Center of Alabama, Inc. v. Riley, 318 F. Supp. 2d 1109 (M.D. Ala. 2003); Planned Parenthood of Delaware v. Brady, 2003 U.S. Dist. LEXIS 10099 (D. Del. 2003). Wharton, Frietsche, and Kolbert also cite Planned Parenthood of Middle Tennessee v. Sundquist, 38 S.W.3d 1 (Tenn. 2000), which enjoined such a law on state constitutional grounds.

32. Planned Parenthood v. State, 1999 Mont. Dist. LEXIS 1117 (Mont. 1st Jud. Dist., Lewis and Clark Cty. 1999); Planned Parenthood of Middle Tennessee v. Sundquist, 38 S.W.3d 1 (Tenn. 2000).

33. Pro-Choice Mississippi v. Fordice, 716 So. 2d 645 (Miss. 1998); Clinic for Women, Inc. v. Brizzi, 837 N.E.2d 973 (Ind. 2005); Preterm Cleveland v. Voinovich, 627 N.E.2d 570 (Ohio. App. 1993); Mahaffey v. Attorney General, 654 N.W.2d 104 (Mich. App. 1997); Florida v. Presidential Women's Center, 937 So. 2d 114 (Fla. 2006); Reproductive Health Services of Planned Parenthood of St. Louis Region, Inc. v. Nixon, 185 S.W.3d 685 (Mo. 2006).

34. Planned Parenthood v. Rounds, 375 F. Supp. 2d 881 (D.S.D. 2005).

35. Planned Parenthood v. Rounds, 467 F.3d 716 (8th Cir. 2006), *subsequent opinion on reh'g*, 530 F.3d 724 (8th Cir. 2008) (en banc).

36. Planned Parenthood Minnesota v. Rounds, 653 F.3d 662 (8th Cir. 2011), *rev'd in part*, 686 F.3d 889 (8th Cir. 2012) (en banc).

37. Planned Parenthood Minnesota v. Daugaard, 799 F. Supp. 2d 1048 (D.S.D. 2011).

38. The 2008 ultrasound provision was part of an omnibus abortion statute; the 2010 provision was a stand-alone bill. The decision invalidating the 2008 law was Nova Health Systems v. Edmondson, 233 P.3d 380 (Okla. 2010).

39. Nova Health Systems v. Pruit, 2012 OK 103 (Okla. 2012).

40. Federal District Judge Catherine C. Eagles enjoined the North Carolina law in Stuart v. Huff, 834 F. Supp. 2d 424 (M.D.N.C. 2011). A unanimous Fourth Circuit panel affirmed Judge Eagles's denial of a motion to intervene advanced by a group of pro-life advocates, 706 F.3d 345 (4th Cir. 2013), but has not yet ruled on the merits of the case. A unanimous Fifth Circuit panel upheld the Texas law in Texas Medical Providers Performing Abortion Services v. Lakey, 667 F.3d 570 (5th Cir. 2012).

41. To put the point more precisely, the Court had held that requirements for the consent of one parent, the consent of both parents, or the notification of both parents must include a judicial bypass; it had suggested, but not expressly held, that a requirement for the notification of one parent need not include such a bypass (Silverstein 2007, 20–27).

42. Planned Parenthood v. Miller, 63 F.3d 1452 (8th Cir 1995), *cert. denied*, Janklow v. Planned Parenthood, 517 U.S. 1174 (1996). Justice Scalia, joined by Chief Justice Rehnquist and Justice Thomas, dissented from the denial of certiorari.

43. Barnes v. Mississippi, 992 F.2d 1335 (5th Cir. 1993); Manning v. Hunt, 119 F.3d 254 (4th Cir. 1997); Planned Parenthood of the Blue Ridge v. Camblos, 155 F.3d 352 (4th Cir. 1998) (en banc).

44. Causeway Medical Suite v. Ieyoub, 109 F.3d 1096, 1108, *reh'g denied*, 123 F.3d 849 (5th Cir. 1997) (en banc).

45. Planned Parenthood v. Lawall, 1999 U.S. App. LEXIS 33154, *reh'g denied*, 193 F.3d 1042 (9th Cir. 1999) (en banc).

46. Zbaraz v. Madigan, 572 F.3d 370 (7th Cir. 2009).

47. Memphis Planned Parenthood v. Sundquist, 175 F.3d 456, 468 (6th Cir. 1999).

48. Memphis Planned Parenthood, Inc. v. Sundquist, 184 F.3d 600 (6th Cir. 1999).

49. Wicklund v. Salvagni, 93 F.3d 567 (9th Cir. 1996), *rev'd*, Lambert v. Wicklund, 520 U.S. 292 (1997).

50. Nova Health Systems v. Edmondson, 460 F.3d 1295 (10th Cir. 2006). I have found no record of any such subsequent challenges being filed in Oklahoma. More than a decade earlier, abortion providers in Ohio had argued that the state's parental involvement law, whose facial validity had already been established by SCOTUS, was operating unconstitutionally as applied, but a unanimous Sixth Circuit panel dismissed the challenge in Cleveland Surgi-Center v. Jones, 2 F.3d 686 (6th Cir. 1993).

51. Pro-Choice Mississippi v. Fordice, 716 So. 2d 645 (Miss. 1998).

52. Planned Parenthood League of Massachusetts, Inc. v. Attorney General, 677 N.E.2d 101 (Mass. 1997); American Academy of Pediatrics v. Lungren, 940 P.2d 797 (Cal. 1997); Planned Parenthood of Central New Jersey v. Farmer, 762

A.2d 620 (N.J. 2000); North Florida Women's Health & Counseling Services, Inc. v. State, 866 So. 2d 612 (Fla. 2003); Alaska v. Planned Parenthood of Alaska, 171 P.3d 577 (Alaska 2007). The Florida decision was subsequently reversed by state constitutional amendment. Note also Wicklund v. State, 1999 Mont. Dist. LEXIS 1116 (Mont. 1st Jud. Dist. Ct., Lewis & Clark Cty. 1999), in which a Montana trial court enjoined a parental notice requirement on state constitutional grounds—a requirement that SCOTUS had previously upheld (on federal constitutional grounds) in Lambert v. Wicklund, 520 U.S. 292 (1997). A similar sequence of events took place with respect to Montana's statutory requirement that only doctors (and not, for example, physicians' assistants) may perform abortions in the state. SCOTUS rejected a federal constitutional challenge to this statute in Mazurek v. Armstrong, 520 U.S. 968 (1997), but the state's abortion providers then persuaded the state high court to invalidate it in Armstrong v. State, 989 P.2d 364 (Mont. 1999).

Likewise with restrictions on public funding for abortion. SCOTUS had long ago held that such restrictions were consistent with the federal Constitution, but from 1993 to 2002, abortion rights advocates persuaded the high courts of West Virginia, Minnesota, New Mexico, Alaska, and Arizona to invalidate such restrictions on state constitutional grounds. Women's Health Center of West Virginia, Inc. v. Panepinto, 446 S.E.2d 658 (W. Va. 1993); Women of State of Minnesota by Doe v. Gomez, 542 N.W.2d 17 (Minn. 1995); New Mexico Right to Choose/ NARAL v. Johnson, 975 P.2d 841 (N.M. 1998); State Department of Health & Social Services v. Planned Parenthood of Alaska, Inc., 28 P.3d 904 (Alaska 2001); Simat Corp. v. Arizona Health Care Cost Containment System, 56 P.3d 28 (Ariz. 2002). Similar challenges were unsuccessful (during this same period) in New York, North Carolina, Florida, and Texas. Hope v. Perales, 634 N.E.2d 183 (N.Y. 1994); Rosie J. v. North Carolina Department of Human Resources, 491 S.E.2d 535 (N.C. 1997); Renee B. v. Florida Agency for Health Care Administration, 790 So. 2d 1036 (Fla. 2001); Bell v. Low Income Women of Texas, 95 S.W.3d 253 (Tex. 2002).

53. *In re* Jane Doe, 19 S.W.3d 346 (Tex. 2000).

54. Planned Parenthood v. Owens, 287 F.3d 910 (10th Cir. 2002); Planned Parenthood v. Wasden, 376 F.3d 908 (9th Cir. 2004); Planned Parenthood of Northern New England v. Heed, 390 F.3d 53 (1st Cir. 2004).

55. Ayotte v. Planned Parenthood of Northern New England, 546 U.S. 320 (2006).

56. Carhart v. Ashcroft, 331 F. Supp. 2d 805 (D. Neb. 2004), *aff'd*, 413 F.3d 791 (8th Cir. 2005); Planned Parenthood Federation of America v. Ashcroft, 320 F. Supp. 2d 957 (N.D. Cal. 2004), *aff'd*, 435 F.3d 1163 (9th Cir. 2006); National Abortion Federation v. Ashcroft, 330 F. Supp. 2d 436 (S.D.N.Y. 2004), *aff'd*, National Abortion Federation v. Gonzales, 437 F.3d 278 (2d Cir. 2006).

57. Gonzales v. Carhart, 550 U.S. 124, 169 (2007). Note Clement's Brief for Petitioner, Gonzales v. Carhart (May 22, 2006), along with his Initial Brief for

Appellant-Petitioner, Gonzales v. Planned Parenthood (August 3, 2006), and Reply Brief for Appellant-Petitioner, Gonzales v. Carhart and Gonzales v. Planned Parenthood (October 25, 2006).

58. 550 U.S. at 159. On the emergence of this argument in the pro-life movement during the 1990s, see Siegel (2007); Toner (2007).

59. 550 U.S. at 161. These limiting constructions echoed Judge Easterbrook's opinion in Hope Clinic v. Ryan (7th Cir. 1999) eight years earlier, and Justice Ginsburg ended her impassioned dissent by quoting Judge Posner's dissent from that case.

60. Center for Reproductive Law & Policy v. Bush, 304 F.3d 183 (2d Cir. 2002); Pear (2011).

61. *In re* Advisory Opinion to the Attorney General, 632 So. 2d 1018 (Fla. 1994). For several similar challenges litigated by Lambda Legal, see Andersen (2005, 151–52).

62. Doe v. Montgomery County Board of Elections, 406 Md. 697 (Md. 2008).

63. Albano v. Attorney General, 437 Mass. 156 (Mass. 2002).

64. Schulman v. Attorney General, 447 Mass. 189 (Mass. 2006).

65. Bennett v. Bowen, 2008 Cal. LEXIS 8868 (Cal. 2008).

66. State electorates rejected antigay ballot initiatives in California in 1978, Oregon in 1992, Idaho and Oregon in 1994, Arizona in 2006, and Minnesota in 2012. The Arizona initiative is sometimes described as the first popular defeat of a proposed ban on SSM (Klarman 2013, 115). In fact, however, the 1994 Idaho and Oregon initiatives each included explicit bans on SSM, though the public campaigns focused, in each case, on the initiative's implications for antidiscrimination protections rather than for marriage.

67. Evans v. Romer, 882 P.2d 1335 (Colo. 1994), *aff'd*, Romer v. Evans, 517 U.S. 620 (1996).

68. 517 U.S. at 631–32, 634.

69. Note, in particular, Equality Foundation v. City of Cincinnati, 54 F.3d 261 (6th Cir. 1995), *on remand at* 128 F.3d 289 (6th Cir. 1997), *reh'g denied*, 1998 U.S. App. LEXIS 1765 (6th Cir.) (en banc), *cert. denied*, 525 U.S. 943 (1998).

70. To state the point about state electorates more precisely, thirty voted to enact constitutional bans on SSM, one (Maine's) voted to enact a statutory ban, and one (Hawaii's) voted to authorize the state legislature to enact a statutory ban. Nevada's electorate voted on two separate occasions, in 2000 and 2002, to enact a constitutional ban, as required by the state's constitutional amendment procedures. California voters enacted a statutory ban in 2000 and a constitutional ban eight years later.

71. Neb. Const. art. 1, § 29.

72. Citizens for Equal Protection v. Bruning, 455 F.3d 859 (8th Cir. 2006).

73. Martinez v. Kulongoski, 220 Or. App. 142 (Or. Ct. App. 2008); McConkey v. Van Hollen, 326 Wis. 2d 1 (Wis. 2010); Strauss v. Horton, 46 Cal. 4th 364 (Cal. 2009).

74. Perry v. Schwarzenegger, 704 F. Supp. 2d 921 (N.D. Cal. 2010).

75. Perry v. Brown, 671 F.3d 1052, *en banc reh'g denied*, 681 F.3d 1065 (9th Cir. 2012).

76. Hollingsworth v. Perry, 133 S. Ct. 2652 (2013).

77. Finstuen v. Crutcher, 496 F.3d 1139 (10th Cir. 2007).

78. Diaz v. Brewer, 656 F.3d 1008 (9th Cir. 2011), *en banc reh'g denied*, 676 F.3d 823 (9th Cir. 2012).

79. Department of Human Services & Child Welfare Agency Review Board v. Howard, 238 S.W.3d 1 (Ark. 2006).

80. Arkansas Department of Human Services v. Cole, 2011 Ark. 145 (Ark.2011).

81. Andersen v. King County, 138 P.3d 963 (Wash. 2006).

82. Pub. L. No. 103-160, 107 Stat. 1670 (1993) (codified at 10 U.S.C. § 654).

83. Sheldon Goldman (1993) reports that on November 3, 1992, 63 percent of sitting federal judges had been appointed by Republican presidents. President Clinton signed the Don't Ask, Don't Tell policy into law one year later, on November 30, 1993.

84. Meinhold v. US Department of Defense, 808 F. Supp. 1455 (C.D. Cal. 1993).

85. Meinhold v. US Department of Defense, 62 Empl. Prac. Dec. 42, 619 (C.D. Cal. 1993).

86. US Department of Defense v. Meinhold, 510 U.S. 939 (1993).

87. Steffan v. Aspin, 8 F.3d 57, 70 (D.C. Cir. 1993).

88. Cammermeyer v. Aspin, 850 F. Supp. 910, 920 (W.D. Wash. 1994).

89. Meinhold v. US Department of Defense, 1994 WL 467311 (9th Cir. 1994).

90. In two related cases that went the other way, DC Circuit panels held that the US Information Agency and the Central Intelligence Agency had lawfully terminated employees on the grounds of homosexual conduct. US Information Agency v. Krc, 989 F.2d 1211 (D.C. Cir. 1993); Doe v. Gates, 981 F.2d 1316 (D.C. Cir. 1993).

91. Steffan v. Perry, 41 F.3d 677 (D.C. Cir. 1994) (en banc).

92. Able v. United States, 847 F. Supp. 1038; 863 F. Supp. 112 (E.D.N.Y. 1994).

93. Able v. United States, 880 F. Supp. 968 (E.D.N.Y. 1995).

94. Thomasson v. Perry, 80 F.3d 915 (4th Cir. 1996). Note also Selland v. Perry, 1996 U.S. App. LEXIS 29054 (4th Cir. 1996).

95. Able v. United States, 88 F.3d 1280 (2d Cir. 1996); 968 F. Supp. 850 (E.D.N.Y. 1997), *rev'd*, 155 F.3d 628 (2d Cir. 1998).

96. Richenberg v. Perry, 97 F.3d 256 (8th Cir. 1996); Philips v. Perry, 106 F.3d 1420 (9th Cir. 1997); Holmes v. California Army National Guard, 124 F.3d 1126 (9th Cir. 1997). The federal courts continued to hear cases arising from discharges under the pre-Clinton policy as well. Note, for example, Jackson v. US Department of the Air Force, 1997 U.S. App. LEXIS 34666 (9th Cir. 1997), in which a Ninth Circuit panel upheld such a discharge dating to 1988.

97. SCOTUS denied certiorari in Krc v. US Information Agency, which involved the pre-Clinton ban on homosexual conduct by Foreign Service officers,

in February 1994. In cases involving DADT, the Court denied certiorari in Thomasson, Selland v. Cohen, Richenberg and Holmes from October 1996 through January 1999.

98. Brief for the *Cook* Respondents, Opposing Cert. *in* Pietrangelo v. Gates (January 2009), 6.

99. Cook v. Gates, 528 F.3d 42 (1st Cir. 2008).

100. Brief for the *Cook* Respondents, Opposing Cert. *in* Pietrangelo v. Gates (January 2009).

101. Witt v. Department of the Air Force, 527 F.3d 806 (9th Cir. 2008).

102. Witt v. Department of the Air Force, 548 F.3d 1264 (9th Cir. 2008).

103. Log Cabin Republicans v. United States, 2010 U.S. Dist. LEXIS 93612 (C.D. Cal. 2010).

104. Log Cabin Republicans v. United States, 658 F.3d 1162 (9th Cir. 2011).

105. Lungren v. Superior Court of Sacramento County, 48 Cal. App. 4th 435 (3d Dist. 1996).

106. Coalition for Economic Equity v. Wilson, 1996 U.S. Dist. LEXIS 18488 (N.D. Cal. 1996).

107. Coalition for Economic Equity v. Wilson, 946 F. Supp. 1480 (N.D. Cal. 1996).

108. Coalition for Economic Equity v. Wilson, 122 F.3d 692 (9th Cir. 1997).

109. In Florida, where affirmative action in public university admissions was banned by Governor Jeb Bush and the state Board of Regents rather than by ballot initiative, the NAACP filed an unsuccessful legal challenge as well (Selingo 2000b).

110. Coalition to Defend Affirmative Action v. Board of State Canvassers, 262 Mich. App. 395 (Mich. Ct. App. 2004).

111. Operation King's Dream v. Connerly, 2006 U.S. Dist. LEXIS 61323 (E.D. Mich. 2006).

112. Operation King's Dream v. Connerly, No. 06-2144 (6th Cir. September 11, 2006) (order). After the election took place, the Sixth Circuit panel rejected the suit as moot. 501 F.3d 584 (6th Cir. 2007).

113. In December 2006, Erwin Chemerinsky, Laurence Tribe, and the ACLU filed an additional challenge on behalf of a separate group of plaintiffs consisting of current and prospective students at the University of Michigan, along with several faculty members. The two cases were subsequently consolidated.

114. Coalition to Defend Affirmative Action v. Granholm, 240 F.R.D. 368 (E.D. Mich. 2006).

115. Coalition to Defend Affirmative Action v. Granholm, 473 F.3d 237 (6th Cir. 2006).

116. Coalition to Defend Affirmative Action v. Regents of the University of Michigan, 539 F. Supp. 2d 924 (S.D. Mich. 2008).

117. Coalition to Defend Affirmative Action v. Regents of the University of Michigan, 652 F.3d 607 (6th Cir. 2011).

118. Coalition to Defend Affirmative Action v. Regents of the University of Michigan, 701 F.3d 466 (6th Cir. 2012).

119. Ibid., 480, 485.

120. Schuette v. Coalition to Defend Affirmative Action, 133 S. Ct. 1633 (2013).

121. After unsuccessful preelection challenges in Colorado and Nebraska, Connerly's initiatives appeared on the ballot in November 2008. In Missouri, Connerly's campaign failed to gather sufficient signatures for the 2008 ballot, and when they tried again in 2009, the ACLU responded with a preelection challenge that succeeded in blocking the proposed initiative (Lieb 2009).

122. Coalition to Defend Affirmative Action v. Brown, 674 F.3d 1128 (9th Cir. 2012).

123. Commonwealth v. Wasson, 842 S.W.2d 487 (Ky. 1992).

124. Texas v. Morales, 869 S.W.2d 941 (Tex. 1994); Louisiana v. Baxley, 633 So. 2d 142 (La. 1994); Sawatzky v. City of Oklahoma City, 906 P.2d 785 (Okla. Crim. App. 1995); Rhode Island v. Lopes, 660 A.2d 707 (R.I. 1995). See also Louisiana v. Baxley, 656 So. 2d 973 (La. 1995).

125. The years indicated in the text identify the date at which each state's sodomy law was finally laid to rest, by virtue of either a ruling from the state's highest court or a decision by the state not to appeal an adverse ruling from a lower court. Campbell v. Sundquist, 926 S.W.2d 250 (Tenn. Ct. App. 1996); Gryczan v. Montana, 942 P.2d 112 (Mont. 1997); Powell v. Georgia, 270 Ga. 327 (Ga. 1998); Williams v. State, 1998 Extra LEXIS 260 (Balt. City Cir. Ct. 1998); Missouri v. Cogshell, 997 S.W.2d 534 (Mo. Ct. App. 1999); Doe v. Ventura, 2001 WL 543734 (Minn. Dist. Ct., Hennepin Cty. 2001); Jegley v. Picado, 349 Ark. 600 (Ark. 2002); Gay & Lesbian Advocates & Defenders v. Attorney General, 436 Mass. 132 (Mass. 2002). For decisions that went the other way, see Christensen v. State, 266 Ga. 474 (Ga. 1996); Topeka v. Movsovitz, 960 P.2d 267 (Kan. Ct. App. 1998); Louisiana v. Smith, 766 So. 2d 501 (La. 2000); DePriest v. Commonwealth, 33 Va. App. 754 (Va. Ct. App. 2000); Fisher v. Commonwealth, 2001 Va. App. LEXIS 342 (Va. Ct. App. 2001); Lawrence v. Texas, 41 S.W.3d 349 (Tex. App. 14th Dist. 2001).

126. Lawrence v. Texas, 539 U.S. 558 (2003). On the tears in the courtroom, see Ball (2010, 232); Toobin (2008, 222).

127. Baehr v. Lewin, 74 Haw. 530 (Haw. 1993).

128. Note also Dean v. District of Columbia, 653 A.2d 307 (D.C. 1995), filed around the same time in Washington, DC, again by local counsel and again with eventual amicus support from Lambda Legal and the ACLU.

129. Tumeo v. University of Alaska (Alaska Sup. Ct. 4th Dist. 1995), *aff'd and remanded*, University of Alaska v. Tumeo, 933 P.2d 1147 (Alaska 1997); Brause & Dugan v. Bureau of Vital Statistics, 1998 WL 88743 (Alaska Sup. Ct. 1998). Around the same time, an intermediate appellate court in Oregon ordered the extension of health benefits to the domestic partners of state employees in Tanner v. Oregon Health Sciences University, 971 P.2d 435 (Or. Ct. App. 1998).

130. 170 Vt. 194, 197–98 (1999).

131. Ibid., 227–28, quoting Sunstein (1996, 101).

132. In Massachusetts, the state legislature had been the second in the nation (after Wisconsin's) to extend its antidiscrimination laws to cover sexual orientation, and the high court had been the second in the nation (after Vermont's) to authorize second-parent adoptions by same-sex couples (Andersen 2005, 220). In New Jersey, the state legislature had likewise been an early adopter of antidiscrimination protections for LGBT persons, and the state supreme court had applied that law expansively in its widely noted decision in Dale v. Boy Scouts of America, 160 N.J. 562 (NJ 1999).

133. 440 Mass. 309 (Mass. 2003).

134. Li v. Oregon, 338 Or. 376 (Or. 2005); Morrison v. Sadler, 821 N.E.2d 15 (Ind. Ct. App. 2d Dist. 2005); Lewis v. Harris, 875 A.2d 259 (N.J. App. Div. 2005).

135. Hernandez v. Robles, 7 N.Y.3d 338 (N.Y. 2006); Citizens for Equal Protection v. Bruning, 455 F.3d 859 (8th Cir. 2006); Andersen v. King County, 138 P.3d 963 (Wash. 2006); and In re Marriage Cases, 49 Cal. Rptr. 3d 675 (Ct. App. 1st Dist. 2006).

136. Morrison v. Sadler, 821 N.E.2d 15, 24–25 (Ind. Ct. App. 2d Dist. 2005); Citizens for Equal Protection v. Bruning, 455 F.3d 859, 867 (8th Cir. 2006); Andersen v. King County, 138 P.3d 963, 982, 1002 (Wash. 2006).

137. Hernandez v. Robles, 7 N.Y.3d 338, 391 (N.Y. 2006).

138. Snetsinger v. Montana University System, 104 P.3d 445 (Mont. 2004).

139. Alaska Civil Liberties Union v. Alaska, 122 P.3d 781 (Alaska 2005); Bedford & Breen v. New Hampshire Technical College System, Case No. 04-E-229 and 04-E-230 (N.H. Sup. Ct. May 3, 2006).

140. Lewis v. Harris, 188 N.J. 415 (N.J. 2006).

141. Conaway v. Deane, 932 A.2d 571 (Md. 2007); In re Marriage Cases, 43 Cal. 4th 757 (Cal. 2008). A decade earlier, the Hawaii Supreme Court had observed in dicta that sexual orientation was a suspect classification, but the 2008 California decision was the first to clearly so hold. For the Hawaii decision, see Baehr v. Miike, 1999 Haw. Lexis 391, p. 6, n.1 (Haw. 1999).

142. Kerrigan v. Commissioner of Public Health, 289 Conn. 135 (Conn. 2008); Varnum v. Brien, 763 N.W.2d 862 (Iowa 2009).

143. Lewis v. Harris, 202 N.J. 340, 340 (N.J. 2010).

144. Note also Donaldson v. Montana, 2012 MT 288 (Mont. 2012), in which a divided state high court declined to hold that same-sex couples were constitutionally entitled to the legal rights and benefits of marriage.

145. Massachusetts v. US Health & Human Services, 682 F.3d 1 (1st Cir. 2012).

146. "Statement of the Attorney General on Litigation Involving the Defense of Marriage Act," Press Release, Department of Justice (February 23, 2011), available at http://www.justice.gov/opa/pr/2011/February/11-ag-222.html.

147. Windsor v. United States, 699 F.3d 169 (2d Cir. 2012).

148. United States v. Windsor, 133 S. Ct. 2675 (2013).

149. Note, for example, Golinski v. US Office of Personnel Management, 2013 U.S. App. LEXIS 15631 (9th Cir. 2013); DeBoer v. Snyder, 2013 U.S. Dist. LEXIS 98382 (E.D. Mich. 2013); Cooper-Harris v. United States, 2013 U.S. Dist. LEXIS 125030 (C.D. Cal. 2013).

150. Cox v. State Department of Health & Rehabilitative Services, 656 So. 2d 902 (Fla. 1995).

151. Lofton v. Secretary of the Department of Children & Family Services, 358 F.3d 804, *reh'g en banc denied*, 377 F.3d 1275 (11th Cir. 2004).

152. Florida Department of Children & Families v. Matter of Adoption of X.X.G. & N.R.G., 45 So. 3d 79 (Fla. Dist. Ct. App. 3d Dist. 2010).

153. Note also Adar v. Smith, 597 F.3d 697 (5th Cir. 2010), *rev'd*, 639 F.3d 146 (5th Cir. 2011) (en banc), in which a divided Fifth Circuit rejected a constitutional challenge to Louisiana's refusal to recognize out-of-state adoptions granted to unmarried couples. The plaintiff couple, represented by Lambda Legal, initially received a favorable ruling from a three-judge panel, but the full circuit reversed, rejecting Lambda's equal protection and full faith and credit clause arguments.

154. "Statewide Employment Laws & Policies," Human Rights Campaign, available at http://www.hrc.org/files/assets/resources/employment_laws_072013.pdf (last updated July 22, 2013).

155. Some years later, antiabortion extremists took yet another life, with Dr. Tiller murdered in his Wichita church in May 2009 (Barstow 2009).

156. National Organization for Women v. Operation Rescue, 726 F. Supp. 1483, 1486 (E.D. Va. 1989). On appeal, the Fourth Circuit upheld the DC-area injunction in National Organization for Women v. Operation Rescue, 914 F.2d 582 (4th Cir. 1990). Note also Pro-Choice Network of Western New York v. Project Rescue Western New York, 799 F. Supp. 1417 (W.D.N.Y. 1992), in which a federal district judge issued a similar injunction limiting disruptive protests against abortion providers in and around Rochester and Buffalo, New York. A Second Circuit panel vacated this injunction in September 1994, but an en banc panel reinstated it the following year. Pro-Choice Network v. Schenck, 67 F.3d 359 (2d Cir. 1994), *vacated in part*, 67 F.3d 377 (2d Cir. 1995).

157. Bray v. Alexandria Women's Health Clinic, 506 U.S. 263, 268–69 (1993).

158. In *Bray*'s wake, some once-promising suits were dismissed. Note, for example, West Hartford v. Operation Rescue, 991 F.2d 1039 (2d Cir. 1993), and Women's Health Services v. Operation Rescue, 24 F.3d 107 (10th Cir. 1994), in which federal appellate panels vacated injunctions on the authority of *Bray*. Some courts continued to allow abortion providers to pursue their claims under a different section of the KKK Act—see, for example, National Abortion Federation v. Operation Rescue, 8 F.3d 680 (9th Cir. 1993), and Libertad v. Welch, 53 F.3d 428 (1st Cir. 1995)—but this provision required them to prove that antiabortion protesters had conspired "for the purpose of preventing or hindering the constituted

authorities . . . from giving or securing to all persons . . . the equal protection of the laws." In short, the need for targeted legislation remained (Banks 1994).

159. National Organization for Women v. Scheidler, 510 U.S. 249, 253 (1994).

160. National Organization for Women v. Scheidler, 765 F. Supp. 937 (N.D. Ill. 1991), *aff'd*, 968 F.2d 612 (7th Cir. 1992).

161. National Organization for Women v. Scheidler, 510 U.S. 249 (1994).

162. Scheidler v. National Organization for Women, 537 U.S. 393 (2003).

163. National Organization for Women, Inc. v. Scheidler, 91 Fed. App'x 510 (7th Cir. 2004), *rev'd*, Scheidler v. National Organization for Women, Inc., 547 U.S. 9 (2006). In addition to the KKK Act and RICO suits, abortion providers relied on state law grounds to appeal for judicial protection in a number of cases as well. In 1991, for example, the Aware Woman Center for Choice in Melbourne, Florida, petitioned a state trial court to enjoin Operation Rescue from blocking access by patients and staff. The court issued an injunction in September 1992 and amended it eight months later in response to continued harassment, and the Florida Supreme Court upheld this injunction in Operation Rescue v. Women's Health Center, 626 So. 2d 664 (Fla. 1993).

164. S. 636, 103d Cong., 1st Sess., § 2(a) (1993).

165. 49 CQ Almanac, 103d Cong., 1st Sess. (1993); Cong. Q. 354, 327 (1994).

166. This suit, filed by the City of Cleveland in 2006, was rejected by a divided state high court in City of Cleveland v. State, 128 Ohio St. 3d 135 (Ohio 2010).

167. As I note below, when state and federal legislators began preempting these local government lawsuits—just as they had so often preempted local legislation— city and county officials challenged some of these statutes in court as well.

168. Hamilton v. Accu-Tek, 62 F. Supp. 2d 802 (E.D.N.Y. 1999).

169. The Second Circuit's 2001 decision dismissing the suit brought by victims of gun violence was Hamilton v. Beretta USA Corp., 264 F.3d 21 (2d Cir. 2001).

170. People v. Sturm, Ruger & Co., 309 A.D.2d 91, 95 (N.Y. App. Div. 1st Dept. 2003), *appeal denied*, 100 N.Y.2d 514 (N.Y.2003).

171. NAACP v. Acusport, 271 F. Supp. 2d 435 (E.D.N.Y. 2003).

172. City of New York v. Beretta USA Corp., 401 F. Supp. 2d 244 (E.D.N.Y. 2005).

173. City of New York v. Beretta USA Corp., 524 F.3d 384 (2d Cir. 2008).

174. In addition to the Second Circuit's holding in New York v. Beretta, note the similar holdings from the Ninth Circuit, the DC Court of Appeals, and the Illinois Supreme Court, respectively, in Ileto v. Glock, Inc., 565 F.3d 1126 (9th Cir. 2009); District of Columbia v. Beretta, 940 A.2d 163 (D.C. 2008); and Adames v. Sheahan, 233 Ill. 2d 276 (Ill. 2009). SCOTUS denied certiorari in all four of these cases. From one angle, these four suits represent examples of category 1 litigation—that is, suits filed in an effort to enjoin policies that gun rights advocates had won via legislative or administrative channels. For other such examples, note Brady Campaign to Prevent Gun Violence v. Salazar, 612 F. Supp. 2d 1

(D.D.C. 2009), and Wollschlaeger v. Farmer, 880 F. Supp. 2d 1251 (S.D. Fla. 2012), in which the Brady Center persuaded federal judges to enjoin a December 2008 regulatory change issued by the lame-duck Bush administration that would have allowed the carrying of concealed weapons in national parks and a 2011 Florida statute that prohibited doctors from discussing firearms safety with their patients. With regard to legislative efforts to preempt antigun litigation, note also Morial v. Smith & Wesson Corp., 785 So. 2d 1 (La. 2001), in which the Louisiana high court upheld a state statute barring local jurisdictions from pursuing tort claims against firearms manufacturers. At least twenty-two additional state legislatures enacted such preemption laws (Kao 2002, 223).

175. Camden County Board of Chosen Freeholders v. Beretta, USA Corp., 273 F.3d 536 (3d Cir. 2001); City of Philadelphia v Beretta USA Corp., 277 F.3d 415 (3d Cir. 2002).

176. Merrill v. Navegar, 28 P.3d 116 (Cal. 2001); Ganim v. Smith & Wesson Corp., 258 Conn. 313 (Conn. 2001); Penelas v. Arms Technology, Inc., 778 So. 2d 1042 (Fla. Ct. App. 3d Dist. 2001), *review denied*, 799 So. 2d 218 (Fla. 2001).

177. Baker v. Smith & Wesson Corp., 2002 Del. Super. LEXIS 539 (Del. Super. Ct. 2002); City of Chicago v. Beretta USA Corp., 213 Ill. 2d 351 (Ill. 2004). On the same day that it dismissed the Chicago suit, the Illinois high court dismissed a suit brought by victims of gun violence as well. Young v. Bryco Arms, 821 N.E.2d 1078 (Ill. 2004).

178. Smith v. Bryco Arms, 33 P.3d 638 (N.M. Ct. App. 2001), *cert. denied*, 131 N.M. 221 (N.M. 2001).

179. City of Cincinnati v. Beretta USA Corp., 95 Ohio St. 3d 416 (Ohio 2002); City of Gary v. Smith & Wesson, 801 N.E.2d 1222 (Ind. 2003); James v. Arms Technology, Inc., 359 N.J. Super. 291 (App. Div. 2003).

180. Note, for example, Smith & Wesson Corp. v. City of Gary, 875 N.E.2d 422 (Ind. Ct. App. 2007), *transfer denied*, 915 N.E.2d 978 (Ind. 2009).

181. Ileto v. Glock, 349 F.3d 1191 (9th Cir. 2003).

182. Ileto v. Glock Inc., 370 F.3d 860 (9th Cir. 2004), *cert. denied*, China North Industrial Corp. v. Ileto, 543 U.S. 1050 (2005).

183. Ileto v. Glock, 421 F. Supp. 2d 1274 (C.D. Cal. 2006).

184. Ileto v. Glock, 565 F.3d 1126 (9th Cir. 2009), *cert. denied*, 130 S. Ct. 3320 (2010).

185. City of New York v. A-1 Jewelry & Pawn, Inc., 501 F. Supp. 2d 369, 374 (E.D.N.Y. 2007). See also City of New York v. Bob Moates' Sport Shop, Inc., 253 F.R.D. 237 (E.D.N.Y. 2008).

186. City of New York v. Adventure Outdoors, Inc., 644 F. Supp. 2d 201 (E.D.N.Y. 2009).

187. City of New York v. Mickalis Pawn Shop, LLC, 645 F.3d 114 (2d Cir. 2011), *later proceeding at* City of New York v. A-1 Jewelry & Pawn, Inc., 2012 U.S. Dist. LEXIS 62276 (E.D.N.Y. 2012).

188. Note, for example, United States v. Smith, 1998 U.S. App. LEXIS 2038 (6th Cir. 1998); United States v. Scott, 187 F.3d 282 (2d Cir. 1999); and United States v. Burke, 15 F. Supp. 2d 1090 (D. Kan. 1998). See Hull and Hoffer (2001, 264).

189. SCOTUS upheld the Hyde Amendment in Harris v. McRae, 448 U.S. 297 (1980).

190. Planned Parenthood Affiliates v. Engler, 73 F.3d 634 (6th Cir. 1996).

191. Hope Medical Group for Women v. Edwards, 63 F.3d 418 (5th Cir. 1995); Little Rock Family Planning Services v. Dalton, 60 F.3d 497 (8th Cir. 1995); Hern v. Beye, 57 F.3d 906 (10th Cir. 1995); Utah Women's Clinic v. Graham, 892 F. Supp. 1379 (D. Utah 1995). In the Eighth Circuit case, SCOTUS subsequently held that the appellate panel had issued an injunction broader than necessary, but otherwise left the decision standing in Dalton v. Little Rock Family Planning Services, 516 U.S. 474 (1996). Note also Elizabeth Blackwell Health Center for Women v. Knoll, 61 F.3d 170 (3d Cir. 1995), in which a Third Circuit panel enjoined a Pennsylvania law that required women using Medicaid funds for an abortion in cases of rape or incest to report the incident and identify the offender.

192. Planned Parenthood Arizona, Inc. v. Betlach, 2013 U.S. App. LEXIS 17584 (9th Cir. 2013); Planned Parenthood of Indiana, Inc. v. Commissioner of the Indiana State Department of Health, 699 F.3d 962 (7th Cir. 2012); Planned Parenthood v. Brownback, 799 F. Supp. 2d 1218 (D. Kan. 2011).

193. Handgun Control, Inc. v. Lungren, No. 991752 (Cal. Sup. Ct. San Fran. Cty. 1998). See DeConde (2001, 269).

194. "Violence Policy Center Sues Attorney General Ashcroft over Unlawful Suspension of Brady Law Regulation; Further Evidence of Shift in Justice Department Gun Policy," Press Release, Violence Policy Center (June 4, 2001), available at http://www.vpc.org/press/0106suit.htm.

Chapter Two

1. Fisher v. University of Texas, 133 S. Ct. 2411 (2013).

2. Hopwood v. Texas, 78 F.3d 932 (5th Cir. 1996); Gratz v. Bollinger, 539 U.S. 244 (2003).

3. Michigan Civil Rights Initiative v. Board of State Canvassers, 474 Mich. 1099 (Mich. 2006); Coalition to Defend Affirmative Action v. Granholm, 473 F.3d 237 (6th Cir. 2006).

4. As Alexander DeConde (2001) has noted, this Clinton-era litigation campaign was to some extent prefigured by a long-running willingness to challenge state gun control laws on state constitutional grounds.

5. United States v. Lopez, 2 F.3d 1342, 1348–60, 1364, n.46 (5th Cir. 1993), *citing* Levinson (1989). But note United States v. Edwards, 13 F.3d 291 (9th Cir. 1993), in

which a unanimous Ninth Circuit panel rejected a similar challenge to the GFSZA later in the year.

6. United States v. Danks, 221 F.3d 1037 (8th Cir. 1999), *cert. denied*, 528 U.S. 1091 (2000); United States v. Dorsey, 418 F.3d 1038 (9th Cir. 2005).

7. Printz v. United States, 854 F. Supp. 1503 (D. Mont. 1994); Mack v. United States, 856 F. Supp. 1372 (D. Ariz. 1994); Frank v. United States, 860 F. Supp. 1030 (D. Vt. 1994); McGee v. United States, 863 F. Supp. 321 (S.D. Miss. 1994).

8. Mack v. United States, 66 F.3d 1025 (9th Cir. 1995).

9. Frank v. United States, 78 F.3d 815 (2d Cir. 1996); Koog v. United States, 79 F.3d 452 (5th Cir. 1996).

10. Printz v. United States, 521 U.S. 898, 937–38 (1997).

11. On the Second Amendment issue, Thomas noted that "a growing body of scholarly commentary" had marshaled "an impressive array of historical evidence . . . indicat[ing] that the 'right to keep and bear arms' is, as the Amendment's text suggests, a personal right." Printz v. United States, 521 U.S. 898, 937–38 (1997). As Amanda Hollis-Brusky (2013, 148–52) has noted, the opinions by Thomas, Scalia, and Rehnquist in *Lopez* and *Printz* reflected a set of constitutional ideas that had been patiently nurtured by the Federalist Society and the broader conservative legal movement since the early 1980s.

12. United States v. Rybar, 103 F.3d 273, 285–86 (3d Cir. 1996).

13. See United States v. Kirk, 70 F.3d 791 (5th Cir. 1995); United States v. Beuckelaere, 91 F.3d 781 (6th Cir. 1996); United States v. Kenney, 91 F.3d 884 (7th Cir. 1996); United States v. Pearson, 8 F.3d 631 (8th Cir. 1993); United States v. Rambo, 74 F.3d 948 (9th Cir. 1996); United States v. Wilks, 58 F.3d 1518 (10th Cir. 1995).

14. United States v. Rybar, 103 F.3d 273 (3d Cir. 1996); United States v. Kirk, 1997 U.S. App. LEXIS 12670 (5th Cir. 1997) (en banc).

15. Navegar, Inc. v. United States, 192 F.3d 1050 (D.C. Cir. 1999). In addition to *Rybar* and the cases cited therein, the DC Circuit panel noted recent decisions from the Second, Fifth, and Eleventh Circuits that had rejected constitutional challenges to the 1986 machine gun law. See United States v. Franklyn, 157 F.3d 90 (2d Cir. 1998); United States v. Knutson, 113 F.3d 27 (5th Cir. 1997); United States v. Wright, 117 F.3d 1265 (11th Cir. 1997).

16. Navegar, Inc. v. United States, 200 F.3d 868, 871 (D.C. Cir. 2000).

17. Brief for the US in Opposition, Navegar v. United States, No. 99-1874 (July 2000), 7; Navegar, Inc. v. United States, 531 U.S. 816 (2000).

18. Olympic Arms v. Magaw, 91 F. Supp. 2d 1061 (E.D. Mich. 2000), *aff'd*, Olympic Arms v. Buckles, 301 F.3d 384 (6th Cir. 2002).

19. United States v. Emerson, 46 F. Supp. 2d 598 (N.D. Tex. 1999).

20. United States v. Emerson, 270 F.3d 203 (5th Cir. 2001). Five of the cited decisions from sister circuits dated from the Clinton era: United States v. Rybar, 103 F.3d 273 (3d Cir. 1996); Love v. Pepersack, 47 F.3d 120 (4th Cir. 1995); Gillespie

v. City of Indianapolis, 185 F.3d 693 (7th Cir. 1999); Hickman v. Block, 81 F.3d 98 (9th Cir. 1996); and United States v. Wright, 117 F.3d 1265 (11th Cir. 1997). Three years later, Robert Spitzer compiled a list of thirty-seven cases since United States v. Miller in which federal appellate courts had adopted the collective rather than individual rights interpretation of the Second Amendment. Fifteen of these decisions had been appealed to the Supreme Court, which declined to hear all fifteen of them (2004, 169, n.59).

21. See, for example, United States v. Napier, 233 F.3d 394 (6th Cir. 2000); United States v. Bayles, 310 F.3d 1302 (10th Cir. 2002); United States v. Hinostroza, 297 F.3d 924 (9th Cir. 2002); and United States v. Lippman, 369 F.3d 1039 (8th Cir. 2004), each of which adopted the collective rights interpretation of the Second Amendment in upholding the domestic violence restraining order provision; and Gillespie v. Indianapolis, 185 F.3d 693 (7th Cir. 1999); and United States v. Smith, 56 M.J. 711 (A.F.C.C.A. 2001), which did likewise in upholding the closely related ban on gun possession by persons who have been convicted of a misdemeanor crime of domestic violence.

22. Brief for the US in Opposition, Emerson v. United States, No. 01-8780 (May 2002), 19–20, n.3.

23. Steven G. Bradbury, "Whether the Second Amendment Secures an Individual Right," Memorandum Opinion for the Attorney General (August 24, 2004), available at http://www.justice.gov/olc/secondamendment2.pdf.

24. United States v. Emerson, 86 Fed. App'x 696 (5th Cir.), *cert. denied*, Emerson v. United States, 541 U.S. 1081 (2004).

25. The first holding came in Hickman v. Block, 81 F.3d 98 (9th Cir. 1996), in which the panel held that the plaintiff lacked standing because the Second Amendment protects a right held by state governments, not individuals. The second came in Silveira v. Lockyer, 312 F.3d 1052 (9th Cir. 2002), with Circuit Judge Stephen Reinhardt reaffirming the *Hickman* doctrine and offering a lengthy rebuttal of the Fifth Circuit's contrary individual rights holding in *Emerson*. The third came in Nordyke v. King, 319 F.3d 1185 (9th Cir. 2003), with the panel indicating that the gun show advocates' Second Amendment claims continued to be precluded by *Hickman*.

26. In addition to the *Rybar*, *Pepersack*, *Gillespie*, and *Wright* holdings cited above, note United States v. Patterson, 431 F.3d 832 (5th Cir. 2005); United States v. Haney, 264 F.3d 1161 (10th Cir. 2001); United States v. Graham, 305 F.3d 1094 (10th Cir. 2002); and United States v. Parker, 362 F.3d 1279 (10th Cir. 2004).

27. National Rifle Ass'n of America, Inc. v. Reno, 216 F.3d 122, 124 (D.C. Cir. 2000). But note Nordyke v. Santa Clara, 110 F.3d 707 (9th Cir. 1997), in which a Ninth Circuit panel relied on commercial speech grounds in striking down a local ban on gun shows.

28. Note, for example, Arnold v. Cleveland, 616 N.E.2d 163 (Ohio 1993); Benjamin v. Bailey, 662 A.2d 1226 (Conn. 1995); and Mosby v. Devine, 851 A.2d

1031 (R.I. 2004). Note also Kasler v. Lockyer, 23 Cal. 4th 472 (Cal. 2000), which did not involve a right-to-bear-arms claim, but in which the California Supreme Court rejected a state constitutional challenge to a 1989 statutory ban on assault weapons.

29. Fiscal v. City & County of San Francisco, 158 Cal. App. 4th 895 (1st Dist. 2008).

30. The panel upheld the District of Columbia's ban on assault weapons and large-capacity ammunition clips, but remanded for further proceedings on the constitutionality of some of the registration requirements. In dissent, Circuit Judge Brett Kavanaugh insisted that the assault weapons ban and all of the registration requirements were unconstitutional. Heller v. District of Columbia, 670 F.3d 1244 (D.C. Cir. 2011).

31. Ezell v. City of Chicago, 651 F.3d 684 (7th Cir. 2011).

32. Note, for example, 54 Sheriffs v. Hickenlooper, complaint filed in U.S. District Court for the District of Colorado (May 17, 2013), available at http://www.nssf.org/share/PDF/Complaint for Declaratory and Injunctive Relief 05-17-13.pdf.

33. But see Hacker (2005, 74–76, 120–23); Keck (2007a, 171–75).

34. State appellate courts invalidated local domestic partnership policies in City of Atlanta v. McKinney, 454 S.E.2d 517 (Ga. 1995); Connors v. City of Boston, 714 N.E.2d 335 (Mass. 1999); Lilly v. City of Minneapolis, 527 N.W.2d 107 (Minn. App.), *review denied*, 1995 Minn. LEXIS 264 (Minn. 1995); and Arlington County v. White, 528 S.E.2d 706 (Va. 2000). In Atlanta's case, the Georgia Supreme Court subsequently upheld a modified policy in City of Atlanta v. Morgan, 268 Ga. 586 (Ga. 1997). Two other suits were partially successful, with courts in Pennsylvania and Florida, respectively, invalidating some but not all provisions of local domestic partnership policies in Devlin v. City of Philadelphia, 580 Pa. 564 (Pa. 2004); and Lowe v. Broward County, 766 So. 2d 1199 (Fla. Dist. Ct. App. 4th Dist. 2000).

In a helpful survey, Charles W. Gossett (2009) has identified seventeen additional challenges that were unsuccessful. The high courts of Louisiana, Maryland, Michigan, and Washington rejected such challenges in Ralph v. New Orleans, 928 So. 2d 537 (La. 2006); Tyma v. Montgomery County, 369 Md. 497 (Md. 2002); Rohde v. Ann Arbor Public Schools, 479 Mich. 336 (2007); and Heinsma v. City of Vancouver, 29 P.3d 709 (Wash. 2001), respectively; the other thirteen suits cited by Gossett were rejected by state trial or intermediate appellate courts. Note also Irizarry v. Board of Education of City of Chicago, 251 F.3d 604 (7th Cir. 2001); Air Transportation Ass'n of America v. City & County of San Francisco, 266 F.3d 1064 (9th Cir. 2001); S. D. Myers, Inc. v. City & County of San Francisco, 336 F.3d 1174 (9th Cir. 2003); and City of Cleveland Heights *ex rel.* Hicks v. City of Cleveland Heights, 162 Ohio App. 3d 193 (Cuyahoga Cty. 2005).

35. Brinkman v. Miami University, 2007 Ohio 4372 (Ohio Ct. App. 2007); Rohde v. Ann Arbor Public Schools, 479 Mich. 336 (Mich. 2007); Cleveland Taxpayers for Ohio Constitution v. City of Cleveland, 2010 Ohio 4685 (8th App. Dist. 2010).

See also National Pride at Work v. Governor of Michigan, 748 N.W.2d 524 (Mich. 2008), in which the Michigan Supreme Court struck down a domestic partnership policy from Kalamazoo, though this suit had been initiated by supporters of such policies who were responding to the state attorney general's 2005 declaration that they were now unconstitutional.

36. The state legislatures of Hawaii and Vermont extended additional rights to legally recognized same-sex couples during this period as well. See "Marriage Equality & Other Relationship Recognition Laws," Human Rights Campaign, available at http://www.hrc.org/files/assets/resources/marriage_equality_082013 .pdf (last updated August 2, 2013).

37. In California, Illinois, New York, Vermont, and Wisconsin, the legal challenges were unsuccessful. Knight v. Superior Court, 128 Cal. App. 4th 14 (3d Dist. 2005); Campaign for California Families v. Schwarzenegger, 2006 Cal. App. Unpub. LEXIS 751 (3d Dist. 2006); Knight v. Schwarzenegger, 2006 Cal. App. Unpub. LEXIS 2164 (3d Dist. 2006); Catholic Charities of the Diocese of Springfield v. Illinois, No. 2011-MR-254 (Ill. Cir. Ct. 7th Cir. 2011); New Yorkers for Constitutional Freedoms v. New York State Senate, 98 A.D.3d 285 (N.Y. App. Div. 4th Dept. 2012), *appeal denied*, 19 N.Y.3d 814 (NY 2012); Brady v. Dean, 173 Vt. 542 (Vt. 2001); Appling v. Doyle, 2013 WI App 3 (Ct. App. 2012). In Hawaii, the legal challenge significantly curtailed the reach of the state's Reciprocal Beneficiaries Act, with the state agreeing to a Consent Order that disavowed any effort to require public or private employers to provide health insurance benefits to the unmarried partners of their employees. Hawaiian Electric Industries, Inc. v. Akiba, Civil No. 97-00913 (D. Haw. September 30, 1997). See generally Goldberg-Hiller (2002, 100–106). The Reciprocal Beneficiaries Act was superseded by a Civil Union law in 2012. In Rhode Island, the legal challenge remains pending as of this writing (Edgar 2013).

38. Largess v. Supreme Judicial Court, 317 F. Supp. 2d 77 (D. Mass.), *aff'd*, 373 F.3d 219 (1st Cir.), *cert. denied*, 543 U.S. 1002 (2004).

39. State *ex rel.* Ohio Campaign to Protect Marriage v. DeWine, 132 Ohio St. 3d 1401 (Ohio 2012).

40. Lockyer v. City & County of San Francisco, 95 P.3d 459, 464 (Cal. 2004). See Cummings and NeJaime (2010).

41. Matter of Hebel v. West, 25 A.D.3d 172 (N.Y. App. Div. 3d Dept. 2005). See generally Hacker (2005, 120–23). See also Godfrey v. Spano, 13 N.Y.3d 358 (N.Y. 2009).

42. Leskovar v. Nickels, 140 Wash. App. 770 (Div. I 2007), *review denied*, 163 Wash. 2d 1043 (Wash. 2008).

43. Presbytery of New Jersey v. Whitman, 99 F.3d 101 (3d Cir. 1996); Boy Scouts of America v. Dale, 530 U.S. 640 (2000).

44. None of these challenges were successful. See North Coast Women's Care Medical Group, Inc. v. Superior Court, 44 Cal. 4th 1145 (Cal. 2008); Elane

Photography, LLC v. Willock, 2013 N.M. LEXIS 284 (N.M. 2013); deParrie v. Oregon, 133 Or. App. 613 (Or. Ct. App. 1995); Hyman v. City of Louisville, 53 Fed. App'x 740 (6th Cir. 2002); Montgomery County v. Broadcast Equities, Inc., 360 Md. 438 (Md. 2000); Brown v. Todd, 53 S.W.3d 297 (Tex. 2001).

45. California Education Committee v. O'Connell, No. 34-2008-00026507-CU-CR-GDS (Sac. Cty. Sup. Ct. 2009); Thomas v. Anchorage Equal Rights Commission, 220 F.3d 1134 (9th Cir. 2000) (en banc).

46. *In re* M.S., 10 Cal. 4th 698 (Cal. 1995); Minnesota v. Machholz, 574 N.W.2d 415 (Minn. 1998).

47. Saxe v. State College Area School District, 240 F.3d 200, 203 (3d Cir. 2001). Note also California Education Committee v. O'Connell, No. 34-2008-00026507-CU-CR-GDS (Sac. Cty. Sup. Ct. 2009), the legal challenge to California's prohibition of discrimination on the basis of gender identity cited above, which was litigated by ADF and a California-based public interest law firm known as Advocates for Faith and Freedom.

48. Glenn v. Holder, 690 F.3d 417 (6th Cir. 2012); Saxe v. State College Area School District, 240 F.3d 200 (3d Cir. 2001).

49. Operation Rescue v. Women's Health Center, 626 So. 2d 664 (Fla. 1993); Cheffer v. McGregor, 6 F.3d 705 (11th Cir. 1993).

50. Madsen v. Women's Health Center, 512 U.S. 753, 785 (1994).

51. Lawson v. Murray, 515 U.S. 1110, 1111, 1116 (1995). When the abortion provider at issue moved to a new residence and sought and received a new injunction imposing the same restrictions there, the case returned to SCOTUS. Once again, Scalia reluctantly voted not to hear the case, on the grounds that "experience suggests that seeking to bring the First Amendment to the assistance of abortion protesters is more likely to harm the former than help the latter." Lawson v. Murray, 525 U.S. 955, 956 (1998).

52. The case that had gone the other way was Vittitow v. City of Upper Arlington, 43 F.3d 1100 (6th Cir.), *cert. denied*, City of Upper Arlington v. Vittitow, 515 U.S. 1121 (1995).

53. Pro-Choice Network of Western New York v. Project Rescue Western New York, 799 F. Supp. 1417, 1425, 1440 (W.D.N.Y. 1992). The injunction was vacated by a Second Circuit panel in September 1994 but reinstated by an en banc panel the following year. Pro-Choice Network v. Schenck, 67 F.3d 359 (2d Cir. 1994), *adhered to in part, vacated in part*, 67 F.3d 377 (2d Cir. 1995).

54. Schenck v. Pro-Choice Network of Western New York, 519 U.S. 357, 394 (1997). Scalia reiterated this complaint the following month, again joined by Kennedy and Thomas. In Planned Parenthood Shasta-Diablo, Inc. v. Williams, 7 Cal. 4th 860 (Cal. 1994), the California Supreme Court upheld an injunction against a First Amendment challenge from antiabortion protesters. SCOTUS vacated the holding for reconsideration in light of *Madsen*, and after the state high court upheld the injunction again, SCOTUS denied certiorari in March 1997. This prompted a

published dissent from Scalia, who characterized the state court's action as open defiance of SCOTUS. Planned Parenthood Shasta-Diablo, Inc. v. Williams, 10 Cal. 4th 1009 (Cal. 1995), *cert. denied*, Williams v. Planned Parenthood Shasta-Diablo, 520 U.S. 1133, 1136 (1997).

55. American Life League v. Reno, 47 F.3d 642 (4th Cir. 1995); Hoffman v. Hunt, 126 F.3d 575 (4th Cir. 1997); Cheffer v. Reno, 55 F.3d 1517 (11th Cir. 1995); and Terry v. Reno, 101 F.3d 1412 (D.C. Cir. 1996).

56. The partial victory came in United States v. Alaw, 327 F.3d 1217 (D.C. Cir. 2003). Unsuccessful challenges include United States v. Wilson, 73 F.3d 675 (7th Cir. 1995), and United States v. Dinwiddie, 76 F.3d 913 (8th Cir. 1996).

57. Planned Parenthood of the Columbia/Willamette, Inc. v. American Coalition of Life Activists, 244 F.3d 1007 (9th Cir. 2001), *vacated and remanded*, 290 F.3d 1058 (9th Cir. 2002).

58. American Life League v. Reno, 516 U.S. 809 (1995); Skott v. United States, 519 U.S. 806 (1996); Dinwiddie v. United States, 519 U.S. 1043 (1996); Terry v. Reno, 520 U.S. 1264 (1997); Hoffman v. Hunt, 523 U.S. 1136 (1998); American Coalition of Life Activists v. Planned Parenthood of the Columbia/Willamette, Inc., 539 U.S. 958 (2003).

59. The quoted language is from the Santa Barbara ordinance, struck down in Edwards v. City of Santa Barbara, 150 F.3d 1213 (9th Cir. 1998). The language of the Phoenix ordinance, invalidated in Sabelko v. City of Phoenix, 120 F.3d 161 (9th Cir. 1997), was quite similar.

60. Note also Hoffman v. Hunt, 126 F.3d 575 (4th Cir. 1997), in which ACLJ failed to persuade a Fourth Circuit panel to enjoin North Carolina's clinic defense statute, enacted in 1993.

61. Hill v. Colorado, 530 U.S. 703, 762 (2000).

62. McCullen v. Coakley, 571 F.3d 167, 173 (1st Cir. 2009).

63. McGuire v. Reilly, 260 F.3d 36 (1st Cir. 2001).

64. McGuire v. Reilly, 386 F.3d 45 (1st Cir. 2004).

65. McCullen v. Coakley, 571 F.3d 167 (1st Cir. 2009).

66. McCullen v. Coakley, 708 F.3d 1 (1st Cir. 2013).

67. McGuire v. Reilly, 544 U.S. 974 (2005); McCullen v. Coakley, 559 U.S. 1005 (2010); McCullen v. Coakley, 133 S. Ct. 2857 (2013). Note also Brown v. Pittsburgh, 586 F.3d 263 (3d Cir. 2009), in which ADF litigators successfully challenged a 2005 Pittsburgh ordinance that imposed both a fifteen-foot fixed buffer zone around clinic entrances and an eight-foot floating buffer zone around all patients within one hundred feet of such an entrance.

68. Evergreen Ass'n v. City of New York, 2011 U.S. Dist. LEXIS 75422 (S.D.N.Y. 2011); Greater Baltimore Center for Pregnancy Concerns v. Mayor & City Council, 683 F.3d 539 (4th Cir. 2012), *vacated*, 721 F.3d 264 (4th Cir. 2013).

69. For a notable example of a legal challenge to a policy that had been created primarily by judges, consider the unusual Rule 60(b) motion filed by right-to-life

advocates urging reconsideration of Roe v. Wade (1973). Representing the original "Jane Roe"—now litigating under her real name, Norma McCorvey—opponents of legal abortion argued that they had new evidence significant enough to reopen the thirty-year-old landmark decision. A unanimous Fifth Circuit panel denied this motion in McCorvey v. Hill, 385 F.3d 846 (5th Cir. 2004).

70. See, for example, United States v. Sorrentino, 72 F.3d 294 (2d Cir. 1995); United States v. Hernandez, 85 F.3d 1023 (2d Cir. 1996); United States v. Trzaska, 111 F.3d 1019 (2d Cir. 1997); United States v. Gateward, 84 F.3d 670 (3d Cir. 1996); United States v. Wells, 98 F.3d 808 (4th Cir. 1996); United States v. Rawls, 85 F.3d 240 (5th Cir. 1996); United States v. Harkrider, 88 F.3d 1408 (5th Cir. 1996); United States v. Chesney, 86 F.3d 564 (6th Cir. 1996); United States v. Turner, 77 F.3d 887 (6th Cir. 1996); United States v. Murphy, 107 F.3d 1199 (6th Cir. 1997); United States v. Bell, 70 F.3d 495 (7th Cir. 1995); United States v. Lee, 72 F.3d 55 (7th Cir. 1995); United States v. Bradford, 78 F.3d 1216 (7th Cir. 1996); United States v. Williams, 128 F.3d 1128 (7th Cir. 1997); United States v. Wesela, 223 F.3d 656 (7th Cir. 2000); United States v. Hemmings, 258 F.3d 587 (7th Cir. 2001); United States v. Jackubowski, 63 Fed. App'x 959 (7th Cir. 2003); United States v. Rankin, 64 F.3d 338 (8th Cir. 1995); United States v. Shelton, 66 F.3d 991 (8th Cir. 1995); United States v. Bates, 77 F.3d 1101 (8th Cir. 1996); United States v. Barry, 98 F.3d 373 (8th Cir. 1996); United States v. Hanna, 55 F.3d 1456 (9th Cir. 1995); United States v. Collins, 61 F.3d 1379 (9th Cir. 1995); United States v. Nguyen, 88 F.3d 812 (9th Cir. 1996); United States v. Henson, 123 F.3d 1226 (9th Cir. 1997); United States v. Bolton, 68 F.3d 396 (10th Cir. 1995); United States v. McAllister, 77 F.3d 387 (11th Cir. 1996); United States v. Adams, 91 F.3d 114 (11th Cir. 1996).

71. United States v. Chesney, 86 F.3d 564, 574 (6th Cir. 1996); United States v. Rawls, 85 F.3d 240, 243–44 (5th Cir. 1996).

72. Federal District Judge Reggie Walton dismissed the NRA suit in Seegars v. Ashcroft, 297 F. Supp. 2d 201 (D.D.C. 2004), and a divided DC Circuit panel affirmed in Seegars v. Ashcroft, 396 F.3d 1248 (D.C. Cir. 2005). Federal District Judge Emmet G. Sullivan likewise dismissed the wildcat suit in Parker v. District of Columbia, 311 F. Supp. 2d 103 (D.D.C. 2004), but here, a DC Circuit panel reversed. 478 F.3d 370 (D.C. Cir. 2007).

73. Regarding the views of state appellate courts, Silberman cited eight decisions purportedly holding "that the Second Amendment protects an individual right," but in at least half of these cases, that description is misleading. Parker v. District of Columbia, 478 F.3d 370, 380 (D.C. Cir. 2007). In Louisiana v. Blanchard, 776 So. 2d 1165 (La. 2001), the Supreme Court of Louisiana read some limits into a state statute prohibiting the possession of a firearm while also possessing a controlled dangerous substance, but did not directly address the scope or nature of the right protected by the Second Amendment. In Brewer v. Commonwealth, 206 S.W.3d 343 (Ky. 2006), the Kentucky Supreme Court invalidated the automatic forfeiture of firearms as part of a criminal sentence, but mentioned the Second

Amendment only in passing. In Hilberg v. F. W. Woolworth Co., 761 P.2d 236 (Colo. Ct. App. 1988), an intermediate appellate court in Colorado likewise mentioned the Second Amendment only in passing, in the course of dismissing a negligence action brought against a firearms retailer by the victim of an accidental shooting. And in State v. Anderson, 2000 Tenn. Crim. App. LEXIS 60 (Tenn. Crim. App. 2000), an intermediate appellate court in Tennessee did not mention the right to bear arms at all. In the other four cases cited by Silberman—Washington v. Williams, 158 Wash. 2d 904 (Wash. 2006); State v. Nickerson, 126 Mont. 157 (Mont. 1952); Stillwell v. Stillwell, 2001 Tenn. App. LEXIS 562 (Tenn. Ct. App. 2001); and Rohrbaugh v. State, 216 W. Va. 298 (W. Va. 2004)—state appellate courts did appear to endorse an individual right to bear arms, though even these decisions addressed the issue only briefly.

74. Parker v. District of Columbia, 2007 U.S. App. LEXIS 11029 (D.C. Cir. 2007), *cert. granted*, District of Columbia v. Heller, 552 U.S. 1035 (2007).

75. District of Columbia v. Heller, 554 U.S. 570, 635 (2008).

76. Ibid., 638–39.

77. "NRA Settles San Francisco Housing Authority Gun Ban Lawsuit" (January 16,2009), available at http://www.nraila.org/legislation/federal-legislation/2009/nra-settles-san-francisco-housing-autho.aspx?s=&st=&ps=; Jackson v. City & County of San Francisco, 2012 U.S. Dist. LEXIS 116732 (N.D. Cal. 2012).

78. Bach v. Pataki, 408 F.3d 75 (2d Cir. 2005); Love v. Pepersack, 47 F.3d 120 (4th Cir. 1995); Edwards v. City of Goldsboro, 178 F.3d 231 (4th Cir. 1999). Note also Peoples Rights Organization v. City of Columbus, 152 F.3d 522, 538, n.18 (6th Cir. 1998), in which a Sixth Circuit panel noted the nonincorporation of the Second Amendment in passing, but invalidated a local ban on assault weapons as unconstitutionally vague.

79. Maloney v. Cuomo, 554 F.3d 56 (2d Cir. 2009).

80. Nordyke v. King, 563 F.3d 439, 457 (9th Cir. 2009). This case had originated as a pre-*Heller* challenge to a 1999 county ordinance that effectively banned gun shows from the county fairgrounds. As I note in category 1 above, the Ninth Circuit initially rejected this challenge in Nordyke v. King, 319 F.3d 1185 (9th Cir. 2003), on the grounds that the Second Amendment protected a collective right of the people to maintain a citizens' militia. The panel reconsidered this holding in light of *Heller*, leading to the 2009 decision discussed in the text.

81. Three years later, the en banc panel vacated the three-judge panel's holding and dismissed the Second Amendment claim, though still granting the plaintiffs a qualified right to conduct gun shows on county property. Nordyke v. King, 681 F.3d 1041 (9th Cir. 2012) (en banc).

82. NRA v. Chicago, 567 F.3d 856, 860 (7th Cir. 2009).

83. Brief for the Brady Center to Prevent Gun Violence et al. in Support of Neither Party, McDonald v. Chicago, No. 08-1521 (November 2009), 12.

84. McDonald v. Chicago, 130 S. Ct. 3020 (2010).

85. Britt v. State, 363 N.C. 546 (N.C. 2009). For another instance of at least partially successful state constitutional litigation, note Wisconsin v. Cole, 665 N.W.2d 328 (Wis. 2003), and Wisconsin v. Hamdan, 665 N.W.2d 785 (Wis. 2003), in which the Wisconsin Supreme Court upheld the state's long-standing ban on the carrying of concealed weapons, but held that it could not constitutionally be applied to a grocery store owner who kept a handgun on the premises for self-defense.

86. See, for example, United States v. Barton, 633 F.3d 168 (3d Cir. 2011); United States v. Frazier, 314 Fed. App'x 801 (6th Cir. 2008), *cert. denied*, Frazier v. United States, 556 U.S. 1143 (2009); United States v. Williams, 616 F.3d 685 (7th Cir. 2010), *cert. denied*, Williams v. United States, 131 S. Ct. 805 (2010); United States v. Irish, 285 Fed. App'x 326 (8th Cir. 2008); United States v. McCane, 573 F.3d 1037 (10th Cir. 2009), *cert. denied*, 130 S. Ct. 1686 (2010); United States v. Rozier, 598 F.3d 768 (11th Cir.), *cert. denied*, Rozier v. United States, 130 S. Ct. 3399 (2010). Note also United States v. Fincher, 538 F.3d 868 (8th Cir. 2008), in which an Eighth Circuit panel rejected a Second Amendment challenge to the federal ban on possession of machine guns.

87. Justice v. Town of Cicero, 577 F.3d 768 (7th Cir. 2009), *cert. denied*, 130 S. Ct. 3410 (2010).

88. Note also Washington v. Sieyes, 168 Wash. 2d 276 (Wash. 2010), in which the Washington Supreme Court held (prior to *McDonald*) that the Second Amendment applies to the states, but that the state statutory ban on possession of firearms by juveniles was nonetheless constitutional. During the period between *Heller* and *McDonald*, federal appellate panels likewise adopted narrow readings of the Second Amendment's scope in United States v. McRobie, 2009 U.S. App. LEXIS 617 (4th Cir. 2009), and United States v. Richard, 350 Fed. App'x 252 (10th Cir. 2009).

89. United States v. Booker, 644 F.3d 12 (1st Cir. 2011); United States v. Decastro, 682 F.3d 160 (2d Cir. 2012); United States v. Marzzarella, 614 F.3d 85 (3d Cir. 2010); Dutton v. Pennsylvania, 503 Fed. App'x 125 (3d Cir. 2012); United States v. Masciandaro, 638 F.3d 458 (4th Cir. 2011); United States v. Staten, 666 F.3d 154 (4th Cir. 2011); United States v. Chester, 514 Fed. App'x 393 (4th Cir. 2013); United States v. Portillo-Munoz, 643 F.3d 437 (5th Cir. 2011); National Rifle Ass'n, Inc. v. Bureau of Alcohol, Tobacco, Firearms & Explosives, 2012 U.S. App. LEXIS 26949 (5th Cir. 2012), *en banc reh'g denied*, 714 F.3d 334 (5th Cir. 2013); United States v. Griffin, 476 Fed. App'x 592 (6th Cir. 2011); United States v. Skoien, 614 F.3d 638 (7th Cir. 2010); United States v. Yancey, 621 F.3d 681 (7th Cir. 2010); United States v. Seay, 620 F.3d 919 (8th Cir. 2010); United States v. Bena, 664 F.3d 1180 (8th Cir. 2011); United States v. Brown, 436 Fed. App'x 725 (8th Cir. 2011); United States v. Aiello, 452 Fed. App'x 699 (8th Cir. 2012); United States v. Potter, 630 F.3d 1260 (9th Cir. 2011); United States v. Dugan, 657 F.3d 998 (9th Cir. 2011); United States v. Henry, 688 F.3d 637 (9th Cir. 2012); United States v. Molina, 484 Fed. App'x 276 (10th Cir. 2012); Schrader v. Holder, 704 F.3d 980 (D.C. Cir. 2013). Note also United States v. Carter, 669 F.3d 411, 419 (4th Cir. 2012), in which

a Fourth Circuit panel remanded for further proceedings on the government interests served by banning illegal drug users from possessing firearms. The panel indicated that the government's "burden should not be difficult to satisfy," and the
government did, in fact, successfully defend the statute on remand in United States
v. Carter, 2012 U.S. Dist. LEXIS 168011 (S.D. W. Va. 2012). In addition to the federal statutory provisions enumerated in the text, federal appellate panels rejected
Second Amendment challenges to the federal criminal sentence enhancement for
possessing a firearm while engaged in a drug crime and to the federal ban on aiding
and abetting the possession of a gun by a convicted felon. United States v. Greeno,
679 F.3d 510 (6th Cir. 2012); United States v. Huet, 665 F.3d 588 (3d Cir. 2012).

90. Peterson v. Martinez, 707 F.3d 1197 (10th Cir. 2013); Drake v. Filko, 724
F.3d 426 (3d Cir. 2013); Kachalsky v. County of Westchester, 701 F.3d 81 (2d Cir.
2012); GeorgiaCarry.Org, Inc. v. Georgia, 687 F.3d 1244 (11th Cir. 2012). Note
also Heller v. District of Columbia, 670 F.3d 1244 (D.C. Cir. 2011), discussed in
category 1 above, in which a divided DC Circuit panel upheld most provisions of
the new gun control law enacted in the District of Columbia after the SCOTUS
decision in *Heller* came down.

91. Williams v. Maryland, 417 Md. 479 (Md. 2011); Commonwealth v. Mc-
Gowan, 464 Mass. 232 (Mass. 2013); Digiacinto v. Rector & Visitors of George
Mason University, 281 Va. 127 (Va. 2011).

92. Moore v. Madigan, 2012 U.S. App. LEXIS 25264 (7th Cir. 2012).

93. Moore v. Madigan, 708 F.3d 901 (7th Cir. 2013) (en banc).

94. Washington Legal Foundation v. Alexander, 984 F.2d 483 (D.C. Cir. 1993);
Podberesky v. Kirwan, 956 F.2d 52 (4th Cir. 1992).

95. Podberesky v. Kirwan, 38 F.3d 147 (4th Cir. 1994); Adarand Constructors,
Inc. v. Pena, 515 U.S. 200 (1995).

96. In Fullilove v. Klutznick, 448 U.S. 448 (1980), and Metro Broadcasting v.
FCC, 497 U.S. 547 (1990), a sharply divided Court had applied intermediate rather
than strict scrutiny to race-conscious affirmative action policies.

97. Adarand Constructors, Inc. v. Pena, 16 F.3d 1537 (10th Cir. 1994).

98. *Adarand* was not the first case in which Roberts had argued that a federal
affirmative action program was unconstitutional. As acting solicitor general, he
had also done so on behalf of the first Bush administration in *Metro Broadcasting*.

99. Hopwood v. Texas, 78 F.3d 932 (5th Cir. 1996).

100. Brief for Plaintiffs-Appellants Hopwood and Carvell (December 19,
1994), Hopwood v. Texas, US Court of Appeals for the Fifth Circuit, No. 94-50664,
at 17 (emphasis in original).

101. One member of the panel, Circuit Judge Jacques Wiener, concurred with
his colleagues that UT's admissions policies were unconstitutional, but declined to
join their sweeping repudiation of *Bakke*. Two weeks later, Wiener joined several
colleagues in urging en banc rehearing, but they were outvoted 9–7. Hopwood v.
Texas, 84 F.3d 720 (5th Cir. 1996).

102. Brief for the US as Amicus Curiae, Board of Education of Piscataway v. Taxman, Third Circuit Court of Appeals, 1994, at 8.

103. Taxman v. Board of Education of the Township of Piscataway, 91 F.3d 1547 (3d Cir. 1996) (en banc).

104. Texas v. Hopwood, 518 U.S. 1033 (1996); Piscataway Township Board of Education v. Taxman, 521 U.S. 1117 (1997).

105. From 1998 through 2002, the justices issued several affirmative action holdings, but none of them examined the central constitutional issues that remained open. Note, in particular, Texas v. Lesage, 528 U.S. 18 (1999), and Adarand Constructors, Inc. v. Mineta, 534 U.S. 103 (2001).

106. Edwards v. Houston, 78 F.3d 983 (5th Cir. 1996).

107. Dallas v. Dallas Fire Fighters Ass'n, 150 F.3d 438 (5th Cir. 1998), *cert. denied*, 526 U.S. 1046 (1999). When SCOTUS denied certiorari in March 1999, Justices Breyer and Ginsburg dissented, with Breyer indicating that there was sufficient evidence of past discrimination by the local fire department to justify a narrowly tailored race-conscious remedial plan. Note also Stern v. Trustees of Columbia University, 131 F.3d 305 (2d Cir. 1997), in which a divided Second Circuit panel allowed an employment discrimination case brought by a white Columbia University professor to proceed to trial.

108. Quinn v. Boston, 325 F.3d 18 (1st Cir. 2003).

109. Lutheran Church-Missouri Synod v. FCC, 141 F.3d 344, 351–52, 354–56 (D.C. Cir. 1998).

110. Lutheran Church-Missouri Synod v. FCC, 154 F.3d 494 (D.C. Cir. 1998); see also 154 F.3d 487 (D.C. Cir. 1998).

111. MD/DC/DE Broadcasters Ass'n v. FCC, 236 F.3d 13 (D.C. Cir. 2001).

112. Wittmer v. Peters, 87 F.3d 916, 919 (7th Cir. 1996).

113. McNamara v. City of Chicago, 138 F.3d 1219 (7th Cir. 1998); Boston Police Superior Officers Federation v. Boston, 147 F.3d 13 (1st Cir. 1998).

114. University & Community College System of Nevada v. Farmer, 113 Nev. 90 (Nev. 1997).

115. Dynalantic v. US Department of Defense, 115 F.3d 1012, 1016 (D.C. Cir. 1997), quoting Northeastern Florida Chapter of the Associated General Contractors of America v. Jacksonville, 508 U.S. 656, 666 (1993).

116. Rothe Development Corp. v. US Department of Defense, 262 F.3d 1306 (Fed. Cir. 2001). On remand, the trial court granted summary judgment to the government, but the Federal Circuit reversed yet again, holding in Rothe Development Corp. v. Department of Defense, 413 F.3d 1327 (Fed. Cir. 2005), that the case should proceed to trial. When the case returned to the Federal Circuit for a third time in 2008, the appellate court again ruled in favor of the defense contractor, this time finding the policy facially unconstitutional. Rothe Development Corp. v. Department of Defense, 545 F.3d 1023 (Fed. Cir. 2008).

117. Adarand Constructors, Inc. v. Slater, 228 F.3d 1147 (10th Cir. 2000).

118. Concrete Works of Colorado v. City & County of Denver, 321 F.3d 950 (10th Cir. 2003).

119. American Federation of Government Employees v. United States, 330 F.3d 513 (D.C. Cir. 2003).

120. Hunter v. Regents of the University of California, 190 F.3d 1061 (9th Cir. 1999).

121. Brewer v. West Irondequoit Central School District, 212 F.3d 738 (2d Cir. 2000).

122. Swann v. Charlotte-Mecklenburg Board of Education, 402 U.S. 1 (1971).

123. Belk v. Charlotte-Mecklenburg Board of Education, 233 F.3d 232 (4th Cir. 2000).

124. Belk v. Charlotte-Mecklenburg Board of Education, 269 F.3d 305 (4th Cir. 2001) (en banc).

125. Ho v. San Francisco Unified School District, 147 F.3d 854 (9th Cir. 1998).

126. Wessmann v. Gittens, 160 F.3d 790 (1st Cir. 1998).

127. Eisenberg v. Montgomery County Public Schools, 197 F.3d 123 (4th Cir. 1999); Tuttle v. Arlington County School Board, 195 F.3d 698 (4th Cir. 1999).

128. The panel subsequently withdrew this opinion, directing the Washington Supreme Court to answer this state law question in the first instance. Parents Involved in Community Schools v. Seattle School District, No. 1, 285 F.3d 1236 (9th Cir. 2002), *opinion withdrawn*, 294 F.3d 1085 (9th Cir. 2002). As I note below, the Seattle policy was subsequently invalidated by SCOTUS.

129. In August 2002, a similar case from Lynn, Massachusetts, went to trial, drawing national media coverage (Lewin 2002), and in September, the Ninth Circuit dismissed another such case, Scott v. Pasadena Unified School District, 306 F.3d 646 (9th Cir. 2002), on standing grounds.

130. Lesage v. Texas, 158 F.3d 213 (5th Cir. 1998).

131. Texas v. Lesage, 528 U.S. 18 (1999).

132. Wooden v. Board of Regents, 32 F. Supp. 2d 1370 (S.D. Ga. 1999); Tracy v. Board of Regents, 59 F. Supp. 2d 1314 (S.D. Ga. 1999).

133. Johnson v. Board of Regents, 106 F. Supp. 2d 1362 (S.D. Ga. 2000).

134. The UW suit continued for several years, as CIR's lawyers continued to seek damages on behalf of its plaintiffs, who had been rejected under the old race-conscious policy, but once I-200 had banned UW from continuing to consider race, the suit was no longer a good vehicle for the substantive constitutional issue.

135. For an earlier such effort, see Brief Amici Curiae of American Council on Education et al., Board of Education of Piscataway v. Taxman, No. 96-679, 1996 U.S. Briefs 679 (August 25, 1997), 15–30.

136. Gratz v. Bollinger, 122 F. Supp. 2d 811 (E.D. Mich. 2000); Grutter v. Bollinger, 137 F. Supp. 2d 821 (E.D. Mich. 2001).

137. Wooden v. Board of Regents of the University System, 247 F.3d 1262 (11th Cir. 2001); Johnson v. Board of Regents of University of Georgia, 263 F.3d 1234 (11th Cir. 2001).

138. Grutter v. Bollinger, 288 F.3d 732, 747 (6th Cir. 2002).

139. Grutter v. Bollinger, 537 U.S. 1043 (2002); Gratz v. Bollinger, 537 U.S. 1044 (2002).

140. President George W. Bush, "Remarks on the Michigan Affirmative Action Case," The Roosevelt Room (January 15, 2003). See Greenhouse (2003).

141. Brief for the US as Amicus Curiae Supporting Petitioner, Grutter v. Bollinger, No. 02-241 (January 17, 2003), 8, 10, 14.

142. Brief for Respondents, Grutter v. Bollinger, No. 02-241 (February 18, 2003), 1, 12–13.

143. 539 U.S. 306, 323, 325 (2003).

144. Ibid., 329–33.

145. Ibid., 327; 539 U.S. 244, 281 (2003).

146. 539 U.S. 306, 340, 349–50, 358, 366, 371–74 (2003).

147. On the evening of the Court's decisions, Coleman was joined on *The News Hour with Jim Lehrer* by three other public university presidents who echoed her declaration of victory. Transcript available at http://www.pbs.org/newshour/bb /law/jan-june03/sc_6-23.html. See also Cantor (2003, 2004); Laird (2005, 26–27); Lewis (2004); Pelton (2003); Schmidt (2003a).

148. Parents Involved in Community Schools v. Seattle School District No. 1, 72 P.3d 151 (Wash. 2003).

149. Sherbrooke Turf, Inc. v. Minnesota Department of Transportation, 345 F.3d 964, 973 (8th Cir. 2003).

150. Concrete Works of Colorado v. Denver, 540 U.S. 1027, 1027 (2003).

151. Smith v. University of Washington, Law School, 392 F.3d 367 (9th Cir. 2004).

152. For an example of a case that went the other way, note Western States Paving Co. v. Washington State Department of Transportation, 407 F.3d 983 (9th Cir. 2005).

153. Comfort v. Lynn School Committee, 418 F.3d 1 (1st Cir. 2005) (en banc); McFarland v. Jefferson County Public Schools, 416 F.3d 513 (6th Cir. 2005); Parents Involved in Community Schools v. Seattle School District, No. 1, 426 F.3d 1162 (9th Cir. 2005). In a related case involving a different legal issue, a divided Ninth Circuit panel invalidated on federal civil rights grounds a longstanding admissions preference for Native Hawaiians in a private school system funded by a charitable trust dedicated to the education of such persons. The following year, an en banc panel split 8–7 in reversing this holding. Doe v. Kamehameha Schools/Bishop Estate, 416 F.3d 1025 (9th Cir. 2005), *rev'd*, 470 F.3d 827 (9th Cir. 2006) (en banc).

154. Parents Involved in Community Schools v. Seattle School District, No. 1, 426 F.3d 1162, 1196 (9th Cir. 2005).

155. 551 U.S. 701, 748 (2007).

156. Ricci v. DeStefano, 530 F.3d 87, 87 (2d Cir. 2008).

157. Ricci v. DeStefano, 530 F.3d 88 (2d Cir. 2008) (en banc).

158. Ricci v. DeStefano, 129 S. Ct. 2658 (2009).

159. Vivenzio v. City of Syracuse, 611 F.3d 98, 109 (2d Cir. 2010).

160. Robinson v. Shelby County Board of Education, 566 F.3d 642, 656 (6th Cir. 2009).

161. Fisher v. University of Texas, 631 F.3d 213, 218, 231 (5th Cir. 2011).

162. Fisher v. University of Texas, 644 F.3d 301 (5th Cir. 2011) (en banc).

163. Fisher v. University of Texas, 133 S. Ct. 2411, 2420 (2013).

164. Desjarlais v. State, 300 P.3d 900 (Alaska 2013).

165. Lemons v. Bradbury, 538 F.3d 1098 (9th Cir. 2008); Protect Marriage Illinois v. Orr, 463 F.3d 604, 606 (7th Cir. 2006).

166. Hawaii State AFL-CIO v. Yoshina, 84 Haw. 374 (Haw. 1997).

167. Bennett v. Yoshina, 140 F.3d 1218 (9th Cir. 1998).

168. Pawlick v. Birmingham, 780 N.E.2d 466 (Mass. 2002).

169. Doyle v. Goodridge, 444 Mass. 1006 (Mass. 2005); Pinello (2006, 45–72).

170. Doyle v. Secretary of the Commonwealth, 858 N.E.2d 1090 (Mass. 2006).

171. Bowler v. Lockyer, No. 05-CS-01123 (Super. Ct. Cal., Sac. Cty. 2005).

172. Jansson v. Bowen, Case Number: 34-2008-00017351 (Super. Ct. Cal., Sac. Cty. 2008), available at http://ag.ca.gov/cms_attachments/press/pdfs/n1597_ruling_on_proposition_8.pdf. Elsewhere, this sort of legal challenge to the ballot language of a proposed anti-SSM initiative has sometimes proven successful. See, e.g., Limmer v. Ritchie, 819 N.W.2d 622 (Minn. 2012).

173. Bopp had served as general counsel for the National Right to Life Committee since 1978. By 2009, his Indiana-based firm had become a leading litigation outfit for a variety of conservative causes. Its most notable victory came the following year, in Citizens United v. FEC, 558 U.S. 310 (2010).

174. Bopp's California suit was rejected in ProtectMarriage.com v. Bowen, 830 F. Supp. 2d 914 (E.D. Cal. 2011).

175. Perry v. Schwarzenegger, 591 F.3d 1147 (9th Cir. 2010); Hollingsworth v. Perry, 130 S. Ct. 705 (2010). After the Supreme Court's holding, the dispute continued over whether the video recordings of the trial should be released after the fact. In Perry v. Brown, 667 F.3d 1078 (9th Cir. 2012), a Ninth Circuit panel gave Proposition 8's proponents another victory, holding that the recordings should remain sealed.

176. Doe v. Reed, 661 F. Supp. 2d 1194 (W.D. Wash. 2009), *rev'd*, 586 F.3d 671 (9th Cir. 2009).

177. Doe v. Reed, Order #09A356, 130 S. Ct. 486 (2009).

178. Moreover, the Court's June 2010 holding left the door open for the referendum's supporters to demonstrate the likelihood of threats, harassment, or reprisals that would justify an exemption from the state's Public Records Act. Writing separately, Justice Alito indicated that such a narrower challenge was, in his view, highly meritorious. In response, Justice Sotomayor indicated that "any party attempting to challenge particular applications of the State's regulations will bear a heavy burden." Doe v. Reed, 130 S. Ct. 2811, 2829 (2010). On remand, Judge Settle

quoted from Sotomayor's opinion in granting summary judgment to the state and lifting the preliminary injunction. Doe v. Reed, 823 F. Supp. 2d 1195 (W.D. Wash. 2011). In November 2011, a divided Ninth Circuit panel declined to reinstate the injunction, and SCOTUS declined to intervene, over another dissent from Justice Alito. Doe v. Reed, 2011 U.S. App. LEXIS 23327 (9th Cir. 2011), *injunction denied*, 132 S. Ct. 449 (2011). The Ninth Circuit panel then dismissed the appeal as moot, on the grounds that the list of petition signatories had already been released and was now widely available. Doe v. Reed, 697 F.3d 1235 (9th Cir. 2012).

179. National Organization for Marriage v. McKee, 649 F.3d 34 (1st Cir. 2011). Note also National Organization for Marriage v. Daluz, 654 F.3d 115 (1st Cir. 2011); National Organization for Marriage v. McKee, 669 F.3d 34 (1st Cir. 2012); and National Organization for Marriage v. Cruz-Bustillo, 477 Fed. App'x 584 (11th Cir. 2012).

180. Jackson v. D.C. Board of Elections & Ethics, 2010 D.C. App. LEXIS 400 (D.C. 2010). Note also Jackson v. D.C. Board of Elections & Ethics, 559 U.S. 1301 (2010).

181. Michigan Civil Rights Initiative v. Board of State Canvassers, 268 Mich. App. 506 (Mich. Ct. App. 2005).

182. Michigan Civil Rights Initiative v. Board of State Canvassers, 474 Mich. 1099 (Mich. 2006).

183. Asher v. Carnahan, Case No. 07AC-CC00648 (Cole Cty. Cir. Ct. 2008), *appeal dismissed*, 268 S.W.3d 427 (Mo. Ct. App. 2008).

184. Letter from Michael S. Greve, November 24, 1998, on file with author, p. 2.

185. "The UW Law School rejected her. Was it reverse discrimination?" KING 5 Up Front with Robert Mak, original broadcast, April 14, 2002.

186. The case that eventually made it to SCOTUS, National Federation of Independent Businesses v. Sebelius, 132 S. Ct. 2566 (2012), was initially filed by thirteen state attorneys general, all of them Republican; by the time it reached the high Court, twenty-five states had signed on, with twenty-two of them represented by Republican attorneys general and three others by Republican governors. Meanwhile, the Republican Attorney General of Virginia had filed a separate constitutional challenge of his own. See Virginia *ex rel.* Cuccinelli v. Sebelius, 133 S. Ct. 59 (2012).

187. Doyle v. Secretary of the Commonwealth, 858 N.E.2d 1090 (Mass. 2006).

188. Connerly v. State Personnel Board, 92 Cal. App. 4th 16 (3d Dist. 2001); Brinkman v. Miami University, 2007 Ohio 4372 (Ohio Ct. App. 2007).

189. The court dismissed their claims on standing grounds in Alons v. Iowa District Court, 698 N.W.2d 858 (Iowa 2005).

190. Alpha Medical Clinic v. Anderson, 280 Kan. 903 (Kan. 2006).

191. Comprehensive Health of Planned Parenthood of Kansas & Mid-Missouri, Inc. v. Kline, 287 Kan. 372 (Kan. 2008).

192. Ibid., 380–81.

193. Kansas v. Comprehensive Health of Planned Parenthood of Kansas, 291 Kan. 322 (Kan. 2010).

194. The state high court dismissed this suit on standing grounds in Rohde v. Ann Arbor Public Schools, 479 Mich. 336 (Mich. 2007), but subsequently held in National Pride at Work v. Governor of Michigan, 748 N.W.2d 524 (Mich. 2008), that such policies were indeed constitutionally prohibited.

195. Brinkman v. Miami University, 2007 Ohio 4372 (Ohio Ct. App. 2007).

196. Cleveland Taxpayers for Ohio Constitution v. City of Cleveland, 2010 Ohio 4685 (8th App. Dist. 2010); Appling v. Doyle, 2012 Wis. App. LEXIS 1016 (Wis. Ct. App. 2012). Note also Leskovar v. Nickels, 140 Wash. App. 770 (Div. I 2007).

197. American Civil Rights Foundation v. Berkeley Unified School District, 172 Cal. App. 4th 207 (1st Dist. 2009); American Civil Rights Foundation v. Los Angeles Unified School District, 169 Cal. App. 4th 436 (2d Dist. 2008); Connerly v. State Personnel Board, 92 Cal. App. 4th 16 (3d Dist. 2001).

198. Hi-Voltage Wire Works, Inc. v. San Jose, 24 Cal. 4th 537 (Cal. 2000).

199. Connerly v. State Personnel Board, 92 Cal. App. 4th 16 (3d Dist. 2001). This case had originally been filed by Republican governor Pete Wilson; Connerly subsequently intervened as a taxpayer litigant, and he continued the suit after Wilson left office.

200. In addition to the cases already cited, note Crawford v. Huntington Beach Union High School District, 98 Cal. App. 4th 1275 (4th Dist. 2002).

201. Coalition to Defend Affirmative Action v. Granholm, 2006 U.S. Dist. LEXIS 93257 (E.D. Mich. 2006).

Chapter Three

1. For a full accounting of the multiple legal challenges, see ACA Litigation Blog (July 6, 2012), http://acalitigationblog.blogspot.com/.

2. Thomas More Law Center v. Obama, 720 F. Supp. 2d 882 (E.D. Mich. 2010); Liberty University v. Geithner, 753 F. Supp. 2d 611 (W.D. Va. 2010); Virginia v. Sebelius, 728 F. Supp. 2d 768 (E.D. Va. 2010); Florida v. US Department of Health & Human Services, 2011 U.S. Dist. LEXIS 8822 (N.D. Fla. 2011); Mead v. Holder, 766 F. Supp. 2d 16 (D.D.C. 2011).

3. Thomas More Law Center v. Obama, 651 F.3d 529 (6th Cir. 2011); Seven-Sky v. Holder, 661 F.3d 1 (D.C. Cir. 2011); Wilkinson (2012).

4. National Federation of Independent Businesses v. Sebelius, 132 S. Ct. 2566 (2012).

5. Most famously, Justices Scalia, Thomas, Alito, and Kennedy argued that if Congress were constitutionally entitled to mandate the purchase of health insurance, it could also mandate the purchase of broccoli. NFIB v. Sebelius, 132 S. Ct. 2566, 2650 (2012).

6. Confirmation Hearing on the Nomination of John G. Roberts Jr. to be Chief Justice of the United States, 109th Cong., 1st Sess. (September 12–15, 2005), 55–56.

7. As I note below, my own research has likewise found substantial evidence that the Sixth Circuit has been unusually polarized in recent years. Matthew Hall (2010) has argued that some of the intercircuit differences identified by Sunstein were artifacts of methodological errors, but he excludes the Sixth Circuit from his analysis because he claims that that circuit has not adhered to strict norms regarding the random assignment of judges to panels.

8. The literature remains divided on the relative merits of these causal accounts, though Joshua Fischman has recently made a strong case that panel effects are the result of dissent aversion or, in his words, the existence of "a strong and stable norm of consensus on the courts of appeals" (forthcoming, 26; see also Posner 2008b, 31–32).

9. Hall (2010) has argued that methodological errors led Sunstein et al. to slightly understate the effect of partisanship for the total universe of cases and to significantly understate it for abortion cases.

10. On gay rights, Dan Pinello has reported similar results (2003, 151–52).

11. The quoted text is from the Declaration of Independence.

12. More precisely, I cited 332 federal appellate decisions on the issues of abortion, affirmative action, gay rights, and gun rights that were issued from 1993 through August 2013. It is this universe of cases that provides the data discussed in the text here. Appendix A provides a detailed description of my coding procedures.

13. The difference between these figures is due to the presence of two liberal Republican appointees on the Court throughout most of the period covered by this study. Again, my coding procedures here are detailed in appendix A.

14. Gratz v. Bollinger, 122 F. Supp. 2d 811, 824 (E.D. Mich. 2000); Grutter v. Bollinger, 137 F. Supp. 2d 821 (E.D. Mich. 2001).

15. Grutter v. Bollinger, 288 F.3d 732, 776 (6th Cir. 2002).

16. 288 F.3d 732, 758 (6th Cir. 2002).

17. *In re* Complaint of Judicial Misconduct No. 03-6-372-07 (6th Cir. 2003), available at http://www.judicialwatch.org/files/documents/2003/6thcircuitdecision-re-judicialmisconduct-05282003.pdf.

18. Memphis Planned Parenthood, Inc. v. Sundquist, 184 F.3d 600, 605, 608 (6th Cir. 1999).

19. *In re* Byrd, 269 F.3d 578, 582 (6th Cir. 2001). Note also Simmons-Harris v. Zelman, 234 F.3d 945 (6th Cir. 2000), in which the members of a divided panel engaged in what the *New York Times* characterized as a "vitriolic exchange" in a decision concerning the constitutionality of a school vouchers policy from Cleveland (Wilgoren 2000b).

20. *In re* Byrd, 269 F.3d 578, 582–3 (6th Cir. 2001).

21. See, for example, Cooey v. Bradshaw, 338 F.3d 615 (6th Cir. 2003); Ohio Republican Party v. Brunner, 544 F.3d 711 (6th Cir. 2008) (en banc).

22. Coalition to Defend Affirmative Action v. Regents of the University of Michigan, 652 F.3d 607 (6th Cir. 2011).

23. Coalition to Defend Affirmative Action v. Regents of the University of Michigan, 2012 U.S. App. LEXIS 23443 (6th Cir. 2012).

24. Coalition to Defend Affirmative Action v. Regents of the University of Michigan, 701 F.3d 466, 493, 506, 512 (6th Cir. 2012).

25. Planned Parenthood of the Blue Ridge v. Camblos, 116 F.3d 707 (4th Cir. 1997).

26. Planned Parenthood of the Blue Ridge v. Camblos, 125 F.3d 884 (4th Cir. 1997).

27. Planned Parenthood of the Blue Ridge v. Camblos, 155 F.3d 352 (4th Cir. 1998).

28. These votes are tabulated from Women's Medical Professional Corp. v. Voinovich, 130 F.3d 187 (6th Cir. 1997); Richmond Medical Center v. Gilmore, 183 F.3d 303 (4th Cir. 1998); Carhart v. Stenberg, 192 F.3d 1142 (8th Cir. 1999); and Hope Clinic v. Ryan, 195 F.3d 857 (7th Cir. 1999) (en banc). The judges on the Eighth Circuit panel who unanimously invalidated Nebraska's partial birth ban in *Carhart* did the same for Arkansas's and Iowa's bans in the companion cases of Planned Parenthood of Greater Iowa, Inc. v. Miller, 195 F.3d 386 (8th Cir. 1999), and Little Rock Family Planning Services v. Jegley, 192 F.3d 794 (8th Cir. 1999).

29. Lutheran Church-Missouri Synod v. FCC, 141 F.3d 344 (D.C. Cir. 1998).

30. The DC Circuit had a 6–5 Republican majority at the time, but one Democratic appointee (Merrick Garland) did not participate in the case. Lutheran Church-Missouri Synod v. FCC, 154 F.3d 494 (D.C. Cir. 1998).

31. MD/DC/DE Broadcasters Ass'n v. FCC, 236 F.3d 13 (D.C. Cir. 2001).

32. Brief for the US as Amicus Curiae, Board of Education of Piscataway v. Taxman, filed with Third Circuit, 1994, at 8; Taxman v. Board of Education of Piscataway, 91 F.3d 1547 (3d Cir. 1996).

33. Fisher v. University of Texas, 631 F.3d 213, 247 (5th Cir. 2011).

34. Fisher v. University of Texas, 644 F.3d 301 (5th Cir. 2011).

35. Fisher v. University of Texas, 133 S. Ct. 2411 (2013).

36. Steffan v. Aspin, 8 F.3d 57 (D.C. Cir. 1993).

37. Steffan v. Perry, 41 F.3d 677 (D.C. Cir. 1994) (en banc).

38. Lofton v. Secretary of the Department of Children & Family Services, 358 F.3d 804, *reh'g denied*, 377 F.3d 1275 (11th Cir. 2004) (en banc).

39. United States v. Rybar, 103 F.3d 273 (3d Cir. 1996).

40. Ileto v. Glock, 349 F.3d 1191 (9th Cir. 2003).

41. Ileto v. Glock Inc., 370 F.3d 860 (9th Cir. 2004).

42. Parker v. District of Columbia, 478 F.3d 370 (D.C. Cir. 2007).

43. Parker v. District of Columbia, 2007 U.S. App. LEXIS 11029 (D.C. Cir. 2007).

44. Moore v. Madigan, 2012 U.S. App. LEXIS 25264 (7th Cir. 2012); 708 F.3d 901 (7th Cir. 2013) (en banc).

45. The anti-SSM initiatives referenced here were from Nebraska and Nevada in 2000; Arkansas, Georgia, Kentucky, Michigan, Mississippi, Montana, North Dakota, Ohio, Oklahoma, Oregon, and Utah in 2004; Arizona, Tennessee, Virginia, and Wisconsin in 2006; and Arizona, California, and Florida in 2008.

46. For the three LGBT rights measures—a 1994 antigay initiative in Oregon, a 2000 referendum on extending antidiscrimination law to cover sexual orientation in Maine, and a 2008 initiative restricting parenting rights in Arkansas—the mean partisan gap was 31.0 points. For the anti–affirmative action votes that took place in California, Washington, and Michigan in 1996, 1998, and 2006, respectively, the gap was 42.9 points. For the abortion-related measures—a 1998 ban on partial-birth abortion in Washington; two proposals to require parental notice in California, in 2006 and 2008, respectively; a 2008 "human life amendment" in Colorado; and a 2008 abortion ban in South Dakota—the gap was 37.0 points.

47. My coding procedures are detailed in appendix A, and the bills themselves are listed in appendix C (available at http://press.uchicago.edu/sites/keck/).

48. Note, for example, Sojourner T v. Edwards, 974 F.2d 27 (5th Cir. 1992), in which GHWB-appointee Emilio M. Garza sharply criticized Planned Parenthood v. Casey (1992), but nonetheless applied it to strike down Louisiana's sweeping ban on abortion.

49. Isaacson v. Horne, 2012 U.S. App. LEXIS 16390 (9th Cir. 2012); 716 F.3d 1213 (9th Cir. 2013).

50. Planned Parenthood v. Miller, 63 F.3d 1452 (8th Cir. 1995).

51. Planned Parenthood v. Farmer, 220 F.3d 127 (3d Cir. 2000).

52. Luttig's opinion later received some attention for its characterization of *Casey* as "a decision of super-*stare decisis* with respect to a woman's fundamental right to choose whether or not to proceed with a pregnancy." Richmond Medical Center v. Gilmore, 219 F.3d 376, 376 (4th Cir. 2000), *aff'd*, 224 F.3d 337 (4th Cir. 2000). As evidence of Luttig's pre-*Carhart* views, note his June 1998 decision to lift the injunction against Virginia's law. Richmond Medical Center v. Gilmore, 144 F.3d 326 (4th Cir. 1998) (Luttig, J., granting stay), *aff'd*, 183 F.3d 303 (4th Cir. 1998).

53. Eubanks v. Stengel, 224 F.3d 576 (6th Cir. 2000); Causeway Medical Suite v. Foster, 221 F.3d 811 (5th Cir. 2000).

54. Rhode Island Medical Society v. Whitehouse, 239 F.3d 104 (1st Cir. 2001); Hope Clinic v. Ryan, 249 F.3d 603 (7th Cir. 2001).

55. Reproductive Health Services of Planned Parenthood of the St. Louis Region, Inc. v. Nixon, 429 F.3d 803 (8th Cir. 2005).

56. Planned Parenthood Federation of America v. Ashcroft, 435 F.3d 1163 (9th Cir. 2006).

57. Carhart v. Gonzales, 413 F.3d 791 (8th Cir. 2005).

58. National Abortion Federation v. Gonzales, 437 F.3d 278, 290 (2d Cir. 2006).

59. Richmond Medical Center for Women v. Hicks, 409 F.3d 619 (4th Cir. 2005).

60. Richmond Medical Center for Women v. Hicks, 422 F.3d 160 (4th Cir. 2005), *vacated and remanded*, Herring v. Richmond Medical Center for Women, 550 U.S. 901 (2007).

61. Richmond Medical Center for Women v. Herring, 527 F.3d 128 (4th Cir. 2008), *rev'd*, 570 F.3d 165 (4th Cir. 2009) (en banc).

62. United States v. Lopez, 514 U.S. 549, 561 (1995).

63. United States v. Danks, 221 F.3d 1037 (8th Cir. 1999), *cert. denied*, 528 U.S. 1091 (2000). Note also United States v. Dorsey, 418 F.3d 1038 (9th Cir. 2005).

64. The courts faced a similar barrage of commerce clause challenges to the 1986 federal ban on the transfer or possession of machine guns. Unlike the felon-in-possession law and the revised GFSZA, this statute included no explicit jurisdictional element; that is, it banned the possession of machine guns whether or not they had traveled in interstate commerce. With the proper application of *Lopez* less clear in this context, partisan affiliation had a greater influence on judicial votes. In the twelve post-*Lopez* holdings on this issue cited in chapter 2, Democratic judges voted 18–0 to uphold the statute, while their GOP colleagues did so by a closer vote of 21–10.

65. District of Columbia v. Heller, 554 U.S. 570, 626–27 (2008).

66. United States v. McCane, 573 F.3d 1037, 1050 (10th Cir. 2009).

67. Comfort v. Lynn School Committee, 418 F.3d 1 (1st Cir. 2005) (en banc); McFarland v. Jefferson County Public Schools, 416 F.3d 513 (6th Cir. 2005); Parents Involved in Community Schools v. Seattle School District, No. 1, 426 F.3d 1162 (9th Cir. 2005) (en banc).

68. A similar pattern held with regard to affirmative action in higher education. In chapter 2, I cite eleven federal appellate holdings regarding race-conscious policies at colleges and universities. (This count includes holdings involving the constitutionality of race-conscious admissions, financial aid, and hiring policies, but excludes those involving the constitutionality of statewide bans on affirmative action.) In the eight holdings that came down prior to *Grutter*, federal judges were sharply polarized, with GOP appointees voting 24–1 against affirmative action and their Democratic colleagues voting 6–12. In the three holdings after *Grutter*, polarization persisted, but judges of both parties shifted in the direction of greater support for affirmative action, with Republican and Democratic tallies of 7–7 and 0–8, respectively.

69. Bennett v. Yoshina, 140 F.3d 1218 (9th Cir. 1998), *cert. denied*, Citizens for a Constitutional Convention v. Yoshina, 525 U.S. 1103 (1999).

70. Largess v. Supreme Judicial Court, 317 F. Supp. 2d 77 (D. Mass.), *aff'd*, 373 F.3d 219 (1st Cir.), *cert. denied*, 543 U.S. 1002 (2004).

71. Lemons v. Bradbury, 538 F.3d 1098 (9th Cir. 2008).

72. Brady v. Dean, 173 Vt. 542, 542–43 (Vt. 2001).

73. Pawlick v. Birmingham, 780 N.E.2d 466 (Mass. 2002); Doyle v. Goodridge, 444 Mass. 1006 (Mass. 2005); Doyle v. Secretary of the Commonwealth, 858 N.E.2d

1090 (Mass. 2006). The April 2004 denial referenced in the text was issued by a single state high court justice and subsequently ratified by the full court in the 2005 *Doyle* holding. In the 2006 *Doyle* holding, the court held that it was powerless to compel the legislature to vote on the proposal, but that the legislators did indeed have a constitutional duty to do so. As I note in chapter 2, this judicial rebuke led the legislature's leaders to schedule a vote after all.

74. Likewise, when opponents of SSM have relied on expansive conceptions of standing to challenge employer-provided benefits policies and even individual civil unions or domestic partnerships to which they object, state courts have wasted little time in rejecting such efforts. See, for example, Alons v. Iowa District Court, 698 N.W.2d 858 (Iowa 2005); Brinkman v. Miami University, 2007 Ohio 4372 (Ohio Ct. App. 2007).

75. Albano v. Attorney General, 437 Mass. 156 (Mass. 2002); Schulman v. Attorney General, 447 Mass. 189 (Mass. 2006).

76. Bennett v. Bowen, 2008 Cal. LEXIS 8868 (Cal. 2008).

77. Strauss v. Horton, 46 Cal. 4th 364 (Cal. 2009).

78. Lockyer v. City & County of San Francisco, 33 Cal. 4th 1055 (Cal. 2004).

79. The Supreme Court declined to recognize fetuses as Fourteenth Amendment "persons" in Roe v. Wade (1973), and even the Court's sharpest dissenting voices on abortion have acknowledged that there is no constitutional right that prevents a state from permitting abortion. See, for example, Justice Thomas's concurring opinion in Stenberg v. Carhart, 530 U.S. 914, 980 (2000). Prior to *Roe*, two members of New York's high court were willing to hold that the state legislature was constitutionally foreclosed from decriminalizing abortion, on the grounds of a fetal right to life, but I am not aware of any state or federal appellate judges who have supported such a holding since *Roe* (Price and Keck 2013).

80. In a concurring opinion, Fifth Circuit Judge Edith H. Jones (a Reagan appointee) made her own opposition to legal abortion clear—calling explicitly for SCOTUS to reevaluate *Roe* and *Casey*—but nonetheless agreed with her colleagues that the case was moot. McCorvey v. Hill, 385 F.3d 846, 850–53 (5th Cir. 2004), *cert, denied*, 543 U.S. 1154 (2005).

81. Elizabeth Blackwell Health Center for Women v. Knoll, 61 F.3d 170 (3d Cir. 1995); Hope Medical Group for Women v. Edwards, 63 F.3d 418 (5th Cir. 1995); Planned Parenthood Affiliates v. Engler, 73 F.3d 634 (6th Cir. 1996); Planned Parenthood of Indiana, Inc. v. Commissioner of the Indiana State Department of Health, 699 F.3d 962 (7th Cir. 2012); Little Rock Family Planning Services v. Dalton, 60 F.3d 497 (8th Cir. 1995); Planned Parenthood Arizona, Inc. v. Betlach, 2013 U.S. App. LEXIS 17584 (9th Cir. 2013); Hern v. Beye, 57 F.3d 906 (10th Cir. 1995).

82. The votes were closer (and more polarized) in six similar decisions issued by state high courts, but here too, most judges of both parties voted against the claims initiated by local governments. GOP judges did so 13–5, with their Democratic colleagues voting 10–8.

83. 551 U.S. 701, 748 (2007).

84. Coalition for Economic Equity v. Wilson, 122 F.3d 692 (9th Cir. 1997); Coalition to Defend Affirmative Action v. Brown, 674 F.3d 1128 (9th Cir. 2012).

85. Coalition to Defend Affirmative Action v. Regents of the University of Michigan, 701 F.3d 466 (6th Cir. 2012), *cert. granted*, Schuette v. Coalition to Defend Affirmative Action, 2013 U.S. LEXIS 2504 (2013).

86. Arnold v. Cleveland, 616 N.E.2d 163 (Ohio 1993); Benjamin v. Bailey, 662 A.2d 1226 (Conn. 1995).

87. Washington v. Sieyes, 168 Wash. 2d 276 (Wash. 2010).

88. Baker v. Vermont, 170 Vt. 194, 246, 262–63 (Vt. 1999).

89. Lewis v. Harris, 188 N.J. 415 (N.J. 2006).

90. As indicated in appendix A, I coded all votes cast by justices who were appointed by a Democratic or Republican governor or elected in a partisan election. I did not code votes cast by justices who were appointed by an independent or third-party governor or elected in a nonpartisan election. I coded 824 individual judicial votes, including at least one from each of the 124 cited decisions.

91. I calculated the first-term Obama figure from the database of federal judges maintained by the Federal Judicial Center, available at http://www.fjc.gov.

Chapter Four

1. Confirmation Hearing on the Nomination of John G. Roberts Jr. to be Chief Justice of the United States, 109th Cong., 1st Sess. (September 12–15, 2005), 55.

2. Confirmation Hearing on the Nomination of Samuel A. Alito Jr. to be an Associate Justice of the Supreme Court of the US, 109th Cong., 2d Sess. (January 9–13, 2006), 37–38.

3. Confirmation Hearing on the Nomination of Hon. Sonia Sotomayor to be an Associate Justice of the Supreme Court of the US, 111th Cong., 1st Sess. (July 13–16, 2009), 6.

4. The First Gore-Bush Presidential Debate, October 3, 2000, available at http://www.debates.org/index.php?page=october-3-2000-transcript; George W. Bush, "State of the Union Address" (January 20, 2004), available at http://www.americanrhetoric.com/speeches/stateoftheunion2004.htm. See Keck (2007a, 168–69).

5. Steffan v. Aspin, 8 F.3d 57 (D.C. Cir. 1993).

6. Steffan v. Perry, 41 F.3d 677 (D.C. Cir. 1994) (en banc).

7. In addition to the abortion funding cases, six holdings involved (at least temporarily) successful efforts to force antiabortion protesters to comply with federal laws restricting their clinic blockade tactics; two involved temporarily successful efforts to hold firearms manufacturers responsible for the deaths and injuries resulting from notorious mass shootings; and two involved successful efforts by supporters of California's 2008 anti-SSM initiative to resist public disclosure of their internal campaign documents.

8. Log Cabin Republicans v. United States, 716 F. Supp. 2d 884 (C.D. Cal. 2010), *vacated*, 658 F.3d 1162 (9th Cir. 2011).

9. Except where otherwise noted, all public opinion ranges reported in this chapter reflect the full set of relevant poll results from the specified time period (up through September 2013) that are archived in the Roper Center's iPoll data-bank. Here, the relevant polls are ABC News/Washington Post polls (ABC/WaPo) from January and May 1993; a CBS News/New York Times poll (CBS/NYT) from February 1993; and NBC News/Wall Street Journal polls (NBC/WSJ) from April, June, and July 1993.

10. After DADT was enacted, polling on the issue was sporadic throughout the remainder of the 1990s, but support generally fell in the mid-50s range. During the George W. Bush era, support for gays and lesbians serving openly appeared to increase over time, reaching as high as 81 percent in a December 2008 poll from CNN/Opinion Research Corporation (ORC). During Barack Obama's first term, support for this position ranged from 62 to 80 percent when respondents were asked directly whether they believed gays and lesbians should be allowed to serve openly. Support for open service was somewhat lower when pollsters described the DADT policy and asked respondents whether they favored or opposed it, with the latter option sometimes framed explicitly as support for repeal. Even with these questions, however, support for open service (i.e., opposition to DADT) exceeded 50 percent in four out of six national polls. The two exceptions were an April 2009 CNN/ORC poll and a November 2010 Marist Poll, each reporting 48 percent sup-port for DADT, with just 47 percent opposition.

11. The Louisiana statute was invalidated by a Fifth Circuit panel in 1992 (i.e., before Bill Clinton took office), but the dispute was not laid to rest until SCOTUS denied certiorari the following year. Sojourner T v. Edwards, 974 F.2d 27 (5th Cir. 1992), *cert. denied*, 507 U.S. 972 (1993). The Utah statute was invalidated by a Tenth Circuit panel in 1995 and again in 1996, with a partial reversal and remand from SCOTUS in the interim. Jane L. v. Bangerter, 61 F.3d 1493 (10th Cir. 1995), *rev'd*, Leavitt v. Jane L., 518 U.S. 137 (1996), *on remand at* 102 F.3d 1112 (10th Cir. 1996).

12. Personhood Nevada v. Bristol, 245 P.3d 572 (Nev. 2010); *In re* Initiative Petition No. 395, 286 P.3d 637 (Okla. 2012); MKB Management Corp. v. Burdick, 2013 U.S. Dist. LEXIS 102620 (D.N.D. 2013); Edwards v. Beck, 2013 U.S. Dist. LEXIS 75277 (E.D. Ark. 2013).

13. In April 1989, for example, with Webster v. Reproductive Health Services (1989) pending at SCOTUS, CBS/NYT asked: "If the Supreme Court changes its view of the law so each state could make its own decision on abortion, would you want your state to permit abortions under all circumstances, or to only allow abortion in cases of rape, incest or to save the life of the mother, or to outlaw all abortions?"; 53 percent of respondents chose either the second or third options. In the same survey, however, just 48 percent of respondents gave similar answers to a question that did not mention the Supreme Court, and one month earlier,

AP/Medial General had reported that just 44 percent of respondents favored a "Constitutional Amendment that would make abortions illegal nationwide, except in cases of rape, incest or to save the life of the mother." Perhaps the clearest example of question-wording effects on this issue comes from an October 1996 CBS/NYT poll. Dividing their sample in half, the pollsters asked two slightly different questions:

> Which of these comes closest to your view: 1. Abortion should be generally available to those who want it. 2. Abortion should be available but under stricter limits than it is now. 3. Abortion should be against the law except in cases of rape, incest, and to save the woman's life. 4. Abortion should not be permitted at all?

> What is your personal feeling about abortion: 1. It should be permitted in all cases. 2. It should be permitted, but subject to greater restrictions than it is now. 3. It should be permitted in cases such as rape, incest, and to save the woman's life. 4. It should only be permitted to save the woman's life?

In response to the first question, 40 percent of respondents indicated support for option 3 or 4; in response to the second, 61 percent of respondents indicated support for option 3 or 4 or volunteered that abortion should not be permitted at all. CBS asked this latter question fourteen times from 1996 to 2011 and reported results at or above 50 percent on thirteen of those occasions. But NBC/WSJ asked a similar question (with slightly different wording) fifteen times from 1991 to 2009 and never reported majority support. The ranges were 47 to 61 for CBS and 37 to 47 for NBC/WSJ. The iPoll databank's full range of responses to polls along these lines was 42 to 66 percent from 1987 to 1991 and 37 to 61 percent from 1992 to 2012. A single poll reported to date for 2013 indicates a response of 52 percent. On these question-wording effects, see Luks and Salamone (2008).

14. Romer v. Evans, 517 U.S. 620 (1996); *In re* Advisory Opinion to the Attorney General, 632 So. 2d 1018 (Fla. 1994); Doe v. Montgomery County Board of Elections, 406 Md. 697 (Md. 2008).

15. Boy Scouts of America v. Dale, 530 U.S. 640 (2000).

16. In 2012 to 2013, Gallup/USAT and ABC/WaPo reported 42 percent and 55 percent support, respectively, for allowing openly gay troop leaders. During the same period, polls from ABC/WaPo, CBS, and Quinnipiac reported 51 to 63 percent support for allowing openly gay members.

17. Department of Human Services & Child Welfare Agency Review Board v. Howard, 238 S.W.3d 1 (Ark. 2006); Arkansas Department of Human Services v. Cole, 2011 Ark. 145 (Ark. 2011); Florida Department of Children & Families v. Matter of Adoption of X.X.G. & N.R.G., 45 So. 3d 79 (Fla. Dist. Ct.App. 3d Dist. 2010); Finstuen v. Crutcher, 496 F.3d 1139 (10th Cir. 2007).

18. Tumeo v. University of Alaska (Sup. Ct. 4th Dist. 1995), *aff'd and remanded*, University of Alaska v. Tumeo, 933 P.2d 1147 (Alaska 1997); Alaska Civil Liberties

Union v. Alaska, 122 P.3d 781 (Alaska 2005); Diaz v. Brewer, 2011 U.S. App. LEXIS 18467 (9th Cir. 2011); Snetsinger v. Montana University System, 104 P.3d 445 (Mont. 2004); Bedford & Breen v. New Hampshire Technical College System (N.H. Super. Ct. May 3, 2006); Tanner v. Oregon Health Sciences University, 971 P.2d 435 (Or. Ct. App. 1998).

19. Jegley v. Picado, 349 Ark. 600 (Ark. 2002); Powell v. Georgia, 270 Ga. 327 (Ga. 1998); Williams v. State, 1998 Extra LEXIS 260 (Balt. City Cir. Ct. 1998); Gay & Lesbian Advocates & Defenders v. Attorney General, 436 Mass. 132 (Mass. 2002); Doe v. Ventura, 2001 WL 543734 (Minn. Dist. Ct., Hennepin Cty. 2001); Missouri v. Cogshell, 997 S.W.2d 534 (Mo. Ct. App. 1999); Gryczan v. Montana, 942 P.2d 112 (Mont. 1997); Campbell v. Sundquist, 926 S.W.2d 250 (Tenn. Ct. App. 1996); Lawrence v. Texas, 539 U.S. 558 (2003). As I note in chapter 1, the first such holding came several years earlier in Commonwealth v. Wasson, 842 S.W.2d 487 (Ky. 1992).

20. Beginning in 2009, Gallup changed the wording of this question to refer to "gay or lesbian relations" rather than "homosexual relations."

21. Fiscal v. City & County of San Francisco, 158 Cal. App. 4th 895 (1st Dist. 2008); District of Columbia v. Heller, 554 U.S. 570 (2008); McDonald v. City of Chicago, 130 S. Ct. 3020 (2010).

22. Hopwood v. Texas, 78 F.3d 932 (5th Cir. 1996); Johnson v. Board of Regents of University of Georgia, 263 F.3d 1234 (11th Cir. 2001); Gratz v. Bollinger, 539 U.S. 244 (2003).

23. I have excluded all polls that ask about support for preferences for "women and minorities" (or words to that effect) because the invalidated policies that I discuss in the text all focused on race. The questions that focus simultaneously on race and gender provide no clear indication of support for racial preferences alone.

24. Connerly v. State Personnel Board, 92 Cal. App. 4th 16 (3d Dist. 2001); Ricci v. DeStefano, 129 S. Ct. 2658 (2009); Quinn v. Boston, 325 F.3d 18 (1st Cir. 2003); Taxman v. Board of Education of the Township of Piscataway, 91 F.3d 1547 (3d Cir. 1996) (en banc); Robinson v. Shelby County Board of Education, 566 F.3d 642, 656 (6th Cir. 2009); Dallas v. Dallas Fire Fighters Ass'n, 150 F.3d 438 (5th Cir. 1998); Lutheran Church-Missouri Synod v. FCC, 141 F.3d 344 (D.C. Cir. 1998); MD/DC/DE Broadcasters Ass'n v. FCC, 236 F.3d 13 (D.C. Cir. 2001).

25. Again, these ranges exclude polls that ask about support for racial and gender preferences, without distinguishing the two.

26. As I note in chapter 2, state or federal courts invalidated race-conscious contracting policies in Hi-Voltage Wire Works, Inc. v. San Jose, 24 Cal. 4th 537 (Cal. 2000); Connerly v. State Personnel Board, 92 Cal. App. 4th 16 (3d Dist. 2001); Western States Paving Co. v. Washington State Department of Transportation, 407 F.3d 983 (9th Cir. 2005); and Rothe Development Corp. v. Department of Defense, 545 F.3d 1023 (Fed. Cir. 2008). SCOTUS also invalidated such a policy in Richmond v. Croson, 488 U.S. 469 (1989), but I am focused on post-1992 decisions

here. In Adarand Constructors, Inc. v. Pena, 515 U.S. 200 (1995), SCOTUS held that such policies were subject to strict scrutiny, but the policy at issue (as subsequently amended) was eventually upheld on remand.

27. Here, state and federal courts invalidated a range of such policies in Ho v. San Francisco Unified School District, 147 F.3d 854 (9th Cir. 1998); Wessmann v. Gittens, 160 F.3d 790 (1st Cir. 1998); Eisenberg v. Montgomery County Public Schools, 197 F.3d 123 (4th Cir. 1999); Tuttle v. Arlington County School Board, 195 F.3d 698 (4th Cir. 1999); Crawford v. Huntington Beach Union High School Dist., 98 Cal. App. 4th 1275 (4th Dist. 2002), *review denied*, 2002 Cal. LEXIS 5928 (Cal. 2002); Parents Involved in Community Schools v. Seattle School Dist. No. 1, 551 U.S. 701 (2007); and Robinson v. Shelby County Board of Education, 566 F.3d 642 (6th Cir. 2009).

28. In State v. Hamdan, 665 N.W.2d 785 (Wis. 2003), the Wisconsin Supreme Court held that the state's ban on concealed weapons could not constitutionally be applied to a grocery store owner who kept a handgun on the premises for self-defense. In Moore v. Madigan, 2012 U.S. App. LEXIS 25264 (7th Cir. 2012), a Seventh Circuit panel invalidated Illinois's statutory ban on carrying firearms in public.

29. Goodridge v. Department of Public Health, 440 Mass. 309 (Mass. 2003); *In re* Marriage Cases, 43 Cal. 4th 757 (Cal. 2008); Kerrigan v. Commissioner of Public Health, 289 Conn. 135 (Conn. 2008); Varnum v. Brien, 763 N.W.2d 862 (Iowa 2009); Perry v. Schwarzenegger, 704 F. Supp. 2d 921 (N.D. Cal. 2010).

30. Judge Walker's holding in California was affirmed by a Ninth Circuit panel in Perry v. Brown, 671 F.3d 1052 (9th Cir. 2012), but that appellate holding was then vacated by SCOTUS in Hollingsworth v. Perry, 133 S. Ct. 2652 (2013), leaving Judge Walker's injunction in place. SCOTUS invalidated § 3 of DOMA in United States v. Windsor, 133 S. Ct. 2675 (2013).

31. The third row of the table includes all polls assessing support for allowing gay and lesbian couples to legally marry or similar words to that effect, except that I have excluded several polls referencing "constitutional amendments" or "constitutional rights" regarding SSM. The fourth row, regarding the federal nonrecognition of lawful SSMs, includes all polls listed in the third row, except that I have excluded a small number that expressly referenced the legal recognition of marriages by state governments, and I have added several polls referencing the federal recognition issue directly. In March 2011, for example, an HRC poll reported that 34 percent of respondents favored "the law banning federal recognition of legal marriages," with 52 percent opposed.

32. As I note elsewhere, the only exceptions to this pattern are the early to mid-1930s, the mid- to late 1960s, and the period from 1995 to 2005 (Keck 2004, 40).

33. United States v. Windsor, 133 S. Ct. 2675 (2013); United States v. Lopez, 514 U.S. 549 (1995); Printz v. United States, 521 U.S. 898 (1997); Rothe Development Corp. v. Department of Defense, 545 F.3d 1023 (Fed. Cir. 2008). In chapter 1, I

also cite several decisions invalidating either the DADT policy or the full ban on military service by homosexuals that preceded it, but none of those holdings survived on appeal.

34. The language quoted in the text is from a December 1993 Gallup Poll, which found 87 percent support; a January 1994 poll with slightly different question wording found 79 percent support.

35. For a similar assessment of the GFSZA, see Hall (2011, 92).

36. Peoples Rights Organization v. City of Columbus, 152 F.3d 522 (6th Cir. 1998).

37. Britt v. State, 363 N.C. 546 (N.C. 2009).

38. Nordyke v. Santa Clara, 110 F.3d 707 (9th Cir. 1997); Ezell v. City of Chicago, 2011 U.S. App. LEXIS 14108 (7th Cir. 2011). A large number of additional polls have reported supermajority support for requiring background checks for firearms purchases made at gun shows, but the August 1999 PSRA/Newsweek poll is the only one I have found that suggested banning gun shows altogether.

39. Wollschlaeger v. Farmer, 880 F. Supp. 2d 1251 (S.D. Fla. 2012).

40. Planned Parenthood of Delaware v. Brady, 2003 U.S. Dist. LEXIS 10099 (D. Del. 2003); Planned Parenthood v. State, 1999 Mont. Dist. LEXIS 1117 (Mont. 1st Jud. Dist., Lewis & Clark Cty. 1999); Planned Parenthood of Middle Tennessee v. Sundquist, 38 S.W.3d 1 (Tenn. 2000); Planned Parenthood Minnesota v. Daugaard, 799 F. Supp. 2d 1048 (D.S.D. 2011).

41. Stuart v. Huff, 2011 U.S. Dist. LEXIS 123244 (M.D.N.C. 2011); Nova Health Systems v. Edmondson, 233 P.3d 380 (Okla. 2010).

42. Armstrong v. State, 989 P.2d 364 (Mont. 1999); Evergreen Ass'n v. City of New York, 2011 U.S. Dist. LEXIS 75422 (S.D.N.Y. 2011).

43. Planned Parenthood v. Miller, 63 F.3d 1452 (8th Cir 1995); Planned Parenthood League of Massachusetts., Inc. v. Attorney General, 677 N.E.2d 101 (Mass. 1997); American Academy of Pediatrics v. Lungren, 940 P.2d 797 (Cal. 1997); Causeway Medical Suite v. Ieyoub, 109 F.3d 1096, 1108 (5th Cir. 1997); Planned Parenthood v. Lawall, 1999 U.S. App. LEXIS 33154 (9th Cir. 1999); Wicklund v. State, 1999 Mont. Dist. LEXIS 1116 (Mont. 1st Jud. Dist. Ct., Lewis & Clark Cty. 1999); Planned Parenthood of Central New Jersey v. Farmer, 762 A.2d 620 (N.J. 2000); Planned Parenthood v. Owens, 287 F.3d 910 (10th Cir. 2002); North Florida Women's Health & Counseling Services, Inc. v. State, 866 So. 2d 612 (Fla. 2003); Planned Parenthood v. Wasden, 376 F.3d 908 (9th Cir. 2004); State v. Planned Parenthood of Alaska, 171 P.3d 577 (Alaska 2007).

44. Women's Medical Professional Corp. v. Voinovich, 130 F.3d 187 (6th Cir. 1997); Planned Parenthood of Southern Arizona, Inc. v. Woods, 982 F. Supp. 1369, 1378 (D. Ariz. 1997); Evans v. Kelley, 977 F. Supp. 1283 (E.D. Mich. 1997); A Choice for Women v. Butterworth, 54 F. Supp. 2d 1148 (S.D. Fla. 1998); Causeway Medical Suite v. Foster, 43 F. Supp. 2d 604 (E.D. La. 1999); Planned Parenthood of Greater Iowa, Inc. v. Miller, 195 F.3d 386 (8th Cir. 1999); Little Rock Family

Planning Services v. Jegley, 192 F.3d 794 (8th Cir. 1999); Stenberg v. Carhart, 530 U.S. 914 (2000); Planned Parenthood v. Farmer, 220 F.3d 127 (3d Cir. 2000); Richmond Medical Center v. Gilmore, 224 F.3d 337 (4th Cir. 2000); Eubanks v. Stengel, 224 F.3d 576 (6th Cir. 2000); Causeway Medical Suite v. Foster, 221 F.3d 811 (5th Cir. 2000); Rhode Island Medical Society v. Whitehouse, 239 F.3d 104 (1st Cir. 2001); Hope Clinic v. Ryan, 249 F.3d 603 (7th Cir. 2001); Reproductive Health Services of Planned Parenthood of the St. Louis Region, Inc. v. Nixon, 429 F.3d 803 (8th Cir. 2005); Northland Family Planning Clinic, Inc. v. Cox, 487 F.3d 323 (6th Cir. 2007).

45. Isaacson v. Horne, 716 F.3d 1213 (9th Cir. 2013); Lathrop v. Deal, Civil Action No. 2012-cv-224423 (Super. Ct. Fulton Cty., Ga., December 21, 2012).

46. State Department of Health & Social Services v. Planned Parenthood of Alaska, Inc., 28 P.3d 904 (Alaska 2001); Simat Corp. v. Arizona Health Care Cost Containment System, 56 P.3d 28 (Ariz. 2002); Women of State of Minnesota by Doe v. Gomez, 542 N.W.2d 17 (Minn. 1995); New Mexico Right to Choose/ NARAL v. Johnson, 975 P.2d 841 (N.M. 1998); Women's Health Center of West Virginia, Inc. v. Panepinto, 446 S.E.2d 658 (W.Va. 1993). As I note in chapter 1, abortion rights advocates have also persuaded federal courts to invalidate a number of state law restrictions on abortion funding as inconsistent with federal Medicaid policy. Because I have characterized these latter holdings as category 3 decisions—with the advocates litigating to enforce policy victories previously won via legislative channels—I do not include them as potentially countermajoritarian exercises of judicial review here.

47. Vittitow v. City of Upper Arlington, 43 F.3d 1100 (6th Cir. 1995); Edwards v. City of Santa Barbara, 150 F.3d 1213 (9th Cir. 1998); Sabelko v. City of Phoenix, 120 F.3d 161 (9th Cir. 1997); Brown v. Pittsburgh, 586 F.3d 263 (3d Cir. 2009).

48. In September 1991, when CBS/NYT provided respondents with a brief description of clinic protests, 80 percent indicated that these actions were an unacceptable form of political protest. In July 2002, the National Constitution Center reported that 73 percent of respondents believed that antiabortion protesters were entitled "to hold a peaceful demonstration across the street from a family planning clinic where abortions take place," but in response to a follow-up question, 64 percent of respondents indicated that if the protests were disrupting business for local store owners, "the courts [should] limit the protest to certain hours of the day." Five national polls from 1994 to 1998 reported 63 to 76 percent support for deploying US marshals or taking other steps to protect abortion providers from violence.

49. Lowe v. Broward County, 766 So. 2d 1199 (Fla. Dist. Ct. App. 4th Dist. 2000), *review denied*, 789 So. 2d 346 (Fla. 2001); City of Atlanta v. McKinney, 454 S.E. 2d 517 (Ga. 1995); Connors v. City of Boston, 714 N.E.2d 335 (Mass. 1999); National Pride at Work v. Governor of Michigan, 748 N.W.2d 524 (Mich. 2008); Lilly v. City of Minneapolis, 527 N.W.2d 107 (Minn. Ct. App.), *review denied*, 1995 Minn. LEXIS 264 (Minn. 1995); Devlin v. City of Philadelphia, 580 Pa. 564 (Pa. 2004); Arlington County v. White, 528 S.E.2d 706 (Va. 2000).

50. As I noted when reporting the mirror images of these poll results above, I have included here all polls that asked about health insurance or other employee benefits for gay and lesbian partners without mentioning SSM or otherwise suggesting that the same-sex partners would have rights and benefits equivalent to those of opposite-sex spouses.

51. State v. Machholz, 574 N.W.2d 415 (Minn. 1998); Saxe v. State College Area School District, 240 F.3d 200 (3d Cir. 2001).

52. Lieb (2009); Coalition to Defend Affirmative Action v. Regents of the University of Michigan, 701 F.3d 466 (6th Cir. 2012).

53. Stenberg v. Carhart, 530 U.S. 914, 950–51 (2000).

54. "Bans on 'Partial-Birth' Abortion," Guttmacher Institute (October 1, 2013), available at http://www.guttmacher.org/statecenter/spibs/spib_BPBA.pdf.

55. "Counseling and Waiting Periods for Abortion," Guttmacher Institute (October 1, 2013), available at http://www.guttmacher.org/statecenter/spibs/spib_MWPA.pdf.

56. Federal courts have invalidated parental involvement requirements in Arizona, Louisiana, and South Dakota for lacking adequate judicial bypass procedures and in Colorado and Idaho for lacking maternal health exceptions.

57. "Parental Involvement in Minors' Abortions," Guttmacher Institute (October 1, 2013), available at http://www.guttmacher.org/statecenter/spibs/spib_PIMA.pdf.

58. Armstrong v. State, 989 P.2d 364 (Mont. 1999); Mazurek v. Armstrong, 520 U.S. 968 (1997).

59. "An Overview of Abortion Laws," Guttmacher Institute (October 1, 2013), available at http://www.guttmacher.org/statecenter/spibs/spib_OAL.pdf.

60. "State Funding of Abortion Under Medicaid," Guttmacher Institute (October 1, 2013), available at http://www.guttmacher.org/statecenter/spibs/spib_SFAM.pdf.

61. "State Hate Crimes Laws," Human Rights Campaign, available at http://www.hrc.org/files/assets/resources/hate_crimes_laws_062013.pdf (last updated June 19, 2013). A Sixth Circuit panel dismissed a constitutional challenge to the 2009 Matthew Shepard and James Byrd Jr. Hate Crimes Prevention Act in Glenn v. Holder, 690 F.3d 417 (6th Cir. 2012).

62. Saxe v. State College Area School District, 240 F.3d 200 (3d Cir. 2001); "Statewide School Anti-Bullying Laws & Policies," Human Rights Campaign, available at http://www.hrc.org/files/assets/resources/school_anti-bullying_laws_062013.pdf (last updated June 4, 2013).

63. Moore v. Madigan, 708 F.3d 901 (7th Cir. 2013) (en banc).

64. United States v. Danks, 221 F.3d 1037 (8th Cir. 1999), *cert. denied*, 528 U.S. 1091 (2000).

65. I refer here to bans on assault weapons, prohibitions of gun possession by convicted felons, bans on partial-birth abortion, restrictions on public funding of abortion, clinic defense laws, and LGBT-inclusive hate crimes laws.

Chapter Five

1. Klarman has significantly softened this account in a more recent book, concluding that "[o]n balance, litigation has probably advanced the cause of gay marriage more than it has retarded it" (2013, 218).

2. As I note in chapter 1, one of these state electorates (Hawaii's) had enacted a constitutional amendment that did not itself ban SSM but authorized the state legislature to do so via statute.

3. As this number implies, nine states enacted bans on SSM, but subsequently reversed those bans by legislative or judicial action: California, Connecticut, Delaware, Iowa, Maine, Maryland, Minnesota, Vermont, and Washington.

4. "Statewide Marriage Prohibitions," Human Rights Campaign, available at http://www.hrc.org/files/assets/resources/marriage_prohibitions_072013.pdf (last updated July 2, 2013).

5. Compare Klarman (2005, 467–70) and Rosenberg (2008, 369–82) with Ansolabehere and Stewart (2005), Egan and Sherrill (2006), Fiorina et al. (2006, 145–57), and Hillygus and Shields (2005).

6. *In re* T.W., 551 So. 2d 1186 (Fla. 1989).

7. North Florida Women's Health & Counseling Services, Inc. v. State, 866 So. 2d 612 (Fla. 2003).

8. Womancare of Orlando, Inc. v. Agwunobi, 448 F. Supp. 2d 1309 (N.D. Fla. 2006).

9. Planned Parenthood of Middle Tennessee v. Sundquist, 38 S.W.3d 1 (Tenn. 2000).

10. This strategy became more oblique in the case of George W. Bush, who never publicly criticized *Roe* but nonetheless continued to signal to his partisan base that his judicial nominees were skeptical of the decision (McMahon and Keck forthcoming).

11. Nova Health Systems v. Edmondson, 233 P.3d 380 (Okla. 2010).

12. These state legislative changes are documented in the Guttmacher Institute's monthly updates on state policy developments, available at http://www.guttmacher.org/statecenter/.

13. The cases, each discussed in chapter 2, were Tuttle v. Arlington County School Board, 195 F.3d 698 (4th Cir. 1999); Eisenberg v. Montgomery County Public Schools, 197 F.3d 123 (4th Cir. 1999); and Belk v. Charlotte-Mecklenburg Board of Education, 233 F.3d 232 (4th Cir. 2000).

14. Congress sometimes joined the Clinton administration in pushing back against this doctrinal trend. In the contracting context, for example, Congress reenacted the National Defense Authorization Act in 1999, 2002, and 2006, each time including provisions that were the focus of a legal challenge that appeared to be winning. Three separate Federal Circuit panels expressed doubts about the constitutionality of the statute's preferences for disadvantaged businesses, but

on each of the first two occasions, the panels remanded for further proceedings. While the litigation continued, Congress repeatedly reenacted the disputed provisions. This legislative and judicial history is recounted in Rothe Development Corp. v. Department of Defense, 545 F.3d 1023 (Fed. Cir. 2008).

15. Brady Campaign to Prevent Gun Violence v. Salazar, 612 F. Supp. 2d 1 (D.D.C. 2009).

16. "Immunity Statutes Policy Summary," Law Center to Prevent Gun Violence (August 12, 2009), available at http://smartgunlaws.org/immunity-statutes-policy -summary/.

17. There are, of course, exceptions. Note, for example, People v. Uplinger, 460 N.Y.S.2d 514 (N.Y. 1983), in which the New York high court invalidated a state statute prohibiting loitering "in a public place for the purpose of engaging, or soliciting another person to engage, in deviate sexual intercourse or other sexual behavior of a deviate nature." Despite this holding, the NYPD continued to enforce this unconstitutional law, along with several additional loitering statutes that had been invalidated in subsequent state and federal decisions, for decades. See Casale v. Kelly, 710 F. Supp. 2d 347 (S.D.N.Y. 2010).

18. Note, for example, Williams v. State, 1998 Extra LEXIS 260 (Balt. City Cir. Ct. 1998); Missouri v. Cogshell, 997 S.W.2d 534 (Mo. Ct. App. 1999); and Doe v. Ventura, 2001 WL 543734 (Minn. Dist. Ct., Hennepin Cty. 2001), in which state courts held that criminal sodomy laws could not be applied to private, consensual sexual activity. In response to each of these decisions, state officials chose to comply rather than appeal. At the margins, state officials have sometimes argued that certain applications of their invalidated statutes remain constitutional under governing precedent—note, for example, McDonald v. Commonwealth, 645 S.E.2d 918 (Va. 2007), in which Virginia prosecutors alleged that juveniles remained subject to the state's sodomy ban—but with respect to private sexual relations between two consenting adults, I have found no evidence of continued efforts to prosecute under a sodomy statute that has been invalidated by a court of last resort.

19. Tanner v. Oregon Health Sciences University, 971 P.2d 435 (Or. Ct. App. 1998). When a state trial court ordered New Hampshire to do the same in Bedford & Breen v. New Hampshire Technical College System, Case No. 04-E-229 and 04-E-230 (N.H. Sup. Ct. May 3, 2006), state officials there did likewise. See "Victory for Gay New Hampshire Employees Seeking Family Benefits," Press Release, Gay & Lesbian Advocates & Defenders (May 7, 2007), available at http://www.glad .org/current/pr-detail/victory-for-gay-new-hampshire-employees-seeking-family -benefits/. A local school district in Pennsylvania also agreed to settle a federal suit by enacting a domestic partnership policy. Weissmann v. State College Area School District, No. 11-cv-00940 (M.D. Pa. 2011).

20. Martinez v. County of Monroe, 850 N.Y.S.2d 740 (App. Div. 4th Dept. 2008).

21. Florida Department of Children & Families v. In re: Matter of Adoption of X.X.G. & N.R.G, 35 Fla. L. Wkly. D2107 (Fla. Dist. Ct. App. 3d Dist. 2010).

22. Hollingsworth v. Perry, 133 S. Ct. 2652 (2013).

23. "Statement of the Attorney General on Litigation Involving the Defense of Marriage Act," Press Release, Department of Justice, Office of Public Affairs (February 23, 2011), available at http://www.justice.gov/opa/pr/2011/February/11-ag-222.html.

24. Arlington County v. White, 528 S.E.2d 706 (Va. 2000).

25. In Atlanta, the Georgia Supreme Court's holding in City of Atlanta v. McKinney, 454 S.E. 2d 517 (Ga. 1995), forced lawmakers to enact a modified policy, which the court upheld in City of Atlanta v. Morgan, 492 S.E.2d 193 (Ga. 1997). In Minneapolis and Boston, the state high court holdings in Lilly v. City of Minneapolis, 527 N.W.2d 107 (Minn. Ct. App. 1995), and Connors v. City of Boston, 714 N.E.2d 335 (Mass. 1999), prevented city officials from extending benefits to same-sex partners of city employees until subsequent developments allowed those employees to legally marry.

26. When affirmative action has been limited via state ballot initiatives, public university officials have responded in similar fashion. For example, immediately after the enactment of I-200 by Washington State voters in 1998, UW officials announced the suspension of race-conscious admissions practices that had been in place for thirty years. When Michigan voters enacted a similar anti–affirmative action initiative in 2006, UM President Mary Sue Coleman responded with some election-night bravado—"I will not stand by while the very heart and soul of this great university is threatened"—but the university eventually changed its admissions policies to comply with MCRI (Coleman 2006).

27. Grutter v. Bollinger, 137 F. Supp. 2d 821, 826–27, 830–31 (E.D. Mich. 2001).

28. Podberesky v. Kirwan, 38 F.3d 147 (4th Cir. 1994).

29. Hopwood v. Texas, 861 F. Supp. 551, 582, n.87 (W.D. Tex. 1994).

30. University of Texas at Austin Office of Institutional Research, Fall Enrollments of New Students by Group Ethnicity (Law), available at http://www.utexas.edu/academic/ima/sites/default/files/SHB01-02Students.pdf.

31. Johnson v. Board of Regents of University of Georgia, 263 F.3d 1234 (11th Cir. 2001). Around the same time, UGA officials settled a suit challenging their law school's admissions policy as well (Brownstein 2001).

32. Northeastern Florida Chapter of the Associated General Contractors of America v. Jacksonville, 508 U.S. 656 (1993). Note also Vivenzio v. City of Syracuse, 611 F.3d 98 (2d Cir. 2010), in which a Second Circuit panel reinstated a suit by white firefighters, prompting city officials to settle, paying damages and initiating a review of the 1980 consent decree that was at issue (O'Brien 2012).

33. "NRA Settles San Francisco Housing Authority Gun Ban Lawsuit" (January 16, 2009), available at http://www.nraila.org/legislation/federal-legislation/2009/nra-settles-san-francisco-housing-autho.aspx?s=&st=&ps=.

34. The Seventh Circuit invalidated the ordinance in Ezell v. City of Chicago, 651 F.3d 684 (7th Cir. 2011); the city's legislative response is detailed in Ezell v. City of Chicago, 2011 U.S. Dist. LEXIS 110860 (N.D. Ill. 2011).

35. Ayotte v. Planned Parenthood of Northern New England, 546 U.S. 320 (2006).

36. The scope of these preemptive legislative changes varied significantly across states. In Connecticut, the legislature extended all state law rights and benefits of marriage (though not the name) while a marriage equality suit was pending in the state's courts. In New Jersey, a November 2003 trial court holding in Lewis v. Harris prompted quick action on a long-stalled and relatively robust domestic partnership bill, which the legislature enacted in January 2004. In New Mexico and New York, the legislatures extended only a small number of discrete legal rights to unmarried domestic partners while such suits were pending, though New York's legislature enacted full marriage equality five years later.

37. Maine, Maryland, and Washington subsequently legislated full marriage equality, but in the text here, I am referring to earlier incremental steps taken by each legislature.

38. City of Atlanta v. McKinney, 454 S.E.2d 517 (Ga. 1995); City of Atlanta v. Morgan, 268 Ga. 586 (Ga. 1997).

39. United States v. Danks, 221 F.3d 1037 (8th Cir. 1999), *cert. denied*, 528 U.S. 1091 (2000).

40. Heller v. District of Columbia, 670 F.3d 1244 (D.C. Cir. 2011).

41. As I note above, a federal constitutional challenge to the new law's ban on firing ranges within city limits prompted the city council to repeal that ban in July 2011. Meanwhile, city officials have continued to defend other elements of the new law. When neighboring Evanston, Illinois, faced a similar suit after *Heller* came down—like Chicago, Evanston had a sweeping handgun ban on the books—city officials responded by amending their ordinance to allow the possession of registered handguns in the home for purposes of self-defense. Despite this effort at preemptive compliance, the city faced continued legal challenges from the NRA. See National Rifle Ass'n of America, Inc. v. City of Evanston, 2009 U.S. Dist. LEXIS 35563 (N.D. Ill. 2009).

On the other side of the issue, the litigation by gun control advocates that I describe in chapter 1 was almost entirely unsuccessful but did occasionally force some concessions on the part of gun manufacturers. In March 2000, for example, Smith & Wesson settled a suit that had been filed by HUD and several state and local governments, agreeing to make a number of changes to its gun design and distribution practices. But the settlement provoked such outrage on the part of industry competitors, the NRA, and the company's own customers that Smith & Wesson eventually repudiated the settlement (Rostron 2006, 497–98).

42. For an example of full compliance, note the Ninth Circuit decision in Western States Paving Co. v. Washington State Department of Transportation, 407 F.3d 983

(9th Cir. 2005). After the decision, the Federal Highway Administration (FHWA) issued a memo directing all states within the circuit to submit annual statements on minority contracting goals to FHWA's Office of Civil Rights for approval. In May 2006, the California Transportation Authority responded by announcing that it would abandon racial preferences in federally funded construction projects. For an example of resistance, albeit ultimately unsuccessful, see Sweet (2010, 59–75).

43. Brief for the US as Amicus Curiae (opposing petition for writ of certiorari), Piscataway Township Board of Education v. Taxman, No. 96-679, Supreme Court of the US (June 1997), 8; Brief for the US as Amicus Curiae Supporting Affirmance, Piscataway Township Board of Education v. Taxman, No. 96-679, Supreme Court of the US (October 3, 1997), 12.

44. Lutheran Church-Missouri Synod v. FCC, 154 F.3d 494 (D.C. Cir. 1998).

45. The Tenth Circuit holding on remand was Adarand Constructors, Inc. v. Slater, 228 F.3d 1147 (10th Cir. 2000). The administration's response to the holding is recounted in Adarand Constructors, Inc. v. Mineta, 534 U.S. 103, 106 (2001).

46. MD/DC/DE Broadcasters Ass'n v. FCC, 236 F.3d 13 (D.C. Cir. 2001).

47. Brief for the Respondents, Adarand Constructors, Inc. v. Mineta, No. 00-730, Supreme Court of the US, 2000 U.S. Briefs 730 (August 10, 2001), 17.

48. In addition to these changes at UMD's flagship campus, the *Chronicle* reported similar compromise measures at the University's Baltimore County campus and at Clemson University in South Carolina (Lederman 1996c).

49. This change ultimately failed to avoid legal liability. As I note above, an Eleventh Circuit panel invalidated the revised policy in Johnson v. Board of Regents, 263 F.3d 1234 (11th Cir. 2001), at which point the university responded with full compliance.

50. For an example of full compliance, note Ho v. San Francisco Unified School District, 147 F.3d 854 (9th Cir. 1998), in which a Ninth Circuit panel held that the student assignment policy used by the San Francisco Unified School District (SFUSD) was subject to strict scrutiny under *Adarand*. By February 1999, the school district had settled, agreeing with the Chinese American plaintiffs that "the SFUSD will not assign or admit any student to a particular school, class or program on the basis of the race or ethnicity of that student, except as related to the language needs of the student or otherwise to assure compliance with controlling federal or state law." NAACP v. San Francisco Unified School District, 59 F. Supp. 2d 1021, 1025 (N.D. Cal. 1999).

51. American Civil Rights Foundation v. Berkeley Unified School District, 172 Cal. App. 4th 207 (1st Dist. 2009). The account in the text is drawn from Chavez and Frankenberg (2009).

52. Barnes (2010); Bazelon (2008); Jefferson County Public Schools, "No Retreat: The JCPS Commitment to School Integration," available at http://www.jefferson.k12.ky.us/Pubs/NoRetreatBro.pdf; Johnson (2013).

53. The New Jersey domestic partnership law was subsequently displaced by the state's Civil Union Law, which was restricted to same-sex couples. The Maine domestic partnership law survived the subsequent legalization of SSM.

54. Compare Kahlenberg (2012, 8–9, 29–33) with Brief of American Social Science Researchers as Amicus Curiae in Support of Respondents, Fisher v. University of Texas, Supreme Court of the US, No. 11-345 (August 2012), 13–18.

55. Officials at UT Austin had been arguing that enrollments under the policy should be capped at 50 percent of the student body. In 2009, the legislature imposed a cap of 75 percent, which effectively limited automatic admissions to the flagship campus to the top 8 or 9 percent of high school graduates, though the policy continued to be advertised as a top 10 percent plan (Arenson 2003; Glater 2004; Golden 2003; Kahlenberg 2012, 27; Selingo 2003). The legislature had also modified the policy in 2001, requiring students to take a college prep curriculum to be eligible for admission.

56. The first of the skeptical studies was a widely noted 1998 book entitled *The Shape of the River*, coauthored by former presidents of Princeton and Harvard Universities. The second was an October 1999 report issued by a College Board task force that documented persistent racial achievement gaps in standardized test scores within every income level (Bowen and Bok 1998; College Board 1999).

57. For a similar observation, see Kapiszewski and Taylor (2013, 808).

Conclusion

1. In a well-known published debate between Gerald Rosenberg and Michael McCann, Rosenberg suggested that in evaluating the significance of litigation, they differed on whether the glass was half empty or half full; McCann retorted that they were looking at a different glass (Rosenberg 1996, 453; McCann 1996, 479).

2. "State Hate Crimes Laws," Human Rights Campaign, available at http://www.hrc.org/files/assets/resources/hate_crimes_laws_062013.pdf (last updated June 19, 2013).

3. "Statewide Employment Laws and Policies," Human Rights Campaign, available at http://www.hrc.org/files/assets/resources/employment_laws_072013.pdf (last updated July 22, 2013).

4. "Marriage Equality & Other Relationship Recognition Laws," Human Rights Campaign, available at http://www.hrc.org/files/assets/resources/marriage_equality_082013.pdf (last updated August 2, 2013).

5. Acting on Connerly's proposed initiatives, state electorates have banned affirmative action altogether in Arizona, California, Michigan, Nebraska, Oklahoma, and Washington. In Florida, Governor Jeb Bush and the state legislature banned it in an effort to preempt a pending ballot initiative (Kahlenberg 2012, 44; Weissert

1999). Only in New Hampshire has affirmative action been banned by legislative action in the absence of such a campaign.

6. Bennett v. Arrington, 806 F. Supp. 926, 930 (N.D. Ala. 1992).

7. Taxman v. Board of Education of the Township of Piscataway, 91 F.3d 1547, 1550 (3d Cir. 1996).

8. Comfort v. Lynn School Committee, 418 F.3d 1, 7–8 (1st Cir. 2005) (en banc).

9. Adarand Constructors, Inc. v. Pena, 16 F.3d 1537, 1539–41 (10th Cir. 1994).

10. Hopwood v. Texas, 861 F. Supp. 551, 560–62 (W.D. Tex. 1994).

11. Podberesky v. Kirwan, 764 F. Supp. 364, 366 (D. Md. 1991).

12. Systematic data on this point are limited, but a 1994 federal government study reported that almost two-thirds of four-year undergraduate colleges, along with one-third of graduate schools and three-fourths of professional schools, had at least one minority scholarship program at the time. See "Higher Education: Information on Minority Targeted Scholarships," US Government Accountability Office, GAO/HEHS-94-77 (January 1994), 4.

13. "Abortion Policy in the Absence of *Roe*," Guttmacher Institute (October 1, 2013), available at http://www.guttmacher.org/statecenter/spibs/spib_APAR.pdf.

14. "Parental Involvement in Minors' Abortions," Guttmacher Institute (October 1, 2013), available at http://www.guttmacher.org/statecenter/spibs/spib_PIMA.pdf. Of course, as I note in chapter 1, the existence of a judicial bypass procedure on the books does not guarantee that pregnant minors actually have effective access to such a procedure in practice (Silverstein 2007).

15. "State Funding of Abortion under Medicaid," Guttmacher Institute (October 1, 2013), available at http://www.guttmacher.org/statecenter/spibs/spib_SFAM.pdf.

16. "Assault Weapons Policy Summary," Law Center to Prevent Gun Violence (updated June 19, 2013), available at http://smartgunlaws.org/assault-weapons-policy-summary/.

17. "Gun Shows Policy Summary," Law Center to Prevent Gun Violence (updated August 13, 2012), available at http://smartgunlaws.org/gun-shows-policy-summary/.

18. "Waiting Periods Policy Summary," Law Center to Prevent Gun Violence (updated June 24, 2013), available at http://smartgunlaws.org/waiting-periods-policy-summary/.

19. "Licensing of Gun Owners & Purchasers Policy Summary" (updated August 23, 2013); "Registration of Firearms Policy Summary" (updated May 21, 2012); "Open Carrying Policy Summary" (updated July 29, 2013); "Concealed Weapons Permitting Policy Summary" (updated May 21, 2012), Law Center to Prevent Gun Violence, all available at http://smartgunlaws.org/search-gun-law-by-gun-policy/.

20. The 1993 numbers are drawn from "Firearms: State Laws and Published Ordinances," Department of Treasury, Bureau of Alcohol, Tobacco, and Firearms, P5300.5 (1993).

21. "Local Authority to Regulate Firearms Policy Summary," Law Center to Prevent Gun Violence (updated May 18, 2012), available at http://smartgunlaws .org/local-authority-to-regulate-firearms-policy-summary/.

22. "Immunity Statutes Policy Summary," Law Center to Prevent Gun Violence (updated August 12, 2009), available at http://smartgunlaws.org/immunity -statutes-policy-summary/.

23. Planned Parenthood v. Casey, 505 U.S. 833, 995, 1002 (1992).

24. McDonald v. Chicago, 130 S. Ct. 3020, 3052, n.2 (2010).

25. Wilkinson (2009, 295); Romer v. Evans, 517 U.S. 620, 652–53 (1996) (Scalia, J., dissenting).

26. Here, contrast Silverstein's otherwise helpful account, which repeatedly characterizes judicial politics as a "substitute" or "replacement" for "the ordinary political process" (2009, 2, 15, 29).

References

Ackerman, Bruce. 2005. *The Failure of the Founding Fathers: Jefferson, Marshall, and the Rise of Presidential Democracy.* Cambridge, MA: Harvard University Press.

All Things Considered. 2003. National Public Radio, June 23.

Andersen, Ellen Ann. 2005. *Out of the Closets and into the Courts: Legal Opportunity Structure and Gay Rights Litigation.* Ann Arbor: University of Michigan Press.

Andrews, Edmund L. 1995. "F.C.C. Is Ordered to Delay an Auction for Wireless Licenses." *New York Times,* July 28, D4.

Ansolabehere, Stephen, and Charles Stewart III. 2005. "Truth in Numbers: Moral Values and the Gay-Marriage Backlash Did Not Help Bush." *Boston Review,* February 25. http://www.bostonreview.net/truth-in-numbers.

Applebome, Peter. 1996a. "Universities Troubled by Decision Limiting Admission Preferences." *New York Times,* March 21, A1.

———. 1996b. "2 Decisions Reflect Bitter Conflict Surrounding University Affirmative Action Policies." *New York Times,* March 22, A12.

———. 1997. "In Shift, U.S. Tells Texas It Can't Ignore Court Ruling Barring Bias in College Admissions." *New York Times,* April 15, A20.

Arenson, Karen W. 2003. "Impact on Universities Will Range from None to a Lot." *New York Times,* June 25, A22.

Associated Press. 2006. "Judge Dismisses Criminal Case Kline Files against Tiller." Associated Press, December 22. http://www2.ljworld.com/news/2006/dec/22/kline_files_charges_against_wichita_abortion_docto/?breaking.

Ball, Carlos A. 2010. *From the Closet to the Courtroom: Five LGBT Rights Lawsuits That Have Changed Our Nation.* Boston: Beacon Press.

Banks, Lisa J. 1994. "*Bray v. Alexandria Women's Health Clinic*: The Supreme Court's License for Domestic Terrorism." *Denver University Law Review* 71: 449–76.

Barclay, Scott. 2010. "In Search of Judicial Activism in the Same Sex Marriage Cases: Sorting the Evidence from Courts, Legislatures, Initiatives and Amendments." *Perspectives on Politics* 8 (1): 111–26.

Barnes, Jeb, and Mark C. Miller. 2004. "Putting the Pieces Together: American Lawmaking from an Interbranch Perspective." In *Making Policy, Making Law: An Interbranch Perspective,* edited by Mark C. Miller and Jeb Barnes, 3–12. Washington, DC: Georgetown University Press.

Barnes, Robert. 2010. "Three Years after Landmark Court Decision, Louisville Still Struggles with School Desegregation." *Washington Post,* September 20.

Barnum, David G. 1985. "The Supreme Court and Public Opinion: Judicial Decision Making in the Post–New Deal Period." *Journal of Politics* 47 (2): 652–66.

Barstow, David. 2009. "An Abortion Battle, Fought to the Death." *New York Times,* July 25.

Bartlett, Thomas, and Megan Rooney. 2003. "Unilateral Actions at Virginia Tech Raise Questions about the Proper Role of Trustees." *Chronicle of Higher Education,* March 28, 25.

Bazelon, Emily. 2008. "The Next Kind of Integration." *New York Times,* July 20, magazine section.

Becker, Theodore L., and Malcolm M. Feeley. 1973. *The Impact of Supreme Court Decisions.* 2nd ed. New York: Oxford University Press.

Belkin, Lisa. 1998. "She Says She Was Rejected by a College for Being White: Is She Paranoid, Racist, or Right?" *Glamour,* November.

Bell, Dawson. 1997. "Legislators Aim to Sue U-M over Race Policy; 4 Want to Do Battle over Preferences." *Detroit Free Press,* May 2.

Belluck, Pam. 2000. "After Abortion Victory, Doctor's Troubles Persist." *New York Times,* November 7, A18.

Bickel, Alexander M. 1986. *The Least Dangerous Branch: The Supreme Court at the Bar of Politics.* 2nd ed. New Haven, CT: Yale University Press.

Biskupic, Joan. 1997. "Rights Groups Pay to Settle Bias Case." *Washington Post,* November 22, A1–8.

Blackstone, Bethany. 2013. "An Analysis of Policy-Based Congressional Responses to the U.S. Supreme Court's Constitutional Decisions." *Law and Society Review* 47 (1): 199–228.

Blake, William. 2012. "Umpires as Legal Realists." *PS: Political Science & Politics* (April 2012): 271–76.

Bloomberg News. 2001. "F.C.C. Chief Seeks Hiring Rules." *New York Times,* June 22, C12.

Blum, Edward, and Roger Clegg. 2003. "'Okay You Caught Me.'" *National Review Online,* May 27. http://www.nationalreview.com/articles/207031/okay-you-caught -me/edward-blum.

Bonauto, Mary L. 2005. "*Goodridge* in Context." *Harvard Civil Rights-Civil Liberties Law Review* 40 (Winter): 1–69.

Bowen, William G., and Derek Bok. 1998. *The Shape of the River: Long-Term Consequences of Considering Race in College and University Admissions.* Princeton, NJ: Princeton University Press.

Bowen, William G., Martin A. Kurzweil, and Eugene M. Tobin. 2005. *Equity and Excellence in American Higher Education*. Charlottesville: University of Virginia Press.

Brennan, William J. 1977. "State Constitutions and the Protection of Individual Rights." *Harvard Law Review* 90:489–504.

Brown, Robbie. 2010. "School District in North Carolina Considers Ending Busing for Economic Diversity." *New York Times*, February 28, A18.

Brownstein, Andrew. 2001. "U.S. Appeals Court Reinstates White Applicant's Bias Suit Against U. of Georgia." *Chronicle of Higher Education*, May 4, A24.

Buchanan, Patrick. 1992. Speech Delivered at Republican National Convention, Houston, Texas, August 17. http://www.americanrhetoric.com/speeches/patrick buchanan1992rnc.htm.

Bumiller, Elisabeth. 2010a. "Varied Forces Pushing Obama to Drop 'Don't Ask, Don't Tell.'" *New York Times*, February 1, A1.

———. 2010b. "Top Brass and McCain Square Off over Gays." *New York Times*, December 3, A16.

Burgess, Susan R. 1992. *Contest for Constitutional Authority: The Abortion and War Powers Debates*. Lawrence: University Press of Kansas.

Burke, Tom. 2002. *Lawyers, Lawsuits and Legal Rights: The Struggle over Litigation in American Society*. Berkeley: University of California Press.

Bybee, Keith J. 2000. "The Political Significance of Legal Ambiguity: The Case of Affirmative Action." *Law and Society Review* 34 (2): 263–90.

———. 2011. "The Rule of Law Is Dead! Long Live the Rule of Law!" In *What's Law Got to Do with It? What Judges Do, Why They Do It, and What's at Stake*, edited by Charles Gardner Geyh, 306–27. Palo Alto, CA: Stanford University Press.

Cantor, Nancy E. 2003. "A Victory for Justice, and a Vindication." *Chronicle of Higher Education*, July 4, 12.

———. 2004. "Introduction." In *Defending Diversity: Affirmative Action at the University of Michigan*, edited by Patricia Gurin, Jeffrey S. Lehman, and Earl Lewis, 1–16. Ann Arbor: University of Michigan Press.

Carlson, John. 1998. "Initiative 200: The War over Racial Preferences in Washington State." *Egalitarian*, December, 3–7.

Chavez, Lisa, and Erika Frankenberg. 2009. "Integration Defended: Berkeley Unified's Strategy to Maintain School Diversity." Report issued by the Chief Justice Earl Warren Institute on Race, Ethnicity & Diversity and The Civil Rights Project, September. http://civilrightsproject.ucla.edu/research/k-12-education /integration-and-diversity/integration-defended-berkeley-unified2019s-strategy -to-maintain-school-diversity.

Chronicle of Higher Education. 2002. "U. of Florida to Open Its Doors to Top 5% of Each High-School Graduating Class." *Chronicle of Higher Education*, March 22, 22.

————. 2006. "Government & Politics in Brief." *Chronicle of Higher Education,* February 17, 30.

Cohen, Carl. 1996. "Race, Lies, and '*Hopwood.*'" *Commentary* 101 (6): 39–45.

Coleman, Mary Sue. 2006. "Diversity Matters at Michigan." November 8. http://president.umich.edu/speech/speeches/061103div.php.

College Board. 1999. "Reaching the Top: A Report of the National Task Force on Minority High Achievement." http://research.collegeboard.org/sites/default/files/publications/2012/7/misc1999-3-reaching-the-top-minority-achievement.pdf.

Colucci, Frank J. 2009. *Justice Kennedy's Jurisprudence: The Full and Necessary Meaning of Liberty.* Lawrence: University Press of Kansas.

Cox, Adam B., and Thomas J. Miles. 2008. "Judging the Voting Rights Act." *Columbia Law Review* 108 (January): 1–54.

Cross, Frank B. 2007. *Decision Making in the U.S. Courts of Appeals.* Palo Alto, CA: Stanford University Press.

Cummings, Scott L. 2013. "Empirical Studies of Law and Social Change: What Is the Field? What Are the Questions?" *Wisconsin Law Review* 2013:171–204.

Cummings, Scott L., and Douglas NeJaime. 2010. "Lawyering for Marriage Equality." *UCLA Law Review* 57 (June): 1235–1331.

Dahl, Robert A. 1957. "Decision-Making in a Democracy: The Supreme Court as a National Policy Maker." *Journal of Public Law* 6 (Fall): 279–95.

DeConde, Alexander. 2001. *Gun Violence in America: The Struggle for Control.* Boston: Northeastern University Press.

D'Emilio, John. 2007. "Will the Courts Set Us Free? Reflections on the Campaign for Same-Sex Marriage." In *The Politics of Same-Sex Marriage,* edited by Craig A. Rimmerman and Clyde Wilcox, 39–64. Chicago: University of Chicago Press.

den Dulk, Kevin. 2008. "Purpose Driven Lawyers: Evangelical Cause Lawyering and the Culture War." In *The Cultural Lives of Cause Lawyers,* edited by Austin Sarat and Stuart Scheingold, 56–78. New York: Cambridge University Press.

Devins, Neal. 1996. *Shaping Constitutional Values: Elected Government, the Supreme Court, and the Abortion Debate.* Baltimore: Johns Hopkins University Press.

————. 2003. "Explaining *Grutter v. Bollinger.*" *University of Pennsylvania Law Review* 152 (November): 347–83.

————. 2009. "How *Planned Parenthood v. Casey* (Pretty Much) Settled the Abortion Wars." *Yale Law Journal* 118 (May): 1318–54.

Doherty, Kathleen, and Ryan Pevnick. 2014. "Are There Good Procedural Objections to Judicial Review?" *Journal of Politics* 76 (1): 86–97.

Edgar, Randal. 2013. "Same-Sex Marriage: Cities, Towns Prepare for New Law." *Providence Journal,* July 31, 1.

Editors. 1995. "Defending Affirmative Action." *New York Times,* July 20, A22.

Edsall, Thomas B., and Michael A. Fletcher. 1997. "Coalition Feared Disaster in Affirmative Action Court Case." *Washington Post,* November 22, A8.

Edwards, Harry T. 1985. "Public Misperceptions Concerning the 'Politics' of Judging: Dispelling Some Myths about the D.C. Circuit." *University of Colorado Law Review* 56:619–46.

Egan, Patrick J., and Kenneth Sherrill. 2005. "Neither an In-Law nor an Outlaw Be: Trends in Americans' Attitudes toward Gay People." *Public Opinion Pros*, February. http://www.publicopinionpros.norc.org/features/2005/feb/sherrill_egan.asp.

———. 2006. "Same-Sex Marriage Initiatives and Lesbian, Gay and Bisexual Voters in the 2006 Elections." Research report, National Gay and Lesbian Task Force. http://www.thetaskforce.org/downloads/reports/reports/MarriageAndLGBVoters2006.pdf.

Ely, John Hart. 1980. *Democracy and Distrust: A Theory of Judicial Review*. Cambridge, MA: Harvard University Press.

Epps, Daniel. 2012. "In Health Care Ruling, Roberts Steals a Move from John Marshall's Playbook." *Atlantic Monthly,* June 28. http://www.theatlantic.com/national/archive/2012/06/in-health-care-ruling-roberts-steals-a-move-from-john-marshalls-playbook/259121/.

Epstein, Lee, William M. Landes, and Richard A. Posner. 2013. *The Behavior of Federal Judges: A Theoretical and Empirical Study of Rational Choice.* Cambridge, MA: Harvard University Press.

Equal Justice Society. 2004. "Facts and Fantasies About UC Berkeley Admissions: A Critical Evaluation of Regent John Moores' Report." *Hastings Race and Poverty Law Journal* 2 (Fall): 53–81.

Eskridge, William. 2002. *Equality Practice: Civil Unions and the Future of Gay Rights.* New York: Routledge.

———. 2013. "Backlash Politics: How Constitutional Litigation Has Advanced Marriage Equality in the United States." *Boston University Law Review* 93: 275–323.

Farhang, Sean. 2010. *The Litigation State: Public Regulation and Private Lawsuits in the United States.* Princeton, NJ: Princeton University Press.

Fiorina, Morris P., with Samuel J. Abrams and Jeremy C. Pope. 2006. *Culture War? The Myth of a Polarized America.* 2nd ed. New York: Pearson Longman.

Fischman, Joshua B. 2011. "Estimating Preferences of Circuit Judges: A Model of Consensus Voting." *Journal of Law & Economics* 54 (November): 781–809.

———. Forthcoming. "Interpreting Circuit Court Voting Patterns: A 'Social Interactions' Framework." October 22. *Journal of Law, Economics, and Organization.*

Fischman, Joshua B., and David S. Law. 2009. "Empirical Research on Decision-Making in the Federal Courts: What Is Judicial Ideology, and How Should We Measure It?" *Washington University Journal of Law & Policy* 29:133–213.

Fontana, David, and Donald Braman. 2012. "Judicial Backlash or Just Backlash? Evidence from a National Experiment." *Columbia Law Review* 112 (May): 731–99.

Ford, Gerald R. 1999. "Inclusive America, Under Attack." *New York Times,* August 8, sec. 4, p. 15.

Foster, Heath, and Ruth Schubert. 1998. "Two UW Law School Applicants, Two Paths." *Seattle Post-Intelligencer,* October 15, A1.

Franklin, Charles H., and Liane C. Kosaki. 1989. "Republican Schoolmaster: The U.S. Supreme Court, Public Opinion, and Abortion." *American Political Science Review* 83 (3): 751–71.

Friedman, Barry. 2004. "William Howard Taft Lecture: The Importance of Being Positive: The Nature and Function of Judicial Review." *University of Cincinnati Law Review* 72 (Summer): 1257–1303.

———. 2009. *The Will of the People: How Public Opinion Has Influenced the Supreme Court and Shaped the Meaning of the Constitution.* New York: Farrar, Strauss & Giroux.

Fry, Steve. 2011. "Recommended Sanction a Virtual Loss of Law License." *Topeka Capital-Journal,* October 14.

Frymer, Paul. 2008. *Black and Blue: African Americans, the Labor Movement, and the Decline of the Democratic Party.* Princeton, NJ: Princeton University Press.

Garrow, David J. 1994. *Liberty and Sexuality: The Right to Privacy and the Making of* Roe v. Wade. New York: Macmillan.

———. 1999. "Abortion before and after *Roe v. Wade*: An Historical Perspective." *Albany Law Review* 62:833–52.

———. 2007. "Significant Risks: *Gonzales v. Carhart* and the Future of Abortion Law." *Supreme Court Review* 2007:1–50.

Gifford, Donald G. 2010. *Suing the Tobacco and Lead Pigment Industries: Government Litigation as Public Health Prescription.* Ann Arbor: University of Michigan Press.

Gillman, Howard. 2002. "How Political Parties Can Use the Courts to Advance Their Agendas: Federal Courts in the United States, 1875–1891." *American Political Science Review* 96 (3): 511–24.

———. 2006. "Party Politics and Constitutional Change: The Political Origins of Liberal Judicial Activism." In *The Supreme Court and American Political Development*, edited by Ronald Kahn and Ken I. Kersch, 138–68. Lawrence: University Press of Kansas.

Glaberson, William. 2000. "Dueling Scholars Join Fray over a Constitutional Challenge to Gun Control Laws." *New York Times,* September 21, A26.

Glater, Jonathan D. 2004. "Diversity Plan Shaped in Texas Is Under Attack." *New York Times,* June 13, sec. 1, p. 1.

Goldberg-Hiller, Jonathan. 2002. *The Limits to Union: Same-Sex Marriage and the Politics of Civil Rights.* Ann Arbor: University of Michigan Press.

Golden, Daniel. 2003. "Not Black and White: Colleges Cut Back Minority Programs after Court Rulings." *Wall Street Journal,* December 30, A1.

Goldman, Sheldon. 1989. "Reagan's Judicial Legacy: Completing the Puzzle and Summing Up." *Judicature* 72 (April–May): 318–30.

———. 1993. "Bush's Judicial Legacy: The Final Imprint." *Judicature* 76 (April–May): 282–97.

Goldman, Sheldon, Elliot Slotnick, Gerry Gryski, and Sara Schiavoni. 2005. "W. Bush's Judiciary: The First Term Record." *Judicature* 88 (May–June): 244–75.

Goldman, Sheldon, Elliot Slotnick, and Sara Schiavoni. 2011. "Obama's Judiciary at Midterm: The Confirmation Drama Continues." *Judicature* 94 (May–June): 262–303.

Gordon, Michael R. 2013. "New U.S. Policy Gives Equal Treatment to Same-Sex Spouses' Visa Applications." *New York Times,* August 3, A8.

Gose, Ben. 2005. "The Chorus Grows Louder for Class-Based Affirmative Action." *Chronicle of Higher Education*, February 25, B5–6.

Goss, Kristin A. 2006. *Disarmed: The Missing Movement for Gun Control in America.* Princeton, NJ: Princeton University Press.

Gossett, Charles W. 2009. "Pushing the Envelope: Dillon's Rule and Local Domestic-Partnership Ordinances." In *Queer Mobilizations: LGBT Activists Confront the Law,* edited by Scott Barclay, Mary Bernstein, and Anna-Maria Marshall, 158–86. New York: New York University Press.

Graber, Mark A. 1993. "The Non-Majoritarian Difficulty: Legislative Deference to the Judiciary." *Studies in American Political Development* 7 (Spring): 35–73.

———. 1999. "Law and Sports Officiating: A Misunderstood and Justly Neglected Relationship." *Constitutional Commentary* 16 (Summer): 293–313.

———. 2006a. "Does It Really Matter? Conservative Courts in a Conservative Era." *Fordham Law Review* 75 (November): 675–708.

———. 2006b. Dred Scott *and the Problem of Constitutional Evil.* New York: Cambridge University Press.

Greenhouse, Linda. 2000a. "Doctor Spurns Euphemism in Pursing Abortion Rights." *New York Times,* April 8, A7.

———. 2000b. "Court Rules That Governments Can't Outlaw Type of Abortion." *New York Times,* June 29, A1.

———. 2002. "U.S., in a Shift, Tells Justices Citizens Have a Right to Guns." *New York Times,* May 8, A1.

———. 2003. "Bush and Affirmative Action: Muted Call in Race Case," *New York Times,* January 17, A1.

Greenhouse, Linda, and Reva B. Siegel. 2010. *Before* Roe v. Wade: *Voices That Shaped the Abortion Debate before the Supreme Court's Ruling.* New York: Kaplan.

———. 2011. "Before (and After) *Roe v. Wade:* New Questions about Backlash." *Yale Law Journal* 120 (June): 2028–87.

Greve, Michael S. 2004. Personal interview with author, September 4.

Guerrero, Andrea. 2002. *Silence at Boalt Hall: The Dismantling of Affirmative Action.* Berkeley: University of California Press.

Hacker, Hans J. 2005. *The Culture of Conservative Christian Litigation.* Lanham, MD: Rowman & Littlefield.

Hall, Matthew E. K. 2010. "Randomness Reconsidered: Modeling Random Judicial Assignment in the U.S. Courts of Appeals." *Journal of Empirical Legal Studies* 7 (3): 574–89.

———. 2011. *The Nature of Supreme Court Power.* New York: Cambridge University Press.

Haltom, William, and Michael McCann. 2008. "Litigation, Radiation, and Communication: How Newspapers Construct Firearms Lawsuits." Paper presented at the annual meeting of the Western Political Science Association, San Diego, California, March 20–22.

Hanley, John, Michael Salamone, and Matthew Wright. 2012. "Reviving the Schoolmaster: Reevaluating Public Opinion in the Wake of *Roe v. Wade*." *Political Research Quarterly* 65 (2): 408–21.

Haworth, Karla. 1998. "University of Minnesota May Alter Program Used to Recruit Minority Students." *Chronicle of Higher Education,* February 6, A33.

Healy, Patrick. 1997a. "U. of Illinois at Chicago Will End Controversial Affirmative-Action Program." *Chronicle of Higher Education*, September 12, A41.

———. 1997b. "Education Department Sends Strong Warning on Race-Exclusive Scholarships." *Chronicle of Higher Education,* October 31, A47.

———. 1999. "U. of Mass. Limits Racial Preferences, Despite Vow to Increase Minority Enrollment." *Chronicle of Higher Education,* March 5, A30.

Hebel, Sara. 2001. "U. of Georgia Won't Appeal Affirmative-Action Case to Supreme Court." *Chronicle of Higher Education,* November 23, 23.

Hilbink, Lisa. 2008. "Assessing the New Constitutionalism." *Comparative Politics* (January): 227–45.

Hillygus, D. Sunshine, and Todd G. Shields. 2005. "Moral Issues and Voter Decision Making in the 2004 Elections." *PS: Political Science and Politics* 38:201–9.

Hollis-Brusky, Amanda. 2013. "'It's the Network': The Federalist Society as a Supplier of Intellectual Capital for the Supreme Court." *Studies in Law, Politics, and Society* 61:137–78.

Holmes, Steven A. 1996a. "Moratorium Called on Minority Contract Program." *New York Times,* March 8, A1.

———. 1996b. "In New Guide, U.S. Retreats on Contracts for Minorities." *New York Times,* May 23, A26.

———. 1998. "Administration Cuts Affirmative Action While Defending It." *New York Times,* March 16, A17.

Hoover, Eric. 2011. "DePaul U. to Drop Standardized Tests as a Requirement." *Chronicle of Higher Education,* February 25, A1.

———. 2013. "Colleges Contemplate a 'Race Neutral' Future." *Chronicle of Higher Education,* October 18, A30–32.

Hull, N. E. H., and Peter Charles Hoffer. 2001. Roe v. Wade: *The Abortion Rights Controversy in American History*. Lawrence: University Press of Kansas.

Jelen, Ted G., and Clyde Wilcox. 2003. "Causes and Consequences of Public Attitudes toward Abortion: A Review and Research Agenda." *Political Research
Quarterly* 56 (4): 489–500.

Johnson, Charles A. 1987. "Law, Politics, and Judicial Decision Making: Lower
Federal Court Uses of Supreme Court Decisions." *Law & Society Review* 21
(2): 325–40.

Johnson, Rebecca Page. 2013. "Desegregation in a 'Color-Blind' Era: Parents Nav-
igating School Assignment and Choice in Louisville, Kentucky." Dissertation
submitted in partial fulfillment of the requirement of the degree of Doctor of
Philosophy in Education, Syracuse University (May).

Kahlenberg, Richard D. 1996. *The Remedy: Class, Race, and Affirmative Action.*
New York: Basic Books.

———. 2012. "A Better Affirmative Action: State Universities That Created Alternatives to Racial Preferences." A Century Foundation Report, October 3. http://
tcf.org/assets/downloads/tcf-abaa.pdf.

Kao, Annie Tai. 2002. "A More Powerful Plaintiff: State Public Nuisance Lawsuits
against the Gun Industry." *George Washington Law Review* 70 (February):
212–27.

Kapiszewski, Diana, and Matthew M. Taylor. 2013. "Compliance: Conceptualizing,
Measuring, and Explaining Adherence to Judicial Rulings." *Law and Social
Inquiry* 38 (4): 803–35.

Keck, Thomas M. 2004. *The Most Activist Supreme Court in History: The Road to
Modern Judicial Conservatism.* Chicago: University of Chicago Press.

———. 2007a. "The Neoconservative Assault on the Courts: How Worried Should
We Be?" In *Confronting the New Conservatism: The Rise of the Right in America,* edited by Michael Thompson, 164–93. New York University Press.

———. 2007b. "Party, Policy, or Duty: Why Does the Supreme Court Invalidate
Federal Statutes?" *American Political Science Review* 101 (2): 321–38.

———. 2009. "Beyond Backlash: Assessing the Impact of Judicial Decisions on
LGBT Rights." *Law and Society Review* 43 (1): 151–85.

Keller, Josh, and Eric Hoover. 2009. "U. of California Adopts Sweeping Changes
in Admissions Policy." *Chronicle of Higher Education,* February 13, A33.

Klarman, Michael J. 1994. "*Brown,* Racial Change, and the Civil Rights Movement." *Virginia Law Review* 80 (February): 7–150.

———. 1996. "Rethinking the Civil Rights and Civil Liberties Revolutions."
Virginia Law Review 82 (February): 1–67.

———. 1997. "Majoritarian Judicial Review: The Entrenchment Problem."
Georgetown Law Journal 85 (February): 491–553.

———. 2004. *From Jim Crow to Civil Rights: The Supreme Court and the Struggle
for Racial Equality.* New York: Oxford University Press.

———. 2005. "*Brown* and *Lawrence* (and *Goodridge*)." *Michigan Law Review* 104
(December): 431–89.

————. 2013. *From the Closet to the Altar: Courts, Backlash, and the Struggle for Same-Sex Marriage.* New York: Oxford University Press.

Klein, Alyson. 2004. "Affirmative-Action Opponents Suffer Setbacks in Colorado and Michigan." *Chronicle of Higher Education,* April 9, A23.

Klein, Ezra. 2012. "Unpopular Mandate." *New Yorker,* June 25. http://www.new yorker.com/reporting/2012/06/25/120625fa_fact_klein.

Knowles, Helen J. 2009. *The Tie Goes to Freedom: Justice Anthony M. Kennedy on Liberty.* Lanham, MD: Rowman & Littlefield.

Kolbert, Kathryn, and Andrea Miller. 1998. "Legal Strategies for Abortion Rights in the Twenty-first Century." In *Abortion Wars: A Half Century of Struggle, 1950–2000,* edited by Rickie Solinger, 95–110. Berkeley: University of California Press.

Kolbo, Kirk. 2006. Personal interview with author, March 2.

Laird, Bob. 2005. *The Case for Affirmative Action in University Admissions.* Berkeley, CA: Bay Tree.

Landau, Brent W. 2000. "State Bans on City Gun Lawsuits." *Harvard Journal on Legislation,* Summer, 623–38.

Lane, Charles. 2001. "Disorder in the Court: Judges Squabble over Proceedings Surrounding Ohio Man's Stay of Execution." *Washington Post,* November 12, A3.

————. 2003. "Appeals Court's Feud in Mich. Case Grows; Senior Judge Decries Charges of 'Rigging.'" *Washington Post,* June 12, A37.

Lax, Jeffrey R., and Justin H. Phillips. 2009. "Gay Rights in the States: Public Opinion and Policy Responsiveness." *American Political Science Review* 103 (August): 367–86.

Le, Loan, and Jack Citrin. 2008. "Affirmative Action." In *Public Opinion and Constitutional Controversy,* edited by Nathaniel Persily, Jack Citrin, and Patrick J. Egan, 162–83. New York: Oxford University Press.

Lederman, Douglas. 1996a. "Affirmative Action Is under Growing Attack in Several States." *Chronicle of Higher Education,* April 26. http://chronicle.com /article/Affirmative-Action-Is-Under/94389/.

————. 1996b. "Appeals Court Suspends Order Barring Use of Race in Admissions." *Chronicle of Higher Education,* May 3. http://chronicle.com/article/Appeals -Court-Suspends-Order/94543/.

————. 1996c. "1994 Ruling against Minority Scholarships Continues to Resound." *Chronicle of Higher Education,* October 25. http://chronicle.com/article /1994-Ruling-Against-Minority/78249/.

————. 1997a. "Northern Virginia Community College Will End Race-Based Scholarships." *Chronicle of Higher Education,* October 24, A33.

————. 1997b. "U. of North Carolina Reviews Policies Based on Race." *Chronicle of Higher Education,* December 5, A45.

Lehman, Jeffrey S. 2004. "The Evolving Language of Diversity and Integration in Discussions of Affirmative Action from *Bakke* to *Grutter.*" In *Defending*

Diversity: Affirmative Action at the University of Michigan, edited by Patricia Gurin, Jeffrey S. Lehman, and Earl Lewis, 61–96. Ann Arbor: University of Michigan Press.

Lemieux, Scott. 2004. "Constitutional Politics and the Political Impact of Abortion Litigation: Judicial Power and Judicial Independence in Comparative Perspective." PhD diss., University of Washington.

Lemieux, Scott E., and George Lovell. 2010. "Legislative Defaults: Interbranch Power Sharing and Abortion Politics." *Polity* 42 (April): 210–43.

Levey, Curt A. 2003. "Colleges Should Take No Comfort in the Supreme Court's Reprieve." *Chronicle of Higher Education,* July 18, B11–14.

Levinson, Sanford. 1989. "The Embarrassing Second Amendment." *Yale Law Journal* 99 (December): 637–59.

Levy, Robert A. 2008. "Anatomy of a Lawsuit: *District of Columbia v. Heller.*" *Engage* 9 (3): 27–31. http://www.fed-soc.org/doclib/20090107_LevyEngage93.pdf.

Lewin, Tamar. 2002. "School Desegregation Policy Is Challenged." *New York Times,* August 12, A8.

Lewis, Earl. 2004. "Why History Remains a Factor in the Search for Racial Equality." In *Defending Diversity: Affirmative Action at the University of Michigan,* edited by Patricia Gurin, Jeffrey S. Lehman, and Earl Lewis, 17–60. Ann Arbor: University of Michigan Press.

Lieb, David A. 2009. "Mo. Judge Strikes Down Affirmative Action Measure." *Associated Press State & Local Wire,* June 26.

Lipson, Daniel N. 2007. "Embracing Diversity: The Institutionalization of Affirmative Action as Diversity Management at UC-Berkeley, UT-Austin, and UW-Madison." *Law and Social Inquiry* 32 (4): 985–1026.

———. 2008. "For Whom Does the Affirmative Action Bell Toll? The Legal Deconstruction of Racial Classifications in Post-Civil Rights America." Paper presented at the annual meeting of the Western Political Science Association, San Diego, California, March 20–22.

Liptak, Adam. 2013. "Court Is One of 'Most Activist,' Ginsburg Says, Vowing to Stay." *New York Times,* August 24.

Littau, Stephen. 2008. "Presidential Candidates Respond to *D.C. v. Heller* Ruling." *The Liberty Papers* (blog). June 26. http://www.thelibertypapers.org/2008/06/26/presidential-candidates-respond-to-heller-vs-dc-ruling/.

Lovell, George I., and Scott E. Lemieux. 2006. "Assessing Juristocracy: Are Judges Rulers or Agents?" *Maryland Law Review* 65 (1): 100–114.

Luks, Samantha, and Michael Salamone. 2008. "Abortion." In *Public Opinion and Constitutional Controversy,* edited by Nathaniel Persily, Jack Citrin, and Patrick J. Egan, 80–107. New York: Oxford University Press.

Lytton, Timothy D. 2008. "Using Tort Litigation to Enhance Regulatory Policy Making: Evaluating Climate-Change Litigation in Light of Lessons from

Gun-Industry and Clergy-Sexual-Abuse Lawsuits." *Texas Law Review* 86 (June): 1837–76.

Maguire, Timothy. 1992. "My Bout with Affirmative Action." *Commentary* 93 (April): 50–52.

McCann, Michael. 1994. *Rights at Work: Pay Equity Reform and the Politics of Legal Mobilization.* Chicago: University of Chicago Press.

———. 1996. "Causal versus Constitutive Explanations (or, On the Difficulty of Being So Positive . . .)." *Law and Social Inquiry* 21 (Spring): 457–82.

———. 1999. "How the Supreme Court Matters in American Politics: New Institutionalist Perspectives." In *The Supreme Court in American Politics: New Institutionalist Interpretations*, edited by Howard Gillman and Cornell Clayton, 63–97. Lawrence: University Press of Kansas.

McMahon, Kevin J. 2011. *Nixon's Court: His Challenge to Judicial Liberalism and Its Political Consequences.* Chicago: University of Chicago Press.

McMahon, Kevin J., and Thomas M. Keck. Forthcoming. "Why *Roe* Still Stands: Abortion Law, the Supreme Court, and the Republican Regime." *Studies in Law, Politics & Society*.

Melvin, Joshua, Eric Kurhi, and Thomas Peele. 2013. "Prop. 8 Stay Lifted, Same-Sex Weddings Can Resume Immediately." *San Jose Mercury News,* June 28.

Menand, Louis. 2003. "The Thin Envelope; Why College Admissions Has Become Unpredictable." *New Yorker,* April 7, 88.

Mezey, Susan Gluck. 2007. *Queers in Court: Gay Rights Law and Public Policy.* Lanham, MD: Rowman & Littlefield.

Miksch, Karen. 2008. "Widening the River: Challenging Unequal Schools in Order to Contest Proposition 209." *Chicano-Latino Law Review* 27:111–47.

Miles, Thomas J., and Cass R. Sunstein. 2008a. "The Real World of Arbitrariness Review." *University of Chicago Law Review* 75 (Spring): 761–814.

———. 2008b. "The New Legal Realism." *University of Chicago Law Review* 75 (Spring): 831–51.

Montejano, David. 1998. "Maintaining Diversity at the University of Texas." In *Race and Representation: Affirmative Action,* edited by Robert Post and Michael Rogin, 359–69. New York: Zone.

Mucciaroni, Gary. 2008. *Same Sex, Different Politics: Success and Failure in the Struggles over Gay Rights.* Chicago: University of Chicago Press.

Mulroy, Quinn. 2012. "Public Regulation through Private Litigation: The Regulatory Power of Private Lawsuits and the American Bureaucracy." PhD diss., Columbia University.

Nagourney, Adam. 2008. "Marriage Ruling Vaults Issue Back to Stage in Presidential Bids." *New York Times,* May 16, A19.

Neff, Christopher L., and Luke R. Edgell. 2013. "The Rise of Repeal: Policy Entrepreneurship and Don't Ask, Don't Tell." *Journal of Homosexuality* 60:232–49.

NeJaime, Douglas. 2011. "Winning through Losing." *Iowa Law Review* 96 (March): 941–1012.

New York Times. 1995. "Pentagon Halts an Affirmative Action Rule." *New York Times,* October 22, sec. 1, p. 22.

Obama, Barack. 2008. "The American Promise." Speech delivered to Democratic National Convention, Denver, Colorado, August 28. http://www.huffington post.com/2008/08/28/barack-obama-democratic-c_n_122224.html.

O'Brien, John. 2012. "City Settles Reverse Discrimination Suit." *Syracuse Post-Standard,* July 15, B1.

Paris, Michael. 2010. *Framing Equal Opportunity: Law and the Politics of School Finance Reform.* Palo Alto, CA: Stanford University Press.

Pear, Robert. 2011. "A Bush Rule on Providers of Abortions Is Revised." *New York Times,* February 19, A11.

Pelton, M. Lee. 2003. "This Issue Has a Human Face." *Chronicle of Higher Education,* July 4, 10.

Peretti, Terri. 1999. *In Defense of a Political Court.* Princeton, NJ: Princeton University Press.

Perry, H. W., Jr., and L. A. Powe Jr. 2004. "The Political Battle for the Constitution." *Constitutional Commentary* 21 (Winter): 641–96.

Peters, Jeremy W. 2013. "Effects of Ruling on Same-Sex Marriage Start Rippling Out through Government." *New York Times,* July 10, A14.

Peterson, Todd David. 2005. "Oh, Behave!" *Legal Affairs,* November/December, 16–18.

Pickerill, J. Mitchell. 2004. *Constitutional Deliberation in Congress: The Impact of Judicial Review in a Separated System.* Durham, NC: Duke University Press.

Pinello, Daniel. 2003. *Gay Rights and American Law.* New York: Cambridge University Press.

———. 2006. *America's Struggle for Same-Sex Marriage.* New York: Cambridge University Press.

Posner, Richard A. 2008a. "In Defense of Looseness." *New Republic,* August 27. http://www.newrepublic.com/article/books/defense-looseness.

———. 2008b. *How Judges Think.* Cambridge, MA: Harvard University Press.

Post, Robert, and Reva Siegel. 2007. "*Roe* Rage: Democratic Constitutionalism and Backlash." *Harvard Civil Rights-Civil Liberties Law Review* 42:373–433.

Powe, Lucas A., Jr. 2000. *The Warren Court and American Politics.* Cambridge, MA: Harvard University Press.

Pralle, Sarah. 2009. "News Coverage of State Climate Change Litigation." Paper presented at the annual meeting of Midwest Political Science Association, Chicago, Illinois, April 2–5.

Price, Richard S. 2013. "Arguing *Gunwall*: The Effect of the Criteria Test on Constitutional Rights Claims." *Journal of Law and Courts* 1 (2): 331–62.

Price, Richard, and Thomas M. Keck. 2013. "Movement Litigation and Unilateral Disarmament." Paper presented at the annual meeting of Western Political Science Association, Hollywood, California, March 28–30.

Reed, Douglas S. 1999. "Popular Constitutionalism: Toward a Theory of State Constitutional Meanings." *Rutgers Law Journal* 30:871–932.

Revesz, Richard. L. 1997. "Environmental Regulation, Ideology, and the D.C. Circuit." *Virginia Law Review* 83 (November): 1717–72.

Rimmerman, Craig A. 1996. "Promise Unfulfilled: Clinton's Failure to Overturn the Military Ban on Lesbians and Gays." In *Gay Rights, Military Wrongs: Political Perspectives on Lesbians and Gays in the Military,* edited by Craig A. Rimmerman, 111–26. New York: Garland.

———. 2002. *From Identity to Politics: The Lesbian and Gay Movements in the United States.* Philadelphia: Temple University Press.

Robinson, Beth. 2001. "The Road to Inclusion for Same-Sex Couples: Lessons from Vermont." *Seton Hall Constitutional Law Journal* 11 (Spring): 237–57.

Robinson, Dorothy K. 2003. "Race-Sensitive Programs after the Michigan Decisions." *Trusteeship* 11 (5): 37.

Rohter, Larry. 1994. "Abortion Clinic Fight Heads to Court." *New York Times,* April 28, A16.

Rolnick, Joshua. 1998. "Minority Enrollment Drops in Graduate Science Programs." *Chronicle of Higher Education,* September 18, A48.

Rosen, Jeffrey. 2006. *The Most Democratic Branch: How the Courts Serve America.* New York: Oxford University Press.

———. 2007. "Robert's Rules." *Atlantic Monthly,* January/February.

Rosenbaum, David E. 1998. "White House Revises Policy on Contracts for Minorities." *New York Times,* June 25, A1.

Rosenberg, Gerald N. 1991. *The Hollow Hope: Can Courts Bring about Social Change?* Chicago: University of Chicago Press.

———. 1996. "Positivism, Interpretivism, and the Study of Law." *Law and Social Inquiry* 21 (Spring): 435–56.

———. 2008. *The Hollow Hope: Can Courts Bring about Social Change?* Rev. ed. Chicago: University of Chicago Press.

Rostron, Allen. 2005. "Shooting Stories: The Creation of Narrative and Melodrama in Real and Fictional Litigation against the Gun Industry." *UMKC Law Review* 73 (Summer): 1047–72.

———. 2006. "Lawyers, Guns, & Money: The Rise and Fall of Tort Litigation against the Firearms Industry." *Santa Clara Law Review* 46:481–511.

———. 2009. "Protecting Gun Rights and Improving Gun Control after *District of Columbia v. Heller.*" *Lewis & Clark Law Review* 13 (Summer): 383–418.

Sargent, Greg. 2012. "On Gay Marriage, Mitt Romney Veers Hard to the Right." *Washington Post Opinions* (blog). February 7. http://www.washingtonpost.com/blogs/plum-line/post/on-gay-marriage-mitt-romney-veers-hard-to-the-right/2012/02/07/gIQALE48wQ_blog.html.

Scheingold, Stuart A. 2004. *The Politics of Rights: Lawyers, Public Policy, and Political Change,* 2nd ed. Ann Arbor: University of Michigan Press.

Schemo, Diana Jean. 2001a. "Head of U. of California Seeks to End SAT Use in Admissions." *New York Times,* February 17, A1.

———. 2001b. "U. of Georgia Won't Contest Ruling on Admissions Policy." *New York Times,* November 10, A10.

Scherer, Nancy. 2005. *Scoring Points: Politicians, Activists, and the Lower Federal Court Appointment Process.* Palo Alto, CA: Stanford University Press.

Schmidt, Peter. 1998. "State Legislatures Show Little Enthusiasm for Measures to End Racial Preferences." *Chronicle of Higher Education,* March 13, A44.

———. 1999a. "With No Lawsuit in Sight, U. of Virginia Dives into the Affirmative-Action Fray." *Chronicle of Higher Education,* October 15, A40.

———. 1999b. "U. of Virginia Halts Use of Scoring System That Helped Black Applicants." *Chronicle of Higher Education,* October 22, A42.

———. 2003a. "Affirmative Action Survives, and So Does the Debate." *Chronicle of Higher Education,* July 4, 1.

———. 2003b. "Affirmative-Action Fight Is Renewed in the States." *Chronicle of Higher Education,* July 18, A19–22.

———. 2003c. "New Admissions System at U. of Michigan to Seek Diversity through Essays." *Chronicle of Higher Education,* September 5, 28.

———. 2003d. "Affirmative Action Remains a Minefield, Mostly Unmapped." *Chronicle of Higher Education,* October 24, A22–25.

———. 2004a. "Not Just for Minority Students Anymore." *Chronicle of Higher Education,* March 19, A17–20.

———. 2004b. "Federal Pressure Prompts Washington U. in St. Louis to Open Minority Scholarship Program to All Races." *Chronicle of Higher Education,* April 16, 23.

———. 2004c. "Federal Civil-Rights Officials Investigate Race-Conscious Admissions." *Chronicle of Higher Education,* December 17, A26.

———. 2005a. "NIH Opening Minority Programs to Other Groups." *Chronicle of Higher Education,* March 11, A26.

———. 2005b. "Justice Dept. Is Expected to Sue Southern Illinois U. over Minority Fellowships." *Chronicle of Higher Education,* November 25.

———. 2006. "From 'Minority' to 'Diversity.'" *Chronicle of Higher Education,* February 3, A24–26.

———. 2007a. "Preference Lawsuit Is Settled in Michigan." *Chronicle of Higher Education,* February 16, 32.

———. 2007b. "Dow Jones Fund Opens Journalism Programs to White Students after Lawsuit." *Chronicle of Higher Education,* February 23, 18.

———. 2007c. "UCLA Reverses Decline in Black Admissions but Rejects More Asians." *Chronicle of Higher Education,* April 20, A42.

———. 2007d. "4 States Named as New Targets in Affirmative-Action Fight." *Chronicle of Higher Education,* May 4, A34–35.

———. 2009. "Asian-Americans Give U. of California an Unexpected Fight over Admissions Policy." *Chronicle of Higher Education,* April 10, A21–22.

———. 2010. "California's Proposition 209 Is Challenged in Effort to Derail Similar Measures." *Chronicle of Higher Education,* February 15, A31.

Schmidt, Peter, and Patrick Healy. 1999. "U. of Virginia Poised to Limit Race-Based Admissions; U. of Georgia Keeps Its Preferences." *Chronicle of Higher Education,* October 8, A40.

Schmidt, Peter, and Jeffrey R. Young. 2003. "MIT and Princeton Open 2 Summer Programs to Students of All Races." *Chronicle of Higher Education,* February 21, A31–32.

Schmitt, Eric. 1993. "U.S. Opposes Court Interference in Gay Troop Ban." *New York Times,* March 5, A14.

Selingo, Jeffrey. 1997. "Task Force Suggests That U. of California Drop SAT as Admissions Requirement." *Chronicle of Higher Education,* October 3, A37.

———. 1999a. "U. of Texas at Austin Ends Minority-Hiring Program." *Chronicle of Higher Education,* January 15, A38.

———. 1999b. "Affirmative Action without Numerical Goals." *Chronicle of Higher Education,* May 28, A34.

———. 1999c. "Florida Plan to End Racial Preferences in Admissions Attracts Attention—and Criticism." *Chronicle of Higher Education,* November 26, A34.

———. 2000a. "Lawmakers' Sit-In Spurs Delay in Florida Affirmative-Action Vote." *Chronicle of Higher Education,* January 28, A37.

———. 2000b. "Judge Upholds Florida Plan to End Affirmative Action." *Chronicle of Higher Education,* July 21, A23.

———. 2001. "Broader Admissions Criteria Near Approval at U. of California." *Chronicle of Higher Education,* November 23, 24.

———. 2003. "Decisions May Prompt Return of Race-Conscious Admissions at Some Colleges." *Chronicle of Higher Education,* July 4, special report sec., p. 5.

———. 2005. "Michigan: Who Really Won?" *Chronicle of Higher Education,* January 14, 21.

Shapiro, Martin. 1964. *Law and Politics in the Supreme Court: New Approaches to Political Jurisprudence.* New York: Free Press of Glencoe.

———. 1981. *Courts: A Comparative and Political Analysis.* Chicago: University of Chicago Press.

Siegel, Neil S. 2006. "Race-Conscious Student Assignment Plans: Balkanization, Integration, and Individualized Consideration." *Duke Law Journal* 56 (December): 781–860.

Siegel, Reva B. 2007. "The New Politics of Abortion: An Equality Analysis of Woman-Protective Abortion Restrictions." *University of Illinois Law Review* 2007:991–1053.

———. 2008. "Dead or Alive: Originalism as Popular Constitutionalism in *Heller.*" *Harvard Law Review* 122 (November): 191–245.

Silverstein, Gordon. 2009. *Law's Allure: How Law Shapes, Constrains, Saves, and Kills Politics.* New York: Cambridge University Press.

Silverstein, Helena. 2007. *Girls on the Stand: How Courts Fail Pregnant Minors.* New York: New York University Press.

Skrentny, John David. 1996. *The Ironies of Affirmative Action: Politics, Culture, and Justice in America.* Chicago: University of Chicago Press.

———. 2001. "Republican Efforts to End Affirmative Action: Walking a Fine Line." In *Seeking the Center: Politics and Policymaking at the New Century,* edited by Martin A. Levin, Marc K. Landy, and Martin Shapiro, 132–71. Washington, DC: Georgetown University Press.

———. 2002. *The Minority Rights Revolution.* Cambridge, MA: Harvard University Press.

Spitzer, Robert J. 2004. *The Politics of Gun Control.* Washington, DC: CQ Press.

Steeh, Charlotte, and Maria Krysan. 1996. "The Polls—Trends: Affirmative Action and the Public, 1970–1995." *Public Opinion Quarterly* 60 (Spring): 128–58.

Stephenson, Donald Grier, Jr. 1999. *Campaigns and the Court: The U.S. Supreme Court in Presidential Elections.* New York: Columbia University Press.

Stohr, Greg. 2005. *A Black and White Case: How Affirmative Action Survived Its Greatest Legal Challenge.* Princeton, NJ: Bloomberg Press.

Stout, David, and Richard Perez-Pena. 1999. "Housing Agencies to Sue Gun Makers." *New York Times,* December 8, A1.

Sulzberger, A.G. 2010. "Ouster of Iowa Judges Sends Signal to Bench." *New York Times,* November 4, A1.

Sunstein, Cass R. 1996. "Foreword: Leaving Things Undecided." *Harvard Law Review* 110 (November): 4–101.

———. 1999. *One Case at a Time: Judicial Minimalism on the Supreme Court.* Cambridge, MA: Harvard University Press.

Sunstein, Cass R., and Thomas J. Miles. 2009. "Depoliticizing Administrative Law." *Duke Law Journal* 58 (May): 2193–2230.

Sunstein, Cass R., David Schkade, Lisa M. Ellman, and Andres Sawicki. 2006. *Are Judges Political? An Empirical Analysis of the Federal Judiciary.* Washington, DC: Brookings Institution Press.

Sweet, Martin J. 2010. *Merely Judgment: Ignoring, Evading, and Trumping the Supreme Court.* Charlottesville: University of Virginia Press.

Teles, Steven M. 2008. *The Rise of the Conservative Legal Movement: The Battle for Control of the Law.* Princeton, NJ: Princeton University Press.

Thompson, E. P. 1975. *Whigs and Hunters: The Origin of the Black Act.* New York: Pantheon Books.

Tienda, Marta, and Teresa A. Sullivan. 2009. "The Promise and Peril of the Texas Uniform Admission Law." In *The Next Twenty-Five Years? Affirmative Action and Higher Education in the United States and South Africa,* edited by Martin Hall, Marvin Krislov, and David L. Featherman, 155–74. Ann Arbor: University of Michigan Press.

Toner, Robin. 2007. "Abortion Foes See Validation for New Tactic." *New York Times,* May 22, A1.

Toobin, Jeffrey. 2008. *The Nine: Inside the Secret World of the Supreme Court.* New York: Anchor Books.

———. 2012. *The Oath: The Obama White House and the Supreme Court.* New York: Doubleday.

Waldron, Jeremy. 1999. *Law and Disagreement.* New York: Oxford University Press.

———. 2006. "The Core of the Case against Judicial Review." *Yale Law Journal* 115:1346–1406.

Walker, John M., Jr. 2007. "Politics and the Confirmation Process: Thoughts on the Roberts and Alito Hearings." In *Bench Press: The Collision of Courts, Politics, and the Media,* edited by Keith J. Bybee, 123–30. Stanford, CA: Stanford University Press.

Wasby, Stephen L. 1981. "Arrogation of Power or Accountability: 'Judicial Imperialism' Revisited." *Judicature* 65 (4): 208–19.

———. 1984. "How Planned Is 'Planned Litigation'?" *American Bar Foundation Research Journal* 1984 (1): 83–138.

Weissert, Will. 1999. "Florida's Universities Keep Careful Watch on Statewide Review of Affirmative Action." *Chronicle of Higher Education,* September 17, A50.

Wertheimer, Linda K. 2002. "New Diversity Law Complicates Texas Graduate Schools' Admissions Policies." *Dallas Morning News,* February 25.

Wharton, Linda J. 2009. "*Roe* at Thirty-Six and Beyond: Enhancing Protection for Abortion Rights through State Constitutions." *William and Mary Journal of Women and Law* 15 (Spring): 469–534.

Wharton, Linda J., Susan Frietsche, and Kathryn Kolbert. 2006. "Preserving the Core of *Roe*: Reflections on *Planned Parenthood v. Casey*." *Yale Journal of Law and Feminism* 18:317–86.

Whittington, Keith E. 1999. *Constitutional Construction: Divided Powers and Constitutional Meaning.* Cambridge, MA: Harvard University Press.

———. 2007. *Political Foundations of Judicial Supremacy: The Presidency, the Supreme Court, and Constitutional Leadership in U.S. History.* Princeton, NJ: Princeton University Press.

Wilgoren, Jodi. 2000a. "Mount Holyoke Drops SAT Requirement." *New York Times,* June 7, A28.

———. 2000b "A Ruling Voids Use of Vouchers in Ohio Schools." *New York Times,* December 12, A1.

Wilkinson, J. Harvie, III. 2009. "Of Guns, Abortions, and the Unraveling Rule of Law." *Virginia Law Review* 95 (April): 253–323.

———. 2012. "Cry, the Beloved Constitution." *New York Times,* March 12, A21.

Winerip, Michael. 2011. "Seeking Integration, Whatever the Path." *New York Times,* February 28, A11.

Winkler, Adam. 2011. *Gun Fight: The Battle over the Right to Bear Arms in America.* New York: W. W. Norton.

Winter, Greg. 2003. "Colleges See Broader Attack on Their Aid to Minorities." *New York Times,* March 30, A16.

Yardley, Jim. 2000. "Bush's Choices for Court Seen as Moderates." *New York Times,* July 9, sec. 1, p. 1.

Yoshino, Kenji. 2006. "Too Good for Marriage." *New York Times,* July 14, A19.

Zackin, Emily. 2008. "Popular Constitutionalism's Hard When You're Not Very Popular: Why the ACLU Turned to Courts." *Law and Society Review* 42 (June): 367–96.

Zeleny, Jeff. 2007. "Obama Says He'd Roll Back Tax Cuts for the Wealthiest." *New York Times,* May 14.

Index

Abbott, Greg, 90

Able v. United States, 40–41, 271n95

abortion rights and restrictions: abortion on demand and, 196–97; abortion procedures and, 33, 270n59; adherence to Supreme Court precedent and, 150–52, 157, 297n48; antiabortion violence and, 58–61, 81–82, 121, 275n155; ballot initiatives and, 25, 148, 266n21, 297n46; broad vs. narrow rulings and, 193–94; clinic protests and, 82–86, 194, 283n51, 283–84n54, 284n67, 306n48; commerce clause and, 84; compliance with judicial decisions and, 223; courts as veto points and, 20–34, 81–86, 249; courts clearing way for policy change and, 112, 121, 167, 172–73, 300n7; courts dismantling existing policies and, 168–69, 178, 188–91, 193–94; courts supporting existing policies and, 250; defense of clinics and, 59–61, 81–82, 188, 191, 195, 275n156, 275–76n158, 276n163, 307n65; exceptions to abortion bans and, 21, 24–25, 32–33, 173, 175, 301–2n13; extreme legal claims and, 157–58; fetal legal rights and, 157, 299n79; fetal personhood and, 25, 81, 175, 266n21, 299n79; Hyde Amendment and, 158, 278n188; informed consent and waiting periods and, 26–31, 189, 194, 207–9, 231, 249, 266–67n25, 267n31, 267n38, 268nn40–41; judicial polarization and, 137, 144–45, 149–52, 295n9; legal compromises and, 159; litigation vs. legislation and, 81; maternal life and health and, 23, 33, 175, 224; Mexico City policy and, 34; near-total bans and, 207, 208–9, 249; parental involvement laws and, 29–32, 143–45, 169, 188, 190, 194, 206–8, 224, 249–50, 268n50, 268–69n52, 307n56, 314n14; partial-birth abortion and, 20–25, 32–33, 145, 151–52, 159, 188, 190, 193, 195, 208, 231, 265nn9–10, 266nn15–18, 307n65; personnel and locations approved for, 188, 189–90, 194, 268–69n52; pre- and postviability, 33, 265n8; pregnancy centers and, 85; provider conscience regulations and, 34; public funding and, 66–67, 158, 188, 191, 194–95, 250, 268–69n52, 278n191, 306n46, 307n65; public opinion and, 172–73, 175–76, 189–91, 301–2n13, 306n48; rape and incest and, 158; resistance to judicial and legislative decisions and, 206–9, 212–13; right to life amendment and, 206–7, 308n10; robust vs. modest readings of rights claims and, 257; spousal notification and, 207; state-level abortion restrictions and, 21–23, 24–32, 207–9; trigger laws and, 208; undue burden and, 25–27; weeks of gestation and, 175, 188, 190–91, 196, 231, 249, 308n11

Academics for the Second Amendment, 72

Ackerman, Bruce, 133–34

ACLJ. *See* American Center for Law and Justice (ACLJ)

ACLU. *See* American Civil Liberties Union (ACLU)

ACRF. *See* American Civil Rights Foundation (ACRF)

ACRI. *See* American Civil Rights Institute (ACRI)

activist judges. *See* judges as tyrants; judicial activism

Adams, John, 133–34

Adams, Michael F., 102

Adarand Constructors, 93, 98

Adarand Constructors v. Mineta, 228, 289n105

Adarand Constructors v. Pena: affirmative action as unconstitutional and, 288n98; conservative public interest law movement and, 94–95, 199; Department of Justice response to, 210; judicial impact and, 246–48; opinion polls and, 182; strict scrutiny and, 94, 96–98, 100, 154–55, 303–4n26

Adarand Constructors v. Slater, 98–99, 289n117, 312n45

Adar v. Smith, 275n153

ADF. *See* Alliance Defense Fund (ADF)

Advocates for Faith and Freedom, 283n47

affirmative action: adherence to Supreme Court precedent and, 154; anti–affirmative action strategy and, 100–101, 119–20; ballot initiatives and, 42, 44–45, 69, 100, 117–19, 122–24, 231, 234, 247, 273n121, 310n26, 313–14n5; bans on, 159, 196–97, 246–47, 272n109, 313–14n5; beneficiaries of, 237–38; in broadcasting, 97, 228; California's Proposition 209 and, 43; centrist legal compromises and, 159; color blindness and, 12, 92, 95, 119–20, 123, 158, 221, 246; compliance with judicial decisions and, 217–23, 311–12n42, 312n50; compromise in response to decisions and, 226–29, 312n49; courts' blocking function and, 42–46; courts clearing way for policy change and, 117–18, 120, 122–23, 238; courts dismantling existing policies and, 92–112, 168–69, 171, 178, 180–86, 188, 192; discriminatory impact and, 211; discriminatory university admissions policies and, 235–37; disparate treatment vs. disparate impact and, 110; diversity as compelling interest and, 96, 102–7, 109, 212, 228, 232, 237; drop in minority enrollment in absence of, 210–11, 219, 233; elite consensus supporting, 105–7; extreme legal claims and, 158–59; faculty diversity and, 98,

145, 223; fire and police departments and, 97–98, 110–11, 247, 289n107, 310n32; Fourteenth Amendment and, 45–46, 141; grounds for, 237, 248; innovation in response to decisions and, 229–38; judicial polarization and, 137, 140–46, 149–50, 154–55, 298n68; legacy admissions and, 237; legislation vs. litigation and, 8–9; level of scrutiny and, 94, 96–97, 100, 109, 154–55, 288n96, 303–4n26, 312n50; liberal-initiated lawsuits and, 42; local business interests' challenge of, 93; mending not ending, 227–28; Michigan's Proposal 2 and, 44–46, 69, 124, 144; minority contractors and, 93–95, 98–99, 108, 123, 154–55, 182, 186, 210, 223, 226–27, 227, 247, 289n116, 303–4n26, 308–9n14, 311–12n42; minority employees and, 97–98, 181, 228, 247; minority scholarships and, 93–94, 169, 183–84, 218, 220–22, 228–29, 248, 314n12; origins of, 92; political backlash after judicial decisions and, 209–12; preemptive policy changes and, 217–19, 223; private school admissions preferences and, 291n153; public opinion and, 180–84, 185, 192; race-conscious hiring and promotion and, 181–82; race-conscious public school student assignments and, 99–100, 108–9, 111, 154–55, 182–83, 212, 219, 229, 247, 290nn128–29, 298n68, 304n27, 312n50; race-neutral alternatives to achieve diversity and, 105, 111, 233–34; robust vs. modest reading of rights claims and, 257; shift in doctrinal landscape on, 245–46; socioeconomic vs. racial diversity and, 229–30, 234–35; standardized test scores and, 235–37, 313n56; Super Tuesday for racial equality and, 46; Supreme Court's shifting balance and, 108, 109–11; Texas Top Ten Percent and similar policies and, 105, 11, 232–34, 313n55; Title VII and, 110; Washington's I-200 law and, 102, 108, 118–19; wildcat vs. movement litigation and, 10–11. See also *Gratz v. Bollinger*; *Grutter v. Bollinger*; *Hopwood v. Texas*; *various universities*

Affordable Care Act (ACA), 1, 120, 129–30, 132–33, 163, 293n186

Air Transportation Ass'n of America v. City and County of San Francisco, 281n34

Alaska Civil Liberties Union v. Alaska, 52, 179, 274n139, 302–3n18
Alaska v. Planned Parenthood of Alaska, 31, 268–69n52
Albano v. Attorney General, 35, 157, 270n63, 299n75
Alito, Samuel: adherence to Supreme Court precedent and, 151; affirmative action and, 145; Affordable Care Act and, 130, 294n5; antiharassment legislation and, 81; appointment of, 32, 108, 109; composition of Supreme Court and, 208; confirmation process for, 2, 164–65; gay rights and, 292–93n178; gun rights and, 73, 146; judges as tyrants and, 3; partial-birth abortion and, 33, 151, 152
Alliance Defense Fund (ADF): antiabortion legislation and, 283n47; antiabortion protests and, 85, 284n67; gay rights and, 78, 113, 115, 117, 120–22, 156
Alons v. Iowa District Court, 120–21, 293n189, 299n74
Alpha Medical Clinic v. Anderson, 121, 293n190
American Academy of Pediatrics v. Lungren, 31, 190, 268–69n52, 305n43
American Center for Law and Justice (ACLJ), 78, 84, 85, 284n60
American Civil Liberties Union (ACLU): abortion restrictions and, 25; affirmative action and, 272n113, 273n121; California's Proposition 209 and, 43; *Cox v. Florida Department of Health and Rehabilitative Services* and, 54; Don't Ask, Don't Tell and, 39; fetal personhood and, 266n21; same-sex marriage and, 36–37, 52; wildcat vs. movement litigation and, 48–49, 273n128
American Civil Rights Foundation (ACRF), 123
American Civil Rights Foundation v. Berkeley Unified School District, 122–23, 229, 294n197, 312n51
American Civil Rights Foundation v. Los Angeles Unified School District, 122–23, 294n197
American Civil Rights Institute (ACRI), 43–44, 122–23, 220, 231
American Coalition of Life Activists v. Planned Parenthood of the Columbia/Willamette, Inc., 84, 284n58

American Family Association, 79, 81, 206
American Federation of Government Employees v. United States, 99, 119
American Life League v. Reno, 84, 284n55, 284n58
Amestoy, Jeffrey L., 49–50, 160, 161
Amherst College, 222
Andersen, Ellen Ann, 50
Andersen v. King County, 38, 51, 271n81, 274nn135–36
Andrew W. Mellon Foundation, 222
Appling v. Doyle, 122, 282n37, 294n196
Apprendi v. New Jersey, 80
Arcara, Richard J., 83
Areen, Judith, 93–94
Arkansas Department of Human Services v. Cole, 38, 178–79, 271n80, 302n17
Arlington County v. White, 191, 217, 281n34, 306n49, 310n24
Armstrong v. State, 189–90, 194, 268–69n52, 305n42, 307n58
Arnold v. Cleveland, 160, 280–81n28, 300n86
Ashcroft, John, 67, 75–76
Asher v. Carnahan, 117–18, 293n183
Associated General Contractors of America, 95
Association of American Law Schools, 106–7
Atkinson, Richard C., 234–36
Aware Woman Center for Choice (Melbourne, Florida), 82, 276n163
Ayotte v. Planned Parenthood of Northern New England, 32–33, 224, 269n55, 311n35

Bach v. Pataki, 88–89, 286n78
Baehr v. Lewin, 48–49, 78, 87, 113, 160–61, 199, 204, 273n127
Baehr v. Miike, 274n141
Baker v. Smith & Wesson Corp., 64, 277n177
Baker v. Vermont, 49–50, 78–79, 148, 160–61, 199, 205, 300n88
Bakke decision. See *Regents of the University of California v. Bakke*
ballot initiatives: abortion and, 25, 148, 266n21, 297n46; affirmative action and, 42, 44–45, 69, 100, 117–19, 122–24, 231, 234, 273n121, 310n26, 313–14n5; courts clearing way for policy change and, 118; gay rights and, 13, 34–35, 57, 79, 113, 122,

ballot initiatives (*cont.*)
148, 156, 270n66, 297n46; polarization and, 148; Republicans' 2004 electoral victories and, 205; same-sex marriage and, 113–17, 122, 148, 205, 270n66, 297n45; signature verification and, 156. *See also* California's Proposition 8; California's Proposition 209; Michigan Civil Rights Initiative (MCRI)
Barnes, Jeb, 202
Barnes v. Mississippi, 29, 268n43
Barnes v. Moore, 26, 266n23
Barrientos, Gonzalo, 232
Batchelder, Alice M., 86, 142, 143
Bedford and Breen v. New Hampshire Technical College System, 52, 179, 274n139, 302–3n18, 309n19
Belk v. Charlotte-Mecklenburg Board of Education, 99–100, 212, 290nn123–24, 308n13
Bell v. Low Inome Women of Texas, 268–69n52
Bell v. Maryland, 264n3
Benjamin v. Bailey, 160, 280–81n28, 300n86
Bennett v. Arrington, 247, 314n6
Bennett v. Bowen, 35, 157, 270n65, 299n76
Bennett v. Yoshina, 113, 155, 292n167, 298n69
Bickel, Alexander, 240, 252
Blackmun, Harry, 23
Blake, William, 134
Bloomberg, Michael, 65
Blum, Edward, 69
Board of Education of Piscataway v. Taxman, 102–3, 145, 289n102, 290n135, 296n32
Boggs, Danny, 141–42, 143–44
Boies, David, 37, 58, 116
Bollinger, Lee, 102–4, 217–23
Bonauto, Mary, 49
Bopp, James, Jr., 115, 116–17, 292nn173–74
Boston Police Superior Officers Federation v. Boston, 98, 289n113
Bowen, William, 234–35
Bowers v. Hardwick, 39, 41–42, 47–48, 154
Bowler v. Lockyer, 115, 292n171
Boy Scouts of America, 80, 178, 302n16
Boy Scouts of America v. Dale, 79–80, 178, 282n43, 302n15
Bradbury, Steven G., 76

Brady Bill (1993), 7, 70, 72–73, 120, 186–88, 195–96, 250
Brady Campaign to Prevent Gun Violence v. Salazar, 213, 276–77n174, 309n15
Brady Center to Prevent Gun Violence, 62, 64, 67, 90
Brady v. Dean, 156, 282n37, 298n72
Brause and Dugan v. Bureau of Vital Statistics, 48–49, 273n129
Bray v. Alexandria Women's Health Clinic, 59–61, 275–76nn157–58
Brewer, Jan, 38
Brewer v. Commonwealth, 285–86n73
Brewer v. West Irondequoit Central School District, 99, 290n120
Breyer, Stephen, 23–24, 32, 107, 109, 289n107
Brinkman v. Miami University, 78, 120, 122, 281–82n35, 293n188, 294n195, 299n74
Britton, John, 59
Britt v. State, 91, 187, 287n85, 305n37
Broad, Molly C., 218
Brown, Janice Rogers, 123
Brown, Jerry, 115
Browne, Sharon, 123
Brown v. Board of Education, 199–200, 203, 244, 264n2
Brown v. Pittsburgh, 191, 284n67, 306n47
Brown v. Todd, 282–83n44
Bryant, Anita, 54, 213
Buchanan, Pat, on culture wars, 4–5, 7
Bureau of Alcohol, Tobacco, and Firearms, 67
Burgess, Susan, 201
Bush, George H. W., and George H. W. Bush years: affirmative action and, 96; gun control and, 70, 71; judicial appointments of, 7, 137, 141–42, 144–46, 151–52, 297n48; 1992 election and, 5
Bush, George W., and George W. Bush years: abortion and, 12, 21, 24–25, 28, 30–34, 85, 175, 208, 308n10; affirmative action and, 104–5, 221–22, 228; control of Congress during, 33; Don't Ask, Don't Tell and, 41, 42, 301n10; gay rights and, 244; gun rights and, 62–64, 70, 75–77, 212, 276–77n174; on judicial activism, 165; judicial appointments of, 2, 129, 141, 144–47, 153, 156–57, 164, 208, 257, 308n10; legislation vs. litigation and, 7–9; Mexico City policy and, 34; propor-

tion of judges from each party and, 163;
Supreme Court turnover and, 32–33;
Texas Top Ten Percent policy and, 232;
2000 presidential campaign and, 31;
2004 elections and, 205
Bush, Jeb, 234, 272n109, 313–14n5
Bush v. Gore, 156
Bybee, Keith, 163

Cabranes, Jose, 110
California Civil Rights Initiative (CCRI).
See California's Proposition 209
*California Education Committee v.
O'Connell*, 80, 283n45, 283n47
Californians against Discrimination and
Preferences (CADP), 43
California's Proposition 8: approval of, 115,
215; ballot language and, 115, 292n172;
extreme legal claims and, 157; gay rights
strategy and, 37, 58; judicial activism
and, 165–66; vs. judicial decisions, 35;
lawsuit challenging, 37, 115–16; opinion
polls and, 184; resistance to judicial vs.
legislative decisions and, 213; San Fran-
cisco's "winter of love" and, 57
California's Proposition 22, 57
California's Proposition 209, 43–46, 117,
122–24, 210, 233
Cal Tech, 222
*Camden County Board of Chosen Freehold-
ers v. Beretta USA Corp.*, 64, 277n175
Cammermeyer, Margarethe, 40
Cammermeyer v. Aspin, 40, 271n88
*Campaign for California Families v.
Schwarzenegger*, 282n37
Campbell v. Sundquist, 48, 179, 273n125,
303n19
Cannon, James M., 103
Cantu, Norma, 211
Carhart, Leroy, 23
Carhart I. See Stenberg v. Carhart (Carhart I)
*Carhart II. See Gonzales v. Carhart (Car-
hart II)*
Carhart v. Ashcroft, 33, 269n56
Carhart v. Gonzales, 151, 297n57
Carhart v. Stenberg, 21–22, 145, 265n9,
296n28. See also *Stenberg v. Carhart
(Carhart I)*
Carlson, John, 119
Carnahan, Robin, 117–18

Carnegie Mellon University, 222
Carter, Jimmy, 137, 141, 142, 143, 145, 146
Casale v. Kelly, 309n17
Casey v. Planned Parenthood, 26, 266n22.
See also *Planned Parenthood v. Casey*
Catholic Action League, 155–56
*Catholic Charities of the Diocese of Spring-
field v. Illinois*, 282n37
Cato Institute, 87
Causeway Medical Suite v. Foster, 24, 151,
190, 265n9, 266n15, 297n53, 305–6n44
Causeway Medical Suite v. Ieyoub, 30, 190,
268n44, 305n43
Cayetano, Ben, 113
Center for Equal Opportunity, 220
Center for Individual Rights (CIR), affirma-
tive action and, 94–95, 100–108, 118–19,
141, 219–23, 231–32, 237, 290n134;
California's Proposition 209 and, 43;
"color-blind" vision of, 69; impact of
work of, 246–47; Michigan's Proposal 2
and, 69, 124; strategy of, 248
Center for Reproductive Law and Policy
(CRLP), 21, 23, 25, 29–30, 144
*Center for Reproductive Law and Policy v.
Bush*, 33–34, 270n60
Center for Reproductive Rights. *See* Center
for Reproductive Law and Policy (CRLP)
Central Intelligence Agency, 271n90
Chase, Samuel, 132–33, 134
Cheffer v. Reno, 84, 284n55
Chemerinsky, Erwin, 272n113
A Choice for Women v. Butterworth, 190,
265n9, 305–6n44
Christensen v. State, 273n125
CIR. *See* Center for Individual Rights
(CIR), affirmative action and
*Citizens for a Constitutional Convention v.
Yoshina*, 155, 298n69
Citizens for Equal Protection v. Bruning, 36,
51, 264n4, 270n72, 274nn135–36
Citizens United v. FEC, 292n173
City of Atlanta v. McKinney, 191, 225,
281n34, 306n49, 310n25, 311n38
City of Atlanta v. Morgan, 225, 281n34,
310n25, 311n38
City of Chicago v. Beretta USA Corp., 64,
277n177
City of Cincinnati v. Beretta USA Corp., 64,
277n179

City of Cleveland Heights ex rel. *Hicks v.
    City of Cleveland Heights*, 281n34
City of Cleveland v. State, 62, 276n166
City of Gary v. Smith & Wesson, 64,
    277n179
*City of New York v. A-1 Jewelry and Pawn,
    Inc.*, 65, 277n185
*City of New York v. Adventure Outdoors,
    Inc.*, 65, 277n186
City of New York v. Beretta USA Corp.,
    63–64, 276–77nn172–74
*City of New York v. Bob Moates' Sport
    Shop, Inc.*, 277n185
*City of New York v. Mickalis Pawn Shop,
    LLC*, 65, 277n187
City of Philadelphia v. Beretta USA Corp.,
    64, 277n175
civil rights, 19, 137, 264n3
Civil Rights Act of 1964, 43, 200
Clay, Eric L., 141–42, 143–44
Clegg, Roger, 220–21, 222
Cleland, Robert H., 74
Clement, Paul, 90
Clemson University, 312n48
Cleveland Surgi-Center v. Jones, 268n50
*Cleveland Taxpayers for Ohio Constitution
    v. City of Cleveland*, 78, 122, 281–82n35,
    294n196
Clinic for Women, Inc. v. Brizzi, 28, 267n33
Clinton, Bill, and Clinton years: abortion
    and, 8, 20–21, 23–33, 59, 66, 81–82, 84,
    158, 175, 207–8, 301n11; affirmative ac-
    tion and, 92, 96, 98–99, 145, 210–12, 226–
    27, 308–9n14; California's Proposition
    209 and, 43, 210; declaration of culture
    wars and, 5; discriminatory university
    admissions policies and, 235; Don't Ask,
    Don't Tell and, 38–40, 41, 170, 271n83;
    gay rights and, 146, 244–45; gun control
    and, 7, 62–63, 67, 70–72, 74–76, 152–53,
    187, 278n4, 279–80n20; judicial appoint-
    ments of, 23–24, 129, 137, 141, 143–45,
    147, 151–52; Mexico City policy and, 34;
    proportion of judges from each party
    and, 163
Clinton, Hillary, 5
CLP. *See* American Family Association
Coakley, Martha, 62
Coalition for Economic Equity v. Wilson,
    43–44, 158–59, 272nn106–8, 300n84

Coalition to Defend Affirmative Action
    by Any Means Necessary (BAMN),
    44–45, 46
*Coalition to Defend Affirmative Action v.
    Board of State Canvassers*, 44, 272n110
*Coalition to Defend Affirmative Action v.
    Brown*, 46, 158–59, 273n122, 300n84
*Coalition to Defend Affirmative Action v.
    Granholm*, 45, 69, 123–24, 272nn114–15,
    278n3, 294n201
*Coalition to Defend Affirmative Action v.
    Regents of the University of Michigan*,
    45–46, 144, 159, 192, 272–73nn116–19,
    296nn22–24, 300n85, 307n52
Cohen, Carl, 101, 104, 217–18
Cole, R. Guy, Jr., 45, 143–44
Coleman, Mary Sue, 107, 291n147, 310n26
Colorado's Amendment 2, 35, 56
Comfort v. Lynn School Committee, 108–9,
    155, 247, 291n153, 298n67, 314n8
Commonwealth v. McGowan, 91, 288n91
Commonwealth v. Wasson, 47–48, 265n5,
    273n123, 303n19
*Comprehensive Health of Planned Parent-
    hood of Kansas and Mid-Missouri, Inc.
    v. Cline*, 121, 293nn191–92
Conaway v. Deane, 52, 274n141
*Concrete Works of Colorado v. City and
    County of Denver*, 99, 108, 290n118
Connerly, Ward: American Civil Rights
    Institute (ACRI) and, 122, 220; bal-
    lot initiatives organized by, 273n121;
    California Civil Rights Initiative (CCRI)
    and, 43; *Hi-Voltage Wire Works, Inc. v.
    City of San Jose* and, 294n199; Michigan
    campaign against affirmative action and,
    46, 69, 119; Pacific Legal Foundation
    and, 123; strategy of, 246–47, 313–14n5;
    Washington's I-200 law and, 119
Connerly v. State Personnel Board, 120,
    122–23, 181, 293n188, 294n197, 294n199,
    303n24, 303–4n26
Connor, Bull, 200
Connors v. City of Boston, 191, 281n34,
    306n49, 310n25
Constitution: judicial independence in, 138;
    Republican vs. Democratic views on,
    160; right to life amendment and, 206.
    See also specific amendments
Cooey v. Bradshaw, 295n21

Cook v. Gates, 41, 272n99
Cooper-Harris v. United States, 275n149
courts as veto points: abortion and, 20–34,
  81–86, 249; affirmative action and 42–46;
  gay rights and, 34–42, 77–81, 303n19;
  gun control and, 70–77; reversal of veto
  points and, 201
courts clearing way for policy change: abortion and, 112, 121, 167, 172–73, 300n7;
  affirmative action and, 117–18, 120,
  122–23, 233, 235, 238; Affordable Care
  Act and, 120; ballot access and language
  and, 118; to call attention to need for
  legislation, 58–61, 118–20; conditions
  under which status quo is altered and,
  200–201; countermajoritarian local
  legislation and, 173; to enforce electoral
  and legislative victories, 65–68, 122–24;
  fragmented policy process and, 112,
  172, 233; fragmented political authority
  and, 55–56, 61; gay rights and, 112–17,
  120–21, 173–74; gun rights and, 120;
  ineffectiveness of rights-protecting
  judicial decisions and, 199; initiative
  and referendum campaigns and, 118;
  innovation in response to decisions and,
  233, 235, 238; judicial activism and, 167;
  judicial polarization and, 140; legislative inattentiveness and, 174; litigation
  to enable legislative politics and, 55–58,
  112–18; majoritarian vs. countermajoritarian decisions and, 174; same-sex
  marriage and, 238; Supreme Court as
  catalyst and, 202; when other policy
  avenues are closed off, 61–65, 120–22;
  to win piecemeal protections, 118–20
courts dismantling existing policies: abortion and, 178, 188, 189–91; affirmative
  action and, 92–112, 171, 178, 180–84,
  185–86, 188, 192; broad vs. narrow decisions and, 193–96; following the public
  and, 174–83; fragmented policy process
  and, 172; gay rights and, 47–54, 176, 178–
  80, 186, 188, 191–92, 194–95; gun rights
  and, 86–92, 171, 178, 180, 185, 186–89,
  195; across ideological spectrum, 168–
  69; judicial polarization and, 140; laws
  with public support and, 188; leading
  the public and, 183–86; legislative unresponsiveness and, 200–201; same-sex

marriage and, 48–54, 170–71, 184–86;
  status quo resistant to change and, 46–
  47; thwarting public will and, 186–96,
  199; trend vs. distribution of public
  opinion and, 183; unpopular legislation
  and, 169–72
courts supporting democratic politics,
  112–13, 124, 140, 167, 171, 174–83, 250,
  306n46
Cox, Mike, 45
*Cox v. State Department of Health and
  Rehabilitation Services*, 54, 275n150
Crabb, Barbara, 27
*Crawford v. Huntington Beach Union High
  School District*, 294n200, 304n27
CRLP. See Center for Reproductive Law
  and Policy (CRLP)
Croson case. See *Richmond v. Croson*
Cuccinelli v. Sebelius, 293n186
culture wars, 4–7, 150
Cummings, Sam R., 74–75
Cummings, Scott, 213
Cuomo, Andrew, 63
Custred, Glynn, 43

Dahl, Robert, 3–4, 198
Dale v. Boy Scouts of America, 274n132.
  See also *Boy Scouts of America v. Dale*
Dallas v. Dallas Firefighters Ass'n, 96–97,
  181, 289n107, 303n24
*Dalton v. Little Rock Family Planning
  Services*, 278n191
Daughtrey, Martha Craig, 45
Davis, Gray, 56–57
Days, Drew S., III, 82, 210
Dean, Howard, 78, 205
Dean v. District of Columbia, 273n128
DeBoer v. Snyder, 275n149
DeConde, Alexander, 278n4
Defense of Marriage Act (DOMA), 53, 62,
  184, 204, 215, 304n30
Dellinger, Walter, 211
Den Dulk, Kevin, 264n13
deParrie v. Oregon, 282–83n44
Department of Defense, 98–99, 227
Department of Education, 210–11, 218, 222,
  229, 235
*Department of Human Services and Child
  Welfare Agency Review Board v. How-
  ard*, 38, 178–79, 264n4, 271n79, 302n17

Department of Justice: affirmative action and, 210–12, 222, 227–28; controversial appointments to, 211–12; gay rights and, 53–54; gun control and gun rights and, 75–76, 87

Department of Transportation, 93, 98, 108, 228

DePaul University, 236

DePriest v. Commonwealth, 273n125

Desjarlais v. State, 112, 292n164

Devins, Neal, 171, 201

Devlin v. City of Philadelphia, 191, 281n34, 306n49

Diaz v. Brewer, 38, 179, 271n78, 302–3n18

Digiacinto v. Rector and Visitors of George Mason University, 91, 288n91

Dinwiddie v. United States, 84, 284n58

District of Columbia v. Beretta, 276–77n174

District of Columbia v. Heller: adherence to Supreme Court precedent and, 153–54; centrist legal compromises and, 159, 160; city's response to, 215; collective vs. individual rights and, 286n80; compliance with, 223, 311n41; compromise in response to, 225–26; courts dismantling existing policies and, 171, 180; judicial activism and, 255; judicial impact and, 202; judicial polarization and, 147; Obama's praise of decision in, 5; Scalia's opinion in, 153; sea change in gun rights and, 77, 87–92

Doe v. Kamehameha Schools/Bishop Estate, 291n153

Doe v. Montgomery County Board of Elections, 34, 176, 270n62, 302n14

Doe v. Reed, 12–13, 116, 292–93nn176–78

Doe v. Ventura, 48, 179, 273n125, 303n19, 309n18

DOMA. *See* Defense of Marriage Act (DOMA)

Donaldson v. Montana, 274n144

Douglass, Frederick, 107

Doyle v. Goodridge, 114, 156, 292n169, 298–99n72

Doyle v. Secretary of the Commonwealth, 114–15, 120, 156, 292n170, 293n187, 298–99n72

Drake v. Filko, 91, 288n90

Driver, Shanta, 46

Duggan, Patrick, 103, 104, 140–41

Dutton v. Pennsylvania, 91, 287–88n89

Dwyer, Ruth, 205

Dynalantic Corporation, 98

Dynalantic v. US Department of Defense, 98, 289n115

Eagles, Catherine C., 268n40

Easterbrook, Frank, 22, 27, 89–90, 270n59

Edenfield, B. Avant, 102, 103

Edwards, Harry, 146

Edwards v. Beck, 25, 175, 266n19, 301n12

Edwards v. City of Goldsboro, 88–89, 286n78

Edwards v. City of Santa Barbara, 84, 191, 284n59, 306n47

Edwards v. Houston, 96, 289n106

Eisenberg v. Montgomery County Public Schools, 100, 212, 290n127, 304n27, 308n13

Elane Photography, LLC v. Willock, 282–83n44

Eleventh Amendment, polarization of judiciary and, 137

Elizabeth Blackwell Health Center for Women v. Knoll, 158, 278n191, 299n81

Ellsworth, Oliver, 133

Emanuel, Rahm, 223

Emerson v. United States, 75–76, 280n22

Employment Non-Discrimination Act, 173

EOF. *See* Equal Opportunity Foundation (EOF)

Epstein, Lee, 136–37

Equal Employment Opportunity Commission, 96

Equality Foundation v. City of Cincinnati, 35, 270n69

Equal Opportunity Foundation (EOF), 94–95

Eskridge, William, 205, 225

Eubanks v. Stengel, 24, 151, 190, 266n15, 297n53, 305–6n44

Evans v. Kelley, 190, 265n9, 305–6n44

Evans v. Romer, 35, 270n67

Evergreen Ass'n v. City of New York, 85, 189–90, 284n68, 305n42

Ezell v. City of Chicago, 77, 187, 189, 281n31, 305n38, 311n34

Ezra, David, 113

FACE Act. *See* Freedom of Access to Clinic Entrances Act (1994)

Family Research Council, 85

Fargo Women's Health Organization v. Schaffer, 26–27, 266–67nn24–25
FCC. *See* Federal Communications Commission (FCC)
Federal Bureau of Investigation (FBI), 67
Federal Communications Commission (FCC), 145, 227–28
Federal Highway Administration, 311–12n42
Federalists, 133–34
Federalist Society, 279n11
54 Sheriffs v. Hickenlooper, 281n32
Finneran, Thomas, 174
Finstuen v. Crutcher, 37–38, 178–79, 271n77, 302n17
First Amendment: antiabortion protests and, 82–84, 191, 283–84n54, 283n51; *Doe v. Reed* and, 12–13; gay rights and, 116–17, 292–93n178; hate crimes legislation and, 80–81; same-sex marriage and, 156; speech condemning homosexuality and, 79–80
Fiscal v. City and County of San Francisco, 76–77, 180, 281n29, 303n21
Fischman, Joshua, 295n8
Fisher v. Commonwealth, 273n125
Fisher v. University of Texas, 69, 111, 145–46, 155, 159, 237, 248, 278n1, 292nn161–63, 296nn33–35
Florida Department of Children and Families v. Matter of Adoption of X.X.G. and N.R.G., 54, 178–79, 216, 275n152, 302n17, 310n21
Florida v. Presidential Women's Center, 28, 267n33
Florida v. US Department of Health and Human Services, 129, 294n2
Focus on the Family, 85
Ford, Gerald, 103, 144
Fourteenth Amendment: affirmative action and, 45–46, 107, 141; color-blind reading of, 212, 308–9n14; fetal personhood and, 299n79; gay marriage and, 53; gun rights and, 89, 90, 160; state deprivations of liberty and, 89
Franklin, Charles H., 202
Frank v. United States, 72, 279n7, 279n9
Freedom of Access to Clinic Entrances Act (1994), 8, 59, 61, 66, 81–82, 84
Friedman, Barry, 199, 253
Friedman, Bernard, 103–4, 106, 140–41

Frietsche, Susan, 267n31
Frymer, Paul, 174
Fullilove v. Klutznick, 288n96

Ganim v. Smith & Wesson Corp., 64, 277n176
Garland, Merrick, 296n30
Garrow, David, 59
Garwood, William, 71, 72
Garza, Emilio M., 145–46, 297n48
Gates, Robert, 215, 221, 237
Gay and Lesbian Advocates and Defenders (GLAD), 35, 49, 50, 53
Gay and Lesbian Advocates and Defenders v. Attorney General, 48, 179, 273n125, 303n19
gay rights: antidiscrimination laws and, 79–80, 274n132, 283n47; antigay violence and, 188, 194–95; awareness raising efforts and, 41; ballot initiatives and, 13, 34–35, 57, 79, 113, 122, 148, 156, 270n66, 297n46; benefits for same-sex partners and, 10, 38, 51–53, 78–79, 122, 174, 179, 191–92, 215, 217, 224, 273n129, 282nn26–37, 299n74, 310n25, 311n36; Boy Scouts of America and, 178; centrist legal compromises and, 159; civil rights laws and, 34; civil unions and, 52–53, 78, 120–21, 156, 160–61, 185–86, 205, 224–25, 230–31, 299n74; compliance with judicial decisions and, 215–17, 224; compromise in response to decisions and, 224–25; constitutional vs. statutory bans and, 36–37; countermajoritarian local legislation and, 173; courts as veto points and, 34–42, 77–81; courts clearing way for policy change and, 112, 120–21, 173–74; courts dismantling existing policies and, 168–69, 176, 178–80, 186, 188, 191–92, 194–95; discrimination and, 173, 176, 178, 245; domestic partnerships and, 57, 78–79, 122, 173–74, 185, 188, 191–92, 215, 217, 225, 230–31, 281–82nn34–35, 294n194, 299n74, 309n19, 310n25, 311n36, 313n53; Don't Ask, Don't Tell and, 38–42, 170, 173, 215, 245, 263–64n9, 271n83, 271–72n97, 301n10, 304–5n33; First Amendment and, 116–17, 292–93n178; gays in the military and, 146; gender identity and, 80; hate crimes legislation and, 80–81, 192, 194–95,

gay rights (*cont.*)
244–45, 307n61, 307n65; innovation in response to decisions and, 230–31; judicial polarization and, 146, 149–50, 154; judicial removal campaigns and, 132; legislation vs. litigation and, 8–9, 78; litigation challenging status quo and, 19, 265n5; litigation in strategy for, 19–20, 244; loitering statutes and, 309n17; National Coming Out Day and, 80; necessity of litigation and, 254; Obama on, 6; parenting rights and, 36, 38, 51–52, 54, 146, 178–79, 213–15, 274n132, 275n153; polarization of judiciary and, 137, 295n10; political backlash and, 245; political cover for legislators and, 225; pre-Clinton gays in the military policy and, 38–40, 167, 271nn96–97, 304–5n33; preemptive policy changes and, 311n36; public opinion and, 176, 178–80, 184–86, 191–92, 302n16, 303n20, 304n31, 307n50; rapid change in, 7, 244–45; resistance to judicial and legislative decisions and, 199, 200, 204–6, 213–14, 308n1; robust vs. modest reading of rights claims and, 257; San Francisco's "winter of love" and, 57; sexual orientation as suspect classification and, 274n141; sodomy laws and, 12, 47–48, 159, 179–80, 204, 245, 265n5, 273nn125–26, 309n18; speech condemning homosexuality and, 79–80; timing of litigation and, 47; transgender persons and, 245; wildcat litigation and, 36–37, 47–49, 80–81; wrongful termination and, 271n90. *See also* same-sex marriage
General Motors, 103, 105, 106
George III (king of England), 138
Georgetown University, 93–94
GeorgiaCarry.Org, Inc. v. Georgia, 91, 288n90
GFSZA. *See* Gun-Free School Zones Act (GFSZA)
Gillespie v. City of Indianapolis, 279–80nn20–21
Gillman, Howard, 198
Ginsburg, Ruth Bader, 23, 166, 270n59, 289n107
GLAD. *See* Gay and Lesbian Advocates and Defenders (GLAD)
Glenn v. Holder, 81, 283n48
Godfrey v. Spano, 282n41

Goldman, Sheldon, 271n83
Golinski v. US Office of Personnel Management, 275n149
Gonzales, Alberto: affirmative action challenges and, 104–5; Priscilla Owen nomination and, 32
Gonzales v. Carhart (Carhart II): adherence to Supreme Court precedent and, 152; centrist legal compromises and, 159; composition of Supreme Court and, 208; effects of, 25, 266n18; opinions in, 33, 269–70n57; public opinion and, 190, 193
Gonzales v. Planned Parenthood, 269–70n57
Goodridge v. Department of Public Health: ballot initiatives and, 35, 148; compliance with, 215; efforts to block implementation of, 50–51, 114, 155–57; judicial impact and, 202; opinion polls and, 184; political backlash and, 199, 200
Gore, Al, 165
Gossett, Charles W., 281n34
Graber, Mark, 171, 198, 257–58
Gramm, Phil, 211
Gratz, Jennifer, 101, 107, 119, 218, 247
Gratz v. Bollinger: centrist legal compromises and, 159; decisions and actions following, 111, 119, 221; holdings in, 106–8; innovative responses to, 236–37; judicial impact and, 202, 246, 248; judicial polarization and, 140, 295n14; litigators' maneuvering in, 104–6; origins of case and, 217–18; procedural dispute and, 142, 144; public face of, 247; public opinion and, 103, 181, 303n22; social and political pressure on court and, 171; strict enforcement of, 221–22
Greater Baltimore Center for Pregnancy Concerns v. Mayor and City Council, 85, 284n68
Green v. County School Board of New Kent County, 264n1
Greve, Michael, 119
Griffin, Chad, California's Proposition 8 and, 37
Griffin v. County School Board of Prince Edward County, 264n1
Griffith, Thomas, 147
Grutter, Barbara, 101, 105, 119, 141, 218
Grutter v. Bollinger: calls for reversal of, 145–46; centrist legal compromises and,

159; decisions and actions following, 109, 111, 119, 145, 155, 221, 291n147, 298n68; Democratic vs. Republican appointees and, 141; diversity as government interest and, 212; grounds for affirmative action and, 237; holdings in, 106–8; innovative responses to, 236–37; judicial polarization, 140, 295n14; litigators' maneuvering in, 104–6; origins of case and, 217–18; procedural dispute in, 141–44; public opinion and, 103, shift in affirmative action landscape and, 246; social and political pressure on court and, 171; strict scrutiny and, 155

Gryczan v. Montana, 48, 179, 273n125, 303n19

Guam Society of Obstetricians and Gynecologists v. Ada, 265n7

Gun Control Act of 1968, 86

Gun-Free School Zones Act (GFSZA): adherence to Supreme Court precedent and, 153, 298n64; challenge to, 71, 72, 278–79n5; vs. Gun Control Act of 1968, 86; Supreme Court invalidation of, 186–87, 188, 195–96, 215, 225, 238

Gunn, David, 59, 82

gun rights and gun control: adherence to Supreme Court precedent and, 152–54; assault weapon bans and, 7, 67, 71, 73–74, 76–77, 146, 187–88, 195, 225–26, 250–51, 279n15, 280–81n28, 281n30, 286n78, 287n86, 298n64, 307n65; background checks and, 67, 70–72, 76, 187, 195, 250–51, 305n38; ban on firing ranges and, 77, 223, 311n34, 311n41; centrist legal compromises and, 159, 160, 161; collective vs. individual rights and, 160; commerce clause and, 71, 73–74, 84, 90, 146, 195, 298n64; compliance with judicial decisions and, 215, 223, 311n41; compromise in response to decisions and, 225–26; concealed carry and, 76, 183–84, 195, 212, 251, 276–77n174, 287n85, 304n28; courts as veto points and, 70–77; courts clearing way for policy change and, 120; courts dismantling existing policies and, 86–92, 168–69, 171, 178, 180, 185–89, 195; crime rates and, 70; domestic violence and, 11–12, 71, 74, 76, 280n21; extreme legal

claims and, 158; gag rules for doctors and, 188, 189, 276–77n174; gun manufacturers' concessions and, 311n41; gun sale restrictions and, 76, 77, 153; gun shows and, 188, 189, 251, 286nn80–81, 305n38; handgun bans and, 12, 77, 87, 88–90, 120, 147, 153, 225–26, 287n85, 311n41; immunity for gun manufacturers and, 63–65, 276–77n174; informed consent and waiting periods and, 188; interstate commerce and, 153; judicial polarization and, 137, 146–47, 149–50, 152–54; legislation vs. litigation and, 8–9, 250; mass shootings and, 6, 64, 70, 77, 146–47, 250; mental health and, 153, 187; necessity of litigation and, 255; nunchucks and, 89; Obama on, 5–6; open carry and, 251; parental liability and, 71; possession by convicted felons and, 86, 90–91, 153, 187–88, 195, 298n64; possession by juveniles and, 160, 161, 250; possession in public housing and, 223; preemptive laws protecting gun rights and, 276–77n174; public opinion and, 180, 183–89, 305n34, 305n38; registration requirements and, 77, 90, 281n30; resistance to decisions and, 212; rights advocates' tactics and, 10; robust vs. modest readings of rights claims and, 257; rules for storage and, 226; scholars' positions on, 90; in school and government buildings, 153; state constitutions and, 74–75, 76, 278n4, 287n85; straw purchasers and, 65; tort suits against gun manufacturers and, 62–64, 212, 251, 276n167, 276–77n174, 277n177; unfettered right to carry and, 196–97; waiting periods and, 70–71, 72, 188, 226, 251; wildcat vs. movement litigation and, 71–72, 87. *See also* Second Amendment; *specific legislation and cases*

Gura, Alan, 87, 91–92, 154

Hall, Cynthia Holcomb, 147

Hall, Matthew, 214–24, 295n7, 295n9

Hamacher, Patrick, 101

Hamilton, Alexander, 138

Hamilton, David F., 27

Hamilton v. Accu-Tek, 63, 276n168

Hamilton v. Beretta USA Corp., 63, 276n169

Handgun Control, Inc. v. Lungren, 67, 278n193
Harris v. McRae, 278n189
Hatter, Terry J., Jr., 39, 40
Hawaiian Electric Industries, Inc. v. Akiba, 282n37
Hawaii Commission on Sexual Orientation and the Law, 160
Hawaii State AFL-CIO v. Yoshina, 113, 292n166
Heinsma v. City of Vancouver, 281n34
Heller, Simon, 23, 144
Heller v. District of Columbia, 226, 281n30, 288n90, 311n40. See also *District of Columbia v. Heller*
Henderson, Karen LeCraft, 147
Henderson, Thelton, 43, 44
Hentoff, Nat, 118
Hernandez v. Robles, 51, 274n135, 274n137
Hern v. Beye, 66, 158, 278n191, 299n81
Herring v. Richmond Medical Center for Women, 152, 266n18, 297–98n60
Heston, Charlton, 88
Hickman v. Block, 279–80n20, 280n25
Hilberg v. F. W. Woolworth Co., 285–86n73
Hilbink, Lisa, 171
Hill v. Colorado, 84–85
Hi-Voltage Wire Works, Inc. v. City of San Jose, 123, 303–4n26
Hjorth, Roland, 118
Hobbs Act, 60
Hoffman v. Hunt, 84, 284n55, 284n58, 284n60
Holder, Eric, 54
Hollingsworth v. Perry, 37, 87, 116, 216, 271n76, 292n175, 304n30, 310n22
Hollis-Brusky, Amanda, 279n11
Holmes v. California Army National Guard, 41, 271–72nn96–97
Hope Clinic v. Ryan, 21–22, 24, 145, 151, 190, 265nn9–10, 266n15, 270n59, 296n28, 297n54, 305–6n44
Hope Medical Group for Women v. Edwards, 66, 158, 278n191, 299n81
Hope v. Perales, 268–69n52
Hopwood, Cheryl, 246
Hopwood v. Texas: anti–affirmative action strategy and, 100–102; drop in minority enrollment and, 211, 219; *Gratz v. Bollinger* and, 236–37; *Grutter v. Bollinger*

and, 111, 145–46; innovative responses to, 232–33; judicial impact and, 97–97, 202; preemptive policy changes and, 217–19; pre-*Hopwood* admissions policies and, 69, 278n2, 95, 247–48; public opinion and, 181, 303n22; race-conscious public school student assignments and, 99; resistance to decision in, 210–11; university actions following, 221
Ho v. San Francisco Unified School District, 100, 290n125, 304n27, 312n50
Hunter v. Erickson, 45–46
Hunter v. Regents of the University of California, 99, 290n120
Huyett, Daniel H., 26
Hyde Amendment, 66, 158
Hyman v. City of Louisville, 282–83n44

Ileto v. Glock, Inc., 64–65, 146–47, 276–77n174, 277nn181–84, 296nn40–41
Indiana University, 222
In re Advisory Opinion to the Attorney General, 34, 270n61
In re Byrd, 143, 295nn19–20
In re Initiative Petition No. 395, 25, 266n20
In re Jane Doe, 31, 269n53
In re Marriage Cases, 51, 52, 184, 274n135, 274n141, 304n29
In re M.S., 80, 283n46
In re T.W., 206, 308n6
Institute for Justice, 87
Irizarry v. Board of Education of City of Chicago, 281n34
Isaacson v. Horne, 25, 150–51, 190, 266n19, 297n49, 306n44

Jackson v. DC Board of Elections and Ethics, 117, 293n180
Jackson v. US Department of the Air Force, 271n96
James v. Arms Technology, Inc., 64, 277n179
Jane L. v. Bangerter, 21, 175, 265n7, 301n11
Janklow v. Planned Parenthood, 29, 268n42
Jansson v. Bowen, 115, 292n172
Jaye, David, 101
Jefferson, Thomas, and Jeffersonians, 132–34
Jeffords, James, 33
Jegley v. Picado, 48, 179, 273n125, 303n19
Johnson, Lyndon, 137

Johnson v. Board of Regents, 102, 103, 181, 220, 290n133, 290n137, 303n22, 310n31, 312n49

Jones, Edith H., 299n80

Jones, Elaine, 141

Jones, Nathaniel, 143–44

judges as sideshows, 3–4, 12, 198–99, 202

judges as tyrants, 3, 14–15, 164–66, 198, 252–53. *See also* judicial activism

judges as umpires: baseball analogy for, 164; baseline for assessing, 147–48; centrist legal compromises and, 159, 160–62; claims for own party's judges and, 166; fiction of impartiality and, 163; judges' self-description and, 198; judicial bipartisanship and, 147, 163; judicial centrism and, 159–60; political polarization vs., 138–47; Supreme Court and, 1–3, 131, 164

judicial activism: abortion restrictions and, 31–32; basis for charges of, 252–53; bipartisan, 256–57, 258; category 1 lawsuits and, 70; by conservatives vs. liberals, 70, 81, 85–86; courts as legislatures and, 164–65; vs. democratic governance, 240, 255; vs. favoring extreme legal claims, 157; finality of judicial decisions and, 253; history of judicial review and, 255–56; across ideological spectrum, 168–69; judges as tyrants and, 3, 14, 164–66; language about, 164–66; legislative inattentiveness and, 174; limited results of judicial review and, 196–97; popular sentiment and, 172; protection of rights and, 166–71; Republican vs. Democratic charges of, 166; *Roe v. Wade* and, 172–73; unnecessary handwringing about, 124; Warren and Burger Courts and, 47

judicial polarization: abortion and, 144–45, 149–52; adherence to Supreme Court precedent and, 136–37, 150–55; affirmative action and, 140–46, 149–50, 154–55, 298n68; Affordable Care Act and, 163; appointing president as proxy for judicial ideology and, 135, 136; asymmetrical character of, 139, 149, 154; baseline for assessing, 147–48; coding of decisions and, 159–60; constitutional courts vs. constitutional theory and, 257–58; cul-

ture wars and, 150; deference to trial court decisions and, 136–37; differences across circuits and, 135–36, 144–45, 295n7; escalating pressure for, 162–63; extreme legal claims and, 155–59, 298–99nn73–74, 299n82; federal appellate courts vs. Supreme Court and, 135, 136, 138–39; gay rights and, 146, 149–50, 154; gun rights and, 146–47, 149–50, 152–54; judicial circuits and, 135, 295n7; vs. legislative polarization, 13–14, 148–50; *Marbury v. Madison and*, 132–34; media coverage of, 162–63; national sentiment vs. local outliers and, 200; nature of umpiring and, 134; nomination and confirmation process and, 137; panel effects and, 135–37, 295n8; partisan judging and, 131–38, 256; partisan senators on, 2–3; partisanship by issue and, 137–38; John Roberts on, 1; rule of law and, 131–38; shifts in law and, 152; Sixth Circuit and, 141–44, 295n7, 295n19; Sonia Sotomayor on, 2; state high courts and, 160–62; studies of judicial partisanship and, 138–40; over time, 139; vs. voter polarization, 148; voting by party on federal appellate courts and, 139

Judiciary Act (1801), 132

Justice v. Town of Cicero, 91, 287n87

Kachalsky v. County of Westchester, 91, 288n90

Kahlenberg, Richard, 234–35

Kansas v. Comprehensive Health of Planned Parenthood of Kansas, 121, 294n193

Karlin v. Foust, 27, 267nn29–30

Kasler v. Lockyer, 280–81n28

Kavanaugh, Brett, 281n30

Kaye, Judith, 51

Keith, Damon, 30, 142, 143–44

Kennedy, Anthony: affirmative action and, 105, 107, 109–10, 158–59; Affordable Care Act and, 130, 294n5; buffer zones at abortion protest sites and, 83, 84, 85, 283–84n54; on Colorado's Amendment 2, 35; gay rights and, 48; partial-birth abortion and, 23–24, 33

Kennedy, Edward, 141

Kerrigan v. Commissioner of Public Health, 52, 184, 274n142, 304n29

Kilgore, Jerry, 220
Klarman, Michael, 198–201, 203, 205, 241, 245, 308n1
Kline, Phill, 121–22
Knight v. Schwarzenegger, 282n37
Knight v. Superior Court, 282n37
Kohl, Herb, 2
Kolbert, Kathryn, 267n31
Kollar-Kotelly, Colleen, 212
Koog v. United States, 72, 279n9
Kosaki, Liane C., 202
Kozinski, Alex, 109
Krc v. US Information Agency, 271–72n97
Krislov, Marvin, 103
Ku Klux Klan Act, 59–60, 61, 82, 275–76n158, 276n163

Lambda Legal Defense and Education Fund, 34, 36–39, 48–50, 52–53, 273n128, 275n153
Lambert v. Wicklund, 30, 268–69n52, 268n49
Landes, William, 136–37
Largess v. Supreme Judicial Court, 79, 155–56, 282n38, 298n70
Lathrop v. Deal, 25, 190, 266n19, 306n44
Law and Society Association, 222
Lawrence v. Texas: adherence to Supreme Court precedent and, 54, 154; centrist legal compromises and, 159; courts as veto points and, 303n19; courts dismantling existing policies and, 179–80; Don't Ask, Don't Tell and, 42; federal appellate courts and, 54, 146; reaction to decision in, 48; sodomy laws and, 273nn125–26
Lawson, David M., 45
Lawson v. Murray, 83, 283n51
Leavitt v. Jane L., 21, 265n7
Lee, Bill Lann, 211–12
Lehman, Jeffrey, 237
Lemieux, Scott, 172–73, 213, 214, 215
Lemons v. Bradbury, 112–13, 156, 292n165, 298n71
Lesage, Francois Daniel, 102
Lesage v. Texas, 101–2, 290n130
Leskovar v. Nickels, 79, 282n42, 294n196
Levey, Curt, 221
Levinson, Sanford, on Second Amendment, 71

Lewis v. Harris, 50–53, 161, 274n134, 274n140, 274n143, 300n89, 311n36
LGBT rights. *See* gay rights
Libertad v. Welch, 275–76n158
Liberty Counsel, 78, 79, 82, 155–56
Liberty University v. Geithner, 129, 294n2
Lilly v. City of Minneapolis, 191, 281n34, 306n49, 310n25
Lingle, Linda, 52
Lipson, Daniel, 237–38
litigation: awareness raising and, 58–61; category 1, 11–12, 47, 70, 140, 148, 276–77n174, 288n90; category 2, 12–13, 47, 118, 123, 140, 148; category 3, 12–13, 67, 112–13, 124, 140, 148, 306n46; challenges to vs. facilitation of democratic politics, 67; challenges to vs. vindication of democratic authority and, 123–24; as channel for policy change, 61–65, 69, 112–18; to enforce electoral and legislative victories, 65–67, 122–24, 276–77n174; evaluating significance of, 313n1; by friend vs. foe, 242–43; in gay rights strategy, 244; judicial polarization by category of, 139–40; vs. legislation, 8–9, 20, 58, 243, 249, 250; litigation that works vs. litigation that matters, 242–44; necessity of, 254–55; policy goals and, 242–43; preservation vs. disruption of status quo and, 19–20, 264–65nn4–5; purpose of for rights advocates, 124; removal of obstacles to legislative change and, 55; scholarship on, 11, 264n13; state constitutional amendments and, 58; in support of democratic action, 19, 69, 264n3; test case strategy and, 50; vs. unilateral disarmament, 251; unintended consequences of, 243–44; when other policy avenues are closed off, 120–22; widespread historical use of, 255–56; wildcat, 36–37, 47–49, 71–72, 80–81, 86–87, 243, 264n12; to win piecemeal protections, 58–61
Little Rock Family Planning Services v. Dalton, 66, 158, 278n191, 299n81
Little Rock Family Planning Services v. Jegley, 21–22, 190, 265n9, 296n28, 305–6n44
Livingston, Debra Ann, 110–11
Li v. Oregon, 50–51, 274n134
Lockyer, Bill, 115

Lockyer v. City and County of San Francisco, 79, 157, 282n40, 299n78
Lofton v. Secretary of the Department of Children and Family Services, 54, 146, 275n151
Log Cabin Republicans, 42
Log Cabin Republicans v. United States, 42, 170, 272nn103–4, 301n8
Lopez case. See *United States v. Lopez*
Louisiana v. Baxley, 48, 273n124
Louisiana v. Blanchard, 285–86n73
Louisiana v. Smith, 273n125
Lovell, George, 215
Love v. Pepersack, 88–89, 279–80n20, 286n78
Lowe v. Broward County, 191, 281n34, 306n49
Luks, Samantha, 172
Lungren, Dan, 67
Lungren v. Superior Court of Sacramento County, 43, 272n105
Lutheran Church–Missouri Synod v. FCC, 97, 145, 181, 228, 289nn109–10, 296nn29–30, 303n24, 312n44
Luttig, J. Michael, 144, 151, 152, 297n52

Mack, Richard, 72–73
Mack v. United States, 72, 279nn7–8
Madison, James, 132
Madsen v. Women's Health Center, 82–83, 84, 283–84n54
Mahaffey v. Attorney General, 28, 267n33
Maloney v. Cuomo, 89, 286n79
Manning v. Hunt, 29, 268n43
Marbury, William, 132, 134
Marbury v. Madison, 132–34
marriage equality. See same-sex marriage
Marriage Project, 49, 50
Marshall, John, 131–34
Martin, Boyce, 104, 141, 143
Martinez v. County of Monroe, 216, 309n20
Martinez v. Kulongoski, 36, 270–71n73
Massachusetts Citizens for Life, 85
Massachusetts Institute of Technology, 220
Massachusetts v. US Health and Human Services, 53, 274n145
Matter of Hebel v. West, 79, 282n41
Matthew Shepard and James Byrd Jr. Hate Crimes Prevention Act, 81, 245, 263–64n9, 307n61

Mazurek v. Armstrong, 194, 268–69n52, 307n58
McCann, Michael, 202, 264n13, 313n1
McCollum, Bill, 215
McConkey v. Van Hollen, 36, 270–71n73
McCorvey, Norma, 157, 284–85n69
McCorvey v. Hill, 284–85n69, 299n80
McCullen v. Coakley, 85, 284n62, 284nn65–67
McDonald v. Chicago: city's response to, 215, 226; compliance with judicial decisions and, 223; courts dismantling existing policies and, 171, 180; interpretation of due process and, 253, 315n24; judicial compromise and, 160; judicial impact and, 202; litigation when other policy avenues are closed off and, 120; sea change in gun rights and, 77, 90–92
McDonald v. Commonwealth, 309n18
McFarland v. Jefferson County Public Schools, 108–9, 155, 291n153, 298n67
McGee v. United States, 72, 279n7
McGreevey, James E., 161
McGuire v. Reilley, 67, 85, 284nn63–64
McMillian, Theodore, 266–67n25
McNamara v. City of Chicago, 98, 289n113
MCRI. *See* Michigan Civil Rights Initiative (MCRI)
MD/DC/DE Broadcasters Ass'n v. FCC, 97, 145, 181, 228, 289n111, 296n31, 303n24, 312n46
Mead v. Holder, 129, 294n2
Meinhold, Keith, 39–40
Meinhold v. US Department of Defense, 39, 40, 271n89, 271nn84–85
Mellon Foundation, 236
Memphis Planned Parenthood, Inc. v. Sundquist, 30, 143, 268nn47–48, 295n18
Merrill v. Navegar, 64, 277n176
Metro Broadcasting v. FCC, 288n96, 288n98
Mexican American Legal Defense and Educational Fund (MALDEF), 211, 235
Miami University, 122
Michael, M. Blane, 144–45
Michigan Civil Rights Initiative (MCRI), 44–46, 117, 119, 144, 159, 192, 247, 310n26
Michigan Civil Rights Initiative v. Board of State Canvassers, 69, 117, 278n3, 293nn180–82

Michigan's Proposal 2. *See* Michigan Civil Rights Initiative (MCRI)

Mikva, Abner, 40, 146

Miller, Mark C., 202

Minnesota v. Machholz, 80, 283n46

Missouri Civil Rights Initiative, 118

Missouri v. Cogshell, 48, 179, 273n125, 303n19, 309n18

MKB Management Corp. v. Burdick, 25, 175, 266n19, 301n12

Montgomery County v. Broadcast Equities, Inc., 282–83n44

Moore, Karen Nelson, 141–42

Moore v. Madigan, 91, 147, 154, 195, 288nn92–93, 296n44, 304n28, 307n63

Morial v. Smith & Wesson Corp., 276–77n174

Morrison, Paul, 121

Morrison v. Sadler, 50–51, 274n134, 274n136

Mosby v. Devine, 280–81n28

Mountain States Legal Foundation (MSLF), 93, 94, 98

Mount Holyoke College, 222, 236

MSLF. *See* Mountain States Legal Foundation (MSLF)

Murray, Susan, 49

NAACP: affirmative action and, 272n109; California's Proposition 209 and, 43; desegregation suits by, 224; discriminatory university admissions policies and, 235–36; gun control litigation and, 62, 63; litigation for policy change and, 19, 69; membership lists of, 264n3; timing of judicial confirmations and, 141

NAACP Legal Defense and Education Fund. *See* NAACP

NAACP v. Acusport, 63, 276n171

NAACP v. Alabama, 264n3

National Abortion Federation v. Ashcroft, 33, 269n56

National Abortion Federation v. Gonzales, 33, 151–52, 269n56, 297n58

National Abortion Federation v. Operation Rescue, 275–76n158

National Association of Scholars, 94

National Center for Lesbian Rights (NCLR), 49, 53

National Defense Authorization Acts, 98, 186, 308–9n14

National Federation of Independent Businesses v. Sebelius, 1, 129, 293n186, 294nn4–5

National Institutes of Health, 222

National Organization for Marriage, 116

National Organization for Marriage v. Cruz-Bustillo, 206, 293n179

National Organization for Marriage v. Daluz, 293n179

National Organization for Marriage v. McKee, 116–17, 293n179

National Organization for Women v. Operation Rescue, 59–60, 275n156

National Organization for Women v. Scheidler, 60, 276nn159–61, 276n163

National Pride at Work v. Governor of Michigan, 122, 191, 281–82n35, 294n194, 306n49

National Rifle Ass'n, Inc. v. Bureau of Alcohol, Tobacco, Firearms, and Explosives, 91, 287–88n89

National Rifle Ass'n of America, Inc. v. City of Evanston, 311n41

National Rifle Ass'n of America, Inc. v. Reno, 76, 280n27

National Rifle Association (NRA): background checks and, 76; Brady Bill and, 72–73; handgun bans and, 311n41; litigation strategy of, 70; local gun restrictions and, 77, 88; San Francisco Housing Authority and, 223; Second Amendment incorporation and, 90; Smith & Wesson concession and, 311n41; wildcat vs. movement litigation and, 87, 285n72

National Right to Life Committee, 292n173

Navegar, Inc. v. United States, 74, 279nn15–17

NCLR. *See* National Center for Lesbian Rights (NCLR)

NeJaime, Douglas, 213

New Haven Fire Department, 110

New Mexico Right to Choose/NARAL v. Johnson, 191, 268–69n52, 306n46

Newsom, Gavin, 57, 79, 157

Newtown, Connecticut, school shooting, gun control legislation and, 6

New Yorkers for Constitutional Freedoms v. New York State Senate, 282n37

New York v. United States, 72

Nickerson, Eugene, 41

Nixon, Richard, 69, 137, 144, 156

Nordyke v. King, 89, 280n25, 286nn80–81
Nordyke v. Santa Clara, 187, 189, 280n27, 305n38
Norris, Alan, 141
North Coast Women's Care Medical Group, Inc. v. Superior Court, 282–83n44
Northeastern Florida Chapter of the Associated General Contractors of America v. Jacksonville, 223, 310n32
Northern Virginia Community College, 218
North Florida Women's Health and Counseling Services, Inc. v. State, 31, 190, 206, 268–69n52, 305n43, 308n7
Northland Family Planning Clinic, Inc. v. Cox, 190, 266n18, 305–6n44
Norton, Gale, 73
Nova Health Systems v. Edmondson, 30, 189, 209, 267n38, 268n50, 305n41, 308n11
Nova Health Systems v. Pruit, 29, 268n39
NOW Legal Defense and Education Fund, 60
NRA. *See* National Rifle Association (NRA)
NRA v. Chicago, 89–90, 91, 286n82

Obama, Barack, and Obama years: abortion and, 21, 25, 28, 34, 66–67, 158, 190–91, 208; affirmative action and, 234–35; Affordable Care Act and, 129, 130; culture wars and, 5, 6, 7; Defense of Marriage Act (DOMA) and, 62; Don't Ask, Don't Tell and, 42, 263–64n9, 301n10; end of Republican era and, 69; gay rights and, 6, 53, 244–45, 263–64n9; gun rights and, 5–6, 8, 70, 250; hate crimes legislation and, 81, 263–64n9; judicial appointments of, 165; proportion of judges from each party and, 163; 2008 convention speech of, 5, 7
Obamacare. *See* Affordable Care Act (ACA)
O'Connor, Sandra Day: abortion and 23, 26–27, 32, 152; affirmative action and, 95; *Gratz v. Bollinger* and, 107; *Grutter v. Bollinger* and, 106–7, 237; retirement of, 32, 108, 109, 152; *Stenberg v. Carhart (Carhart I)* and, 33, 193
OCR (Department of Education Office of Civil Rights). *See* Department of Education

Ohio Republican Party v. Brunner, 295n21
Ohio State University, 236
Olson, Ted, 37, 58, 95, 104, 115, 228
Olympic Arms v. Magaw, 74, 279n19
Operation King's Dream v. Connerly, 44–45, 272nn111–12
Operation Rescue, 58–60, 62, 83, 276n163
Operation Rescue v. Women's Health Center, 82, 276n163, 283n49
Oregon Citizens Alliance, 113
Orr, Valery Pech, 119
Orthodox Presbyterian Church, 79–80
O'Scannlain, Diarmuid F., 89
Owen, Priscilla, 32

Pacific Legal Foundation (PLF), 72, 95, 123, 229
Parents Involved in Community Schools v. Seattle School District, No. 1, 108–11, 155, 158–59, 229, 246, 248, 290n128, 291n148, 291nn153–4, 298n67, 304n27
Paris, Michael, 215
Parker v. District of Columbia, 87, 147, 285–86n73, 296nn42–43
Parks, A. Lee, 102
Paterson, David, 215
Patient Protection and Affordable Care Act. *See* Affordable Care Act (ACA)
Patrick, Deval, 96
Pawlick v. Birmingham, 114, 156, 292n168, 298–99n72
Penelas v. Arms Technology, Inc., 64, 277n176
Peoples Rights Organization v. City of Columbus, 187, 286n78, 305n36
People v. Sturm, Ruger & Co., 63, 276n170
People v. Uplinger, 309n17
Peretti, Terri, 198, 258
Perry, H. W., 160
Perry v. Brown, 37, 271n75, 292n175, 304n30
Perry v. Schwarzenegger, 7, 37, 58, 116, 264n10, 271n74, 284, 292n175, 304n29
Personhood Nevada v. Bristol, 175, 266n21, 301n12
Peterson v. Martinez, 91, 288n90
Philips v. Perry, 41, 271n96
Phillips, Virginia A., 42, 170
Pickerill, Mitch, 201, 238
Pickering, John, 132
Pietrangelo v. Gates, 41–42, 272n98, 272n100

Pinello, Dan, 225, 295n10

Piscataway Township Board of Education v. Taxman, 96, 227–28, 289n104, 312n43

Planned Parenthood, 28, 66–67, 121, 144–45, 158

Planned Parenthood Affiliates v. Engler, 66, 158, 278n190, 299n81

Planned Parenthood Arizona, Inc. v. Betlach, 66–67, 158, 278n192, 299n81

Planned Parenthood Federation of America v. Ashcroft, 33, 151, 269n56, 297n56

Planned Parenthood League of Massachusetts, Inc. v. Attorney General, 31, 190, 268–69n52, 305n43

Planned Parenthood Minnesota v. Daugaard, 28–29, 189, 267n37, 305n40

Planned Parenthood Minnesota v. Rounds, 28, 267n36

Planned Parenthood of Central New Jersey v. Farmer, 31, 190, 268–69n52, 305n43

Planned Parenthood of Delaware v. Brady, 27, 189, 267n31, 305n40

Planned Parenthood of Greater Iowa, Inc. v. Miller, 21–22, 190, 265n9, 296n28, 305–6n44

Planned Parenthood of Indiana, Inc. v. Commissioner of the Indiana State Department of Health, 66–67, 158, 278n192, 299n81

Planned Parenthood of Middle Tennessee v. Sundquist, 27–28, 189, 206, 267nn31–32, 305n40, 308n8

Planned Parenthood of Northern New England v. Heed, 32, 269n54

Planned Parenthood of Southern Arizona, Inc. v. Woods, 190, 265n9, 305–6n44

Planned Parenthood of the Blue Ridge v. Camblos, 29, 144–45 268n43, 296nn25–27

Planned Parenthood of the Columbia/ Willamette, Inc. v. American Coalition of Life Activists, 84, 284n57

Planned Parenthood Shasta-Diablo, Inc. v. Williams, 283–84n54

Planned Parenthood v. Brownback, 66–67, 278n192

Planned Parenthood v. Casey: abortion bans prevented by, 122; adherence to, 151, 297n48; calls for reversal of, 299n80; centrist legal compromises and, 159;

characterizations of, 297n52; courts as veto points and, 20–21; dissenting arguments in, 265n14; failure to reverse, 33; foreclosure of democratic deliberation and, 253, 315n23; informed consent and waiting periods and, 26–28; legal personhood for fetuses and, 25; parental involvement laws and, 29; partial-birth abortion and, 21, 23–24; public opinion and, 172–73; *Roe v. Wade* reaffirmed in, 7, 21; state-level abortion restrictions and, 207–8; undue burden on right to abortion and, 25–27

Planned Parenthood v. Farmer, 24, 151, 190, 266n15, 297n51, 305–6n44

Planned Parenthood v. Lawall, 30, 190, 268n45, 305n43

Planned Parenthood v. Miller, 27, 29, 151, 190, 267n26, 268n42, 297n50, 305n43

Planned Parenthood v. Owens, 32, 190, 269n54, 305n43

Planned Parenthood v. Rounds, 28, 267nn34–35

Planned Parenthood v. State, 28, 189, 267n32, 305n40

Planned Parenthood v. Wasden, 32, 190, 269n54, 305n43

PLCAA. *See* Protection of Lawful Commerce in Arms Act (PLCAA)

PLF. *See* Pacific Legal Foundation (PLF)

Podberesky, Daniel, 93

Podberesky v. Kirwan, 93–94, 183, 218, 228, 246, 248, 288nn94–95, 314n11

Posner, Richard, 22–23, 91, 97, 136–37, 270n59

Post, Robert, 201, 212–13

Powe, Lucas, 160

Powell, Lewis, 92–93, 95–96, 102–6, 141, 212, 237

Powell, Michael, 228

Powell v. Georgia, 48, 179, 273n125, 303n19

Presbytery of New Jersey v. Whitman, 79–80, 282n43

Presser v. Illinois, 89

Preterm Cleveland v. Voinovich, 28, 267n33

Princeton University, 220

Printz v. United States, 72–73, 76, 120, 186, 279n7, 279nn10–11, 304–5n33

Pro-Choice Mississippi v. Fordice, 28, 30–31, 267n33, 268n51

Pro-Choice Network of Western New York v. Project Rescue of Western New York, 83, 275n156, 283n53
Pro-Choice Network v. Schenck, 275n156, 283n53. See also *Schenck v. Pro-Choice Network of Western New York*
Project on Fair Representation, 69
Proposal 2 (Michigan). *See* Michigan Civil Rights Initiative (MCRI)
Proposition 8 (California). *See* California's Proposition 8
Proposition 209 (California). *See* California's Proposition 209
Protection of Lawful Commerce in Arms Act (PLCAA), 63–65, 212
ProtectMarriage.com v. Bowen, 292n174
Protect Marriage Illinois v. Orr, 112–13, 292n165
Pryor, William, 146

Quinn v. Boston, 97, 181, 289n108, 303n24

Ralph v. New Orleans, 281n34
R.A.V. v. St. Paul, 80
Reagan, Ronald, and Reagan years: judicial appointments of, 93, 129, 137, 141, 144–45, 147, 151; Mexico City policy and, 34; Second Amendment and, 88
Reed, Douglas, 113, 120
Regents of the University of California v. Bakke: adherence to, 217; binding nature of, 103, 106, 141; George W. Bush administration's position on, 104–5; grounds for affirmative action and, 212, 237–38; Lewis Powell's compromise in, 92–93, 95–96, 102–6, 141; repudiation of, 288n101
Rehnquist, William, 32, 82–83, 106–8, 265n8, 265n14, 268n42, 279n11
Reinhardt, Stephen, 280n25
Rell, Jodi, 215
Renee B. v. Florida Agency for Health Care Administration, 268–69n52
Reno, Janet, 75
Reproductive Health Services of Planned Parenthood of St. Louis Region, Inc. v. Nixon, 24, 28, 151, 190, 266n15, 267n33, 297n55, 305–6n44
Rhode Island Medical Society v. Whitehouse, 24, 151, 190, 266n15, 297n54, 305–6n44

Rhode Island v. Lopes, 48, 273n124
Ricci v. DeStefano, 110, 155, 181, 182, 303n24
Rice, Walter Herbert, 24
Richenberg v. Perry, 41, 271–72nn96–97
Richmond Medical Center for Women v. Herring, 152, 266n18, 298n61
Richmond Medical Center for Women v. Hicks, 152, 266n18, 297–98nn59–60
Richmond Medical Center v. Gilmore, 21, 24, 145, 151, 190, 265n8, 266n15, 296n28, 297n52, 305–6n44
Richmond v. Croson, 93, 95, 96, 108, 303–4n26
RICO Act, 60, 82, 276n163
rights and rights advocates: categories of litigation and, 13; compliance with judicial decisions and, 214–24, 238–39, 309nn18–19, 310n25; compromise in response to decisions and, 224–29, 238–39; countermajoritarian rights-protecting decisions and, 201; courts' uneven protection of rights and, 125; holding policy stable and, 250; across ideological spectrum, 168–69; ineffectiveness of rights-protecting judicial decisions and, 199; innovation in response to decisions and, 229–39; judicial activism and, 14, 166–71, 240; left-liberal advocates' litigation strategies and, 67–68; legislation vs. litigation and, 8–9; limited results of judicial review and, 196–97; litigation to challenge vs. facilitate democratic politics and, 67; litigation vs. legislation and, 243; majoritarian vs. countermajoritarian decisions and, 174–75; paths of policy contestation and, 202–3; policymakers' reactions to judges and, 14–15; political backlash after judicial decisions and, 199–200, 245; purposes of litigation and, 124; range of goals and, 10–12; resistance to judicial and legislative decisions and, 203–14, 238–39, 309n17; robust vs. modest readings of rights claims and, 257, 258; wildcat vs. movement litigation and, 10–11, 243. *See also* abortion rights and restrictions; affirmative action; gay rights; gun rights and gun control
Rios v. Regents of the University of California, 235–36

Roberts, John: affirmative action and, 95, 109–11, 155, 158, 246, 288n98; Affordable Care Act and, 129–30, 133; appointment of, 32; composition of Supreme Court and, 208; judges as umpires and, 1, 3, 131, 164; judicial activism and, 166; on judicial bipartisanship, 147; judicial strategy of, 133; judicial style of, 109; John Marshall as model for, 131–33; nomination process for, 1; partial-birth abortion and, 33; Republicans' 2004 electoral victories and, 205

Robinson, Beth, 49

Robinson v. Shelby County Board of Education, 111, 181, 292n160, 303n24, 304n27

Roeder, Scott, 121

Roe v. Wade: authorship of, 23; calls for reversal of, 33, 299n80; efforts to provoke reconsideration of, 206–7; fetal personhood and, 299n79; finality of, 253; foreclosure of democratic deliberation and, 201, 253, 255; judicial activism and, 172–73; judicial impact and, 202; legislative alternative to, 213; litigation prior to, 81; litigation vs. legislation and, 243; *McCorvey v. Hill* and, 157, 284–85n69, 299n80; possibility of overturning, 249; pre-*Roe* abortion laws and, 173; public opinion and, 172–73; reaffirmations of, 21, 150–51, 172; Republicans' judicial appointment strategy and, 206–7, 308n10; Supreme Court balance of power on, 23–24; Supreme Court refusal to overturn, 7, 21, 157; statutory codification of, 81. *See also* abortion rights and restrictions

Rohde v. Ann Arbor Public Schools, 78, 122, 281–82nn34–35, 294n194

Rohrbaugh v. State, 285–86n73

Romer v. Evans: adherence to Supreme Court precedent and, 154; centrist legal compromises and, 159; courts' blocking function and, 35, 270n67; courts dismantling existing policies and, 176, 302n14; Don't Ask, Don't Tell and, 41; enabling of legislative politics and, 56; federal appellate courts and, 146; judges as legislators and, 254, 315n25; litigation vs. legislation and, 19–20, 265n6; plaintiffs in, 62

Romney, Mitt, 114, 120, 165–66

Rosen, Jeffrey, 131, 172, 199

Rosenberg, Gerald, 4, 199–201, 203, 205, 225, 241, 245, 264n13, 313n1

Rosie J. v. North Carolina Department of Human Resources, 268–69n52

Rosman, Michael, 108

Rostron, Allen, 91

Rothe Development Corp. v. US Department of Defense, 98, 186, 289n116, 303–4n26, 304–5n33, 308–9n14

Russell, Eric, 45

Rybar, Raymond, Jr., 73. See also *United States v. Rybar*

Sabelko v. City of Phoenix, 191, 284n59, 306n47

Salamone, Michael, 172

same-sex marriage: ballot initiatives and, 113–17, 122, 148, 205, 270n66, 297n45; centrist legal compromises and, 160–62; compliance with legalization and, 215–16; compromise in response to decisions and, 224, 225, 311nn36–37; courts as veto points and, 34–38, 79; courts clearing way for policy change and, 238; courts dismantling existing policies and, 48–54, 170–71 178, 184–86; Defense of Marriage Act (DOMA) and, 53, 62, 184; denial of constitutional entitlements and, 274n144; domestic partnerships and, 230–31, 313n53; extreme legal claims and, 155–57, 298–99nn73–74; full marriage equality and, 196–97; innovation in response to decisions and, 230–31; litigation challenging status quo and, 19, 265n5; necessity of litigation and, 254; Obama's support for, 263–64n9; public opinion and, 6, 178, 184–86, 304n31; rapid change in, 245; resistance to judicial and legislative decisions and, 204–6, 213; state constitutional bans and, 78, 113–15, 155–56, 170, 205–6, 270n70, 308nn2–3; state legalization of, 10, 62, 78–79, 170; strategies for achieving legalization of, 56–58, 113; strategies of opponents of, 113, 115–17; wildcat litigation and, 87. *See also* California's Proposition 8; gay rights

Sawatzky v. City of Oklahoma City, 48, 273n124

Saxe v. State College Area School District, 81, 192, 194–95, 283nn47–48, 307n51, 307n62

Scalia, Antonin: affirmative action and, 110, 154; Affordable Care Act and, 130, 294n5; Brady Bill challenge and, 73; in *Bray v. Alexandria Women's Health Clinic,* 60; buffer zones at abortion protest sites and, 83, 84–85, 283–84n54; *Carhart II* and, 33; *Concrete Works of Colorado v. City and County of Denver* and, 108; on due process clause, 253; Federalist Society and, 279n11; on finality of judicial decisions, 253; *Lawson v. Murray* and, 283n51; parental involvement in abortion and, 268n42; partial-birth abortion and, 33; on *Planned Parenthood v. Casey,* 33, 265n14; postviability abortion and, 265n8; on *Roe v. Wade,* 33, 253; Second Amendment and, 87–88

Scheidler v. National Organization for Women, 60, 276n162

Schenck v. Pro-Choice Network of Western New York, 83–84

Scherer, Nancy, 137

Schmidt, John, 210

school vouchers, 295n19

Schrader v. Holder, 91, 287–88n89

Schreier, Karen, 28–29

Schuette, Bill, 45

Schuette v. Coalition to Defend Affirmative Action, 46, 159, 273n120, 300n85

Schulman v. Attorney General, 35, 157, 270n64, 299n75

Schumer, Charles, 3, 164–65

Schwarzenegger, Arnold, 57, 213

Scott v. Pasadena Unified School District, 290n129

S. D. Myers, Inc. v. City and County of San Franscisco, 281n34

Second Amendment: assault weapon bans and, 73, 287n86; Brady Bill and, 73; collective vs. individual rights and, 74–77, 87–89, 147, 279n11, 279–80nn20–21, 280n25, 285–86n73, 286n80; convicted felons and, 90–91, 287–88n89; courts dismantling existing policies and, 171; *District of Columbia v. Heller* and, 153, 159; domestic violence and, 74; failure of litigation based on, 76; Gun-Free School Zones Act and, 72; gun rights goals and, 10; handgun bans and, 120; illegal drug users and, 287–88n89; incorporation of, 88–92; militia service and, 75–76; National Rifle Association strategy and, 70; original meaning of, 88; as orphan of Bill of Rights, 71; as ripe for litigation, 71, 72; state appellate courts on, 285–86n73; state vs. local governments and, 88–92, 161, 226, 286n78, 286n81, 287n88

Sedition Act, 134

Seegars v. Ashcroft, 87, 285n72

Sekulow, Jay, 82, 83–84

Selland v. Cohen, 271–72n97

Selland v. Perry, 271n94

Sensenbrenner, F. James, 142

Sentelle, David, 74, 145

Service Members Legal Defense Network (SLDN), 39, 41

Sessions, Jeff, 165

Settle, Benjamin, 116, 292–93n178

Seven-Sky v. Holder, 129, 294n3

Shapiro, Martin, 258

Shelby County v. Holder, 166, 263n8

Sherbrooke Turf, Inc. v. Minnesota Department of Transportation, 108, 291n149

Siegel, Reva, 88, 201, 212–13

Silberman, Laurence, 87, 97, 129, 145, 147, 285–86n73

Silveira v. Lockyer, 280n25

Silverstein, Gordon, 20, 47, 201, 244, 264n13, 315n26

Silverstein, Helena, 30

Simat Corp. v. Arizona Health Care Cost Containment System, 191, 268–69n52, 306n46

Simmons-Harris v. Zelman, 295n19

Skott v. United States, 84, 284n58

Skrentny, John, 237–38

SLDN. *See* Service Members Legal Defense Network (SLDN)

Small Business Administration, 98, 227

Smith, Katuria, 118–19, 247

Smith & Wesson, 311n41

Smith & Wesson Corp. v. City of Gary, 277n180

Smith v. Bryco Arms, 64, 277n178

Smith v. University of Washington Law School, 108, 118–19, 291n151

Snetsinger v. Montana University System, 51–52, 179, 274n138, 302–3n18
Sojourner T v. Edwards, 21, 150, 175, 265n7, 297n48, 301n11
Sotomayor, Sonia, 2–3, 34, 89, 110, 165, 292–93n178
Souter, David, 26
Spitzer, Eliot, 63
Spitzer, Robert, 279–80n20
State Department of Health and Social Services v. Planned Parenthood of Alaska, Inc., 191, 268–69n52, 306n46
State ex rel. Ohio Campaign to Protect Marriage v. DeWine, 79, 282n39
State v. Anderson, 285–86n73
State v. Hamdan, 304n28
State v. Machholz, 192, 307n51
State v. Nickerson, 285–86n73
State v. Planned Parenthood of Alaska, 190, 305n43
Staver, Mathew, 82, 155–56
Steelcase Inc., 103
Steffan, Joseph, 146
Steffan v. Aspin, 40, 146, 167, 271n87, 296n36
Steffan v. Perry, 40, 146, 167, 271n91, 296n36, 300n6
Stenberg v. Carhart (Carhart I): abortion methods and, 23, 265nn11–12; adherence to Supreme Court precedent and, 151–52, 297n52; centrist legal compromises and, 159; failure to reverse, 33; fetal personhood and, 299n79; immediate impact of, 24; medically necessary abortions and, 32; Sandra Day O'Connor's opinion in, 33, 193; partial-birth abortion and, 190, 305–6n44
Stern v. Trustees of Columbia University, 289n107
Stevens, John Paul, 84, 88
Stillwell v. Stillwell, 285–86n73
St. Louis University, 222
Stohr, Greg, 108
Story, Joseph, 73
Strauss v. Horton, 36–37, 58, 157, 270–71n73, 299n77
Stuart v. Huff, 189, 268n40, 305n41
Suhrheinrich, Richard, 141
Sullivan, Emmet G., 87
Sullivan, Teresa A., 233

Summit Medical Center of Alabama, Inc. v. Riley, 27, 267n31
Sunstein, Cass, 50, 135–37, 295n7, 295n9
Supreme Court of the United States: adherence to precedents of, 136–37, 150–55, 157, 297n48; as catalyst for policy change, 202; centrist legal compromises and, 159; First Amendment and gay rights and, 116, 292–93n178; founding myth of, 132; invalidation of federal statutes by, 187, 201, 238, 304n32; judicial activism and, 47, 166; judicial polarization and, 138–39, 152, 295n13; public support for decisions of, 171; *Roe v. Wade* balance of power on, 23–24; sea change in affirmative action and, 109–11; sea change on gun rights and, 250; size of, 133; terms of, 132. *See also* judges as sideshows; judges as tyrants; judges as umpires; *specific cases*
Sutton, Jeffrey, 129
Swann v. Charlotte-Mecklenburg Board of Education, 99, 290n122

Tanner v. Oregon Health Sciences University, 179, 216, 273n129, 302–3n18, 309n19
Tarnow, Arthur, 44–45
Taxman, Sharon, 96
Taxman v. Piscataway Board of Education, 96, 145, 181, 223, 227–28, 246, 247, 303n24, 314n7
Tea Party Republicans, 130
Teles, Steven, 93, 264n13
Tenth Amendment, 10, 72, 76, 120
Terry v. Reno, 84, 284n55, 284n58
Texas A&M, 221, 237
Texas Medical Providers Performing Abortion Services v. Lakey, 268n40
Texas v. Hopwood, 96, 289n104. See also *Hopwood v. Texas*
Texas v. Lesage, 102, 289n105, 290n131
Texas v. Morales, 48, 273n124
Thomas, Clarence: Affordable Care Act and, 130; buffer zones at abortion protest sites and, 83, 84, 283–84n54; Federalist Society and, 279n11; *Grutter v. Bollinger* and, 107; parental involvement in abortion and, 268n42; partial-birth abortion and, 33; on *Planned Parenthood v. Casey*, 33, 265n14; postviability

abortions and, 265n8; on *Roe v. Wade,*
33; Second Amendment and, 72, 73,
279n11; *Stenberg v. Carhart (Carhart I)*
and, 299n79
Thomas More Law Center, 81, 122
Thomas More Law Center v. Obama, 129,
294nn2–3
Thomasson, Paul, 41
Thomasson v. Perry, 41, 271n94, 271–72n97
Thomas v. Anchorage Equal Rights Commission, 80, 283n45
Thompson, E. P., 163
Tienda, Marta, 233
Tiller, George, 58–59, 121, 275n155
tobacco industry, litigation against, 62
Topeka v. Movsovitz, 273n125
Tracy v. Board of Regents, 102, 290n132
Tribe, Laurence, 87, 272n113
Tufts University, 222
Tumeo v. University of Alaska, 48–49, 179,
273n129, 302–3n18
Tuttle v. Arlington County School Board,
100, 212, 290n127, 304n27, 308n13
Tyma v. Montgomery County, 281n34
Tymkovich, Timothy M., 153

United States v. Adams, 285n70
United States v. Aiello, 91, 287–88n89
United States v. Alaw, 284n56
United States v. Barry, 285n70
United States v. Barton, 287n86
United States v. Bates, 285n70
United States v. Bayles, 280n21
United States v. Bell, 285n70
United States v. Bena, 91, 287–88n89
United States v. Beuckelaere, 73, 279n13
United States v. Bolton, 285n70
United States v. Booker, 91, 287–88n89
United States v. Bradford, 285n70
United States v. Brown, 91, 287–88n89
United States v. Burke, 278n188
United States v. Carter, 287–88n89
United States v. Chesney, 86, 285nn70–71
United States v. Chester, 91, 287–88n89
United States v. Collins, 285n70
United States v. Danks, 72, 153, 195, 225,
279n6, 298n63, 307n63, 311n39
United States v. Decastro, 91, 287–88n89
United States v. Dinwiddie, 284n56
United States v. Dorsey, 72, 279n6, 298n63

United States v. Dugan, 91, 287–88n89
United States v. Edwards, 278–79n5
United States v. Emerson, 74–77, 87, 91,
279–80nn19–20
United States v. Fincher, 287n86
United States v. Franklyn, 279n15
United States v. Frazier, 287n86
United States v. Gateward, 285n70
United States v. Graham, 280n26
United States v. Greeno, 287–88n89
United States v. Griffin, 91, 287–88n89
United States v. Haney, 280n26
United States v. Hanna, 285n70
United States v. Harkrider, 285n70
United States v. Hemmings, 285n70
United States v. Henry, 91, 287–88n89
United States v. Henson, 285n70
United States v. Hernandez, 285n70
United States v. Hinostroza, 280n21
United States v. Irish, 287n86
United States v. Jackubowski, 285n70
United States v. Kenney, 73, 279n13
United States v. Kirk, 73–74, 279nn13–14
United States v. Knutson, 279n15
United States v. Lee, 285n70
United States v. Lippman, 280n21
United States v. Lopez, 71–74, 76, 153,
278–79n5, 298n64; commerce clause
and, 84; compliance with, 223; compromise in response to, 225; congressional
response to, 215; courts dismantling
existing policies and, 186, 304–5n33;
gun rights strategy and, 86–87
United States v. Marzzarella, 91, 287–88n89
United States v. Masciandaro, 91, 287–88n89
United States v. McAllister, 285n70
United States v. McCane, 287n86, 298n66
United States v. McRobie, 287n88
United States v. Miller, 73, 75, 88, 279–80n20
United States v. Molina, 91, 287–88n89
United States v. Murphy, 285n70
United States v. Napier, 280n21
United States v. Nguyen, 285n70
United States v. Parker, 280n26
United States v. Patterson, 280n26
United States v. Pearson, 73, 279n13
United States v. Portillo-Munoz, 91,
287–88n89
United States v. Potter, 91, 287–88n89
United States v. Rambo, 73, 279n13

United States v. Rankin, 285n70
United States v. Rawls, 86, 285nn70–71
United States v. Richard, 287n88
United States v. Rozier, 287n86
United States v. Rybar, 73–74, 146, 164–65, 279n15, 279–80n20, 296n39
United States v. Scott, 278n188
United States v. Seay, 91, 287–88n89
United States v. Shelton, 285n70
United States v. Skoien, 91, 287–88n89
United States v. Smith, 278n188, 280n21
United States v. Sorrentino, 285n70
United States v. Staten, 91, 287–88n89
United States v. Trzaska, 285n70
United States v. Turner, 285n70
United States v. Wells, 285n70
United States v. Wesela, 285n70
United States v. Wilks, 73, 279n13
United States v. Williams, 285n70, 287n86
United States v. Wilson, 284n56
United States v. Windsor, 54, 154, 186, 215, 263n8, 275n148, 304n30, 304–5n33
United States v. Wright, 279n15, 279–80n20, 279n15
United States v. Yancey, 91, 287–88n89
University and Community College System of Nevada v. Farmer, 98, 289n114
University of California, 233–37
University of Florida, 234
University of Georgia, 102, 219, 220, 229, 237, 310n31
University of Illinois at Chicago, 219
University of Maryland, 93–94, 218, 228, 248, 312n48
University of Massachusetts, 236
University of Michigan. See *Gratz v. Bollinger*; *Grutter v. Bollinger*
University of Minnesota, 219
University of North Carolina, 218
University of Texas School of Law. See *Hopwood v. Texas*
University of Virginia, 218–20
University of Washington, 101, 102, 108, 118, 247, 290n134. *See also* Washington's I-200 law
University of Wisconsin, 219
US Department of Defense v. Meinhold, 39–40, 271n86
US Information Agency, 271n90
US Information Agency v. Krc, 271n90
Utah Women's Clinic v. Graham, 66, 278n191

Varnum v. Brien, 52, 184, 205–6, 274n142, 304n29; compliance with, 215
Violence Policy Center, background checks for gun purchasers and, 67
Virginia Commonwealth University, 223
Virginia Tech, 220
Virginia v. Sebelius, 129, 294n2
Vittitow v. City of Upper Arlington, 83, 191, 283n52, 306n47
Vivenzio v. City of Syracuse, 110–11, 292n159, 310n32
Voinovich v. Women's Medical Professional Corp., 265n8

Wake Forest University, 236
Wald, Patricia, 146
Waldron, Jeremy, 240–41, 252–53
Walker, John M., Jr., 152
Walker, Vaughn R., 37, 184, 215, 304n30
Walton, Reggie, 87
Washington Civil Rights Initiative. *See* Washington's I-200 law
Washington Legal Foundation (WLF), 93, 94
Washington Legal Foundation v. Alexander, 93, 288n94
Washington's I-200 law, 102, 108, 118, 119, 247, 290n134, 310n26
Washington University, 222
Washington v. Seattle School District No. 1, 45–46
Washington v. Sieyes, 160, 287n88, 300n87
Washington v. Williams, 285–86n73
Webb, Rodney S., 26
Webster v. Reproductive Health Services, 301–2n13
Weicker, Lowell, 161, 162
Weinstein, Jack B., 63–64, 65
Weissmann v. State College Area School District, 309n19
Wessmann v. Gittens, 100, 290n126, 304n27
Western States Paving Co. v. Washington State Department of Transportation, 291n152, 303–4n26, 311–12n42
West Hartford v. Operation Rescue, 275–76n158
Wharton, Linda J., 267n31
White, Byron, 23
Whitman, Christine Todd, 161
Whittington, Keith, 173, 198, 240–41
Whyman, Deborah, 101
Wicklund v. Salvagni, 30, 268n49

Wicklund v. State, 190, 268–69n52, 305n43

Wiener, Jacques, 288n101

Wilkinson, J. Harvie, 41, 254, 255

Williams, Ann Claire, 265n10

Williams, Stephen, 145

Williams College, 222

Williams v. Maryland, 91, 288n91

Williams v. State, 48, 179, 273n125, 303n19, 309n18

Wilson, Pete, 56–57, 120, 174, 294n199

Windsor v. United States, 54, 265n5, 274n147

Wisconsin v. Cole, 287n85

Wisconsin v. Hamdan, 287n85

Wisconsin v. Mitchell, 80

Wittmer v. Peters, 97–98, 289n112

Witt v. Department of the Air Force, 42, 272nn101–2

Wollschlaeger v. Farmer, 189, 276–77n174, 305n39

Womancare of Orlando, Inc. v. Agwunobi, 206, 308n8

A Woman's Choice—East Side Women's Clinic v. Newman, 27, 267nn27–28

Women of State of Minnesota by Doe v. Gomez, 191, 268–69n52, 306n46

Women's Health Center of West Virginia, Inc. v. Panepinto, 191, 268–69n52, 306n46

Women's Health Services v. Operation Rescue, 275–76n158

Women's Medical Professional Corp. v. Taft, 24, 266nn16–17

Women's Medical Professional Corp. v. Voinovich, 21, 145, 190, 265n8, 296n28, 305–6n44

Wood, Diane, 27, 90

Wood, Thomas, 43

Wooden v. Board of Regents of the University System, 102, 103, 290n132, 290n137

Yale University, 222

Yoo, John, 44

Yoshino, Kenji, 51

Young v. Bryco Arms, 277n177

Zackin, Emily, 174

Zbaraz v. Madigan, 30, 268n46

Zilly, Thomas S., 40